walking a tightrope aboriginal people and their representations

Ute Lischke and David T. McNab, editors

Aboriginal Studies Series

Wilfrid Laurier University Press

We acknowledge the financial support of the Government of Canada through the Book Publishing Industry Development Program for our publishing activities.

Library and Archives Canada Cataloguing in Publication

Walking a tightrope : aboriginal people and their representations / Ute Lischke and David T. McNab, editors.

(Aboriginal studies series)
Includes bibliographical references

ISBN-10: 0-88920-484-5 (pbk.)
ISBN-13: 978-0-88920-484-3 (pbk.)

1. Native peoples — Canada — Historiography. 2. Native peoples in literature. 3. Native peoples in motion pictures. 4. Native peoples—Canada—Ethnic identity. I. Lischke, Ute II. McNab, David, 1947- III. Series: Aboriginal studies series (Waterloo, Ont.)

E78.C2W35 2005   305.897'071   C2005-900151-8

© 2005 Wilfrid Laurier University Press
Waterloo, Ontario, Canada N2L 3C5
www.wlupress.wlu.ca

Book cover image: "A Rattle Speaks," by Teresa A. Altiman. Cover designed by Leslie Macredie. Book series colophon by Hugh McKenzie. Text design by P.J. Woodland.

Goodbye, Wild Indian

Lenore Keeshig-Tobias

1   Goodbye, Wild Indian, Goodbye.

I know it's time
       for you to go.
It's a good day too,
       to go.

I want you to know I always
       rooted for you—
       all those times.

All those times when
       the cavalry and cowboys
were kicking your ass and
shooting you with their silver bullets.
All those times the history
books were saying
you were doomed
to die, to vanish
from the face of the earth—
that meant
Mom and Dad and me too—
my whole family, eh—
And when you died, each time
you died, up there
on that silver screen
and in the paperbacks
and in the comics
and on the airwaves,
little bits of me
died too.

Actually, they just went
on reserve—
Waiting for this day, Nyah.

I remember—
Dad and mom always went
to those dark movie places
and rooted for you.

Took me too, sometimes
and I'd crane my neck
when the shooting started
because they always covered my eyes
and held me tight
as the whiteman's fear and fury
whizzed through the air,
slamming into our spirits
again and again.

And I'd look up
and see their scarlet tears
and I'd feel their sobs
caught hard and silent
between heart beats and
dry throats.

But they kept their vigil,
mom and dad did,
time and again
because
you were still part of us
and we were still part of you
and, I think, they hoped
it would all end
some day,
and you would be free.

Yeah, I rooted for you
all those times—
after I got over
the negative part of
being "Indian,"
of playing Cowboys

and Indians
and not wanting to be
the "bad guy,"
the Indian.
It's the truth. It happened.
And I ain't ashamed
to admit that either.
Those were tough times.
We didn't know any better.

2   Goodbye, Wild Indian, Goodbye.

I know it's time
for you to go.
It's a good day too,
to go.

Oh you red devil, you.
What a ham you've been.
Bloodthirsty.
Savage fiend.

And how could you?

How could you ravage
those white bosoms, those
swan-like necks,
those frail pale
voiceless women?

Yeah, I know.
They made you do it,
those whitemen.

What a novel idea.
And they wanted you to,
to do it,
those whitewomen.
Imagine that!

Deepening the intimacy—
he captured her mouth—
incredible!

Fantastic!
She moaned—
I cannot help but touch you—
Now what an imagination!
What a story!

Oh you handsome breed, you.
You raider.
You killer.
You scalper.
You wagon-burner.
You red de-flowerer of whiteman's women.
You shooter of whiteman's turkeys.
You poacher of whiteman-made fish.
You speaker of red-man's wisdom,
and whiteman's folly.
Golly.
You soothsayer.
You smooth-sayer.
You perpetual fucking conservationist.

Oh, they're out to get you now. They're all looking
to bury you.
Aaay, as if 112 million dead
over 500 years
wasn't enough already.

"We have created a monster!"
they say, "*Let's bury the noble*
savage. He has out-lived his
usefulness (the old derelict)."

"*Indian can't be noble. That's*
a stereotype," they say. "*This is the new millennium.*
We've got to be politically
correct. Besides, they never
had any royalty."
Can't you just hear
those shovels picking at the earth,
bulldozers arumbling
ready to gouge out great pile of clay?
Red clay... Red Earth Man ...

Say, ever run into that guy, Adam? Nyah.

Hey, maybe 60 years from now
they'll dig you up again
and crush your bones into bricks.

Wouldn't be the first time
neither,
wouldn't be the first time they
dug up Indian braves
from their graves, aaay.

Like the Nawash and the city of Owen Sound—
a fine Canadian city
founded on dead Indians, and
built of dead Indians.
Imagine Indian DNA in the walls of
their oldest, most important and
prestigious buildings—
courthouses, churches, city hall,
mansions, tenement buildings and stores.

Some brick work! Aaay.
What technique!
Nyah! And how about us Indians
being trustworthy, reliable!
Solid as a brick.
Solid as a red brick Nyah.

Hits you doesn't it?
Like a ton. Nyah.

Nyah, what a diatribe?
Diatribe, eh?
You know,
die-a-tribe,
die-tribe, aaay.
Like the only good one
is a dead one.

Nyah.
Feeling bitter? Besieged?
Sat on? Aaay.

3   Goodbye, Wild Indian, Goodbye.

I know it's time
for you to go.
It's a good day too,
to go.

On the other hand, maybe
they'll just make you into
a stupid cup or something.

Bona fide bone china
Bric-a-brac
Kitsch
O Kitchi-Manidou
What will they do to you next?

But I know
you're not going to go.
Not with them anyway...
Down the old garden path.
Or is it up?

Either way
it is still a rut,
one paved with our
treaty money.
Like how many other Canadian highways?

On the other hand,
they might just march
you off in shackles.
It wouldn't be the first
time neither.

Hey, can't you just see
a pair of empty shackles
walking down the street—
all by themselves. Nyah.

And you'll just let them think
what they've always thought—
that what's best for them is best

for you,
that what's best for them is best
for us,
and that you're following,
and that we're all following you.

"It looks we're done for, Tonto."
"What you mean *we*, whiteman?" Aaay.

You know, I think they never
think about how they
could be like us unless
it is for money, some financial
investment down the line
or a much higher level
of communion with
the Great Spirit
than any real "Indian"
could ever achieve.

I know—old Indian trick.
Just let them think
what they want.
They always do anyway.
That's their problem, aaay.

And just between you and me ...
It's been fun.
Hair-raising, in fact.
I'll miss you—sometimes.
But not much, honest.
You must be real
tired by now.
Five hundred years
of whoopin' it up
is one helluva party, eh.

Goodbye,
Wild Indian.
Rest in Peace.

I'll always love you. Nyah.

Contents

For<e>ward

Lenore Keeshig-Tobias

INDIAN HEAD COVE IS AN AWESOME bit of northern shoreline where the Niagara Escarpment rises high out of the water to present its aged limestone and dolomite layers to the blue-green waters of Georgian Bay, summer sunrises, the north wind, and the multitude of summer visitors. Along this wave-cut shoreline, as elsewhere along the escarpment, are incredible promontories: this place bears the name of a perceived resemblance to an "Indian" face. And yes, one can vaguely discern, there on the cliff, the profile of a human face with a big hooked nose. I thought it appropriate that I should sit here and contemplate this for<e>ward.

A number of years ago, I was deeply involved in the issue of cultural appropriation, the taking of stories, "voice," and aspects of other cultures by "white" Canadian writers for their own use. It was also an issue of whose work got published and whose didn't. More often than not, Native writers and writers of colour had their work constantly overlooked, and set and judged against the backdrop of the English-Canadian literary canon. This was in the late 1980s. I wrote an opinion piece for the *Globe and Mail*, which appeared in January 1990. The piece was intended as a challenge to the larger audience for discourse. This was a challenge I was prepared for; however, what ended up being published, when the *Globe and Mail* finished editing it, was declaration of war. My challenge song, *Hiya ho / Make way / In a sacred manner I come / The stories are mine*, which ended the piece and came after my arguments, had been moved to the beginning of the piece before the arguments. The *Globe and Mail* had me declare war on the writing community. I lost the battle and retreated to the reserve.

Now, many years later, having mellowed somewhat, I am still inclined to say, *Oh boy, here we are again re-presenting ourselves. Let x = x. This is not a Canadian experience, because the treaties were for land, not citizenship. Forever means forever. Nawash was never approached to be partners in confederation. Who the heck wants to be part of a dysfunctional relationship anyway? Not me.*

Now, I am truly glad to see that there is real and meaningful discourse about Aboriginal images and representations, from both Aboriginal and non-Aboriginal writers. It's a coming together that brings about necessary healing, so that together we can work for the common good. Miigwech to all of you.

As for the wild and noble stereotype, ten years ago, after all the quincentennial celebrations and anti-celebrations, I took it upon myself to respond to Robert Fulford's "Let's bury the noble savage," published in *Rotunda* (Fall 1992). This piece was a complement to the late Deborah Doxstator's "Fluffs 'n Feathers" exhibit. As the curator for this incredibly funny and satirical exhibit of mostly non-Aboriginal symbols of Indianness, Deborah had pulled together posters, city crests, biscuit tins, food labels, and all kind of kitsch and bric-a-brac: horribly funny Indian stuff. It was fun.

Back on the rez, I was listening to CBC radio. Robert Fulford was talking to the interviewer about burying the noble savage. Interesting. Good show. Very informative. I was indignant (not really). I thought, *Well finally... but it's too late. It's too late because we, Aboriginal peoples, have embraced the noble stereotype, adopted him, and he is now one of us, and has been for a very long time. So, back off.* I cast Robert into the role of the great white Indian agent whose whole reason for living was to make decisions for and about the Indians. Sorry, Robert, I'm just having a little bit of fun here (thanks for all the inspiration). Now, if anyone is going to bury the wild Indian ... it is going to be me, I said to my kitchen. Thus I began my "Dear John" letter, waiting for this day, nyah.

Lenore Keeshig-Tobias
Neyasshinigmiing ndoonjibaa

[*Translation:* This beautiful point of land
that is partially surrounded by water is
where my sound is coming from.]

Chippewas of Nawash Unceded
First Nation (aka Cape Croker)
September 2003

Preface

Ute Lischke and *David T. McNab*

IN 2003 WE PUBLISHED AN EDITED VOLUME—the first in the new series of Aboriginal Studies—with Wilfrid Laurier University Press, entitled *Blockades and Resistance: Studies in Actions of Peace and the Temagami Blockades of 1988–89.* One theme in that volume was how non-Aboriginal governments and peoples characterized those blockades and resistance movements. Generally, Aboriginal peoples who participated or supported blockades and engaged in other forms of resistance were perceived as "Bad Indians" derived from the "wild or savage Indians" of Canada's written histories who enjoyed torching the Christian missionaries. On the other hand, "Good Indians" were those who remained colonized, civilized, and peaceful. One finding of our study was that the "Bad Indians" were involved in such actions as blockades and resistance out of actions of peace—to protect their lands and Mother Earth. We believed that it was also necessary to explore, on a wider scale, the theme of the stereotypes about "Indians" in a separate volume. This event led to the next Wanapitei Colloquium on "Representations of Aboriginal People by Themselves and Others," held in August 2000 on Lake Temagami and Bear Island. Many of the papers from that colloquium are included in this volume.

In Elizabeth Hay's novel *A Student of Weather,* the protagonist, Norma Joyce Hardy, ponders Duncan Campbell Scott's poem "At Gull Lake: August 1810." Her teacher had introduced the poem as a love poem about a young Indian woman whose love for a down-and-out white trader precipitates her ostracism by her own people. Her teacher suggests that she is Tess, "an Indian Tess of the D'Urbervilles. She's the Highwayman's daughter. An Indian Tess braiding a loveknot into her long dark hair." The novel takes place in the early 1930s when Scott was still the deputy superintendent general of Indian Affairs. Just as Hay drew the example of a disinherited young Indian woman and compared her to Tess of the D'Urbervilles,[1] Scott, as an Aboriginal person himself,[2] has also been known to represent different views of Aboriginal people. As an administrator, he attempted to assimilate the "Bad Indians" and their "senseless drumming and dancing." But as a poet, he also romanticized them. Similar ambiguous and contradictory points of view abound in white society about the notion of the "Indian."

Over the last five hundred years, various representations of Aboriginal peoples have evolved, not only in North America but also in Europe. Aboriginal societies have always held a charm for Europeans, and Germans especially have often romanticized the notion of the wilderness and Aboriginals. Many Germans, for example, have attempted to live in their own re-created "aboriginal" communities. Franz Kafka, presents this image of a wild and free "Indian":

> If one could be an Indian, up and ready, askew, high in the air, atop a speedy horse, quivering excitedly above the shaking earth, shedding one's spurs, for there really were no spurs, throwing off the reins, since one needed no reins, barely seeing the land ahead, a barren heath, as horse and rider disappeared.[3]

Kafka's representation of the "Indian" as a disappearing "noble savage" is startlingly vivid, but hardly unique. Leaving behind the stereotypes embodied in these European/Western representations, we need to hear and examine the multiplicity and distinctiveness of Aboriginal voices. It is hoped that this volume will present to the reader a fascinating exploration of perspectives on and approaches to the representations of Aboriginal peoples, as well as to time, history, land, cultures, identities, and literacies.

We would like to thank all the contributors, the editors at WLU Press, and above all, the Social Sciences and Humanities Research Council that provided the funding for the conference and subsequently the publication of this volume.

Ute Lischke and *David T. McNab*
Keeshigonong, "The Place of Cedars"
Cape Croker

Notes

1 See Elizabeth Hay, *A Student of Weather* (Toronto: McClelland and Stewart, 2000), 101–102. Duncan Campbell Scott's study of the Saulteaux woman in his poem "At Gull Lake: August 1810" is misrepresented as being like "Tess of the D'Urbervilles."

2 See David McNab, *Circles of Time: Aboriginal Land Rights and Resistance in Ontario* (Waterloo: Wilfrid Laurier University Press, 1999), 195; "'A Lurid Dash of Colour': Powassan's Drum and Canada's Mission, the Reverend William and Duncan Campbell Scott," in *Aboriginal Cultural Landscapes*, ed. Jill Oakes, Rick Riewe, et al. (Winnipeg: Aboriginal Issues Press, 2004), 258–71. See also Daniel Francis, *The Imaginary Indian: The Image of the Indian in Canadian Culture* (Vancouver: Arsenal Pulp Press, 1992), 196–213, who, like many others, does not recognize that Scott was an Aboriginal person and thus misinterprets his life and misrepresents him.

3 Franz Kafka, *Erzählungen* (Stuttgart: Reclam, 1995), 43. Translation by Ute Lischke.

Bibliography

Francis, Daniel. *The Imaginary Indian: The Image of the Indian in Canadian Culture*. Vancouver: Arsenal Pulp Press, 1992.

Hay, Elizabeth. *A Student of Weather*. Toronto: McClelland and Stewart, 2000.

Kafka, Franz. *Erzählungen*. Stuttgart: Reclam, 1995.

McNab, David. *Circles of Time: Aboriginal Land Rights and Resistance in Ontario*. Waterloo: Wilfrid Laurier University Press, 1999.

Introduction

Ute Lischke and *David T. McNab*

"THE MOST WE CAN HOPE FOR is that we are paraphrased correctly."[1] In this quotation, Lenore Keeshig-Tobias points to one of the issues in how Aboriginal people are represented by non-Aboriginal peoples. Frequently, Aboriginal people are not understood in their own contexts. Non-Aboriginal people often fail to understand the sheer diversity and multiplicity and the shifting identities of Aboriginal people. Unless that is understood, Aboriginal people will continue to be misrepresented as individuals and as groups. Even a paraphrase is better than a stereotype of "good" or "bad" Indians, which has been the case only too often in the past.

From the very first contacts with Europeans, Aboriginal people have been presented in two distinct ways: one as the noble savage and the other not so noble. Randy Fred, a member of the Tseshaht First Nation in British Columbia, concluded in his foreword to *The Imaginary Indian*, after talking about his experiences in a residential school, that "Native people live within a world of imagery that isn't their own." Daniel Francis goes on to point out in his book that "Indians, as we think we know them, do not exist. In fact, there may well be no such thing as an Indian."[2] Yet stereotypes, often accepted uncritically as true representations of "Indians," have proliferated over the last five hundred years, in Europe, North America, and elsewhere.

Since the publication of *The Imaginary Indian*, numerous studies have appeared that deal with stereotyping of Aboriginal peoples. These stereotypes, however, have seldom gone beyond the contradictions found in them. One could well argue that everything is in fact represented or constructed in the practice of life writing, the writing of history, literature or presented in cinematic forms. The fact is that many Aboriginal voices need to be heard and explored. The themes of non-Aboriginal representations and self-representation of Aboriginal peoples raise the question of which voices we are listening to: European or Aboriginal? And how are these voices constructed? Can Aboriginal voices appear in a European context? Can we get beyond the stereotypes, to the idea and problems inherent in the recognition of multiple and distinct Aboriginal voices? Moreover, can we not also examine representations of all peoples and their voices, the land, and time, from different and Indigenous and European/North American perspectives? Indeed, the notion of many Aboriginal voices has recently been theorized by several critics, thus opening onto "highly meaningful and symbolic 'worlds' populated with fantastic, inanimate, animal, human and spirit characters who act out some of the most fascinating tales in world literature today. The body of natural scientific knowledge encompassed in the concept of Aboriginal Voices also contains valuable paradigms, teachings and information that can benefit all of the world family of nations." Aboriginal voices, and the knowledge embedded in them, have always been an "integral part of the key to human survival."[3] These voices must be presented in their own context as stories flowing ceaselessly and naturally from Indigenous knowledge itself. The founding of Native Studies programs and departments at Canadian institutions—for example the First Nations University (formerly the Saskatchewan Federated Indian College affiliated with the University of Regina), Universities of Saskatchewan, Manitoba, and Alberta, and Trent University—reflect the importance of the development of Aboriginal knowledge and recognition of it in its own right. The latter has also become the first Canadian university (and only the second in North America) to offer a doctorate in Native Studies.

There are unique Aboriginal voices from many different nations. When Columbus arrived on the shores of present-day North America, he thought he had reached the East Indies, and called the inhabitants "Indians." But the people he first met were Arawaks, who had "as much in common with the Iroquois of the northern Woodlands as the Iroquois had in common with the Blackfoot of the western Plains or the Haida of the Pacific Coast." There were many different and distinct cultures— but no category of "Indians." This category was the "invention of the European."[4] A similar parallel can be found in the "northern experience" of Canada, which is one of the central myths of Canadian culture in which the Inuit voices are appropriated as part of the "Canadian experience." It is significant that, although "we forget what we know about the arbitrariness of representation in order to get on with everyday life, that arbitrariness is no excuse for making everything we see in our own images, and it is certainly no excuse for speaking on behalf of others."[5]

Representations of others are usually social and political acts. These acts are problematic and need to be contested. As Francis deftly put it, "The Indian began as a White man's mistake, and became a White man's fantasy. Through the prism of White hopes, fears and prejudices, indigenous Americans would be seen to have lost contact with reality and to have become Indians; that is, anything non-Natives wanted them to be."[6] Similarly, as John M. MacKenzie has also persuasively demonstrated,[7] European imperialism, especially German imperialism strongly rooted in the nineteenth century, aided and abetted by the literature of Karl May (itself a branch of popular culture), retained a powerful hold upon German popular culture, especially about the "other," in particular about "Indians" in North America. European representations of "Indians" as the "other" have become embedded in European-based knowledge systems and in the history of North America. Representations of non-Aboriginal people have forced Aboriginal people to walk a tightrope in terms of their identities.

Representations by Aboriginal people have become grounded in the independent histories of each. Aboriginal histories written by Aboriginal people differ significantly from those written by non-Aboriginals. In addition, these historical representations affect how Aboriginal people see themselves and how they continue to be seen by others to this day. In order for Aboriginal people to see themselves in a light more consistent with their own cultures, these representations must be changed. This is slowly starting to happen and it is hoped that this book will assist in that transformation. Unless this is done, as Dale A. Turner, a citizen of the Temagami First Nation and a professor of Native Studies at Dartmouth College, pointed out in his "History and Aboriginal Rights after Delgamuukw," Aboriginal people will continue to be "walking a tightrope."

Another notion of representation is to present again. Representation is the act or an instance of representing or being re-presented and is also a statement made by allegation or to convey opinion. Aboriginal people have always presented themselves in their own (but many different) cultural contexts to Europeans, usually with a public display of their context, but those viewing such a representation would not usually have known this Aboriginal context. Europeans frequently neglected to inquire about this context and instead assumed it away and substituted a European imperial context. This manner of representation has effectively been the same for hundreds of years, and through it, Aboriginal people today still continue to be represented in it. The most obvious result is racism. In this very real sense, Aboriginal people are still walking a tightrope with the European noose of representations around their necks. Only very slowly has this begun to change in incremental ways. For example, Aboriginal people are now beginning to publish their own books and to represent themselves and their literatures in them. The multiplicity and distinctiveness of their voices are now being heard, and the silence has been broken.[8]

One of the most significant assumptions about representations of Aboriginal people is revealed in how histories are constructed and the concepts of history that Aboriginal and non-Aboriginal people have about "Indians." The German scholar Christian Feest has argued, "'Indians' are not a people inhabiting the wide expanses of the American continent. Their place of origin and residence lies in the realm of the imagination of the Europeans (and later the white Americans) who were taken by surprise to discover 'new' people in a 'new' world following its 'discovery' in 1492. With their confusing diversity and contradictions, the 'Indians' quickly became the embodiment of the 'other,' providing a counter example of what was good and of what was bad in the observer's culture." These representations of the "Indian" have continued to this day and reflect the "changes in Western society's perception of Native Americans and show how much the imagined world of 'the Indians' is due to our own situation." Feest explains that while "in the 19th century 'the Indians' stood for exemplary courage in war, for masculinity, and for leadership, by the late 20th century they had become representatives of peace, feminism, and environmental awareness. Just as the famous 'environmental' speech by Chief Seattle had never been delivered by the historic Duwamish leader but was written in 1969 by a white American for a film on environmental destruction in the United States, other aspects of the 'Indian' image are also nothing but figments of our imagination."[9] This has nothing to do with Aboriginal histories, which are sovereign and independent in their own right. To be clearly represented, Aboriginal peoples must tell their own stories about themselves.

Shepard Krech, in his controversial book *The Ecological Indian: Myth and History*, has also provided the example of Iron Eyes Cody being used as the image for the Crying Indian on a poster in 1971 by Keep America Beautiful Inc. This Cherokee actor's face became one of the most recognizable Indians as noble ecologist. Krech questions the notion of the Indian being the representative of ecology. He argues that it was an advertising invention of Madison Avenue that helped to reduce the "Indian" to a simplistic stereotypical image as ecologist and conservationist.[10] Simply put, non-Aboriginal peoples have always represented '"Indians" as European categories of thought rather than as human beings.[11]

In the 1990s the Royal Commission on Aboriginal Peoples, in the context of public education of Canada about Aboriginal peoples, investigated these categories of thought as stereotypes. The commission published its final report in 1996. It gave an opportunity for the distinctiveness of Aboriginal voices to be heard—some for the first time. These voices were embedded in Aboriginal histories. For example, the 1996 *Report of the Royal Commission on Aboriginal Peoples* (RCAP) drew attention to the diverse concepts of history among Aboriginal and non-Aboriginal people in Canada. Chief Eli Mandamin spoke eloquently to the commission at Kenora, Ontario, on October 28, 1992: "Prejudice has prevented non-Aboriginal society from recognizing the depth, sophistication and beauty of our culture.... But this must change, or there will be immense suffering in the future in this beautiful land which the Creator has bestowed upon us." The RCAP stated bluntly that the public held two views of "Indians" and their relationship to the rest of Canada as exemplified in the framework of treaty relationships. Pierre Elliott Trudeau represented the first in a speech on the white paper in 1969: "We will recognize treaty rights. We will recognize forms of contract which have been made with the Indian people by the Crown and we will try to bring justice in that area and this will mean that perhaps the treaties shouldn't go on forever. It's inconceivable, I think, that in a given society one section of the society have a treaty with the other section of society. We must all be equal under the laws and we must not sign treaties amongst ourselves."[12]

The false views of treaties in the public mind were characterized by a static view of Aboriginal cultures that were anachronistic and outdated: "The view described earlier—that treaties are no more than outdated scraps of paper—has led many Canadians to consider that the specific obligations described in the treaty documents are trivial and can therefore be easily discharged."[13] In this view, treaties are ancient and anachronistic documents with no relevance today. Like Prime Minister Trudeau (who was also an Aboriginal person, an Elliott, Mohawk, Bear clan, on his mother's side)[14] in 1969, many Canadians still do not understand how, in a modern democratic society, treaties can continue to exist between different parts of society. The second view is that "old treaty obligations might have to be fulfilled—grudgingly—but that the making of new ones is anathema to a vital and modern nation."[15]

To understand Aboriginal voices means that we must listen to their stories. In this volume David Newhouse represents himself as a middle-aged Onondaga man and reminds us that we must tell our own story about ourselves if we are to represent ourselves in our context. Likewise, Marcia Crosby, a Tsimpsian/Haida woman, has observed that the representations of the "Indians" she encountered were "euro centric constructions of either the bloodthirsty savage, or passive, colonized Indian-as-landscape; both representations reflect the new Canadians' fear of the hostile forces of nature/indigene."[16] The RCAP summed this view up as follows: "If, as Justice Reid said, 'every schoolboy knows' that the treaties were a sham used to disguise the expropriation of land, then this is the direct result of schoolboys having been misled or at least deprived of the truth about the treaties and about the people that made them."[17] This has had profound political consequences for how non-Aboriginal Canadians view Aboriginal nations as equal partners in the Canadian Confederation.[18]

Part of this cultural context of Aboriginal peoples' representing themselves in their own contexts lies in a better understanding of and respect for Aboriginal oral traditions. These traditions are now part of Canadian law upheld by the Supreme Court of Canada in its judgments, which for many decades misrepresented the rights of Aboriginal peoples. Daniel Francis emphasized in *The Imaginary Indian*,

"Much public discourse about native people still deals in stereotypes. Our views of what constitutes an Indian today are as much bound up with myth, prejudice and ideology as earlier versions were. If the Indian really is imaginary, it could hardly be otherwise" [emphasis added].[19] One of the best examples is the Delgamuukw trial judgment by Chief Justice McEachern in 1991. Delgamuukw was a British Columbia case involving the Aboriginal title and rights of the Gitksan and Wet'suwet'en peoples. Rejecting Aboriginal oral traditions as well as their cultural context, McEachern wrote, "The plaintiffs' ancestors had no written language, no horses or wheeled vehicles, slavery and starvation was not uncommon, wars with neighbouring peoples were common, and there is no doubt, to quote Hobbs [*sic*] that aboriginal life was, at best, 'nasty, brutish and short.'"[20] This view was completely overturned by the Supreme Court of Canada six years later. In December 1997, the Supreme Court of Canada addressed the issue of the legitimacy of Aboriginal oral traditions in its judgment on Delgamuukw while rejecting McEachern's racist and stereotyped views of the imaginary Indian. The Supreme Court of Canada ordered a new trial. The options for the parties to this case are two-fold: to negotiate a treaty or similar agreement or to begin again at the trial level. Delgamuukw both identified and marked a beginning—a spiritual watershed—not an end, while raising questions about written history and oral traditions. Can Aboriginal oral traditions and written history intersect? What kinds of history can historians use? How do Aboriginal and non-Aboriginal historians try to recreate and understand the past? The answers to these questions are significant and are addressed in part 2 of this volume entitled, "Historical Representations." In this transformation, the Delgamuukw case, as Turner points out above, was pivotal.

Moreover, the principles embodied in that case were also tested and reinforced in the Marshall decision of the Supreme Court of Canada handed down on September 17, 1999. This case was a treaty-rights resource issue regarding the catching of eels for commercial purposes by Donald Marshall Junior, a Mi'kmaq, in Pomquet Harbour in Nova Scotia based on a Mi'kmaq treaty of 1760 negotiated at Halifax. The court ruled that, in understanding and interpreting the spirit and intent of these treaties, the oral and the written records and the testimony of expert witnesses were to be relied upon, whether or not the treaty document was ambiguous on its face. These records should be used so as *not* to define Aboriginal or treaty rights on the basis of a narrow focus on, or interpretation of, a written treaty document. All of the historical evidence, including oral traditions, as written or otherwise, must be equally weighed and equally applied. The historical context, intentions, and result of the treaty negotiations in terms of the integrity and honour of the Crown must be taken into account in deciding Aboriginal and treaty rights. Oral traditions and the context of the Aboriginal context of a treaty were to be now weighted equally with the written record. This decision was a landmark in recogning that Aboriginal peoples and their histories had equal voices and representation about themselves in their context.

These court cases mark the beginning on a macrocosmic scale of a dialogue about Canada and its future. Canada will become a place where both Aboriginal and non-Aboriginal nations will have equal voices, a place to share, and a place where we are all respected as equals.[21]

Part 1 of this volume explores Aboriginal voices through reflections on personal experience. Drew Hayden Taylor, an Anishinabe writer from Curve Lake, writes provocatively in "Seeing Red: The Stoic Whiteman and Non-Native Humour." He takes apart the racist stereotypes about "Indians" and turns them inside out to reveal, with a great deal of humour, what would happen if the white people applied their own stereotypes to themselves. On the other side of the coin, Phil Bellfy, an Anishinabe scholar teaching at Michigan State University, shows how pervasive white images of "Indians" are, and how they are misappropriated and exploited, in chapter 2, "The Identity Tightrope." These corporate logos have been part of North American corporate culture, much like mascots, since at least the early nineteenth century.

In chapter 3, "Telling Our Story," Professor David Newhouse, who teaches in the Department of Native Studies at Trent University, provides a compelling argument on the character of Aboriginal and non-Aboriginal histories, emphasizing their diverse character and uniqueness. Newhouse stresses that our notions of history are ultimately and intimately personal experiences based on our understanding of the world and our roles and responsibilities in it. His comments are reflections based on that of a "contemporary Onondaga middle-aged man" who has been educated in the divergent Western and Iro-quoian traditions of history. Going back to the thirteenth century and the formation of the Iroquois Confederacy, he focuses on the complementary character and richness of Aboriginal histories that already exist in these communities. Newhouse concludes that history is the "story that we tell ourselves about ourselves."

In chapter 4, Dawn T. Maracle, a doctoral student in education at OISE in the University of Toronto, writes about the misrepresentations in her life and her family in "A Story Untold: A Community-based Oral Narrative of Mohawk Women's Voices from Point Anne." This chapter is a series of stories, an Aboriginal tradition, which calls into question the false notions of non-Aboriginal people derived from nineteenth-century scientific racism about "pure-bloodedness." Maracle's chapter is a thoughtful exploration of her family's highly diverse identities within the Tyendinaga Mohawk Territory that defy categorization.

In chapter 5, Mark Dockstator who teaches in the Department of Native Studies at Trent University, writes about the independence and the sovereignty of Aboriginal people. In his "Reflections on Aboriginal Representations of History and the Royal Commission on Aboriginal Peoples, 1996," Dockstator reflects on the groundbreaking work he completed for the Royal Commission on Aboriginal Peoples in the early 1990s, which was published in its 1996 report. The issue for the commission was to reconcile the highly divergent models of history of Western linear knowledge systems with cyclical Indigenous notions based on Aboriginal oral traditions. His paper goes on to show the implications of this divergence of historical paradigms in the periodization of Canada's history. Dockstator also indicates how this divergence affects present and future development of Aboriginal governance in Canada. Recognition of the inherent right of Aboriginal governance will help to end the European-based representations of Aboriginal people by "others."

In part 2, Historical Representations, chapter 6, Olive Patricia Dickason, professor emeritus at the University of Alberta, and an adjunct professor at the University of Ottawa, examines the "Many Faces of Canada's History as It Relates to Aboriginal People in Some Recent Writing." Dickason accurately attributes these "many faces" to the relationships between histories and identities within the framework of our world views. She points out that this is a process. In her article, Dickason does not refer to her own work in this process. In it, as a Metis historian, Dickason has done much in her historical writings to break the silence about Aboriginal histories and to give voice to them in written form. She is herself a watershed in Canadian historical writing about Aboriginal peoples: she has been prominently recognized in the First Peoples Hall in Canada's National Museum of Civilization for her work, as well as receiving a National Aboriginal Achievement Award and the Order of Canada. Dickason's magisterial volume, *Canada's First Nations: A History of Founding Peoples from Earliest Times*, first published more than a decade ago, is now in its third edition (2002) and has made an enormous impact on the process in which the multiplicity and distinctiveness of Aboriginal voices are now heard in the past as well as in the present. It took an Aboriginal voice to break that historical silence.

In her chapter, Dickason refers to convergences and divergences in the writing of histories in the Canadian experience, on the basis of written and oral sources. She consequently posits, "The spoken word can have a range of values that eludes the transposition into print." Dickason concludes that history is living, a "major instrument" in self-discovery, and an accurate representation of the voices of Aboriginal peoples. This is a remarkable achievement, highlighting how important Aboriginal voices are in changing the ways in which Europeans and North Americans view the history of Aboriginal people in the context of North American history.

Karl Hele writes, in chapter 7, about the "Whirlwind of History: Parallel Nineteenth-Century Perspectives on 'Are they savage?'" In it, Hele, an Anishinabe citizen of the Garden River First Nation and an assistant professor of First Nations Studies at the University of Western Ontario, examines the historical perspectives of two individuals— two Methodist ministers: a non-Aboriginal (Thomas Hurlburt) and Kahkewaquonaby (Peter Jones), a Mississauga, as they debated in writing. From this encounter, Hele illustrates that the "Aboriginal concept of history … is a fluid motion, bound by neither time nor space" and that a "basic tool used to teach these conceptualizations is the medicine wheel; its centre remains fixed as the wheel moves with history flowing around the circle." The effect is syncretic. From this whirlwind concept, "history is moving toward an era when Aboriginal and non-Aboriginal peoples will live in mutual respect and cooperation."

Winona Wheeler is a Cree historian, who is dean and teaches at the First Nation's University's campus in Saskatoon. Her chapter, "Reflections on the Social Relations of Indigenous Oral Histories," is a timely evocation of the significance of languages and cultures in relationship to oral traditions. After returning home from graduate school in California, she reaffirmed her discovery of why she had become a Cree historian: "Nêhiyawîhckikêwin, *the Cree way/culture,* is an oral culture, a listening culture. We are a people to whom understanding and knowledge comes by way of relationships—with the Creator, the past, the present, the future, life around us, each other, and within ourselves. And, like my ancestors, I am here on this earth to learn." Wheeler's contribution is a significant chapter in the attempt to understand the differences between European-based and Aboriginal knowledge systems and their disparate world views.

In chapter 9, Stephen Bocking, a political scientist at Trent University, examines European-based knowledge systems, showing their relationships to Indigenous knowledge of the North in his "Scientists and Evolving Perceptions of Traditional Knowledge." Bocking shows just how significant indigenous knowledge is compared to some European-based knowledge, especially in the context of Canada's North. He uses the classic example of the fate of Sir John Franklin to reveal how very lacking European knowledge can sometimes be.

In chapter 10, Dennis Bartels, of Sir Wilfrid Grenfell College, Memorial University of Newfoundland, and Alice Bartels, in their "Representations of Newfoundland Mi'gmaq" show how powerfully community history and identity are related through oral histories among the Mi'kmaq of Newfoundland. This form of resistance is a key to their gaining their status and recognition as Aboriginal peoples within Canada's political and constitutional systems.

What is the relationship between Aboriginal voices and identities, their cultures, and their art? George Morrison, the Anishinabe artist, argued that the "identity of an artist, and in this sense the *anishinabe* artist, does not decide the meaning or determine the merit of the art. Native artists create more than the mere pictures of a culture."[21] This issue of identity further complicates the literary and cinematic forms of representations of Aboriginal peoples.

In part 3, Literary and Cinematic Representations, Ute Lischke, of Wilfrid Laurier University and David T. McNab, of the Atkinson Faculty of Liberal and Professional Studies, York University, lead off in chapter 11, with "Show me the money: Representations of Aboriginal People in East-German Indian Films in the Late Twentieth Century." This is a provocative exploration of the basis for racist stereotypical representations and their exploitive impact on Aboriginal peoples. These films made between 1966 and 1983 in the former East Germany were based on "Indians" of earlier American westerns. Here, however, westerns became "easterns." The plots were often turned on their heads: the "Indians" usually won rather than lost. The bad guys were the American, English, or French imperialists—effectively Cold War propaganda. Notwithstanding this inversion, the "Indians" in the NEFA films in the late twentieth century remained the stereotypical "good Indian" and "noble savage."

Kathryn Bunn-Marcuse, a doctoral student at the University of Washington, in chapter 12 examines the role of the non-Aboriginal and Aboriginal filmmakers in attempting to document their lives: "'This film has been modified from its original version ...,' Films of the Kwakwaka'wakw from Curtis to U'mista Kwakwaka'wakw on Film." She focuses on the films of Edward Curtis, Franz Boas, Robert Gardner, and the U'mista Cultural Society—all of which feature the potlatch and its dramatic dances. The films by Curtis and Boas (*In the Land of the Head-Hunters*, rereleased as *In the Land of the War Canoes*, 1914; *A Documentary on the Kwakiutl*, 1930) are firmly rooted in the salvage ethnography of the early twentieth century. Robert Gardner attempted to capture a more complete picture of Kwakwaka'wakw life in the 1950s (*Blunden Harbour* and *Dances of the Kwakiutl*, 1951) but still omits any presentation of contemporary cultural struggles. Parts of these early documentary films have subsequently been re-appropriated by Kwakwaka'wakw filmmakers to represent their culture through their own creative lens. This paper concludes that the modern U'mista films (*Potlatch...A Strict Law Bids Us Dance*, 1975 and *Box of Treasures*, 1983) reclaim and reinterpret ceremonial imagery from the earlier films as part of a larger Native-directed effort to document Aboriginal history.

In chapter 13, Bernie Harder, who teaches English at the University of Windsor, discusses the poetry of the Anishinabe writer Armand

Ruffo. Entitled "A Way of Seeing the World: Anishinabe in Armand Garnet Ruffo's *Grey Owl: The Mystery of Archie Belaney* (1997)," this chapter explores how an Aboriginal writer can have an impact on the racial stereotypes created by Euro-Canadians, in this case Grey Owl, the Englishman who was adopted by the Anishinabe. In his poetry Ruffo has provided us, Harder explains, with a new perspective on Grey Owl by the use of oral traditions from his family history.

Janne Korkka, a doctoral student at the University of Turku, Finland, focuses on the fiction of Rudy Wiebe in chapter 14 entitled "Representation of Aboriginal Peoples in Rudy Wiebe's Fiction, *The Temptations of Big Bear* and *A Discovery of Strangers*." This study explores the persons and themes of Aboriginal people in the fictional work of Wiebe and then compares them to his collaborative work (with Yvonne Johnson, who is a descendant of Big Bear). Korkka concludes that Wiebe's fiction is part of an overall process which is continuously re-occurring: "Wiebe's novels do not invite readers to view remnants of a story. Instead, readers are invited to engage in an ongoing remaking of neglected or suppressed stories and seek to understand the elements they may not have stopped to consider before."

Christian Feest has aptly observed that "through countless books and movies, the myth of the 'Indian' has been kept alive and continues to exert a considerable influence on our perception of the original inhabitants of America. It is precisely for this reason that we constantly need to remind ourselves how much this distorts our view of the manifold realities of the indigenous American."[23] All of these representations of Aboriginal peoples reveal overwhelmingly how significant Aboriginal people and their distinctive voices are becoming. There is complexity and diversity in individuals and issues. The old categories of Aboriginal people must fall by the wayside. Leaving aside the significant issue of authenticity, it is not impossible for non-Aboriginal people to portray Aboriginal people accurately. The painter Edmund Morris, son of the government negotiator of late-nineteenth-century treaties, was able to accomplish that difficult task early in the twentieth century with his Aboriginal portraits. The ethnographer Edward S. Rogers remarked that these paintings "should be to all Canadians, as they were to Morris, as important as the portraits of prime ministers, lieutenant governors and generals."[24] Lavonne Brown Ruoff has also commented that nearly 500 years later, many people think of American

Indians as curious vestiges of a distant past, waging a futile war to survive in a Space Age society. Even today, our understanding of the history and culture of American Indians is too often derived from unsympathetic, culturally biased, and inaccurate reports. The American Indian, described and portrayed in thousands of movies, televisions programs, books, articles, and government studies, has either been raised to the statues of the "noble savage" or disparaged as the "wild Indian" who resisted the westward expansion of the American frontier. Where in this popular view are the real Indians, the human beings, the families, and the communities whose ancestors can be traced back to ice-age hunters? Where are the creative and indomitable people whose sophisticated technologies used the natural resources to ensure their survival, whose military skill might even have prevented European settlement of North America if not for devastating epidemics and disruption of the ecology?[25]

This volume is part of the dynamic historical process that envisions an ongoing change in the representation of Aboriginal peoples. The issues are difficult and cannot always be easily understood or resolved. Yet a study of these issues is vitally necessary in order to comprehend the relationship between the Aboriginal and First Nation levels of government, and the immigrant population in North America. Only when we begin to understand the complex and unique legal and historical status of Aboriginal peoples, can we begin to understand the cultures of Native Peoples in North America. We can expect more profound change and resistance to new representations in the years ahead. Yet the multiplicity and distinctiveness of Aboriginal voices, no longer silenced, will continue to be heard, and as Keeshig-Tobias has said, in this process for Aboriginal people, the most they can hope for is that they are paraphrased correctly.

Notes

1   Lenore Keeshig-Tobias, quoted in David McLaren, "Lost Words," *Alternatives Journal* 29, 1 (2003): 45.

2   Daniel Francis, *The Imaginary Indian: The Image of the Indian in Canadian Culture* (Vancouver: Arsenal Pulp Press, 1992), xii, 4.

3   Greg Young-Ing, "Aboriginal Text in Context," *(Ad)dressing Our Words: Aboriginal Perspectives on Aboriginal Literature*, ed. Armand Garnet Ruffo (Penticton: Theytus, 2001), 240–41.

4 Francis, *The Imaginary Indian*, 4.

5 Renée Hulan, *Northern Experience and the Myths of Canadian Culture* (Montreal & Kingston: McGill-Queen's University Press, 2002), 17.

6 See, for example, the contributions of Aboriginal voices in *(Ad)dressing Our Words: Aboriginal Perspectives on Aboriginal Literature*, ed. Armand Garnet Ruffo (Penticton: Theytus, 2001).

7 John M. Mackenzie, ed., *Imperialism and Popular Culture* (Manchester: Manchester University Press, 1986), especially MacKenzie, "Introduction," 1-16; *Orientalism, History, Theory and the Arts* (Manchester: Manchester University Press, 1995); *The Empire of Nature, Hunting, Conservation and British Imperialism* (Manchester: Manchester University Press, 1988).

8 Thomas King, *The Truth about Stories: A Native Narrative*, The Massey Lecture Series (Toronto: House of Anansi Press, 2003).

9 Christian F. Feest, ed., *The Cultures of Native North Americans* (Cologne: Könemann Verlagsgesellschaft mbH, 2000), 13.

10 Sheppard Krech III, *The Ecological Indian: Myth and History* (New York: Norton, 1999).

11 Canada. *Report of The Royal Commission on Aboriginal Peoples* (Ottawa: Canada Communications Group, 1996), 13 (hereinafter cited as RCAP).

12 Ibid., 16.

13 Barbara Alice Mann, *Iroquoian Women, The Gantowisas* (New York: Peter Lang, 2000), 156.

14 RCAP, 16-17.

15 Winona Wheeler, "Thoughts on the Responsibilities of Indigenous/Native Studies," *The Canadian Journal of Native Studies* 21, 1 (2001): 97-104.

16 On this subject see Francis, *The Imaginary Indian*.

17 Marcia Crosby, "Construction of the Imaginary Indian," in *Vancouver Anthology: The Institutional Politics of Art*, ed. Stan Douglas (Vancouver: Talonbooks, 1991), 266-91 . Mann, a Seneca woman of the Bear Clan, also shows the extensive misrepresentations of Iroquoian women by Europeans in her book, noted above in endnote 13.

18 RCAP, 17.

19 Kiera L. Ladner, "Visions of Neo-Colonialism? Renewing the Relationship with Aboriginal Peoples," *The Canadian Journal of Native Studies* 21, 1 (2001): 105-36.

20 Francis, *The Imaginary Indian*, 6-7.

21 David T. McNab, "The Spirit of Delgamuukw and Aboriginal Oral Traditions in Ontario," in *Beyond the Nass Valley: National Implications of the Supreme Court's Delgamuukw Decision*, ed. Owen Lippert (Vancouver: The Fraser Institute, 2000), 273-83 . See also Dean M. Jacobs, "'We have but our hearts and the traditions of our old men': Understanding the Traditions and History of Bkejwanong," in *Gin Das Winan Documenting Aboriginal History in Ontario*, Occasional Papers of the Champlain Society,

no. 2, ed. David McNab and S. Dale Standen (Toronto: The Champlain Society, 1996), 1-13 ; Paul Williams, "Oral Traditions on Trial," *Gin Das Winan Documenting Aboriginal History in Ontario*, Occasional Papers of the Champlain Society, no. 2, ed. David McNab and S. Dale Standen (Toronto: The Champlain Society, 1996), 29-34.

22 Gerald Vizenor, *The Everlasting Sky, Voices of the Anishinabe People* (St. Paul: Minnesota Historical Society Press, 2000 (1972), ix.

23 Feest, *Cultures of Native North Americans*, 13.

24 E.S. Rogers, "Introduction," in *The Diaries of Edmund Montague Morris: Western Journeys, 1907-10*, ed. Mary Fitzgibbon (Toronto: The Royal Ontario Museum, 1985), 6.

25 A. Lavonne Brown Ruoff. *Literatures of the American Indian* (New York: Chelsea House, 1991), 8.

Bibliography

Canada. *Report of The Royal Commission on Aboriginal Peoples*. Ottawa: Canada Communications Group, 1996.

Crosby, Marcia. "Construction of the Imaginary Indian." In *Vancouver Anthology: The Institutional Politics of Art*. Ed. Stan Douglas. Vancouver: Talonbooks, 1991. 266-91.

Feest, Christian F., ed. *The Cultures of Native North Americans*. Cologne: Könemann Verlagsgesellschaft mbH, 2000.

Francis, Daniel. *The Imaginary Indian: The Image of the Indian in Canadian Culture*. Vancouver: Arsenal Pulp Press, 1992.

Hulan, Renée. *Northern Experience and the Myths of Canadian Culture*. Montreal and Kingston: McGill-Queen's University Press, 2002.

Jacobs, Dean M. "'We have but our hearts and the traditions of our old men': Understanding the Traditions and History of Bkejwanong." In *Gin Das Winan Documenting Aboriginal History in Ontario*. Ed. David T. McNab and S. Dale Standen, 1-13. Toronto: The Champlain Society, 1996.

Keeshig-Tobias, Lenore. "Lost Words." *Alternatives Journal* 29, 1 (2003): 45.

King, Thomas. *The Truth about Stories: A Native Narrative*. The Massey Lecture Series. Toronto: House of Anansi Press, 2003.

Krech, Sheppard III. *The Ecological Indian: Myth and History*. New York: Norton, 1999.

Ladner, Kiera L. "Visions of Neo-Colonialism? Renewing the Relationship with Aboriginal Peoples." *The Canadian Journal of Native Studies* 21, 1 (2001): 105-36.

Mackenzie, John M., ed. *The Empire of Nature, Hunting, Conservation and British Imperialism*. Manchester: Manchester University Press, 1988.

———. *Imperialism and Popular Culture*. Manchester: Manchester University Press, 1986.

———. *Orientalism, History, Theory and the Arts*. Manchester: Manchester University Press, 1995.

Mann, Barbara Alice. *Iroquoian Women, The Gantowisas*. New York: Peter Lang, 2000.

McNab, David T. "The Spirit of Delgamuukw and Aboriginal Oral Traditions in Ontario." In *Beyond the Nass Valley: National Implications of the Supreme Court's Delgamuukw Decision*. Ed. Owen Lippert. Vancouver: The Fraser Institute, 2000. 273–83.

Rogers, E.S. *The Diaries of Edmund Montague Morris: Western Journeys, 1907–10*. Toronto: The Royal Ontario Museum, 1985.

Ruoff, A. Lavonne Brown. *Literatures of the American Indian*. New York: Chelsea House, 1991.

Vizenor, Gerald. *The Everlasting Sky: Voices of the Anishinabe People*. St. Paul: Minnesota Historical Society Press, 2000.

Wheeler, Winona. "Thoughts on the Responsibilities of Indigenous/Native Studies." *The Canadian Journal of Native Studies* 21, 1 (2001): 97–104.

Williams, Paul. "Oral Traditions on Trial." In *Gin Das Winan Documenting Aboriginal History in Ontario*. Ed. David T. McNab and S. Dale Standen. Toronto: The Champlain Society, 1996. 29–34.

Young-Ing, Greg. "Aboriginal Text in Context." In *(Ad)dressing Our Words: Aboriginal Perspectives on Aboriginal Literature*. Ed. Armand Garnet Ruffo. Penticton: Theytus, 2001. 233–42.

A Reflections on Walking a Tightrope

1

Seeing Red: The Stoic Whiteman and Non-Native Humour

Drew Hayden Taylor

> *A smile is sacred.*
> —Hopi elder

SOME PEOPLE HAVE NO SENSE OF HUMOUR. I am tempted to say "some white people," but that would be racist, though I'm told that it is politically impossible for a member of an oppressed minority to be racist against a dominant culture because of some socio-political reason. But I digress. In December 1999, a play of mine titled *alterNATIVES* was produced in Vancouver. It was about cultural conflicts between Native and non-Native people, and perceived stereotypes, presented in a somewhat comedic manner. Or so I thought. A few days into its run, one lone reviewer referred to it as "witless white-bashing" (though other critics had responded embarrassingly well to this and its previous production), practically accusing me of having it in for white people (even though I am half white—I am still trying to understand that logic). The day the review came out, the theatre received a bomb threat, accusing the company of producing a play that was racist against white people. Some days it just doesn't pay to get out of bed and write a play.

I don't know why I was so surprised. Non-Native reaction to Native humour, specifically that presented in theatre, has always been something of a perception problem, as the art form continues to grow. With the debate over the suitability of political correctness, the dominate culture's willingness to enjoy, appreciate, and accept the unique Native sense of humour quickly becomes a political minefield. Add to that the volatile atmosphere in British Columbia at the time surrounding the fallout over the Nishga Treaty and the turmoil involving the Musqueum landowners, and it's no wonder a few people in Vancouver were less than enthusiastic about a Native comedy/drama and were developing theatre appraisal via chemical interaction.

But this particular reaction to Native humour goes beyond Vancouver and December 1999. Several years ago I was fortunate to have an early play of mine produced at the Lighthouse Theatre in Port Dover, Ontario. It was a small, innocuous comedy called *The Bootlegger Blues*, which detailed the adventures of a fifty-eight-year-old, good Christian Ojibway woman named Martha, who, through a series of circumstances, finds herself bootlegging 143 cases of beer to raise money to buy an organ for the church. Not exactly Sam Shepard, but based on an incident that happened on a reserve that I won't get into or my mother will kill me.

In this play there were no searing insights into the Aboriginal existence, or tragic portrayals of a culture done wrong, that we have grown to expect on the stage. In fact, it was the opposite of that. The director-dramaturge with whom I developed the project, my mentor Larry Lewis, came to me one day after having just directed the premiere of a little play you may have heard of, *Drylips Oughta Move to Kapuskasing*. He was somewhat burnt out by the process and said to me. "Drew, I want you to write something for me that has people leaving the theatre holding their sore stomachs from laughing so much, not drying their eyes from crying or scratching their heads from thinking too much." Thus was born *The Bootlegger Blues*.

This play, I was proud to say, had no socially redeeming qualities whatsoever. It was simply a celebration of the Native sense of humour. Not my best work in retrospect, but it was funny enough to beat the theatre's audience projections and subtly (don't tell anybody) raise some awareness. But the thing I especially remember about that particular production was that it was my introduction to the racially divisive line that sometimes exists when a non-Native audience is presented with Native humour, primarily on stage. Basically put, pigment-challenged audiences didn't quite know how to react to a Native comedy. And since Native theatre was still quite young, many of us Aboriginal theatre practitioners weren't too experienced in that field either. Prior to this production, *The Bootlegger Blues* had been produced on Manitoulin Island by a Native theatre company, so the audience was either primarily Native or sympathetic/interested people of pallor. After a two-week run it went on tour for a month. In fact, it was on that tour where I received what I consider to be the best review of my life. Somewhere in Ottawa, this old man, an elder I believe, shuffled out after seeing the play, walked up to me, and shook my hand, telling me my play had made him homesick. It was then it occurred to me that maybe this play was more then just a frothy comedy.

But in Port Dover, a small town on the shores of Lake Erie, most of the pallid theatre patrons sported white or blue-rinsed hair and were expecting normal summer theatre epitomized by frothy British comedies or mindless musicals. While my humble offering was a comedy (though I hesitate to say mindless), it wasn't the type they were expecting. I still remember the discussions with the artistic director who was concerned about some of the "strong" language in the show. Now those who know my work can attest that I am not one of the more profane playwrights. Hell no!

The strong language consisted of, I think, one "shit" and one "F.O.A.D. (fuck off and die)" in the two-hour play. But that was enough to scandalize. A wall of beer, two Indians climbing into the same bed, and a veritable plethora of jokes about alcohol and drinking from a race of people most of the audience more than likely associated with drunkenness, didn't make the situation any more accessible. And a touch uncomfortable. But what I remember most was the white audience's puzzled reaction to the show. It had a talented cast, and a fabulous director. Overall, it was a very good production. You would never know it from the audience response. The only response to the first fifteen minutes of the play was silence. All you could hear was the cast trying vainly to engage the audience, and the audience's breathing. For all the cast's enthusiasm, this could have been a murder mystery.

I puzzled over the unexpected lack of involvement for some time. I knew it couldn't be the actors or the production. Heaven forbid, was it my writing? But the show had done well on Manitoulin Island. Then after one matinee, it occurred to me: It wasn't me. It was them, the audience. Proving my point, I overheard one pigment-challenged lady coming downstairs from the balcony talking to her friend: "I guess it's funny, but I can't help getting over the fact that if a white man had written that, he'd be in deep trouble." That was it. Political correctness had invaded my career.

Most of the audience was afraid to laugh, or uncomfortable with the prospect of laughing at Native people, regardless of the context. After so many years of being told about the miseries and tribulations we have gone through, the concept of funny or entertaining Aboriginal people (outside the powwow circuit) was problematic. Other plays that had been produced, like Tomson Highway's, had some humour, but were darker, or more critical, and it seems that was what the audience was expecting, and I was failing to provide it. Perhaps in some way they wanted to feel guilty from what they saw, to be kicked in the ribs by social tragedy their ancestors had caused, rather then give in to the healing powers of humour. They did not expect Native people to be funny, let alone laugh at themselves. The audience had landed on Mars.

In this post-Oka society, people were still coming to grips with the concept that Native people were no longer victimized, they could be dangerous and volatile. These are notions of a definitely non-humorous nature. Maybe the wounds of Oka were still healing. As an afterthought I considered a quick rewrite and throwing in a rape or murder somewhere to shake the patrons up. Maybe blockading the bar or bathroom, something as a reference point for the overwhelmed audience. In fact, even though the play was about an aged female bootlegger, nowhere in the play does she or anybody actually drink a beer onstage. I didn't even give the audience that.

The other interesting fact about this production was that, as I've said, it beat the projection for audience attendance. By several important percentage points. So, obviously people must have liked it. I started to watch the audiences more closely, in an attempt to answer this conundrum, and that's where I made my second observation: After twenty minutes into the play, people began to laugh. Finally, the politically correct non-Natives were laughing at the Native actors doing the Native comedy. Laughing a lot, I might add. Above all else, true humour must be universal.

What the audience was waiting for, seeking in fact, was permission. They were looking for permission to laugh at this strange story about oppressed people that political correctness told them shouldn't tickle their funny bone. As fate would have it, in practically every audience were several Native people enjoying the show. Luckily, Port Dover is half an hour from Six Nations, one of the largest Native communities in Canada, if not the largest. And with two members of the cast from that community, needless to say there were always a few trickling in to see their friends and relatives appear onstage. And they needed no permission to laugh. In fact, try and stop them.

In this audience of over two hundred people (on a good night), it was always the Indians who would start the chuckling and giggling. Theirs was the laughter of recognition, because seldom had they seen this world outside their own kitchen. Other than the rare movie like *Pow-wow Highway*, the humorous Indian was a rare though thoroughly enjoyed animal. They were used to seeing the tragic, downtrodden, and victimized Indian. According to the media, that was the only kind out there. The laughter was scattered at first, sometimes from embarrassment at being the only ones laughing, but eventually the rest of the audience got the hint that this was a comedy and they were supposed to laugh. By the end of the performance, the whole audience was enjoying the play. A round of applause and an occasional standing ovation would follow. I think part of the catharsis was a sense of relief from the Caucasian patrons that everything they had seen in the media wasn't always true, the fact that Native people weren't continually depressed, suppressed, and oppressed. Yes, they found out, they have a sense of humour and a joy for life. That production was a learning for me, the cast, and I hope, the audiences.

Several years later I wrote a sequel to *The Bootlegger Blues*, called *The Baby Blues*, part of a four-part series I'm working on called *The Blues Quartet*. Its American premiere was at Pennsylvania Centre Stage, at Penn State University, deep in the heart of Amish country. And everybody knows what theatre animals the Amish are. Not exactly optimum territory for Native theatre, but I was getting paid in American dollars. Again, this play was a celebration of Native humour in a country that knows practically nothing of its Aboriginal inhabitants post-1880 (except for Wayne Newton). Again I witnessed that awesome silence of an audience trying to connect, trying to find some neutral ground. It didn't help that there were numerous Canadianisms in the text—references to *The Beachcombers*, Canadian Tire money, Graham

Greene (for some reason, most American people thought I was referring to the English novelist, not the Iroquois actor), to name a few. But overall, I still felt it should have been an accessible play. It had been in Toronto. I even ended up quickly putting together a glossary of Canadian and Native words with explanations—like for sweet grass, drumming, Oka, fancy dancing—to help the audience. But still a Native comedy was difficult for them to grasp. And there were precious few American Indians around to act as guides for the confused theatre customers. Oddly enough, my production was sandwiched between *Man of La Mancha* and *Forever Plaid*. Maybe if my characters had been insane and wore tartan, it would have been a different story.

One theory about Native comedy that I came up with, then discarded, is that theatre patrons in the city tend to be more accepting and willing to embrace styles and forms of expression that are perhaps not as well known or familiar. I've seen plays with seventeenth-century people trapped in a plastic room with no dialogue, just bouncing back and forth. In comparison, a Native comedy seems almost pedestrian. Yet witness the bomb threat in Vancouver and the success in Port Dover and Kincardine (maybe mad bombers don't have cottages). But urban companies tend to prefer a more serious interpretation of life. As a result, few theatre companies program comedies, because they are often viewed as lightweight and frothy. The phrase I have heard is "It's more summer theatre." Thus I end up in Kincardine or Port Dover trying to explain what an inter-tribal dance is.

Native theatre as a whole has developed a cachet in the last decade. With Ian Ross winning the Governor General's Award for his play *fareWel* (which admittedly had much humour), and the success of Tomson Highway and Daniel David Moses, to name just a few, most major theatre companies (and many of the smaller ones) try to program a certain amount of Aboriginal theatre in their lineup. But again, their preferences are for the angry, dark, and often disheartening view of Native life. Thus I remember one Aboriginal woman telling me that she refused to see any more Native theatre because she found it "too depressing."

More recently, I wrote the play *alterNATIVES*, a comedy-drama this time, produced in that same Port Dover theatre. But this time, it was more than a simple comedy. It was what I called an intellectual satire, meaning it dealt with serious and complex issues, but through humour. I've always thought the best way to reach somebody wasn't through preaching or instructing, but through humour. It seems to make the message more palatable—"a spoonful of sugar" and all that. This time the play premiered in two different small towns with primarily non-Native audiences. The result this time was markedly different. People, again mostly non-Native, laughed from the moment the lights went down. No waiting for permission or dealing with political guilt. In a scant six years, colour-denied people had learned it's OK to laugh at Native comedies. God (who, as some might suggest, is a Mohawk woman) will not strike them down and send them to work at the Department of Indian Affairs if they laugh. It's amazing what can happen in little over half a decade. The public looks at us now as being almost three-dimensional! It's astonishing what a good laugh will get you.

I think part of the reason, if not the whole reason, is the change in perceptions brought about by broadcasting. Witness the number of television and radio programs that have embraced the Native appetite for humour. *Dance Me Outside, The Rez*—both of which were more or less successful—the delightful movie *Smoke Signals*, even the CBC Radio show *Dead Dog Café*, written and hosted by Mr. Amusing, Tom King. Currently a television series of my own is in the stages of early development—a sketch comedy show titled *Seeing Red*. I see it as a combination of *Air Farce* and America's *In Living Color*, Native-oriented humour where we make fun of the perceptions and stereotypes surrounding First Nations culture. It could be dangerous because the other two writers and I plan to pull the leg of white people and Native people to the point of dislocation.

The CBC seems very interested. I think it shows a willingness of the public now not only to embrace the Aboriginal sense of humour, but also to appreciate and revel in it. So much so, in fact, that the powers that be at the CBC have specifically told me to concentrate on Native-based sketches, and if possible to avoid writing any that doesn't deal specifically with Native issues. Perhaps we've gone a little too far in the other direction. Add to that the documentary I recently directed for the National Film Board of Canada on Native humour, called *Redskins, Tricksters, and Puppy Stew*, and by golly, it's almost enough to make you think Canadian society has developed somewhat in the last decade. What was once the exception, has become a widely accepted rule. There is definitely hope.

In my research, I have come across a term used by some Native academics to describe humour, specifically Native humour. They refer to it as "permitted disrespect." You have the other people's permission to tease or joke about them without getting into a fight. Maybe that's what some audiences need to understand. We Native writers are part of a specific community and have to answer to that community. We are allowed a certain amount of "permitted disrespect." But it was Tom King who also told me in a recent interview that most of the negative letters the show receives come from the non-Native population, most of which say something like "If you guys [the producers/writers/actors] are white, you're not funny." When Tom tells them that, in fact, they are Native, they then grudgingly respond, "Oh, that's OK, then."

If I'm to understand the meaning of what they say, it's nice to know finally that you're funny only if you're Native. Finally, people are catching on. Except in Vancouver, I guess.

> *It may be the one universal thing about Native Americans*
> *from tribe to tribe, is the survival humour.*
> —Louise Erdrich[1]

Note

1 Interview with Louise Erdrich, in Bill Moyers's *World of Ideas*, quoted in Kenneth Lincoln, *Indi'n Humour: Bicultural Play in Native America* (New York: Oxford University Press, 1993), 209.

Bibliography

Lincoln, Kenneth. *Indi'n Humour: Bicultural Play in Native America.* New York: Oxford University Press, 1993.

2

Permission and Possession:
The Identity Tightrope

Philip Bellfy

A FUNNY THING HAPPENED ON THE WAY TO THIS FORUM. I'm sure that almost everyone who is reading this is well-versed in the concept of "academic freedom," that elusive but necessary adjunct to the teaching profession. But academic freedom is partly myth, and in the case of this essay in particular, barely even alive. Let me explain.

The first "permission" I had to obtain in order for you to have the opportunity to read what you are reading right now was from the organizers of the conference, where Version 1.0 of this essay was presented. Then I had to get permission (and a promise of funding) from my department at Michigan State University.

As this conference was being held in Canada and I reside in Michigan, I had to be allowed to enter your country[1] to attend the conference. After the conclusion of the conference, my essay had to be accepted by the editors of this volume,[2] which it was. But *their* academic freedom is also more illusory than real; their judgments must be "reviewed" by others, and those judgments reviewed by the Press itself, which I assume is under the control of an editorial board. And then there are changes made to the essay as it moves through the editorial system and as permissions are granted or denied. What you are now reading is perhaps Version 5.2, which may be only tangentially related to the original Temagami Conference presentation.

As this essay is laden with images I have encountered an "extra" requirement: the "owners" of these images had to grant me "permission" to use the images in this wholly academic, non-commercial essay. So, after all the hoops of permission-seeking listed above were jumped,[3] I was faced with this last hurdle, mind-numbing in its absurdity—or at least this is how it appeared to me. I tried to rally everyone to the call of academic freedom by trotting out the well-known American concept of academic "fair-use," which allows for the limited use of copyrighted material for educational purposes. And this is where the statement that opened this essay arose—it is a funny thing that we (in this case, we refers to the Aboriginal people of what is called North America) don't own or control our own images, either historical or contemporary. As a consequence, we don't control our own identity.

Of course, I said *a funny thing happened on the way to this forum*, but it is far from funny, except in a tragicomic kind of way. We lost most of our land, most of our "Aboriginal" rights, many of our languages, most of our traditional cultural ways, our religion, our relationship to the land and the spirits of this land, and, it seems, that we've even lost control of much of our identity through the process of "trade-marking" images of us, and elements of our culture, as someone else's "intellectual property," owned by some corporate (or individual) entity that claims exclusive use of that image through the concept of "private property."

The "Washington Redskins" and Other Offensive Acts

During most of the time that this essay was being written (and rewritten), the Washington *Redskins* were operating without the benefit of US trademark protection. They had lost this government "protection" when the Trademark and Patent Office determined that the *word* "redskins" was demeaning to a specific group of people and was thus outside government protection as a "registered trademark."

So, just what image does the "Washington Redskins" bring to mind? A football player being brought down by a fierce opponent? An Indian in a feathered headdress, letting out a blood-curdling war-whoop? Or some settler "bounty hunter" holding up a bloody scalp—a "red skin"? What image is evoked by hearing someone say "Atlanta Braves" or the "Cleveland Indians"?

For Indigenous people, walking that tightrope between who we really are and who we are perceived to be by those who create popular

Top left, Washington Redskin; *top centre,* Atlanta Braves; *top right,* Chief Wahoo of the Cleveland Indians; *lower right,* Frito Bandito

culture, the issue of identity is forever in our minds. And for those who know what the meaning of the "redskin" is, these and other images we see of ourselves in the dominant society are profoundly disturbing. As this essay unfolded, it became increasingly clear to me that, as Indigenous people, we could do very little to counter these images—in fact, we are not now, nor have we ever been, in control of how we are perceived by the dominant culture.

A federal court in the United States has now reversed the original Trademark Office determination that the use of the term "redskins" was demeaning. Consequently, the court has reinstated US federal protection to the team based in the capitol of the United States, Washington, DC.[4]

As Indigenous people in North America, we are bombarded by "Indian" images every day of our lives, be it through the use of Indian mascots in sports or the portrayal of "savage Indians" in popular culture. The use of Indian imagery is one of the most persistent and ubiquitous "American" cultural practices, and only recently has the dominant society been asked to take a long, hard look at the prevalence of these stereotypical images and the damage they do.

Of course, "Frito Bandito" and "Little Black Sambo," iconic hispanic and black cultural commodities, have been quite appropriately relegated to the dustbin of history. But the image of the full-headdress, horse-riding, buffalo-killing, Custer-killing, teepee-dwelling "Indian" is still very much with us, and the use of these stereotypical images is vigorously defended quite by those who claim to "honour" the memory of forgotten tribes and people by adopting them as sport mascots or as corporate logos.

While the controversy over the use of Indians as sport mascots is well known and hotly debated, the ubiquitous use of Indian and Eskimoi[5] imagery in corporate logos and by governments hardly merits a simple mention; yet, I the damage these images do to Indigenous identity is as widespread and pernicious as any portrayal of any "redskin" of the Washington, or any other, variety.

In his book *Playing Indian*,[6] Philip Deloria does a magnificent job of tracing the North American fascination with all things Indian, from the dumping of tea into Boston Harbor by "American" patriots dressed as Indians, through organizations like the Boy Scouts and the Improved Order of Red Men, to the radical "hippie tribes" of the 1960s and the way sports fans have come to "play Indian" on football weekends or at basketball games. Deloria's is a fascinating history, made all the more relevant by the fascination he describes. Deloria suggests that "Americans" adopt the "Indian" image because, in the popular mind, Indians *are* America, and because of the immigrant nature of American society, most people long for an "authentic" identity, one where, as Ward Churchill titled one of his many books, *Indians-Are-Us*.[7]

Early immigrants to North America were forced to adopt an "American" identity, and the only role models were Indigenous people. Yet they had to reject "going Native," identifying too closely with the "Savage" lifestyle or worldview,[8] according to the Christian dictum to shun the devil and convert the pagan. Therein lies a paradox: in order to survive in this hostile environment—hostile to the immigrant, that is—immigrants had to learn from, as well as displace, the Indian. Once displaced, the Indian could then serve very well, as the image of all that is truly "American," an ideology (in)famously summarized, as "The only good Indian is a dead Indian."

Early Stereotypes

The image of the Indian was used in commerce very early in the English colonial experiment. Not surprisingly, the earliest uses of "Indian" imagery were by tobacco merchants. The "cigar-store" image is repre-

Top left, Black Boy; *top centre,* Nova Scotia Coat of Arms; *lower centre,* Savage Arms; *right,* female cigar-store Indian

sentative of those used in England in the early 1600s. Early carvers used African slave boys as models, and, as a consequence, this image is referred to as a "Black Boy or Virginian." The North American cigar-store Indian was not popular here until the eighteenth century, and in these early uses, the figure was often female.[9] As can be seen in this late 1800s female cigar-store Indian, even the women cannot escape the "warrior" image so prevalent in popular images and logotypes depicting Americn Indians.

"New World" governments also wished to create an identity associated with the Indian image. An early example of this government imagery can be found in the coat of arms of Nova Scotia, adopted in 1625, which makes it the oldest coat of arms in Canada. It might be assumed that the motto, "One defends and the other conquers," refers to the two figures in the image: the crowned unicorn represents the province's Scottish settlers (the image is taken from Scotland's royal coat of arms); the Native on the coat of arms represents perhaps, the "defenders" who are "conquered" by the colonial settlers.[10]

These early images are, of course, stereotypical, evolving, as we see in both the "black boy" and the coat of arms, almost exclusively from ignorance and ideology, little reference to what actual Native people may have looked like, let alone what they might have worn. These early images were later adopted by myriad businesses and governments, most often utilizing male "savage" imagery. Below, we see an early 1900s image from the firearms company, Savage Arms.[11]

The Great Plains Warrior

The warrior in full headdress is perhaps the world's most enduring "Indian" image. Based on Plains warrior regalia, the image became fixed in the world's collective mind. The "winning of the West" was a relatively brief phenomenon in American history—beginning right after the US Civil War and ending with the slaughter of the Lakota at Wounded Knee in 1890 (the next year Frederick Jackson Turner declared that there was no more frontier in America). Of course, within this twenty-five-year period the images of Crazy Horse and Sitting Bull and "Custer's Last Stand," were created. It often seems that these Indians are the only ones who exist (or are worth remembering) in popular culture; made (in)famous, worldwide, by the Hollywood "western."

Of course, the Great Plains imagery has migrated far from its original home, finding its way into virtually everyone's Indian fantasy, including that of Quebec.[12] The Eugene Cloutier Company manufactures moccasins in Saint-Émile (notice the "savage" war paint on this, and in the previous, image).

While certainly widespread, the corporate imagery of the Indian Chief is not all savage; some, while still stereotypical, seem a bit more dignified, like an early logo for Walters Axe, which made a wide variety of axes in its factory in Hull, Quebec. This image is from the 1940s (the Ottawa Chief was one type of axe head they made).

Ronson Lighter of Rexdale, Ontario, made the clear connection between Indians and tobacco and their image contains the now-standard full headdress, but with a clever stylized *R* forming the warrior's body, taking the stereotypical image to a level of almost surreal abstraction. This too is from the 1940s.[13]

Famous Names—Famous Faces

So far, the images of warriors are typically generic, if wholly fanciful. The following graphic advertising the Hiawatha Horse Park and Enter-

Top left, Laurentian Chief; *top centre*, Walters Axe Company; *top right*, Tecumseh Products Company; *lower left*, Hiawatha Horse Park®; *lower centre*, Ronson Lighter Company

tainment Centre®, near Sarnia, Ontario, attempts to cash in on the readily recognizable name of Hiawatha, founder of the Iroquois Confederacy. Oddly enough, one of the most well-known confederacy leaders was Joseph Brant, whose Iroquois name, Thayendanegea, means He Places Together Two Bets,[14] creating, perhaps, an obscure but fitting connection among Hiawatha, the Iroquois Confederacy, and racetrack betting.[15]

Another important figure from Canadian history is Tecumseh, the military leader of the War of 1812, killed in southern Ontario on October 5, 1813. The contemporary image here is that of the Tecumseh Products Company, based in Tecumseh, Michigan, known for its lawnmower engines.

Women and Children

As mentioned earlier, the majority of cigar store Indians were originally carved female figures, and that tradition of Indian maiden imagery has been carried down to contemporary society. Just as it is difficult for young Aboriginal men to escape the stereotypical Indian warrior imagery, Native women are being brought up in a culture that casts them as romantic objects—in both senses of that word. Perhaps the most widely know of these logotypes is that of the Land O' Lakes lady. The Land O' Lakes is, of course, a reference to Minnesota dairy country, where the co-operative company got its start (although it is now a national company, it still calls Arden Hills, Minnesota, its home). This image, now world famous, was adopted in an earlier form in 1928.[17] Unfortunately, the Land O' Lakes company denied me permission to use their image in this essay, but, as it is so well-known, I'm sure you can conjure up the image at will.

As we are concerned about identity, it's interesting to note that images of our children and young people have also been appropriated by the corporate world. One very notable example is that of "Tommy Tomahawk," a "spokesman" for the Mohawk Carpet Company. The company still uses "Tommy" as part of its corporate image, notably as an integral part of their Mohawk Color Center Division logo. Developed by Disney in 1951, this example shows how Native children are also in danger of being reduced to mere "savage" cartoon characters in the public's mind.[19]

"Eskimos"

Several thousand other logotypes employ Indian images, but before turning to examples of a more symbolic nature, I'd like to present a few "Eskimo" images: first, stereotypical "warrior" images. In the logo of the Valenti Shoe Company of Toronto, maker of winter boots.[20] It is not necessary to show a person behind that hooded figure—the stereotypical image conveys all the information needed to lead the viewer to believe in the value of this company's product.

Again, women are prevalent in these images of the far north. The Jean Dansereau Company of Quebec manufactured automotive antifreeze during the time that this logo was developed.[21]

Children of the far north have not escaped stereotyping either; perhaps the best example is that of the "Eskimo Pie" logo. While the modern logo emphasizes the name at the expense of the child's face, the image of that immutable smile is the one that comes to mind. Of

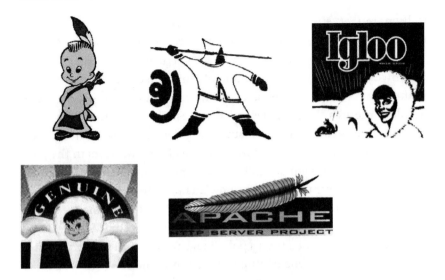

Top left, "Tommy Tomahawk"; *top centre*, Valenti Shoe Co.; *top right*, Igloo brand antifreeze; *lower left*, Eskimo Pie; *lower right*, Apache Software Foundation

course, other than the parka that outlines the face, nothing in the logo gives the viewer to gain any insight into who Inuit children really are—the stereotype will have to suffice.[22]

Often fragments of a culture stand in for the whole. Indeed, that is the nature of stereotypes, as can be seen in the next few examples.

The "Indian" As Abstraction

This essay introduced a few examples of Indian warriors with full head-dress, but what if just one feather is presented—is it sufficient to conjure images of savage warriors? Well, probably not just one feather, unless it can be associated with some other stereotypical image. In this case, what if the feather is paired with the word "Apache"?[23]

It is interesting that the Apache Web site provides a link to a Web site devoted to the Apache people, providing "stereotypical proof" that the feather symbol and the foundation name are designed to evoke images of the Apache people. This is all the more interesting in light of the fact that perhaps history's most photographed Indigenous warrior—the Apache Geronimo—was not inclined to adorn himself in this fashion. In fact, even Hollywood depictions of Geronimo eschew the feather look. Yet the stereotypical image of the feathered Indian persists.

Other stereotypical abstractions derive from the imagery of the Northwest Coast, perhaps most notably in the use of the "totem pole" in the logos of corporations that have no connection to the Indigenous people of the area. Totem poles in Northwest Coast communities were, indeed, widespread, so it is not surprising that totem poles have often come to serve the same function as full-headdress warriors in the popular culture—evoking *historic* images of Indigenous people. This phenomenon is relevant to both US and Canadian stereotypes.

I had originally begun this discussion of Northwest imagery using a totem pole by the British Columbian vintner, Blossom Winery. I was intrigued by the use of a totem pole image to sell, of all things, mostly wild berry wines. Maybe it's the connection with the "wild" aspect of the wine that compelled the vintner to use this imagery, but, for whatever reason, the connection exists, and the stereotype persists. Given that the winery refused me permission to use "their" totem-pole image, I am presenting another similar image, this from the Alaska Fish Fertilizer Company[24] which looks surprisingly (or, because we're dealing with stereotypes here, not surprisingly) similar to that used by the Blossom Winery.

Other industries are apparently eager to be associated with images of Indigenous Northwest cultures. Consider the logo of the Totem Ginseng Trading Company. According to the notice this company filed with the Canadian trademark office, the Chinese characters translate as "chief."[25] It should be obvious from the use of these Chinese characters that the company is looking to the ethnic Chinese market for its sales, yet it uses a "Western" Indian chief—complete with a stylized, full-headdress, stereotypic image of a Great Plains warrior—to do so. The result is an odd mix of the Chinese and the Indigenous, the Eastern and the Western, all the while remaining faithful to popular culture norms, which are designed to remind everyone, Native and non-Native alike, that the *dominant culture* has determined how Indigenous identity is to be constructed, and, of course, who owns and controls those images.

Top left, Alaska Fish Fertilizer Company; *top centre*, Totem Ginseng Trading; *top right*, Canadian quarter, 22 October 1999; *lower centre*, souvenir pin

Canadian Cultural Identity

This souvenir pin is not really "official" in the sense that it has been issued by the Canadian government, but it integrates the full-head-dress warrior image and the Canadian flag to suggest that Canada is Indian, and the Indian is Canada.[26] I suspect that anyone who enters the Canadian Museum of Civilization, in Hull, Quebec, will be struck by the fact that it is an "Indian" village scene from the Northwest that has been chosen to occupy the most prominent public space in this very "national" museum.

In this essay, images used by corporations have been presented, yet Indigenous imagery is also widely used by governments on coins, paper money, stamps, flags, and coats of arms (as we saw, above). The Canadian quarter pictured here, minted in October 1999, was one of a series of quarters issued that year to celebrate the millennium, several of which contained Aboriginal imagery.[27] Again, the Canadian government is asking all of us to interpret *Aboriginal* imagery as equal to *Canadian* identity—quite a radical answer to the question of who am I?

Conclusion

Although the use of Indian mascots gets most of the publicity when the stereotypical use of Indians is raised in public discourse, the more widespread use of Aboriginal imagery in daily commerce is seldom recognized, even though companies doing business in virtually all fields—from chemicals to clothing—have registered and claimed ownership of literally thousands of logos that contain Indian and Eskimo stereotypes.[28] It's unlikely that you could walk into a convenience store anywhere in North America and not be confronted by the image of the "Pemmican Chief" staring at you from that beef jerky package. As you walk down the aisle of a local American grocery store, you can look at the images companies present to you: Argo cornstarch, Calumet baking powder, Big Chief sugar, Sioux Bee honey, Red Man tobacco, Trail's End popcorn—the list goes on and on.

Even though it appears that the Sioux Bee honey image—a young Native girl, surrounded by the phrase "Sioux Honey Assn"—has dropped the single feather in her hair, the company denied me permission to use their image in this essay. I find this very intriguing. The fact that they dropped the feather suggests to me that they have recognized that using Native imagery is inappropriate; I would have been very happy to show you how the elimination of such a stereotype in no way diminishes the value of their logo. It's just the right thing to do, and this company has done it.

Another image that was to be used in this "parade of products" was the logo of the Big Chief Sugar brand, but the Monitor Sugar Company, owners of the logo, also denied me permission to use their image. As a perfect example of how corporate ownership of our imagery works, the company wanted to know the context in which it would be used; after I sent an outline of this paper to them for their review, they declared that they would need to read the entire paper before they would make a decision. After reading an earlier draft of this essay, permission was denied. In the letter of denial, they implied that they would reconsider if I agreed to reprint their "official" corporate statement on the use of a Plains Indian image as their corporate logo. I agreed to consider their demands, but they never responded to my request for a copy of their official position.[29]

Top left, Pemmican; *top centre,* Argo corn starch; *top right,* Calumet baking powder; *middle left,* Red Man tobacco; *middle centre,* Trail's End popcorn; *middle right,* Leinenkeugel's beer; *lower left,* Dos Equis beer

So, even though you can't see all of those Native-based images in this paper, you could continue your grocery market stroll down the beer aisle (or at the government beer distributor) to see the Indigenous figures used by the Leinenkeugel and Dos Equis breweries.

By its nature, the use of Aboriginal stereotypes by sport teams, corporations, and governments leads to the denigration of Aboriginal culture, not only in North America, where the current mascot controversy rages, but throughout the world, as these stereotypical images can literally be found all over the world from China to South Africa, from Fiji to Finland. *Who am I?* is a question asked by everyone in our society, be they American, Canadian, Irish, Ukrainian, Indian, Aboriginal, Indigenous, or multi-ethnic; it is not a trivial issue; it comprises the core of each and every person. I am often asked if we don't have something better to do—fight poverty and unemployment, combat alcoholism and drug abuse—and, of course, the answer is that we, as Indigenous people, fight those fights everyday. But many, if not all, of the problems facing Aboriginal people can be traced back to a question of identity. We all ask—Native and non-Native alike—who am I? How do I fit into this mosaic? What is my role in society? Until the question of stereotypes—be they in sports mascots, corporate logos, or national identities—is addressed, Indigenous people will continue to be pushed to the fringes of the dominant society, viewed as, and often called, chief, or the squaw, not recognized as, for example, Anishnabe, Lakota, Inuit, Métis, or Dene. We have to be careful as we walk this identity tightrope, careful not to falter as we struggle toward our goal: a desire to be recognized simply for who we are, who we know we are, the flesh-and-blood version, not the corporatized cardboard cut-out.

Notes

1 As an Indigenous person, I was all prepared to shake my fist at the border guard, clutching a crumpled copy of Jay's Treaty in her face as I sped across the border. Article III of the treaty gives me the right to "pass and repass" the border without hindrance, although neither the Canadian nor the US governments are willing to recognize that "Aboriginal right" (see *Mitchell v. M.N.R.*; 2001 SCC 33. File No.: 27066; June 16, 2001, for the Canadian Supreme Court ruling on "cross-border" rights under Jay's Treaty).

2 I should make it clear that I do not consider the editors of this volume to be in the category of "permission grantors" inasmuch as they too are merely academics doing academic work under the same rules that govern all of us; they are essentially at the same level as I am—that of "permission seekers."

3 I have made a "good faith effort" by phone, letter, or e-mail, to obtain the proper permissions for all the images included and in some cases I received no response. Governments, generally, do not "trademark" their images (coins, etc.); they are considered to be in the "public domain."

4 For more on this case, see "Washington plaintiffs file notice of appeal in Redskins trademark case." Jerry Reynolds, *Indian Country Today*, 19 November 2003.

5 I need to make it clear that when I use the terms "Indian" and "Eskimo" I am doing so with full awareness of the inappropriateness of such terminology. But as this paper deals with the *stereotypical* use of Indigenous imagery by corporations and governments, it seems to me that the images are truly those of "Indians" and "Eskimos," and much less so the images of Indigenous people.

6 Philip J. Deloria, *Playing Indian* (New Haven: Yale University Press, 1998).

7 Ward Churchill, *Indians Are Us?: Culture and Genocide in Native North America* (Monroe, ME: Common Courage Press, 1994).

8 For a more thorough discussion see Phil Bellfy, "Savage, Savages, Savagism."

Encyclopedia of North American Indians, ed. Frederick Hoxie (Boston: Houghton Mifflin, 1996), 568–70.

9 Frederick Fried, *Artists in Wood: American Carvers of Cigar-Store Indians, Show Figures, and Circus Wagons* (New York: Clarkston N. Potter, 1970), 10–11. Also, see my contribution on "Cigar-store Indians" in the *Encyclopedia of North American Indians,* ed. Frederick Hoxie (Boston: Houghton Mifflin, 1996), 123.

10 See *Symbols of Canada,* Department of Canadian Heritage (Ottawa: Canadian Government Publishing, 1999), 24–25.

11 From a reprint catalog offered for sale by a Michigan company doing Internet business at <http://www.savage99.com/catalog24.htm>.

12 This image was adopted in the 1940s, and can be found at <http://www.eugene-cloutier.qc.ca>.

13 This image was taken from the US Trademark and Patent Office Web page at <http://www.uspto.gov/>.

14 Bellfy, Phil, *Indians and Other Misnomers* (Golden, CO: Fulcrum Press, 2001), 343.

15 The image is from a photograph taken by the author.

16 From the USPTO Web site.

17 The history of the company and the logo can be found on the corporate Web site <http://www.landolakes.com/ourCompany/LandOLakesHistory.cfm>

18 From the USPTO Web site.

19 In 1951, the famous Walt Disney Studios designed "Tommy," one of the most identifiable and effective company mascots in the history of American business. The "Tommy Mohawk" character was created for a series of animated television commercials with titles such as "Tommy Tests Carpets," "Tommy Plants Carpet Seeds," "Tommy Falls for Minnie," "Birds Use Waterfall for Loom," and others. This image is taken from the Web site of the Mohawk Carpet Company <http://www.mohawk-colorcenter.com/>.

20 The company is currently doing business as the Star Valenti Company (information from the Canadian trademark database Web site).

21 Information from the Canadian trademark database Web site.

22 From a product carton scan by the author.

23 From the Apache Software Foundation Web site <http://httpd.apache.org/index2.html>.

24 From the USPTO Web site <http://tess2.uspto.gov/>; serial number 75277680.

25 See the company's filing, trademark registration number TMA498553, at the Canadian trademark Web site <http://strategis.ic.gc.ca/SSG/0774/trdp0774254000e.html>.

26 From scan by author.

27 From the Canadian government Web site <http://www.rcmint.ca/en/millennium>.

28 See the complete list of all "Goods and Services" at the US government trademark site at <http://www.uspto.gov/web/offices/tac/doc/gsmanual /manual.html>. Military and government "services" are classified in the "Miscellaneous services" category (no. 42). It may just be that clothing companies are the largest group of corporate entities, but clothing companies seem overly represented in the use of Indians in company logos.

29 The document in question is titled "Legend of Big Chief," and I was told that I would have to include it in my text, "word-for-word as presented." Although I did ask that a copy be sent to me, it never was, so I can't tell you what the "official" position of the Monitor Sugar Company is vis-a-vis the use of Indian imagery, but you can see the logo at <http://www.unitedway- baycounty.org/images/MonitorSugar.jpg>.

Bibliography

Bellfy, Philip. *Indians and Other Misnomers*. Golden, CO: Fulcrum Press, 2001, 343.

————. "Savage, Savages, Savagism." *Encyclopedia of North American Indians*. Ed. Frederick Hoxie, 568–70. Boston: Houghton Mifflin, 1996.

Churchill, Ward. *Indians-Are-Us?: Culture and Genocide in Native North America*. Monroe, ME: Common Courage Press, 1994.

Department of Canadian Heritage. *Symbols of Canada*. Ottawa: Canadian Government Publishing, 1999, 24–25.

Deloria, Philip J. *Playing Indian*. New Haven: Yale University Press, 1998.

Fried, Frederick. *Artists in Wood: American Carvers of Cigar-Store Indians, Show Figures, and Circus Wagons*. New York: Clarkston N. Potter, 1970, 10–11.

3

Telling Our Story
David Newhouse

I WAS PROFOUNDLY UNCOMFORTABLE, living as I do in the most post-modern country in this postmodern world, with the idea of giving "Aboriginal reflections." What I am really going to talk about are reflections of a contemporary Onondaga middle-aged man, educated in both the Western and Iroquoian tradition, on the idea of histories as they might be created from Aboriginal pasts. I often have the pleasure of driving from Ottawa to Peterborough. If I drive in the evening, I take the opportunity to listen to *As It Happens*. In May 1998, the show had invited the member of parliament who had sponsored a private member's bill to overturn the conviction of Louis Riel and to declare him a Father of Manitoba as well as a Father of Confederation, to talk about his reasoning. They also asked a professor who taught Canadian history at the University of Toronto to offer his comment. The MP presented his case and was quite rudely rebuffed by the professor, who said that the whole case was silly, would not make a bit of difference to Louis Riel, and was imbecilic. He argued that Louis Riel was indeed insane and that it was not good form to honour someone who had killed so many people in a rebellion against the Canadian state. (Completely lost on him was the argument that we honour many people who have killed thousands of people all the time.)

It's hard for me to judge the merits of the case, as I simply don't know enough about the various interpretations of Louis Riel's actions. I know the basic outline of the story of Riel but I simply don't know enough about the ideological forces influencing these stories. I was quite simply struck by the rudeness of the history professor and his absolute refusal to deal with what clearly is an alternative thesis. There was open hostility. The interview ended with a shouting match between the two, with the *As It Happens* moderator saying at one point, "You can't understand each other if you keep talking all at once." Great historical debate, I must admit! And great radio.

Now I have some background in psychology and I begin to ask questions when people have reactions that seem out of all proportion to the issue under discussion. I wonder what it is they are reacting to. My experience has taught me that the reaction is often to something that is not on the table. Not knowing the professor, however, I can only speculate. Somehow challenging the idea that Louis Riel was a rebel and a traitor struck a deep chord, and my speculation is that his mainstream ideas about Louis Riel challenge ideas about the formation of Canada and all those sorts of things. Could Louis Riel have contributed in some fundamental way to the development of Canada? That was a question he was unwilling to consider. He wanted his history, I think, to confirm something about himself or more likely to affirm something that he held dearly: that the orderly development of Canada was somehow disrupted by the actions of Louis Riel. I must admit that he was almost American in his reaction to this attack on the national myth (or at least as we have been led to believe most Americans would behave).

I grew up on the Six Nations of the Grand River community eighty or so kilometres from Toronto. I grew up with a strong sense of self as Onondaga, and I learned a history of my people that dated from the founding of the Confederacy in the early thirteenth century. The date for the founding of the Confederacy has been constantly pushed back from the middle of the fifteenth century to its now current early thirteenth-century date. That date has been established through the correlation of star patterns passed down through oral traditions and contemporary astronomical charts. I learned the traditional history of my people throughout my public school career. It is only recently that this history is being made visible to many people. This, despite the fact that the Iroquois are probably one of the most researched Aboriginal groups in North America. The amount of scholarship on Iroquoian peoples is simply astounding. The history that most Canadians hear of the Iroquois is about their wars with the Hurons, the burning of Father Brebeuf, their wars with the French, their alliance with the British and Dutch, their move from the Finger Lakes region of upper New York state to southwestern Ontario sometime vaguely after the American War of Independence. The story of the formation of the Confederacy and the Great Peace, the story of the Peacemaker and Hiawatha is not generally known to Canadians. Nor are the continuous attempts to ensure the integrity of Iroquoian land and culture. I would hazard the guess that most contemporary Iroquoian peoples also have only a rudimentary understanding of their own history.

I have the pleasure of teaching an introductory course in Native studies at Trent. One of the first assignments is for students to investigate and prepare a short report on their home communities. I call it the Homelands Report. What I ask students to do is to go back to their own communities, find out who the original Aboriginal inhabitants were, what they called the area, what languages they spoke, construct a short history of the Aboriginal peoples in the area, identify the contemporary issues that are facing the Aboriginal communities, and report on how Aboriginal and newcomer communities see each other. The students go home, back to the historical societies, museums, archives, etc., to search for material. They come back after a short while telling us that they can't find any information. We send them to look again and with some diligence and digging, they find some material. They then report that Indians are there but just at the start of their communities. They then disappear from historical and contemporary sight. I ask them, "How is it that you had such a hard time finding material on the Aboriginal peoples in your area?" We discuss this absence and its meaning.

I did a quick review of overview Canadian history texts from the 1960s to the 1990s to see how Aboriginal history was portrayed. In the 1994 text *A Short History of Canada* by Desmond Morton, of McGill University, we appear at the start in part 1, chapter 1, and then a few times throughout the text. In a section on the First World War, he mentions that the regulations for enlisting in the First World War were relaxed to let Aboriginal peoples—at that time, Indians—enrol. Our next mention is in part 5, chapter 4 (the last chapter) where we are credited with killing the Meech Lake accord. Oka is described as a "distraction," which forced Canadians to consider Native concerns. Metis people are given slightly better treatment. Metis identity, he says, develops out of a hatred for the HBC, spurred on by the North West Company. I'm certain that many Metis people would disagree. An older text, *Canada: A Story of Challenge*, subtitled *Revised Edition of the Popular History of Canada—with Maps written by J.M.S. Careless*, first in 1953 and then again in 1963 treats Indian people in a fashion similar to that in the 1994 Morton text: Indian people are described at the beginning and then disappear from the rest of the text. Here are his conclusions about Indians:

> Tribal organization and customs decayed. The tide of settlement spread over their remnants, until in the end some of the Indian hunting life was only preserved in the fur-trapping far North, or on the reservations, the tracts of land guaranteed at last to the remaining tribes by white governments. And even here, on eastern reservations, the Indians have largely adopted the same ways as neighboring white farmers. Thus, for better or worse (for remember that the "noble red man" had often lived a life of squalor and near-starvation) the Indian world gradually but inevitably collapsed, as Europeans entered the Canadian scene.

He describes Metis as being caught between a battle between the North West Company and the Hudson Bay Company and as "being stirred up" to commit acts of violence, thefts, and threats against Lord Selkirk's settlers, eventually leading to open battle: the massacre of Seven Oaks. Later in the same text, Louis Riel is described as "clever but unbalanced, a French-speaking inhabitant of Red river with a dash of Indian blood." Both of these texts won praise from their reviewers. Of Morton's book, the *Quill and Quire* reviewer wrote, "General readers will be pleasantly surprised to find that a professional historian has written a book that is a joy to read, succinct, sensible and well balanced in its viewpoint as well as its coverage." Of the Careless book, the reviewer for *The Canadian Historical Review* said, "The student and general reader alike will be grateful for an introduction to Canadian history which, while giving satisfactory answers to obvious questions, offers a pleasant invitation to further study and research." The back cover states, "This is history as it should be written."

A more recent (1996) two-part text, *Origins: Canadian History to Confederation and Destinies: Canadian History since Confederation* written by Douglas Francis, Richard Jones, and Donald Smith, attempts to be more inclusive of Aboriginal peoples and succeeds. Yet in the final chapter on contemporary challenges, reconciliation with Aboriginal peoples is not listed as a chapter. Somehow, even in recent Canadian history texts, we have a tendency to disappear. The entire treaty-making process, central to the creation of Canada, is given four half pages. These are examples of the texts that Canadians see. These are the stories that Canadian historians tell about us. They are not the stories that we tell. Nor can they be.

I am happy, however, to note that there has emerged over the last decade much scholarship in the area of Aboriginal history. This scholarship is slowly making its way into overview Canadian history texts. A good example of the influence of this recent scholarship is a 2002 text, *History of the Canadian Peoples*, in two volumes, by Alvin Finkel and Margaret Conrad. It provides a more balanced and respectful view of Aboriginal peoples as well as continued Aboriginal visibility throughout the 125-year period it covers. The story of Canada is changing and becoming more complex.

History is the official set of stories that we tell ourselves about ourselves. Today, we conceive of history as many stories. In a postmodern age, the idea of one grand narrative is losing ground. One narrative is simply not complex enough to present the multitude of stories that we now want to include. "There are a million stories in the naked city" is what we used hear it on a popular fifties television show. History is also the story that tells us who we are, where we came from, what we did, why we did what we did, and sometimes where we're going. History defines us and makes us human. In fact, I would say that the ability to construct and to think historically—to link past with present and to speculate on possible futures—is a fundamental characteristic of humanity.

History is also a continuing story that changes as our understanding of ourselves changes and as we ask different questions about the past. The meaning of the story changes with time and with perspective. Yet we must remember that not all stories are given equal time. We cannot separate the telling of history from issues of power. It is still a fact that those who have power still get to write their version of the story and to have it accepted as "truth," to have other plausible stories pushed from the table, so to speak. The Aboriginal set of stories is one that is only starting to be told. The telling of it from our perspectives is difficult because we don't have power to make others listen. But why should it be so difficult to extend the rafters, to use an Iroquoian term, to include these other stories?

It seems to me, then, that as historians write at this moment in Canada, two intellectual projects should be of interest. The first I call "the visibility project." What I mean by this is a critical examination and rewriting of the history of Canada to ensure the visibility of Aboriginal peoples in it. The presence of Aboriginal peoples and the response of the British and French to that presence is what defines Canada in its present form. Aboriginal participation in the formation of Canada is ignored. The treaty process is central to Canada. Without the treaties and the transfer of most of Canada from Aboriginal control to Canadian control, Canada would not exist in its present form. A significant portion of the history of Canada is defined by its relationship to the Aboriginal peoples within its borders. To ignore that ongoing relationship is to render Aboriginal peoples inhuman. Canada simply would not be Canada without us, despite the attempts at erasure.

The second project is what I call the "tribal history project." What I mean is the writing of histories of Aboriginal nations/communities through community effort. For example, despite all the scholarship, there is not yet a history of the Six Nations community written by community members. If we view history as the way in which we come to understand ourselves through our past, then this project is critical for Aboriginal peoples. We simply must begin to understand ourselves through histories that we create for ourselves. If not, then we continue to let others define us. And if we do that, then we simply cannot govern ourselves in any meaningful manner. These histories already exist in every community and Aboriginal nation across the country. These histories are not simply the oral histories resident in the minds of a few old people and elders. These histories are contained within the songs, dances, rituals, and ceremonies of each people. These things tell the history of a particular group and people in the same way that written histories do.

It is this second project that I think is the most important at this time and is the most intellectually challenging. What does it mean to write a national/community history from Aboriginal perspectives? I think it is here in this project that we will begin to see the humanity of Aboriginal people come through. We will portray ourselves as active agents in the world that we find ourselves. We will challenge the notion, I hope, of us lying down in front of the steamroller of Western civilization and letting it crush us into the ground as it moves across the land. It will also be interesting to see if Aboriginal peoples use traditional prophecies as the interpretive framework for these histories. For example, the Anishnaabe prophecy of the seven fires tells us that we will almost lose our culture and languages before a revival or the eighth fire is lit. Could we interpret the events of the last hundred years as part of the seventh fire, as part of the dark ages before the renaissance and enlightenment? We then interpret all that has happened as something that had to be endured. Is it wrong to give people hope that an eighth and final fire, promising everlasting peace, may arrive soon? How different is this from the various interpretations of Christian teachings, which tell us that we are now in a time of waiting before the Second Coming? Or how different is this from its secular equivalent: the idea of progress?

The Royal Commission on Aboriginal Peoples, in the first volume of its final report, laid out its conception of the history of the relationship between Aboriginal peoples and the newcomers as consisting of four distinct phases: separate worlds, contact and co-operation, displacement and assimilation, and negotiation and renewal. Is this how we see our shared history on this continent? Are we indeed in the negotiation and renewal phase? Some would argue that we are still in the assimilation and displacement phase. Yet despite the debate about where we are, does the interpretive framework hold?

Olive Dickason, a Metis scholar and National Aboriginal Achievement Award winner, writes in her seminal text *Canada's First Nations: A History of Founding Peoples from Earliest Times* that the theme of persistence of identity and the adaptability of Aboriginal peoples is key to understanding Aboriginal history. I must admit that I like that interpretive framework. It resonates within me and probably resonates with most Aboriginal peoples. Is this the story that we will come to tell

ourselves? It certainly is one very different from the one in the Canadian history texts.

I come back to the idea that history is the official story that we tell
ourselves about ourselves. What happens when your story is missing
or the story is told wrongly or is missing significant parts? If the story
is missing, then our humanity is denied. If the story is told wrongly,
then our understanding of ourselves is incorrect. If parts are missing,
then the story is incomplete and our understanding of ourselves is
skewed. We do have opportunities and I would add duties and responsibilities to add the story where it's missing, to correct the story where
it's wrong, and to complete the story where parts are left out. In doing
so, we will admit the humanity of Aboriginal peoples, four hundred
years after the debates in Europe over whether or not we had souls.

We are the original inhabitants of this country. For the last five
hundred years or so, our journey on this continent has been a shared
journey, our pasts are shared pasts, and our history is now the history
of our sharing of this land. We are still alive, albeit in some diminished form and a bit the worse for wear, but we are alive. We now move
forward to tell our story in our way. We only ask that you listen, pay
attention, and work to create a future different from that past.

Bibliography

Canada. *Report of the Royal Commission on Aboriginal Peoples*. Ottawa:
    Canada Communications Group Publishing, 1996.

Careless, J.M.S. *Canada: A Story of Challenge*. Toronto: Macmillan, 1963.

Dickason, Olive. *Canada's First Nations: A History of Founding Peoples
    from Earliest Times*. 3rd ed. Don Mills, ON: Oxford University
    Press, 2002.

Francis, Douglas, Richard Jones, and Donald Smith. *Origins: Canadian
    History to Confederation and Destinies: Canadian History since
    Confederation*. Toronto: Holt, Rinehart and Winston of Canada,
    1988.

Morton, Desmond. *A Short History of Canada*. Toronto: McClelland and
    Stewart, 1994.

4

A Story Untold: A Community-Based Oral Narrative of Mohawk Women's Voices from Point Anne, Ontario

Dawn T. Maracle

My Story: Introduction

THIS STORY STARTS WITH THE DEATH of my father, long before I was born, and encompasses a portion of my paternal history that has shaped my existence, my psyche, and my identity as a Mohawk band member of Tyendinaga. The focus of this story includes an oral narrative of female Mohawk relatives of mine belonging to the Mohawks of the Bay of Quinte but who grew up in Point Anne, Ontario, which was part of the original Tyendinaga Reserve.

I have found that in my travels Native people ask me where I am from and who my family is. I have had some difficulty in answering their questions. For although I am, indeed, a status Indian under the meaning of the Indian Act, chapter 27, Statutes of Canada, 1985, and do belong to the Mohawks of the Bay of Quinte (otherwise known as Tyendinaga), and although my father was Mohawk and was born on the reserve, and my grandfather lived on the reserve numerous times including the last twenty years of his life, the story is much more complex than that. My response has often been to say,

> My grandfather was the Leonard Maracle who lived next to the other Leonard Maracle on the Slash Road in Shannonville, whose wife was Ethel. My father was Lloyd Maracle. His siblings are Benny, Linda, Brenda, and Helen, but they grew up in Point Anne, between Tyendinaga and Belleville. But my father, grandfather, Ethel, Brenda, and Uncle Benny have all passed away. Do you know them?

And the response was usually a bewildered look. I have found a couple of people on the reserve who also grew up in Point Anne, but my encounters with them have been brief. I found the need to ask questions about my family and the community in which they grew up so that I in turn may understand more about myself. Also, the need to be able to explain and know my family story at any given time is a necessary one, not only as a Mohawk woman, but also as a Native person in Canada. It is important to learn about the telling of stories by people in Point Anne *as they are connected to* Tyendinaga. Although there are about 2500 registered band members living on the current Tyendinaga Mohawk Territory, and another 4000 living off reserve, the group of people who regularly partake in Haudenosaunee tradition is relatively small. The people who live on the traditional spectrum struggle to learn, maintain, and pass on Mohawk culture and language while the other residents seem to pretend the culture does not exist, and some even feel that the language isn't very important. In reality, the area is full of stories of places, people, and information, but it is not accessible to most of those from school-aged children up to retirees. The stories are there, but they are rarely ever told.

The community as a whole has not fully supported the culture or language in the past, although it is gaining in popularity and financial support (as evidenced by immersion in Aboriginal Head Start day care, for example). As an off-reserve band member, I found I have often had to work very hard to gain access to stories and facts about my family and community. That is why I thought I would try to make the information more accessible to myself, as well as anyone who may read or find out about this piece. Beth Brant (1995) compiled a small book of the narratives of elders in Tyendinaga, and Rona Rustige (1988) attempted a simple book of *Tyendinaga Tales*, but her title is misleading: the stories are *Iroquois* stories, not Tyendinaga community stories, and none of them is attributed to the teller *she* heard them from. The stories are not written in an oral storytelling voice, and only in the English language.

Although little has been published on Tyendinaga other than these two books, even less has been published on Point Anne, the little cement-company hamlet nestled in between it and the city of Belleville to the west. Numerous local newspaper clippings on the Canada

Cement Plant abound, but information about the people and relationships there seems non-existent. Buck Burshaw had taken it upon himself in 1988 to begin collecting information on Point Anne for a book, but died before the manuscript seemed to have been completed. Now, no one knows where the manuscript is, or to what degree it had been written.

It is important to learn the effects of the stories on some Mohawk people of Tyendinaga at Point Anne. In learning their personal and community stories, we can begin to understand what it was like to live during that time and why some relationships in the family and between the local communities are the way they are today. For me, learning the stories of those relatives who still remain help to fill a void that was created not when my father, aunt, uncle, and grandparents died, but during the whole time I grew up, when no one in my family talked about being Native, Mohawk, or Indian, or of the current Tyendinaga Territory or Point Anne. They help me to understand who I am and where I come from, so that I in turn may provide better access to my children, nieces, and nephews on the topic. No one should have to do graduate work to find out about his or her family. The time for silence has passed; the time to sit and listen to the stories has begun.

At present, storytelling is used to dispense cultural knowledge in events ranging from informal meetings and socials, to formal ceremonies and capital S Storytelling. It is also used in kindergarten and primary classes in Quinte Mohawk School in Tyendinaga in an attempt to enable students to learn. It is interesting, though, that storytelling is used informally in *everyone's* life on this earth, including all of the Mohawks of the Bay of Quinte (Tyendinaga) and Point Anne. Drama is used in the school to tell a story, as is dance, show-and-tell, artwork of all varieties, creative writing, and journalistic writing. There is a story in every movie that is rented, every book that is read, and in every bit of gossip that is spread throughout the territory. Let's not forget the fact that children tell their parents, as do spouses tell each other, a story on how their day went. Our society is built on stories. Why aren't the traditional and community stories also being maintained? It would not be so difficult to make it more available to the residents and visitors of the territory. Why isn't it being done?

Reflection

This work is reflexive, so I will start with "me." Let me explain. I am a Mohawk-Irish-English woman from southern Ontario who was raised in the city next to my reserve, and whose relatives did not speak of being Native until the late 1980s. When I was four I vaguely remember my grandfather "dressing up as an Indian" for the local Santa Claus parade, but my perception was that it was a costume he wore. Other than that, it was easy to miss the fact that I was not Native until my sixteenth birthday: my father had blue eyes, I had fair skin and blonde hair as a child, and although my grandparents lived on the reserve, it was always referred to as "the country."

In public school there was a group of boys who had the same thing to say in every class about Native people for that one week a year we "learned" about them in history class: "Indians are welfare alcoholics who lush off the government and get their schooling paid for." I remember my responses clearly. "That is not true!" I would shout out. But the teacher would do nothing. Not a single teacher would support me or even foster a positive, open discussion and learning environment. Usually the boys would laugh and the teacher would tell them to stop interrupting the class. In the process, I was consistently left powerless, voiceless, and lacking in self-esteem and knowledge. I knew their comments were not true, only I did not have the knowledge from which I could argue the point. It is clear that this group got these very prejudiced, limited, and stereotypical views of "Indians" from somewhere, though. I didn't even have any conception of whom I could talk to about the subject—I felt very alone. It was clear in the mid-1980s that I did not have any Native role models to look up to, let alone positive ones. Every year, it seemed that I refuted the boys' statements, but the education system in Ontario, as well as the teachers I had, made no attempt to give me the skills I needed to present my own viewpoint on the subject. And the teachers made no attempt to point out to the students that their arguments were shallow, vague, racist, stereotypical, and without substance.

My interest in Aboriginal education, Native studies, and Haudenosaunee storytelling stems from that experience. I was then, and still am, appalled by the ignorance and racism towards Native people in the educational system in Ontario and within the greater Canadian/North

American society. Ironically, however, I can be thankful such ignorance has enabled me to start my journey to self-, cultural, and spiritual realizations that have made me the proud Mohawk woman I am today. I am a student who thrives on academic learning. I am a child in this world, awed by all I see, and perplexed that my world isn't full of happiness. I am these and more.

Growing up, my grandfather, my father, and the rest of my relatives for that matter, never spoke to me about anything related to Mohawks. This weighed heavily upon me, and I found myself asking questions about my father's background, about Tyendinaga. The more I asked, the less I heard from my father or grandfather. The Native liaison at my high school helped put some things into perspective: he said I was Native. And although I argued with him that I was only half Native (on my father's side), he said I was Mohawk and that's all that mattered. I suddenly felt myself become very self-conscious and sputtered that I didn't know anyone in the community. He told me where to go and whom to see. It was as simple as that, so I thought.

One year before I graduated from high school, my father contracted cancer. He lived three painful years and died eventually from many brain tumours. Unfortunately, I have learned more about my father from stories than I ever did when he was alive. I realize that while growing up, the public school system did not offer him *or* me any realistic, positive, or holistic stories about the Native people in North America, Canada, or even in the Quinte area. I have since been driven to learn stories of local Haudenosaunee (people of the longhouse, or Iroquois peoples). It took some time for me to sort out who my family was and what my racialized minority background was that had been hidden from my siblings and me. (I already knew that I was Irish-English on my mother's side.) I took a history survey course at Queen's University where I had the misconception that the majority of people had social and intellectual awareness, yet I found my peers expressing every stereotype you could imagine about Native people. I remained a spy as long as I could, biting my lip all the while, then I had to finally put a stop to it by whipping out my band card. Yes, I took part in the time-honoured tradition by light-skinned Onkwehonwe (Natives) everywhere. Upon careful inspection of the card, one student looked at me and said, "You can't be Native ... you don't look like one." So I knew that I had to have a card and flowing black hair around my dark skin and brown eyes. I learned that some people thought I wasn't Native. And I transferred to Trent for Native studies.

While graduating from Trent University with my BA, a first-year Anishnawbe student came up to me and said, "Dawn, I am glad you came to my classes last September to tell me and the other Native students what was available to us from Native clubs, socials, and counsellors. I had to really wonder then just how Native you were, but now it's cool." A teaching says that every word is a gift, but people should be more careful with the "gifts" they give. By this point, I learned that some others thought that if looks were the only factor, I was not Native, but since I do work with Native people, on health, well-being, and learning, and since my dad was Native and I have a Mohawk last name *and* a status card, well then I *was* an acceptable candidate. It seemed better that others at least based my identity on the work I did and the person I was. The outsiders' view of me was beginning to become more acceptable. I worked with that view as well as with my own over the years, as I traced the history of my community, Tyendinaga, worked and lived there for awhile, and continued learning about it through school.

While at Trent I experienced Native stories from my courses, elders, and other extracurricular experiences. I also learned that many Native people have maintained colonized attitudes about how the Anishnawbe (Ojibwe) warred with the Haudenosaunee (Iroquois), and were prepared to continue acting such scenarios out. It was and is still very unfortunate that some people believe that Ojibwe have to be better than Mohawk, etc. In any case, at Trent I began writing stories on my own for several audiences, about experiences, families, communities, and Iroquois stories. Then I went back to Queen's to the Aboriginal Teacher Education Program and received my Bachelor of Education. I taught kindergarten for four months and I learned an immense amount about myself and my community, and I illustrated a book based on an Iroquois legend, "The Three Sisters." I found out that five year olds are much more accepting of who is or isn't Native. I found that I was a person, just like they were, who both told stories and listened to the stories of others. There I felt at home, part of the community, and very open to discussing issues of who I was. Show-and-tell was a great time for that—to learn about each other and our families. If the children made fun of others, we talked about it and how we would feel if it happened to us. Then we talked about respect, caring, and sharing. Eventually, though, I still had to deal with adults.

I decided that I didn't learn enough in teacher's college, so I decided to do my Master of Education, looking at Haudenosaunee narrative voices. I find that as I learn about my culture and the traditional and contemporary education of our people, I learn more about myself. I have become a better person for it, and I still fight to improve knowledge, attitudes, and self-esteem for Native students and other Canadians in the country.

However, I received an interesting comment a while ago. I was back at Trent University for a dinner at a college master's home. One of the Native women there went into great detail about how *privileged* my life is because I have fair skin.

I told her, "You don't understand, I am prejudiced against, too." It is not just dark-skinned Native people, or what the government calls "visible minorities" who have to deal with racism, sexism, ageism, and prejudice. The grass isn't always greener on the other side.

But she would not hear a word of it. "You are privileged and you have had an easier life than my family, most of whom have darker skin than yours," she said quite emphatically.

I could not convince her otherwise. All I could think was that I have come all this way, I try to learn about my people, the Haudenosaunee, and other Native nations; I live with them, I try to live as honestly I can with respect, trust, generosity, love, caring, sharing, gentleness, and kindness, and yet people are still telling me who I am. Fifteen years ago, I was told that I was Native. Thirteen years ago, I was told I wasn't Native unless I could produce a status card; at Trent, people discussed behind my back how Native I was or was not. The truth of it is, we are all human beings; we are all part of Mother Earth. The story of the Great White Roots of Peace (Wallace) states that whoever follows the roots (of Haudenosaunee culture) to the source of the Great Tree of Peace may take protection under its branches. I have followed the root to the source with an open mind. Shouldn't I belong, regardless of my physical appearance?

Graduate studies in education is part of a natural progression in the work I am doing in Native education, Native health, and oral narrative/

storytelling. It has given me a more formal background in the roles that culture and language play in education and learning, while allowing me to include play, language, and visual displays within storytelling. However, my focus here will be to continue my story by placing it in the context of my family and the community they grew up in: Point Anne.

My main goal as a writer and educator is to help lessen the ignorance in Canada about Native people. I would also like to help improve the chance of success, through formal education, of Native youth. The key to accomplishing this is by empowering through telling and listening to stories that are traditional, contemporary, and futuristic, as well as based on nation, community, and the self. Today it takes more than a community to raise a child; it also takes people from various educational experiences, formal and traditional, who care. I exist for the quality education of the next seven generations—education that is realistic, holistic, balanced, and healthy. To be balanced, I must include storytelling knowledge and attitudes within a life history context, in order to give a well-rounded view of myself through my aunties' lives in Point Anne.

For a long time, we Native people had to fight people of European descent to protect our families, communities, and nations. Today we are fighting each other. We will move forward only when we all try to be the best that *we* can be and forget about destructive ideas of superiority. Our relationships with other people will tell us where to go from there. We should remember our teachings, or learn them, and try to respect ourselves, for only then can we respect others. Sharing personal narratives seems the least confrontational and most supportive way to learn about ourselves. Learning about others allows us to reflect on ourselves, who we are, and "where we fit."

I know the people whose stories I have included here (Ista'a's Aunt and Great Aunt). The frame of reference for my research was to interview only female family members who are Mohawk who grew up in Point Anne. My uncle was alive when I started this project, but he died of lung cancer during my research. He had a great interest in my work and was very proud of the fact that I was trying to collect family stories. There is one male and one other great aunt (whom I barely know) left who grew up there, but my uncle was sick and was going through treatment. He has since passed away as well. One other aunt refused to be interviewed; she said she didn't want to talk of the past, although she supports my work. The reality is, Native people still have a shorter lifespan than any other minorities in Canada. My family has certainly followed that mode: my grandmother died in her early sixties, my father was fifty-two, my aunt was fifty, and my uncle was fifty-five. My grandfather lived well into his seventies, as did his second wife, but they both died of health complications. The focus here is to speak of issues of narrative context, about my Ista'a's lives and relationships with my family when they lived in Point Anne and after they left it.

Community Profiles: Tyendinaga

The ancestral homeland of the Mohawks of the Bay of Quinte is the former Fort Hunter in present-day New York state. The Mohawks were the easternmost nation in the Iroquois Confederacy and were therefore known as "Keepers of the Eastern Door." West of the Mohawk territory is that of the Oneidas, Onondagas, Cayugas, and Senecas, the last of which are near Niagara Falls. It was the adoption of the Tuscaroras in 1722 that led the Confederacy to be otherwise known as "the Six Nations." The name Mohawk is said to have originated from an Algonkian word, *mohowauuck*, which means "man-eaters." Our own word to describe ourselves is "Kanienkehaka," which means People of the Flint, which was abundant in our traditional territory.

In the Mohawk Valley of New York, the Kanienkehaka lived in villages along the river in longhouses—rectangular houses made of tree branches and bark, identified by a particular clan. The clan is the family unit and is derived from the mother's side of the family. Clans in this nation are Bear, Wolf, and Turtle. Several Mohawks were respected allies of the British Crown before and during the American Revolution, and for their support they were torn from their homelands during the war and forced to temporarily settle in Lachine, Quebec (near present-day Kahnawake) after the war. In compensation, the British Crown promised land to the Mohawks for their loyalty. Through the Haldimand Grant later known as the Simcoe Deed, Captain John Deserontyon and twenty Mohawk families arrived on the shores of the Bay of

Quinte on May 22, 1784. John Graves Simcoe gave Deserontyon and the Mohawks 92,700 acres, but over the years the land has been reduced to about 17,500 acres, after land alienations and surrenders. Yes, that means the government (for example, through land granted to non-Native war veterans, squatters, and illegal leases) minimized the original territory.

Captain John Deserontyon (1740–1811) was a recognized Mohawk leader who fought with the British during the war. There is a town just east of the territory, on the Bay of Quinte, called Deseronto. A Mohawk fair has been held the second weekend in September at the community centre since 1901. The annual powwow is held at Tsitkerhododon Park, meaning "where the trees are standing," during the second weekend in August. There are also two subdivisions close to the southeast end of the territory, built by Mohawks in the territory, complete with parkettes and roads. The rental units all have water and electrical facilities, as well as geared-to-income rent. The library, Ka:nhiote, means "rainbow" and first opened in 1989. It is located right next to the Quinte Mohawk School, and features numerous reading and viewing materials by and about Native people. The flag derives its colours from wampum belts: purple symbolizes civic affairs, and white represents good, peace, and purity. The circle on the flag symbolizes the Great Peace and the Great Law (*Kaienereko:wa*) that was established by the Five Nations (Haudenosaunee/Iroquois) Confederacy. The chiefs stand in a circle with joined hands—to always be strong so that if a tree falls on the circle, it will not weaken or separate the hold they have—that stands for the strength of the confederacy and our community.

Point Anne

It has been a difficult task to find background information on Point Anne. Although I have tried numerous routes to get it, there have been repeated blocks in my way. For instance, it has already been mentioned that Buck Burshaw, a former Point Anne resident, began collecting information on the hamlet and its residents. He passed away and his book does not seem to have been published; there is also some question about what happened to his manuscript. A number of Bellevillians and former Point Anne residents have said they were aware of a pamphlet or booklet published in the 1960s or 1970s, which had a little background information on the community, but no one could remember where they saw it or even what it was called. I have searched for it in vain in the local library and the local newspaper. The only other historian of Point Anne that I know of volunteered to do an interview with me to give me some background information on the subject. He, too, has disappeared and did not show up for two scheduled interviews. I have tried Internet searches, archive searches, and searches through university libraries, and I even contacted the cement companies themselves, with no result. In the process, the mystery of this little company hamlet has continued to grow and intrigue me.

From what I understand about Point Anne from the numerous conversations I have had over the years, it was a farming community, first settled in the mid-nineteenth century when minerals were taken from the quarry there to help build the Trent waterway bridges. As early as 1903, I have been told, Canada Cement began its business there, and people started moving into the cement-company houses built for employees. The information I have collected from the Belleville Public Library includes newspaper clippings on both Canada Cement and Point Anne, but they cover only the period from 1956 to 1995. What I can gather is that before World War II, the hamlet boasted a population of over 600 people. In 1973, when Canada Cement closed its Point Anne operation and moved to a newly computerized Bath (Ontario) plant, the community's population dwindled to less than 150 residents, and it remains at about that number to this day.

Interview with Aunt Betty (Maracle) Young, October 1999

"I don't really know where Point Anne got its name. I heard it one time but I forget now, Dawn. There was a lot of Indians living in Point Anne, although there were more non-Native, but the Native people had an area of their own which was east of the cement plant. They called it 'shacktown' because the homes weren't that big, like, you know, but everybody owned their own home, but the Canada Cement owned the property, and eventually there was mostly all Natives that lived there. All around in there, it was like a little reserve of its own.

And then when the Canada Cement made them get out of there so they had to either tear down or move their places, well, Mom and Dad, they tore theirs down, and that's when they got that place up there across from the school, you know.

"There was racism when we were growing up, yes. Oh, they used to call you Indian, you know, like that, but there was no like fights or anything like that. They'd get mad at you and call you Indian, and some, I was more fair than they were [giggle], but oh yeah, I still got called names though. I've had a lot of people call me that, yep.

"All kinds of nationalities lived there; a lot of Polish lived in Point Anne. They used to call one street 'Honk Town.' There was a lot of different nationalities, and we all went to the same school, so I think we did pretty good [as Indians], you know. Most of the people were really lovely people, and they all helped each other: if we had a wedding, everybody turned out for it in the town, and the same with the baby showers—everybody turned out. That's the way it was: it was like a great big family, you know. And we talk about prejudice, but it wasn't anywheres near what some of them went through, you know.

"Some of the people I remember living there in Point Anne were Mahars, Bennetts, Burna Bennett and all his family. His daughter Colleen, she still lives there, and she lived in Ottawa for quite awhile. But when Mom and Dad died, she moved back there and fixed up the house. But I've known her for awhile—I went to school with her. She's married; I think her last name is Ash now. And Ardra Green, her name used to be Green. She still lives down there. But when I grew up, there was the McCurneys, Sweets, MacDonalds, but I could go on and on, but there's only so many I remember, you know. We weren't the only Maracles there, but towards the end there, I think we were the last ones, mostly, that lived there. And your grandfather lived there right up until, you know, the cement plant closed down. Afterwards, they closed up and made them get out of the company houses, and they tore them down. There were nice homes, too. I think it was in the sixties.

"The family relationships in Point Anne were so close, there wasn't much divorce. And we were a close-knit bunch there: when things went wrong or anything like that, they always gathered together. Like, you know, they were like one big family in Point Anne—they cared about each other, you know. I don't know what clan we are—just know we are Mohawk.

"I only live half an hour from Point Anne now, in Prince Edward County. I used to go down there a lot, still, you know, to see different ones that are still there, stop and talk to them and that. A lot of them died off, you know? But there are a few that went to school with us that's still there, but the children I don't know, 'cause I was away when they were growing up, mostly. There's a Burshaw girl there now—I don't know what her married name is—she lived in the Simmons house, right across from our old house, and there are some Harts there too, but I don't know what the names of the girls [are] though. But I think one girl lives in the school there because they made them into apartments. The Anglican and United churches are gone now, torn down, and the Orange hall is torn down, too. But there are still a few of them, you know. Just can't remember their names right now.

"I was born in Point Anne, at home on February 5, 1928, and Mrs. Dale MacDonald? was ... Mom never had no doctor, she delivered me and she delivered Dick. And they lived across from each other. And Mother delivered one or two of *her* children, too. That's the way they did it in those days. They weren't midwives; they just did it. That's where I was born. And that, in fact your grandmother, when Helen was born, she lived in that same place, but it's not there no more. It was like a big terrace place, like, you know? And it wasn't far from where the Post Office used to be up there, you know, up at that end, up near the highway. So that's where I was born, anyhow. I think Dick was born in Point Anne in the same place too.

"There were seven of us brothers and sisters; I am the second youngest of seven. There was Leonard was first, then Gladys, Garnet, then Audrey, then Dick, then me, and then Mavis. I think the rest of them was born down around Deseronto, around the reserve, down in through there. I don't know my birth story; a lot of people didn't tell it then, but parents are starting to let kids know that now. I don't even know what time I was born or anything like that. My dad was Alfred and my mother was Matilda Anne. Mom's dad was Tom, and Dad's dad was Joseph. Mom's mom was Mary Heaney. And I forget what Dad's mother's name was. Isn't that awful?

"My father worked at Canada Cement. He lived in Deseronto, in the town, or it might have been on the reserve. I don't know. He moved to Point Anne for work. His grandfather, Joseph Maracle, who they

called, 'Joe,' owned about three farms on the reserve and he worked
for his dad a lot of the time. Then after he got married he went, you
know, and got jobs on his own. And then I think when he got the
Cement Plant [job]. That's when they moved to Point Anne, years ago.
My mom's name was Maracle too, you know, Matilda Anne. Her father
was Tom Maracle. 'Course there's still lots of Tom Maracles down
there today, and lots of Dawn Maracles. Yeah, that's the way with my
cousin, [your Uncle] Tom: he was named after his father and then he
got married and they named his son Tom, too. It's not the Tom Maracle that owns the Native Renaissance thing; he's the one who owns a
construction business or something there near Deseronto. His dad was
the chief of police there and he died. Well, that was my first cousin. The
other boys are a cop and a teacher. Tom's [deceased] father and my
mother, Matilda Anne, were brother and sister. There's a lot of Maracles that intertwined there, you know.

"We got the blond hair from Grandma Heaney, my mother's
mother, although all our hair got darker as we got older. She was born
and raised and everything in Ireland. She was light-eyed and that's why
four of us have light eyes, out of seven of us in the family, with three
of us having brown eyes like Mom and Dad.

"Yeah, she died in Belleville Hospital there. She fell and broke her
hip and she never came out, like you know, she never lived through it.
She's buried there now in Deseronto in the cemetery, not on the reserve,
but there, because that's where Mom and Dad and Dick's buried, because Mom wanted to be near her mother. And so I brought the graves
in the Deseronto Cemetery, east of Deseronto there, when I came up
from the States.

"They were nice. My father: he was a gem, the whole set of us
never even remember him ever touching or hitting us or ever laying a
hand on us. He never did, no. Mom used to spank us; that is how we
were disciplined [which was] unusual for the time.

"Then Leonard and his wife, Beulah, moved to Belleville [with the
youngest, Linda]. She left the day Linda got married.

"After the ceremony, she went to Toronto to work. She was either
a maid, cleaning, or she went to live with a family, you know? But I
know she used to go visit my sisters who lived up there. She used to
call them all the time. After she left Leonard, he stayed in that place

for quite a while afterward. He worked for the YMCA for quite a few years; he got a pension and that. He was a janitor there, like he tended pools and everything. It was quite a long time after Grandma left before he got married [to Ethel], but I guess he was going with Ethel for quite a while, or so I heard, anyhow. I was at the wedding. You were born already, 'cause I was living back here [in Canada], too, when they got married. And we didn't move back here until 1975, so yeah, you were born.

"Grandma Heaney came over from Ireland, Mom's mother. She was born in Ireland, I don't know where, but I've heard of it. She came over when she was young, but she still had the Irish accent, though. She was always funny. Teasing and stuff, you know? She used to always say, "Kiss my Irish ass," if we got to teasing her about her accent. I always liked her; in fact, I was right beside her bed a few hours before she died, Dick and I. We didn't know she was dying, but we were with her at Belleville General Hospital before she died. She always wanted me to do her hair. I always took my hairbrush and fixed her hair for her.

"Grandpa owned an awful lot of land. He used to give the Natives an awful lot of stuff, you know. He was very generous with the Natives there, [with] maple syrup, and all kinds of suckers. He used to tap, and give up all kinds of stuff, too, like apples. He also had lots of cattle, too. Yeah, he gave a lot of stuff to the Natives.

"Yeah, Earl Hill's wife, Lorraine, is your grandma's first cousin. Earl was related too. When his father died, the one that adopted them, he willed $200 to Beulah and Genny. They called him Uncle, so he was related to them, too. I don't know where Genny was buried, because her son didn't want anyone to know. Not even Lloyd [your father] or anyone [went] to the funeral. Lloyd, he was upset because [the son] didn't want anyone to know at all. And Genny died a couple of weeks before your grandmother died. And she (Beulah) knew about it, and she cried. She couldn't go, because she was in the hospital. She was very sick, but she knew, and she cried.

"Genny wanted to have a big family reunion, you know, on that side of the family, and I told her, yeah, I would organize it. And you know, your mom and dad were there too, and you could ask them. She phoned up everyone, you know, down by the lake, and we did all kinds of stuff: games and food, you know. You remember that? Yeah, you were a young kid, then. And they took her in the hospital a day or two before, so she couldn't be here for the [reunion]. She was in a wheelchair, you know, and she had arthritis really bad. For years she was slim, but she got larger as she got older. Yeah, that's right; she used to live where the Loyalist Market is now [at Sidney and Bridge Streets].

"When I came back here [to Canada], she'd phone all the time. And when Lloyd [your father] would come over and stay at the cottage [with your family], he brought her over here a couple of times, and she was on portable oxygen here, too. He brought her over to the house so she could visit with me. But she was always close to us, Beulah was. And all our family still has great regards for your grandmother, because they had three children, Helen, Lloyd and Benny, during the war [when] they didn't have much, but she was clean as a pin with the kids and with the house. We always liked her. Even Audrey talks about her today.

"Oh yeah, she stayed with your family for years when you were young, and it was hard on your mother. And it was hard on me, 'cause you kids were all still at home yet, and your mother would come to me because she couldn't take it anymore, and I told her, 'Look, just tell Lloyd, your family comes first, and they gotta get a place for [his] mother. You can't go on like that Gloria.' And a couple of weeks later, she did it, and she knew I was all for it. It was hard on your mom, because [Beulah's] other kids, they wouldn't take her, you know. No, Helen, none of them. [Not in the long-term.] How did she afford the apartments? Well, your dad helped her, oh, he helped her an awful lot. I remember when she got out on her own, your mom would go and get her laundry and do a wash for her. And your dad, too, he was the best on the wall to help her. Oh yeah, he helped her a lot.

"And when your grandpa was sick? Your dad, too, used to go down there and shave him. And [your brother] Craig, too. You and your mom used to help out, too. Dick used to go to Belleville and get Chinese food when he knew Ethel wouldn't be home, and bring it to Leonard, and they would sit there and eat it. I used to visit Leonard a lot, too, yeah. I remember when he was in the hospital for surgery, I sat with him right from the six o'clock surgery, and Ethel left for lunch, and I sat with him right through it. They thought I was his wife! [Both laughing.] And a bunch of stuff went wrong once they got him up to the bed and stuff, and I stayed the whole day and looked after him. And she came after he was all settled in and that, you know? He said, 'God bless my sister!' He said, 'She stayed right there beside me.' His surgery was gallstones, or something like that. He had one monster stone.

"Yeah, I loved my brother, I'll tell you that. I loved all them. The surgery was a long time ago. Six years ago. I saw him a week before he died. We went to visit him in the home. He wanted me to bring him to my home. It was pouring down rain that day. Benny was with me, and his daughter, and we stayed and had dinner with him there at the home, and Benny took movies of us. Yeah, Benny has movies of us. So we went back to his room, and he asked me to take him, but I told him that, you know, I couldn't take him. I told him it was pouring down rain, and I couldn't. 'But don't you worry, I'll come back to see you,' I told him. And that was the last I'd seen him. But at least I shared a little time with him. And we used to go down there, Audrey and I, the first time, we used to bring him outside, and sit there and talk with him. And it was nice.

"I used to go down to the farm [in Tyendinaga] with my grandma and grandpa; so did Dick [otherwise known as Alfred] and Mavis, in the summer. And they used to give us all kinds of stuff during the Depression, and we'd stay there and they'd have everything, like their own butter they'd make, and milk and everything. So we'd stay there for awhile. Garnet still has that one of the three farms, but it's condemned now. And the farm next to it, my cousin lives on it now, back in behind Purple Acres. That was Grandpa's homestead. And then there was another farm up on the airport road there, the daughter [Shirley] got, like you know, she lived there. Dad had one sister, and he had three brothers. So two out of the three were behind Purple Acres, just when you came out of Deseronto. It's got siding on it now. It used to be brick though. And then right across from it you see an old faded boarded home, old, old home right across from it that, that Percy used to live there. But it belonged to Grandpa, and Garnet took, bought it all up. Mom and Dad used to grow squash, and I love squash. Oh, butternut is one of my favourite ones. We got quite a few downstairs yet. That is one of the more tasty squashes. That's Hank's favourite.

"I went to school in Point Anne, at the public school (the only one). It wasn't religious, just regular. Everybody went there whether they were Catholic or Protestant. I went all through the grades in the school. I didn't go to high school because we had to pay to go on the bus and my Mom and Dad couldn't afford to pay for us, so we went to work. You had to pay for the school buses in those days to drive you, and you had to walk no matter how far. We used to live way down near the cement plant. We used to have to walk all that way to school, so we didn't have no transportation at all, and very few had cars. And it was very hard, and you know it was, growing up in the Depression and everything, you know. I think most of my brothers and sisters just went to grade school, so finished to grade 8. I think they did, yeah. I know they couldn't go on because they couldn't afford to pay for buses into Belleville for high school. A lot couldn't afford it, but those who could went to BCI.

"My parents had very little education. In fact, they couldn't hardly read or write very much—only their names and stuff. But they had smarts, you know. I always felt bad because my mother and dad couldn't write and that, you know? We [the children] used to read to them and that, you know, papers and everything for them. They liked that. Mom always wanted to know, so they were open-minded about being read to and stuff. Oh yeah, we used to read them their mail, letters, and everything. We did it all for them, to read and tell them, you know.

"Yeah, Dad worked at the cement plant. When he first went there he was just a labourer on the tracks and everything else, but then as he got older, they put him in janitor work inside, like cleaning washrooms and different things like that. And he worked hard out in the cold for many years, like you know? Mom had a job. She told me she worked in the match factory in Deseronto, though I don't know whether it was after she married, or before she was married. Then she worked in Belleville at a restaurant, and she was part-time cook there for a little while. But it was only a few years. How did she get to Belleville? She had a room there with me. She stayed with me, and she used to go home on the weekends. I worked then, too.

"I worked for Alamite, [where] your Grandfather Leonard worked … as an electrician, and then I went to Northern Telecom. I went to work for Northern Telecom about a week after they came to Belleville, but then I only worked about five, six years. I guess, six years. I was a super-

visor there, although my education ... I was good in electronics and I
went to the States and I was in electronics down there, making organs
and everything. My whole life was in electronics. Yeah, I wired and
taught wiring and soldering and I taught everything, a lot of things. I
learned on my own, and I learned how to read blueprints and everything, you know. I did wiring and soldering at the Alamite, too. During the war, I moved. I went up to Toronto. Well Mavis was up there
then, and Gladys and Audrey, and I went up there and I worked in a
factory there, making walkie-talkie sets. So then, in fact that was the
first job I had. Then I came back down to the Alamite and worked for
the Alamite. [But] then I got very ill, and Mom came up and brought
me back down home, and I had my tonsils and I haemorrhaged and
everything, so she made me come back. So when I came back, I got a
job at Northern, and that's where I stayed till I went to the States. Oh,
I had two children down there. Then I went to work down there. And
didn't you know, I stayed there sixteen years. I went down there because
of [Uncle] Hank, because jobs were hard for him to get this time. And
his family, you know his whole family lived down there at the time, in
Chicago. But they all came back after—they're all back. It was so long
ago I met Hank. I don't remember how, but I knew his sister and that
'cause she worked and Northern, and I think it was through her that
we met. I was twenty-six or twenty-seven when we got married; Hank
was around thirty. That was considered late getting married back then,
but before that people got married really young, you know? But it
wasn't considered too bad to get married that late, 'cause a lot of the
women were working back then, you know. When the war broke out,
they all went to work; they worked a lot, so they never got married so
young. When I went down to the States I worked for Hammond Organs.
First I was a line girl, then I went on to be a supervisor, and then I was,
after that, I transferred to another department and I tested all, you
know, different electrical components.

"When I was younger and grew up in Point Anne, mostly everything
we needed was right there. It was a great place to grow up in. It was wonderful because they had three grocery stores that I know of, and the post
office, but you had to go to Belleville if you wanted clothes or furniture
or something. It was a booming town and it was beautiful—they had
tennis courts there! The cement plant [owned] them and everyone

could use them; they had a big clubhouse there, you know, where you go there and gather on Sundays and chit-chat; they had a canteen there where you could buy pop, this and that. It was a great place to grow up in though, really.

"As for languages, we weren't taught any languages in school. They never even touched it. They did teach French, but you had to go to high school before you learned any French. All the nationalities there spoke English. Maybe at home they spoke their own languages, if they were Polish or Indian or something. We'd be at our friends' houses and hear their parents speaking Polish or whatever, but other than that, they all spoke English. There was Ukrainian there too, you know. I know Dad's family spoke Mohawk, you know his side did, and Dad and Mom could speak some things. Dad could say a lot of different things. And they used to tell us (I don't know whether I'll pronounce it right), they used to say, when my uncle would come in, they'd tell us to say *sekhorikhenaha* [giggle]. It used to mean 'hello' or something like that, anyhow. They were open about the language. I remember living in Point Anne, and some of them used to come up from the reserve, and they used to sing Mohawk songs, and we used to giggle because we never heard it, you know. Only when we'd go down to Grandpa's [we'd hear it], but it wasn't the same, so we used to laugh there, too, because we thought it was funny. So our parents mostly taught us words and stuff like that. They understood more than they passed on—they would understand different things, you know. Even Leonard, your grandfather, could say a lot of different things in Mohawk.

"There was never a time when my parents told us not to speak Mohawk. In fact, they tried to teach us very different things in Mohawk, you know, and they were always proud of their heritage. [We didn't learn as much of the language as they did] because then, the language wasn't around as much except in the band, like on the reserve and that. And they never spoke it that much unless someone came that was relatives or that, and they would [talk], sing songs, or something like that. But it was never spoken as language around us. That's why we never learned a lot, [unless] we went to the band to learn that. All of our relatives were from Tyendinaga, as far as I know.

"Tyendinaga? I still like to go down there, because you know, I still know a few people down there, and I can go and visit. But Point

Anne, there's not much left of it, but that is home to me, 'cause that's where I grew up, you know. But I still like to go down to the reserve, to get my lyed corn soup. Yeah, I make it! [But] then I stopped making it, [because] you could get it in packages. You know Earl Hill, the old chief there? He told me, Dick used to get it for me all the time. He said, 'Betty, you come here any time you want it, I've always got it in the freezer.' And there's a certain kind of bean you can't buy in stores. I don't have a recipe for it; it's all in my head. Yeah, I also made dry corn soup. A lot of people like that; a lot of white people liked it. Lyed corn used to be made [with poison] but they don't do that now. They used to wash them and wash them after soaking them. But I used to love it, I used to crave it, because we grew up on it; Mom used to lye her own corn.

"When I go to Tyendinaga, I still visit the Maracles—Gary's family, you know, who used to go see Dick all the time? Well the parents, I knew [them], 'cause Dick was like family to them. Yeah, he lived with them for awhile, and I knew the grandfather. They just built a newer house for one of the sons, plus they have a couple of shacks on the water [off the Bayshore Road]. The sons, they live all over the reserve now. Chief Earl Hill, when he was younger, his sister Mary and that, their mother died when they were all young and there was an awful big family, and the brother lived in Point Anne. He took them, he adopted them. And he was a Hill, and that is why Earl changed his name to Hill, although he was really a Maracle. We went to school with him, so we know him, you know? He was a good guy; he helped me, no matter what, especially after Dick died. Dick was always close to Earl, all his life. Earl told you one of your great-grandfathers is buried under a tree on his property? [Giggle.] No, they were buried at the church, because I remember when he died, you know, and that, they are both buried at the church.

"I'll tell you anything, 'cause I'm not ashamed of anything."

Interview with Aunt Linda (Maracle) Adams, October 1999

"Basically I don't know how Point Anne got its name, but it's at the point on the Bay of Quinte, and there was a church there named St. Anne. I think the "point" and the "Anne" congregated together and they called it Point Anne 'cause it's right on the very point at the very end of the village. That's where the name, I believe, originated. I think people probably started living there back in the early 1900s.

"Yeah, it originated basically due to Canada Cement, eh, [who] built on it. But prior to that I think it was more of a farming community, and then it built up around the [cement] industry. And then all the Canada Cement houses were built at this point. We lived in a house that belonged to Canada Cement, and most of the houses in the lower part of the village were built by [them, too], so when the cement plant went down, they also tore down most of the main houses [which] were built of cement. They were basically good-size houses. The house that we lived in growing up had two parts; they were almost like you call a "semi" in this area. On our side there were three bedrooms upstairs and then a big living room and a big live-in kitchen. It was so huge with a big cook stove and a pantry, [although] it had no running water or inside conveniences back then. As we progressed, we ended up taking over the whole house, and that gave us another two bedrooms, so we ended up having five bedrooms in the end.

"I think there were a few Indian families in the village, but like the Green family that were down there and they were Indian also, but most of the relatives were in the area of the reserve, you know. Like all of Dad's brothers and sisters and that when we were younger were all from the reserve area. Uncle Garnett lived down there, and Uncle Dickie, and yep, it was Grandpa who got the job at Canada Cement. No, it wasn't all Native people who lived there. Actually, the Natives were the minorities in the village, but like I said, there were Greens down there that were also Indians, and there were some that were married that had come probably from Fullers and Brants, but I didn't know all of that well you know. I think there were about 500 people who lived there when I grew up. So I will give you [the local historian's] number so you can get some background from him—he set up a few of those Point Anne reunions, you know. I think he's basically home on weekends, but through the week he works up at Rama. But his wife, you know, could get a hold of him, then probably set up something to talk to him you know. 'Cause I'm sure he would like to talk—he likes to talk. He went to school with the younger part of the Maracle family, meaning Aunt Brenda and myself—we all went to Point Anne Public School and we basically all grew up together. We all come together in our groups, you know, in the village, and Gerald was one of them that was always with us. No, he's not Native. Now, Mary MacDonald was one of our friends who married a Gord Chisholm. Now his mother's maiden name was Green, so they did have an Indian background.

"So Gerald put some Point Anne reunions together for about five, six years in a row. You know, people just came from all over and got together at different parks that he had set up, and reminisced over the years. The Point Anne family was like a family because it was such a small village and nearly everybody knew each other, and every generation of kids grew up with their own group of people. As the years progressed they all basically looked back on it as sort of like one big family in the village, eh. I didn't make it to any of the reunions, but I know Aunt Helen and Aunt Brenda went, and I don't know if your dad made any or not. I think even Uncle Benny may have made some too, but I know it seems when they were on I was pretty well booked to be working. I never could quite get to them, but I guess they were quite interesting, because like your dad's generation of kids all grew up together and there were many of them there. So it was quite a nice thing.

"I think there was always a bit of underlying racism at Point Anne school at times, you know, but nothing big, 'cause like I said, we were all like one big family, you know. The biggest thing I think was between the Catholics and Protestants. When we were kids in the village [it] was a big thing, you know, if you went with a Catholic and you were a Protestant—it caused a lot of problems because [things were] very, very religious back then. St. Anne's was Anglican and the Catholic church ... I'm trying to think what the name of it was. There was a Catholic school and a Catholic church halfway through the upper part of the village. Yes, in that little village there were two churches, and two schools. The Catholic church was built later on; it wasn't built right in the very beginning. We all sort of started out in the public school and then the Catholic school was built, and a lot of the Catholic kids were transferred of [the name of it] but I guess the other was the Point Anne's Saint Anne's Anglican Church.

"First when we were going to school, religion was a big part of school, back then. Like we always said the Lord's Prayer in the morning before you started school, and most people in the village were very much [of the practice] that you were baptized and you went to church every Sunday. And we were all in the choir growing up, and we were all confirmed. That was always big, big thing, you know—religion sort of went part and parcel with the daily activities of the village, you know. Today a lot of kids aren't baptized or confirmed or anything, but it was part of growing up for us, eh? We went to Sunday school, and there were a lot of different Bible stories and every little thing to go with the Bible that you could possibly learn. Sunday school really didn't change that much. The teachers that taught us Sunday school were Miss Parks and Penny Parks [her daughter]. She was at Auntie Brenda's wake—I don't know whether you seen her or not. Penny was one of the girls that grew up with us and she bought her mother's house. It was right kitty-corner from Point Anne Public School, and there used to be a little store in front of there at one point. Like a little variety store. That was years ago.

"There was a big old farmhouse, and they had horses and chickens, and a little old horse called Joe that was as white as anything that all of us kids used to love. We grew up in a really nice place, 'cause we had everything, like the Bay of Quinte which we could go swimming in. And behind our house, Canada Cement had built a skating rink, so we had a girls hockey team and a boys hockey team. I've got a scar to prove it, in girls hockey with Bobby Hull's sister, Judy. We all played together, and I got a big scar where Judy checked me into the boards. Bobby was in Helen's category. There was Bobby, and then there was Dennis, and then of course the girls who were our age, so we grew up with the girls. And Canada Cement also built a baseball diamond right behind our house, and tennis courts, so we had a baseball team and played tennis. Your Auntie Brenda and myself actually played competition tennis, and we ended up playing in Kingston, Belleville, and Campbellford, and we were quite the tennis players when we were younger. It was very much a sports-oriented town, and everything was basically free for us. Everything was very close.

"I think Canada Cement basically treated everybody the same [including the Mohawks], although I think there was always a little bit of a stigma with the Indian name—I think throughout the Belleville area, at times. I think that's just the way it was. But really for us kids to have a lot of prejudice, we didn't really know what it was. You might get into the odd little argument and somebody would say something, you know, but ... some people interacted very well.

"Some of the names of the people I remember in the village are the Weeses, the Hulls, Hearts, Frasers, the Cooks, and the MacDonalds, oh, and the Greens.

"There were hardships throughout different areas of life, you know, where the plant would go on strike or something, and you'd find life a little rough, you know. But as far as families, they were pretty much well united, like I said when you think in terms of Point Anne as one big family. Certainly when we were young kids growing up, Mom and Dad then had a good relationship, and they were good to us kids, at least in the early years. When we were very little, they used to have card games and have people in, and that was their social. They'd have cards from house to house, and played a lot of euchre and that kind of thing.

"I was born at the Belleville General Hospital on November 18, 1946, four of us were born in Belleville, and just the one, Uncle Lloydie, was born on the Tyendinaga reserve. [He] was born right in a little fishing shack right down by the water as the men were out fishing. Mom had a midwife and Lloyd was born on the water. I don't know the name of the midwife, although she might have been a Hill or Brant, but I'm not just exactly sure. Lloydie was different because he was born when Grandma and Grandpa Maracle were living on the reserve. Mom was really close to her time but really didn't feel it was time, and as I said, the [men] had gone out fishing, and the women were in this little fishing shanty or whatever, right down at the point. It was right at the base of where Grandpa Hill owned the property there [in] Tyendinaga. You were there and one time found part of the cot and a buoy? That's exactly it, and that's where your dad was born. The only thing I know about my birth story is that I was born the smallest child of the whole five—I was only four pounds, three ounces. I could fit in a little shoebox when Mom brought me home. How do I know? They put me in one. I was in a little shoebox for awhile [giggle]. Well, out of the whole five, that's what Mom always said, that I was born the smallest, and remained the smallest. The shortest, anyway, not the smallest but the shortest.

"I don't know much about our names, not too much. Now your dad, he was the only one that was christened Lloyd Maracle, and he never had a middle name. The rest of us all had middle names, but the only thing that was kind of different with our birth names is the way ... I don't know whether it was Mom or Dad. I suspect, I suspect it was probably Mom that had put all our names backwards. And you'll see that on our birth certificates. Like mine is Noreen Linda and Brenda's was Jean Brenda, and Benny's.... Ah, now Benny's may have been Leonard Arthur, but I'm not positive on that, but I know all the girls had their middle names first. Helen's 'middle' name is Gwendolyn. But of course Leonard Arthur never went by Leonard Arthur. As a child he was always called Ben, and I'm not just sure why, whether it was the story of Big Ben the bear or what happened there. He got Benjy as a kid, and then as he started to get older he sort of hated the name Benjy but he liked Ben, so he's always stuck with that name throughout his whole life. He's never been called Leonard, you know, but he was basically named after Dad.

"I can remember grade 9, attending Moira Secondary School. And as I said, your Auntie Brenda and I were always very close, and Mom dressed us almost like twins as we were growing up, eh? And Auntie Brenda used to get into little skirmishes, and of course I'd always have to back her up. I can remember that being the fun times and stuff when we went to school together [both giggling]. I'd be called to the office, and they'd say 'Brenda's got a doctor's appointment, eh?' and I'd say, 'Oh-ooh, I guess so' [both giggling again]. And off she'd go and have a good time, you know. But oh yeah, there was some good times. There was some times during the nursing course where'd you be taking different aspects of nursing and you would have to, you know, learn how to make beds, and learn how to make ... and how to feed babies and bathe them properly. When [your cousin] Lynn was born jaundiced I think, I practised on her all the time. I used to bathe Lynn, and feed her, and all kinds of stuff, so I'd be practising on her for my nursing. It worked out very nice.

"We always knew that we were Native, but like I said, we were never really brought up in the Indian setting, like we never lived on the reserve. So I mean other than that to go and visit the relatives, you remember visiting down there, you know, we did. We were conscious enough to know that it was a reserve, that the other Indians lived down there, but we were never really brought up as having really any real

Indian rights. So I mean as far as the girls went, we all married off and lost our Indian status. And back when they used to take away the Indian rights for the women, eh? And so we all lost that after we got married, though we all got it back. That was a big prejudice in the Indian law, you know, once you married a white man that you immediately [lost] your right to be Indian [including] Indian laws and rights. But if you were a male Indian and you married a white girl, then she gained all the rights. Well, it was very weird for us growing up knowing that we actually had the Indian blood. And say, for instance, not being against your mother, but your mother had the Indian rights and we didn't, because we married white, you know. Anyway, that's the way the laws work[ed], I guess, for the Indian … but then again, I think they were changed in, what, 1987 or something? 1985.

"I don't remember what jobs my grandparents had—I just remember them being old [both giggling]. By the time Brenda and I came along, they were a lot older and they were retired. But I don't know whether or not Grandpa Maracle worked as a farmer or not. I'm not exactly sure, and I don't really know where you could find out that information. But they lived on a big piece of land, like I said, that farm land. His name was Alfred Maracle, and Matilda Anne. I just called her Grandma, though [both giggling]. I never thought of her name other than Grandma, you know. You grew up not knowing that you were Native? Your parents never talked about it, or called it the reserve, or said 'Indian'?

"Oh, I got you a funny story of Helen and Harold when we were just kids. Brenda and I and that, they used to take us to drive-in matinees. We'd get to the sign that said 'Welcome to Tyendinaga Indian Reserve,' and they used to always say, 'Duck, here come the Indians,' and Brenda and I would jump down in the back seat, thinking that we were getting bows and arrows shot at us [giggle]. Oh yeah, we were always conscious of that, but like I said, we were never brought up in the Indian culture. You know, we all lived off the reserve and your dad inherited the Indian culture. You know, we all lived off the reserve and your dad inherited the property from Grandpa Hill, well Grandma, but it was Grandpa Hill's to begin with. She inherited it. And other than that, your dad was born down there. We certainly knew about the Council House and the Mohawk Indian Fair and that kind of stuff, and like with the lot of relatives I can remember going to visit old relatives and that on the reserve. But as far as living the culture, we didn't.

"Well, I was the last child. There was Mom and Dad and myself in the village, and I was close to sixteen, maybe fifteen, when they decided that it was time to move on at that point because the plant had closed down. We moved on up to Belleville, or had the plant closed? No, the plant hadn't closed at that point 'cause Dad still went down after we moved. But it just got to the point where there was just the three of us, and for years we lived with outside water: never had inside toilets or anything in the house. The chance to move to Belleville—which I thought was great—gave us all the inside conveniences in the city. So it wasn't until I was nearly sixteen that we moved to Octavia Street in Belleville. Yeah, the transition was good. I thought it was good [giggle], but then at that point in the relationship between Mom and Dad was not that great. And probably prior to that they weren't even the best, you know, but then it eventually got to them, so that they had very little communication back then. And at the time, Grandma (Beulah) always said I was the last one in the family, so she was sort of staying for that reason, because I was home. When I was getting married and they she'd be gone too. And that's exactly what happened—the day I got married she had her bags packed and she left for Oshawa. She went to the wedding, and right afterwards she packed her bags and away she went, and that was it—that's when they split.

"Nobody knows why she went to Oshawa, but she got a job living in a house in Oshawa and was the housekeeper and that kind of thing. She did that kind of stuff for maybe five or six years. Then after that it was sort of a case of her moving around from family to family, you know. She lived with your family for a few years, and she lived with Auntie Linda for a while, too. She started having different little apartments in Point Anne, and then I moved [to Ajax] in 1973, and I've been here ever since. Why did I move there? I think at that point in my life I was looking for a change, and Betty was moving to Ajax and she gave the opportunity—if I wanted to go and start over, well, then that was the chance I had.

"Grandpa Hill, your grandmother's father, used to love to tell stories about all the old Indians on the reserve and how they all believed very much so in stories of the sort of supernatural and ghost stories and stuff. I think that was sort of inherited to your grandmother. She used to like to tell stories of things happening, and how people you would know died, and for some reason they would have to exhume a grave and then find out the person would be turned over in the coffin. Things like that. But way back then too, they never used to prepare the bodies. Like they never used to put—what is it?—formaldehyde? They never used to put it in the bodies. Yeah. But Grandma Maracle really believed in ghosts and ghost stories, you know. She was really into all that kind of stuff, and I think she learned a lot of that from her father, you know. And we grew up in the village, so us kids didn't really spend a lot of time on the reserve. Now Mom and Dad had grown up on the reserve, and they lived down there for a period of time 'cause Grandpa Hill of course had his property [down there], and Grandma Hill and her sister were brought up on it. But when it came to our generation, we were all sort of born off-reserve except for your dad, and we all lived in the village, near Point Anne.

"I do remember one story. They always gave to the Indians every year a big bag of flour for the winter. And we always got that—from the reserve. Every winter you got a big bag of flour and a bag of corn. We used to make Indian corn soup, which they still do today down there, and you can get it at the Mohawk Fair and places like that. I think Mom did lye the corn to make the Indian corn soup when we were just kids, but I'm going back a lot of years, so it's hard to remember it all, except that I remember eating a lot of corn soup, and it was very good.

"As for the stories, I think that they would go from one generation to the other because it was like a family, so when you're growing up in the public school system, you know, your parents went there, your brothers and sisters went there ahead of you, and then the teachers would have stories about what your siblings did ahead of you and stuff. So that was always quite interesting. If you did something, they'd say, 'Oh yeah, your brother used to do that three or four years ago,' you know [giggle]. Good and bad stuff. Of course the school eventually closed down as well as the cement plant. And I think it was taken over—for a while they ended up with a bit of a flea market in the basement of the school, and I'd go down there a few times. It was interesting to go through it. That was basically our school system.

"I went to Point Anne Public School in the upper part of the village—it went from grade 1 to grade 8. There was more than one room, but you had more than one grade [in each room]. Then I went to Moira Secondary School for two years in the commercial program, and then I switched over to a general course in grade 10, so I actually took two different courses with two different years of grade 10 at Moira. Then I went from there to Quinte Secondary School and took grade 11 and 12 ... of the science, technology, and trade to be a nursing assistant. I knew I wanted to be a nurse, and the nursing assistant course at that point was given in the high schools with year 11 and 12 along with your academic subjects. You had two years with nursing as one of your subjects, and nursing was part of your curriculum into the hospital, where you spent so much time in the hospital, and so much time in the classroom. Once I graduated grade 12, I was a nursing assistant, although they called it a registered nursing assistant then; it's now called a registered practical nurse, an RPN.

"I don't think any of my brothers or sisters got as far as grade 12. I think Auntie Brenda went to 9, and I think your dad may have went to grade 10, but I'm not sure. He went out working early in his lifetime, you know. Auntie Helen did too, and of course Aunt Brenda was married very young. I think your Aunt Linda was the only one that went right through to finish high school. By the time I transferred to Quinte, Mom, Dad, and I had moved to Octavia Street, 'cause the other four [kids] were all married. In between classes I used to go to Earl Street and spend a lot of time with your Aunt Helen 'cause she lived over on Earl Street.

"We bought our groceries and stuff [in Point Anne] at the village McLaren's store, and it was like a grocery/variety store. You could go in there and buy groceries, clothes, camping stuff—they had a little bit of everything in there. And they had a little gas station down there and they had a post office in the front of one of the houses. So as for major, major purchases, of course you'd go in to Belleville. Not everybody had cars, but we always had a car, and maybe a good point of all was when Dad used to let us little kids sit in the front of the car and steer it up through Point Anne and up Point Anne Lane, and once you hit the main highway you're outta there. And he would drive us. Yeah, we used to all do that. It was about a mile from down in the village to the top of the upper part of the village where we went to school, so we used to always hitch. One of the little fellows that had a pickup truck used to stop and pick us all up, and we'd sit in the back of the truck to go to school [giggling]. Closest to Highway 2 is the Upper Village, and Point Anne Lane is what they called the area that stretched from the highway right down until you actually entered the village [that] was Point Anne Lane.

"The cement plant offered the obvious jobs in Point Anne, though it was only men. Your relatives were electricians. Your grandpa was an electrician, and that's how your dad got interested in electricity. And Grandpa worked at the Point Anne plant in the electrical department, as did your dad, until the plant closed, and then that's when he went to Picton. He was a lot like your brother Craig; he grew up and learned how to do electrical work through Dad (Grandpa), then went on to get his licence eventually and be an electrician.

"More worked out into the Belleville area or Napanee area and that kind of thing too, you know. More worked for Canada Cement as the main industry than have gone out of the village to work. It was a big industry back then. If they didn't work for Canada Cement, they may have worked in a company that had some dealings with Canada Cement. So there was different areas that the plant provided, different jobs outside of the village, but most of the people that were there were at Canada Cement. There were also some farmers at the upper part of town. Like your grandparents lived down on an area that was like a farm. In school, we were brought up mostly with the English language. Now Grandpa Hill, Mom's father, used to try to teach us some Indian language 'cause he could talk Mohawk. But being kids and not too interested in a lot of things, we never picked up on much. But we learned *otsikheda*, which means 'sugar' in Mohawk. And *shekon*, which means 'hello,' right? And a few other little words we picked up. But he could talk so very often and revert to some Mohawk language. He would throw in some stories, too, yeah.

"We didn't have to do French in school unfortunately; we should have did more of it as we were growing up, but it wasn't a dominant thing back then, you know. Like reading, writing, arithmetic, and English was your big subjects. There were other languages spoken in the village, too. I think there was a little bit of French spoken down there, because you were heading closer down the area towards, you know, oh, and Ukrainian. There was one whole street in our village over from us where it was all Ukrainian people, which was very, very deep in tradition too. Their Ukrainian foods, and that, you know. They used to make us cabbage rolls and all that kind of stuff—they loved to cook.

"Grandpa Hill could talk Mohawk fairly good, and I think Mom and Aunt Genny may have gotten more than we did. You know, on Dad's side, I don't know whether he got too much [of Mohawk], but he may have known more than he talked, you know. I'm not too sure on those.

"There was the Landing of the Mohawks that happened every year down on the reserve—I don't know if you ever heard about that. They did it for many years. And we used to go to that too and watch them come up the river in the canoes, and that kind of thing, you know. A lot of them were in their traditional clothes. Grandpa Maracle had a whole traditional Indian outfit. I actually have a picture I can look at it right here I think. Your dad had one too, where he's wearing the big headdress. You have the outfit? He said you could have it because he knew you would take care of it? Oh, isn't that nice. He belonged to the Orange Lodge down there on the reserve, and when they had parades, he would always march in them and he would wear his Indian costume, like most of them would traditionally when they were down there. But by the time Dad and Ethel moved back down to the reserve, [we kids] were all basically out on our own, eh? And his parents moved back to Deseronto from Point Anne and that's where they died. They're buried there. Yeah, just as you are going around the bend, there's a cemetery there at Deseronto, and that's where they are, closer to Highway 2. I think Grandma Heaney is buried there, too. That's where your grandparents' parents are too. They'd be your great-grandparents and are buried in Deseronto, too.

"There was some connection between Point Anne and Tyendinaga in the fact that there were some Indians in the village and it was close to the reserve. And certainly everyone in the village knew of the reserve and they've probably been down there. So it was something that was always there."

Discussion of Findings

Point Anne

A number of themes come out of the narratives. It is important to keep in mind, as you read along, that Great Aunt Betty and Aunt Linda are from two different generations, so naturally their experiences in Point Anne were somewhat different. Not a lot changed over the time of their residence there, so I was able to draw a number of parallels and comparisons from their narratives. The community of Point Anne, family life, education, local economy, and employment, as well as story, language, and relationship to the people and place of Tyendinaga were common threads running through the tapestries of their stories.

From what I understand and what Aunt Betty and Aunt Linda have reinforced, both lived in lower Point Anne, near the Canada Cement plant and the water. Aunt Betty notes that they lived in "shacktown," where a lot of other Mohawks lived just east of the plant. She said it was like a little reserve right there in the village, while Aunt Linda said that at her time of residence there were some, but not a lot of Native families living there. She remembers the Greens, Fullers, and Brants.

Both commented on racism and the fact that although it was present at their time in Point Anne, it was never very prominent. Aunt Betty commented that she had been called Indian a number of times, even though she had very fair skin, eyes, and hair, but that physical fights were generally not a result of the comments. Aunt Linda did notice a bit of stigma in having the Indian name, though: she is referring to the name *Maracle*, which all three of us women share (although they go by their married names now). Maracle is a common name in Six Nations, and in Akwesasne Mohawk Territory as well, but is most prevalent in Tyendinaga, where it can be likened to the name *Smith*. It is said on the reserve that three of the original twenty families that moved to Tyendinaga in 1784 at some point changed their names to Maracle. Furthermore, it is said that their previous names were Buck, Papineau, and Pencil. My family came from the Papineaus. It is interesting that there is no record of what our names were before that. This break in record of the name is likely because there were few written records of residents of the Mohawks residing at Fort Hunter, in the Mohawk Valley in present-day New York state because of all the devastation during the American Revolution. In any case, there is a say-ing in Tyendinaga: If you throw a rock over a *Green Hill*, and it doesn't hit a *Brant*, it's a *Maracle*. Maracle, then, is a recognized name in the Quinte area (Belleville, Trenton, Thurlow, and Tyendinaga Townships, Deseronto and Napanee) as a Mohawk name.

Aunt Linda said the biggest prejudice was expressed in the strug-gle between the Catholics and Protestants: if you were from one and went out with someone from the other, it caused big problems, because religion was part of the everyday life of Point Anne. While Linda was living there, a Catholic Church and school were built in Upper Point Anne, and the students and religious factions segregated themselves in the hamlet a little more so than they had previously. There seems to have been a conflict between Anglican and Protestant churches, as opposed to the Catholic church. Both Aunt Betty and Aunt Linda recalled a great variety of people living together in the closely knit community of Point Anne: Mohawk, French, Polish, and Ukrainian. Aunt Betty noted there was a street that was primarily Polish called "Honk Town," while Aunt Linda remembered a street made up mostly of Ukrainians. Perhaps there were two separate streets, or more Ukraini-ans lived there while Linda was there.

MacDonald, Mahar, Green, and Hart are the family names that both women remember, but Linda mentions the Hulls, Frasiers, and Cooks, too. I remember my dad telling me stories while I was growing up about how he played hockey with Bobby Hull—I wonder if he received any scars from a member of the Hull family, as Linda did! Linda emphasized, although Betty mentioned it as well, that Point Anne was a very sports-oriented village, complete with skating rink, tennis courts, and baseball diamond. It was interesting to hear that Brenda and Linda were travelling competitive tennis players!

The only other discrepancy I found was that Betty said that my grandfather, Leonard, lived in Point Anne until the cement plant closed down. Linda said she moved to Belleville with Leonard and Beulah (her parents) when she was sixteen years old, which would have been the early-to-mid-1960s. After the interviews I discovered that Grandpa continued working in Point Anne for awhile and drove back from Belleville, so it is definitely possible that he worked there until the plant closed in 1973.

Family

It is very interesting to see the different family experiences of birthing and community ties. My Aunt Betty was born Matilda Anne on February 5, 1928, aided into this world by Mrs. Dale MacDonald, the neighbour across the street. "They weren't midwives," she said. "They just did that." Can you imagine how much closer *any* community would be if neighbours were involved in helping children to be born? There must be an instantly stronger bond in both family and community when members from *within* help in the birthing. In comparison, Linda was born in the Belleville General Hospital on November 18, 1946. Three of her siblings were born there as well, whereas my father had a different story. He was the only sibling born on the reserve, in a little fishing shack down by the water near their land. Grandma thought she would be fine, and luckily a midwife was there (a Hill or a Brant?) and helped her bring Lloyd into this world on May 24, 1941. Linda noted a peculiarity on the birth certificates of everyone but my father, who incidentally had no middle name: the names by which they are known is actually the *middle* name on the card. Linda is technically called Noreen Linda, and Helen is Gwendolyn Helen, and Brenda was Jean Brenda. We are not sure about my Uncle Benny, though—we think his birth certificate was Leonard Arthur (first name after his father).

Other than the midwife–hospital comparison, Betty does not know her birth story: the details, events, and visitors of the day. The only thing Linda knows is that she was small enough to fit in a shoebox at four pounds, three ounces, and indeed that is where she was kept for a little while. I have learned, in speaking to Native women over the years, that your birth story is important, and it is the responsibility of the mother to share it with her child over the years. It seems that my grandparents' and parents' generation did not have their birth stories passed on to them, which is now becoming a trend again in both Native and mainstream cultures. I was unique in my family as well. I was my mother's only overdue baby, and her largest at seven pounds, five ounces. She also gained the least weight for me: she gained about twenty pounds each for the other four pregnancies, but only nine pounds for me. I think that is why I have been known to get colds a lot—my Mom gave all the other children the antibodies, and couldn't produce enough for me because she didn't gain very much weight! So to continue the story, I was born on March 8, 1973 (International Women's Day!) at 8:27 p.m. in the Belleville General Hospital. You see, I was Gloria's fifth child—she had an idea about what to expect and how to understand what her body was telling her. Three days after the due date, she was in the delivery room, yelling at the doctor and nurse to come into the room because she was ready. The doctor, you see, was having a rather lengthy conversation outside her door, and told her that she was fine. She said, "No, I am not fine. I am ready now!" and so the nurse came in to check on her. Right at that moment I came shooting out of my mother and the nurse caught me, mid-air. Talk about airborne! Mom has always said to me that I was born late, and I will die late. She says how I was born is an indication that I will participate when I am good and ready and won't be rushed by others, but that when I am ready, look out! I am there full speed and doing everything I need to on my own. I would say that is a pretty accurate assessment.

There were seven children in Betty's family: my grandfather, Leonard, being the oldest, and Betty being the second youngest. Linda was the youngest, and I am the youngest in my family as well. Betty and Linda both said that their parents moved to Point Anne because their fathers got jobs at the cement plant. It turns out Betty's mom, Matilda Anne, was a Maracle from one of the other branches of Maracle (Buck or Pencil?) and married my great-grandfather, Alfred, who was a (Papineau) Maracle. It is interesting to note that Betty said everyone agrees that it was her dad who was a gem, and her mother, Matilda Anne, who disciplined them. I wonder if that could be the European influence of her mother, Mary Heaney, who came straight from Ireland. It is a possibility, but only speculation at this point. I firmly believe from learning about traditional stories, oral history, and roles of the parents of the Iroquois that they did not hit their children. Lessons were learned by role modelling, observing, and exercising shame and humility, from what I can understand of conversations I have had with people over the last decade.

Unlike me, Linda said they were always conscious of being Native. It is interesting, though, that when I asked both her and Betty about their connection to being Native, belonging to Point Anne, and being Mohawk, they consistently began their comments with "but." Let me illustrate: "But we were never really brought up in the Indian setting, like we never lived on the reserve, so were conscious enough to know that it was a reserve, that the other Indians lived down there, but we were never really brought up as having any really Indian rights. So I mean, as far as the girls went, we all married off and lost our Indian status." Betty and Linda identify with being Native. However, they do not live in Native communities now nor have they for the majority of their lives, nor do urban Native communities surround them. Aunt Betty's complexion is very fair, and Aunt Linda has dark hair and eyes, and pale brown skin. Whenever I asked them about their identity and consciousness of their heritage from *both* sides of their families, they repeatedly said, "but." Aunt Linda said she was conscious of being Native, "*but* [they] were never really brought up in the Indian setting." At another point in the interview, Linda said, "But like I said, [we were] never brought up in the Indian culture ... your dad inherited the property from Grandma Hill, she was born down there. [They] certainly knew about the Council House and the Mohawk Indian Fair and that kind of stuff, and like with a lot of relatives [she] can remember going to visit ... on the reserve."

In my eyes, with all the learning of Native culture through books, schools, socials, storytelling sessions, listening to elders, ceremonies, and conversations with friends and colleagues, Betty and Linda do not need to explain that they did not grow up "in the Indian culture." It seems they have succumbed to the popular culture's assimilationist version of the only "real Indian" is one who grows up *on* reserve *with* Native culture. Regardless, they are Mohawk to me; both of them had both parents who were Mohawk and who came from Tyendinaga. *I* was not raised in the Indian way, but I have taken it upon myself as *my personal responsibility* to learn, and have been doing so for the last decade of my life. I was still Mohawk before I learned. However, I have purposefully surrounded myself with Native communities in the last eight years of my life in Kingston, Peterborough, Tyendinaga, Curve Lake, Grassy Narrows, and Toronto. I feel that I do not need to preface my being Mohawk anymore. If people want to judge me, they will continue to do so. I have a stronger idea of where I come from, and who I am, from learning about my family through talking, telling stories, and doing research on Tyendinaga and Point Anne. More of this can be seen in the Stories section below.

I thought it was very brave and courageous of my grandmother to leave my grandfather and seek work on her own; I thought it was very humorous that she didn't waste any time and left exactly when she said she was going to—when the last child left. However, Aunt Linda showed me another way of looking at it. It was *her* wedding day, *her* happy day, and to know that her Mom was leaving her dad on *her* day did not make it so happy or so focused on her and the groom. That is true, and I can mourn that moment with her and understand the timing of it. It does not take away the courage and conviction I think Beulah must have had, though.

Stories

Aunt Betty said she doesn't remember if she was told traditional stories as a child, saying they are "foggy" in her mind. That's understandable, because it was a long time ago that she lived in Point Anne. She instantly answered the question with "but my mom never lived that long on the reserve after she got married, and she didn't go down there a lot, because she didn't get along with her mother-in-law." Again, it's interesting that when I asked about cultural influence, she gave a reason, excuse, saying, "but." Aunt Linda said that Grandpa Hill, Beulah's father, used to love to tell stories about the old Indians on the reserve and how they all believed very much in stories of ghosts and the supernatural. I have a feeling that when they say "supernatural," they may indeed be talking about cultural stories, many of which contained what Western civilization today would consider to be events beyond scientific explanation. Grandmother liked to tell stories of bodies being exhumed and of finding the body turned over in the coffin. I vaguely remember my grandmother telling ghost stories when I was a young child, but I don't remember the actual stories, because I think I was too scared! Linda said that Grandma really believed in ghosts and ghost stories, and she probably learned that from her father. She said, "But we grew up in the village so us kids didn't really spend a lot of time on the reserve." Again, she has prefaced her experience by saying "but," by giving reason for her not having stories. It sounds to me as if there was a fair amount of oral tradition flowing around their family, especially with Grandma and her father around.

Aunt Betty said she was not familiar with the Three Sisters story, so I shared it with her. She said she was not familiar with the planting technique, but she grew up on squash and still loves it today. She got her beans and corn often in lyed or dry corn soup, which she still makes, and which is a common food found at any powwow or social gathering, along with fried bread. The funniest stories I have heard her tell me in the interview was about Great Grandma Heaney—she sounds like quite a character. "Kiss my Irish ass!" will forever ring in my mind and bring a smile to my lips.

Aunt Linda said she did remember one story after all, that every year the Indians were given a big bag of flour and of corn for the winter. I think this may have been a result of the 999-year Turton Penn Lease, whose payment was an annual bag of flour to each Indian family belonging to the reserve. (This land claim was settled in the 1990s.) The lessees paid the flour for only a few years, then managed to keep the land until a decade ago, when the land claim was finally settled and the western third of (of the reserve) the Turton Penn Lease was supposedly returned to the band. She also talked about stories of family. Linda was the youngest of her siblings in a school that her parents also attended. Likely she heard a lot of stories of what they did when they were her age, or what she did that was the same or different. That is an interesting point for her to make, and made me realize that stories really are everywhere. As the youngest, I received stories about my siblings in Belleville at my schools, although I am sure there was more teacher turnover there than in Point Anne.

Language

Both Betty and Linda experienced only English in their education in Point Anne, although Aunt Betty noted that other languages were spoken at home such as "Indian," Polish, and Ukrainian. Both her parents could say a lot of things in Mohawk, and she and her siblings would giggle when they heard Mohawk songs or people speaking in Mohawk, but they were taught a number of words in Mohawk that they used with some regularity. Today she remembers how to say "hello" in Mohawk. She was fortunate enough, in my opinion, to be exposed to some language in social settings, such as in the conversations of Mohawks on the reserve, or between her parents and Mohawks who came to visit Point Anne. Clearly, there was more exposure and practical use of the language on the reserve than there was in Point

Anne, where such a diverse community of people used English as their common language.

Linda said that Beulah's dad used to try to teach them some Indian language because he could speak fluent Mohawk, but that they never picked up on it. She remembers how to say the Mohawk words for sugar and hello today, as well as other little words. She said her mom and sister, Genny, also spoke and understood quite a bit that their father had taught them. It has been interesting to learn that Grandpa Hill threw in Mohawk stories as well when he was trying to teach them Mohawk—an experience I regret that I did not have as a child, growing up. That is why I focus so much on the stories now—I do not want my children or nieces or nephews to have that side of their family neglected simply because nobody knows the stories anymore. I have taken it upon myself to learn the old stories, and take part in contemporary stories such as this one, which is both recently historical as well as contemporary. I am even editing the first—ever—anthology of Native science fiction, in hopes of including prophecies and contemporary written stories of the future. They have always been part of the Mohawk tradition, but most people think that stories can only be about the distant past. As I write this story, I am conscious of the fact that it will never be finished, for the Mohawk women in my family will continue to live and experience and have stories to tell. I recognize this as a contextual piece of research on our understandings of our lives now, and during our childhoods, in the context of Point Anne.

Tyendinaga

There is still a connection for both my aunts to Point Anne and Tyendinaga. Aunt Betty said she still likes to go down there and visit friends—distant relatives, second, third, and fourth cousins live there now. Her brothers Dick and Garnet passed away in the late 1990s, and they were the last of Betty's siblings living on the reserve. The bloodline of connections between us and the reserve is becoming more and more faint. I don't even know who Garnet's kids are. And now that I know about them, I would like to seek them out—and not only to be comforted by a *physical* connection to the reserve. I recognize the spiritual, mental, and emotional connections as well, and I have a good number of precious friends and relationships that are based on blood ties, land ties, spiritual experiences, and the like. I feel as if part of the story is missing, and that I never had an opportunity to know Garnet as I grew up—I think the last time I saw him I was a small child, and have only heard the family talk about him in the last few years.

Aunt Betty says she used to go and visit the former chief Earl Hill, who grew up in Point Anne and who was close to my Uncle Dick all his life. He used to give her corn that was already lyed, and special beans for corn soup she couldn't find in any other store. I knew Earl; he was a great man, beloved by the community. Earl has passed away, but his wife is still there, and she ran their restaurant, the Chief's Inn, for some time afterwards. She is my grandma's first cousin, so I plan on going to talk to her soon. Aunt Betty says that Earl had always been especially kind to her, especially since Dick's death. He was chief of Tyendinaga for twenty-two years, and is an extremely well-known, well-liked fellow who will always be a strong part of the history there. He passed away a number of years ago as well.

Aunt Linda says that as a child she used to go to the Landing of the Mohawks in May every year, which was a re-enactment of the twenty families who travelled by canoe to live in Tyendinaga, after being displaced from the Mohawk Valley during the American Revolution. Some of the people, she remarked, wore traditional outfits, and she pointed out that Grandpa Maracle, her father, had an outfit of his own. I have that outfit today, holding it and using it when the need arises. The outfit is not traditional, though. It is all leather with fringe, and has a headdress with flashy brown and bright orange (dyed) feathers, which are not recognized as Mohawk clothing or head gear. I have been there too; the landing still takes place every May. Regardless, it is the outfit that he used to wear when I was a little child and I watched him walk in the Santa Claus Parade, waving and smiling to the kids who were excited to see "real live Indians."

Aunt Linda said that Grandma Heaney, Dick, and both her parents are buried at Deseronto Cemetery. Now that I know, I think I should go and visit. She had an advantage over me when I grew up; she was conscious of the fact that she was Mohawk, and of the connection between Tyendinaga and Point Anne. "Certainly everyone in the village knew of the reserve and they've probably been down there. It was something that was always there."

Conclusions

Much work has gone into this attempt to search into my family history and contemporary reality, and reflect upon its effect on my personal being and professional development as a listener, a storyteller, a researcher, and a teacher. I found during my journey that there does not appear to be anything published on Point Anne, yet the community has a rich and unique history within the Quinte area. Searching out information on it therefore became quite a difficult task—I had to piece together a history based on newspaper clippings from the local *Intelligencer* and what I have been told by my family and local historians. (Interviewing them proved to be quite a feat as well.) It is important to continue trying to contact more local historians.

One reason I was driven to find out more about Point Anne is the lack of knowledge residents and band members of Tyendinaga have about it. When meeting Native people, they always ask you, upon finding out that you are Native, what nation you come from, what community, and what family. Inevitably I explain that I *am* Mohawk although I look very fair and my father *didn't* grow up on the current reserve, but in an adjoining community (Point Anne) with numerous other Mohawk families. It is a unique experience and connection to Tyendinaga, and the story simply hasn't been told yet.

I also wanted to give expression to the voices of my aunties by offering them a safe place to narrate their stories about growing up in Point Anne, and their connections to it since they moved away. One device to make their voices stronger was to include only *their* voices in the narrative; my contribution to their narratives was insignificant enough to exclude, and the main themes of the narratives still manages to be clearly heard.

In my methodology I used interviews with my aunties, as well as literature reviews of Iroquois stories and articles on Point Anne and Canada Cement. I had hoped to hear that my aunts had heard traditional stories, even though they did not grow up on the reserve. Indeed, they received some of the social and practical aspects of the Mohawk language and identity. They were told stories about "Indians" by Grandpa Hill, who had a knack for storytelling and a good grasp of the language. Upon reflection, I am sure they heard many stories as they were growing up, and it is still relevant for me to have asked about them. At first,

I was disappointed that they didn't know any of the traditional stories that I know; but in hindsight, that is not important. *I* learned from the stories, and I also learned that almost all the Iroquois stories found today in print are written by men and are about men and boys. Joseph Bruchac (1985), James Herrick (1995), and the North American Indian Travelling College (1984) all indicated to me that Mohawk women's voices, roles in life, and stories were not being heard. I thought I would start in a very minute way to turn this trend around by beginning with what I know about my family and myself, for our voices and stories to be heard. We have been successful in this endeavour.

The contextual narrative interviews were quite consistent with one another and have urged me to continue communicating with my aunties about new questions and stories. The stories are similar, despite the fact that Aunt Betty lived in Point Anne between the first and second world wars, and Aunt Linda lived there from World War II until the mid-1960s. I feel closer to my aunties, as if we have strengthened our relationship with each other, and gotten to know each other better in the process. It is clear that themes of Point Anne as a community, family, story, schooling/education, economy, language, and relationship to Tyendinaga came out of the narratives and our conversations with each other.

Limitations of This Work

There were a number of limitations to this study. First, I had hoped to interview four of my Mohawk aunties in this study. Unfortunately, my Aunt Brenda had lymphatic cancer for some time and passed away in the summer of 1999. I talked to my other auntie about it, but during the research phase of this work, she declined to take part in the interviews. That left me with two aunts I am close to, from a total of three generations. I decided to include my experiences more throughout the text—not just in the beginning and the end, for in reality I am included *within* the lives of my aunties and our more broad Mohawk family.

I had hoped to come across Mr. Burshaw's manuscript on Point Anne, for which he started research in the late 1980s. To date, the whereabouts and length of the manuscript is unknown. The local historian had agreed to find out more about the manuscript and to share that knowledge with me. Alas, he did not show up for two interviews we set up, and has been unreachable since. Since nothing substantial had been published on Point Anne, the community, Canada Cement, and the residents there, and certainly since nothing has been written on its Mohawk residents, Mr. Mahar is a key resource for my research, especially since he grew up with my aunties. Lastly, I had hoped to interview my aunties in person over a series of visits, but time and health constraints forced us to conduct taped telephone interviews. There were at least ten telephone conversations, and four major phone interviews, which proved to be enough for the scope of this paper.

With this research, I set out to learn more about my family and their experiences in Point Anne. It wasn't until I began to read other Iroquois stories that I learned how many tellers were male and how much emphasis was placed on men and boys. Furthermore, I learned that in what little was shared about Mohawk women in the stories, most of them misbehaved and were difficult role models. I knew that these were betrayals, inaccurate portrayals of the Iroquoian women I know and have existed before me. So I decided to interview the female Mohawk relatives of mine who grew up in Point Anne. I did not choose to neglect my one uncle who grew up there as well; to the contrary, I had hoped to give him this as a gift during his recovery from cancer. The story is never done; it will never have its final version, although it may have been told a last time and lost forever. I hope to gather information from Uncle Benny's family to expand the project in the future.

I learned a wealth of information on the topic. The newspaper articles helped to give me a base on the effects that Canada Cement has had on the community, although the voice of the people and *their* experiences were left out of the articles I found. I learned that not only my brother, but my father, grandfather, and great aunt were all electricians in their own right, and I had thought they were joking when they said we had "electric" personalities!

Once this project is more polished and expanded, I intend to share it with Tyendinaga and what is left of the Point Anne community, so that they each may take what they will from it. The next time I meet a Native person and am asked to explain myself, I can say that I am a Mohawk woman whose family came from Tyendinaga, whose father grew up in Point Anne next to Tyendinaga, and whose family is rich with experiences of language and culture. Well, that sounds a bit dramatic. And what if there are questions about Point Anne? At least now I can direct them to some solid proof of my "Mohawk-ness" and the connection of Tyendinaga Mohawks to Point Anne.

Etho niiowennake. Nia:wen.

Definitions

Acculturated   Combination of traditional and contemporary Western societal values and practices

Assimilated   Living in Canada as a Canadian, denying *or ignorant of* most or all depth, reality, culture meaning, and connection to Native/racialized minority heritage

Off-reserve band member   Someone who is presently on a band list, whose ancestors were around when the original census identified Indians living in the area; the person still qualifies for Indian status, but no longer lives on the reserve

Haudenosaunee   The internally accepted term of the Iroquois Confederacy meaning "People of the Longhouse"

Bibliography

Barreiro, Jose, ed. *Indian Roots of Democracy*. Ithaca: Akwe:kon Press, 1992.

(Belleville) Intelligencer. "Cement Workers Relocation Done." n.d.

———. "Familiar Clubhouse Leaves Pointe Anne." April 14, 1969.

———. "The Ghosts of Quinte Past: Point Anne Has Seen Better Days, Friend." September 15, 1991.

———. "Local Man Seeks Material for Book in Preparation." February 8, 1988.

———. "Point Anne Company House to Be Vacated by Late 1973." July 10, 1972.

———. "Point Anne Firehall Now Open." November 23, 1970.

———. "Point Anne Residents Fear for the Future." October 19, 1972.

———. "Point Anne Water Costs Are Rising." March 15, 1974.

———. "Production Really Booming at Point Anne Cement Plant." December 3, 1971.

———. "Stubborn Stack." December 20, 1974.

———. "Temporary Layoffs Begin: Community of Point Anne Faces Belt Tightening Period." December 30, 1967.

———. "Three Prospects for Point Anne." August 3, 1972.

———. "Time Capsule." November 6, 1995.

———. "Water to Be a Point Anne Problem." December 12, 1973.

———. "Water Route for Mills." March 15, 1974.

Brant, Beth. *I'll Sing 'til the Day I Die: Conversations with Tyendinaga Elders.* Toronto: McGilligan Books, 1995.

Bruchac, Joseph. *Iroquois Stories: Heroes and Heroines, Monsters and Magic.* Freedom, CA: Crossing Press, 1985.

———. *New Voices from the Longhouse: An Anthology of Contemporary Iroquois Writing.* Greenfield Center, NY: Greenfield Review Press, 1989.

Cornplanter, Jesse J. *Legends of the Longhouse.* Oshweken: Iroqrafts, 1938.

Evans, Jack. "Point Anne Residents Split on Condo Plan." *(Belleville) Intelligencer.* June 9, 1988.

Goodleaf, Donna. *Entering the War Zone: A Mohawk Perspective on Resisting Invasions.* Penticton: Theytus, 1995.

Herrick, James W. *Iroquois Medical Botany.* Ed. Dean R. Snow. Syracuse: Syracuse University Press, 1995.

Maracle, David (compiler). "Mohawk Stories: A Compilation of English-Mohawk Translated Stories." Unpublished, 1997.

Mulhall, Harry. "American Firm to Level Pt Anne Cement Plant." *(Belleville) Intelligencer.* December 6, 1973.

———. "Canada Cement Plans Point Anne Shutdown." *(Belleville) Intelligencer.* November 1, 1967.

———. "Canada Cement to Close Point Anne Plant for Two Months." *(Belleville) Intelligencer.* December 16, 1967.

———. "Church Settled in Last Location." *(Belleville) Intelligencer.* February 3, 1973.

North American Indian Travelling College. *Legends of Our Nations.* Cornwall Island, ON: NAITC, 1984.

———. *Traditional Teachings.* Cornwall Island, ON: NAITC, 1984.

Obomsawin, Alanis. *Kahnehsatake: 270 Years of Resistance.* Montreal: National Film Board of Canada, 1993. Film.

Peacock, Roy. "Month's Extension for Canada Cement." *(Belleville) Intelligencer.* 8 September 1973.

Smith, Erminnie A. *Myths of the Iroquois.* Oshweken: Iroqrafts, 1883.

Vecsey, Christopher, and William A. Starna. *Iroquois Land Claims.* Syracuse: Syracuse University Press, 1998.

Wallace, Paul. *The Iroquois Book of Life: White Roots of Peace.* Santa Fe, NM: Clear Light, 1994.

Wright, Ronald. *Stolen Continents: The "New World" through Indian Eyes since 1492.* Toronto: Penguin, 1993.

5

Aboriginal Representations of History and the Royal Commission on Aboriginal Peoples

Mark Dockstator

THE FINAL REPORT of the *Royal Commission on Aboriginal Peoples* (RCAP) in 1996 recommended fundamental change in the relationship between Aboriginal peoples and Canada. To facilitate this change the commissioners emphasized the importance of establishing an appropriate historical framework for the understanding of Aboriginal–Canadian relations. At the outset of the report the RCAP commissioners provide their reasoning for their approach to history by stating that the past is more than something to be recalled and debated intellectually. A complete understanding of the past has important contemporary and practical implications because many of the attitudes, institutions, and practices that took shape in the past significantly influence and constrain the present.[1]

However, attempting to construct a singular interpretation of history that effectively incorporated the perspectives of both Aboriginal and non-Aboriginal societies proved to be, in a word, challenging. After a number of unsuccessful attempts to devise such a history, the commissioners requested that I make a presentation of my doctoral dissertation. Having just graduated a few years earlier with my doctorate in law, I found that the dissertation was attracting a great deal of attention from a number of people and organizations across Canada and internationally.

At the time, the approach taken for the dissertation was somewhat innovative, in some respects groundbreaking. As a specialist in the legal field known as Native law, I adopted the approach that the teachings of Native peoples, that is, the words and wisdom of Native elders and traditional people, should form the foundation for research involving Native peoples and more specifically, the development of the Native law field. Accordingly the model developed for the dissertation was based solely on the traditional teachings of Aboriginal peoples.

From the earliest part of my legal career it became obvious that history, more specifically the historical record, played a critical role in the interpretation of the law, especially in relation to Aboriginal issues. However, the historical record, as it applied to the interpretation and construction of Native legal issues, seemed to be totally devoid of any Aboriginal understandings or perspectives of history. It was with this observation firmly embedded in my mind that I embarked on a dual track of legal education. One track consisted of getting my legal education in the Western world through university. The second track consisted of getting my legal education by studying with elders and traditional people. It was my eventual goal to use both educations, Western and Aboriginal, to provide a more complete and comprehensive understanding of the historical record and of how history, in its many forms, affects the development of contemporary issues relating to Aboriginal peoples. The result of many years of study, both in university and with elders, was the model of societal interaction developed for my doctoral dissertation. It was this model that I presented to the RCAP commissioners and it was this model that now forms the historical foundation for the RCAP report.

The discussion here introduces the model of societal interaction used by the RCAP commissioners. As this model is a composite of differing perspectives drawn from Western and Aboriginal societies, subsequent discussion isolates and examines the origin of each perspective.

A Historical Model of Societal Interaction

Early in its report, the Royal Commission discusses the different conceptions of history and societal development, and the relationship between Aboriginal and Western peoples. For this complex discussion, the commissioners draw on a model that depicts four broad stages in this historical societal interaction.[2] This historical model (appendix 1, fig. 1) offers a means for interpreting the past 500 years of interaction between Western and Aboriginal societies.

The model in figure 1 represents a unique solution to a unique problem. Perhaps most striking and obvious is the fact that "history" is presented diagrammatically. Prior to the introduction of this model by RCAP, histories were presented through words, in written form, and not by a diagram. The fact that the historical model is a diagram, a visual interpretation of history, is reflective of the model's origins that of traditional Aboriginal teachings. Thus another unique feature of the RCAP model is that it is derived from traditional Aboriginal teachings—those ceremonies and oral traditions that have been passed on by elders and traditional Aboriginal people for thousands of years.

As a reflection and combination of various and different Aboriginal teachings, the model is also the first time that Aboriginal knowledge has been presented in this manner for use by the general public. With the adoption of the historical model by RCAP, it is also the first time that both Aboriginal and Western perspectives of history have been presented using Aboriginal knowledge as the basis of those two perspectives.

Another unique feature of the model is the fact that it can be simultaneously classified as theoretical and practical or applied. The model is theoretical to the extent that it attempts to represent the dual societal perspectives of all versions, combinations, and permutations of the historical record over the last 500 years. However, the model is also well rooted in the thousands of years of practical and applied knowledge of Aboriginal peoples and consequently is not purely theoretical, as that term is generally understood. Finally, the model is unique in the fact that RCAP introduces the Aboriginal perspective of history to the wider Canadian public by utilizing a model based on Aboriginal knowledge. In this manner the RCAP report becomes the first practical example of the philosophy represented by the model, that of incorporating the Aboriginal perspective into the contemporary discourse on Aboriginal issues.

Western Perspective

When isolated and extracted from the composite model, the Western perspective of the historical interaction between Western and Aboriginal societies can be shown as in figure 2 (appendix 1). From this perspective, history in North America begins with the arrival of Europeans in stage 2 of the model. The line representing the existence of Aboriginal society is represented as a broken line in stage 1, to indicate the general lack of recognition by Western society of the thousands of years of Aboriginal histories prior to contact.

Proceeding to stage 2 of the model, the line for Aboriginal society splits into two: one part becomes a short dotted line that proceeds straight, and the other remains solid and slants downwards. The dotted line that disappears depicts the Western view that Aboriginal society would soon fade and then disappear. The solid slanting line represents the expected path to be travelled by Aboriginal peoples who, having been displaced from their disappearing culture and way of life, were also to be displaced from the socio-economic mainstream of Canadian society.

Western society would maintain and protect Aboriginal peoples and their societal institutions in the absence of their former powers of nationhood and their temporary displacement by such legal instruments as treaties and the Indian Act. These legal instruments would simultaneously displace Aboriginal nationhood and forms of governance and maintain that temporary displacement until assimilation was complete. Once assimilation was complete, as indicated in the model by the vertical arrow from Aboriginal society up to Western society, it was assumed that the separate and distinct existence of Aboriginal peoples would end. Accordingly, the Western understanding was that temporary support structures, such as treaties and the *Indian Act*, would become historical anomalies disappearing along with any remnants of Aboriginal peoples and their nationhood.

Within this view of history, there is no fourth stage to renew the societal relationship, since a distinct and separate Aboriginal society would no longer exist. Once displaced, the separate existence of Aboriginal peoples is supported only by powers delegated by the Canadian state. Thus the only societal powers of Aboriginal peoples, for example the authority to govern themselves, are those granted and devolved to them from the majority Western society. In the model this is denoted by the vertical downwards arrows labelled "Indian Act" and "Treaties." As Western society can grant and devolve temporary powers to Aboriginal society, there is an assumption that Western society can also take away these powers to achieve assimilation.

This Western conceptualization of the historical interaction includes some key characteristics or attributes that are significant to the analysis of issues flowing from a consideration of Aboriginal nationhood. Of these key characteristics, three in particular have shaped much of the contemporary debate. In the contemporary context, these associations are referred to as the concept of the "imaginary Indian," and they contribute useful insights into the analysis of contemporary events.[3] In summary, the Western perception of Aboriginal peoples as "imaginary Indians" was based on a foundation developed since contact from the assumptions that Indians were: (1) a single homogeneous group; (2) a vanishing race; and, (3) a mixture of simultaneous contrasts. The minimal recognition by the earliest Europeans of societal or cultural differences among the hundreds of Aboriginal nations inhabiting the Americas resulted in the attribution of cultural homogeneity to all Aboriginal peoples. The notion that Aboriginal peoples were disappearing was pervasive among early Europeans and has been maintained since then: "Anyone who paid attention at all to the question agreed that Natives were disappearing from the face of the earth, victims of disease, starvation, alcohol and the remorseless ebb and flow of civilizations."[4]

Armed with these assumptions, Western society manufactured an image of Aboriginal peoples that consisted of simultaneous conflicting dualities. For example, Aboriginal people were noble yet savage. The Indian seen through Western cultural lenses possesses at once admirable characteristics for revering, and pitiable characteristics for despising. Indian society was both robust and dying. Indian nations existed and did not quite exist.[5]

This conflicting duality in the Western image of Aboriginal peoples continues to have an impact on contemporary discussions of Aboriginal issues. This following discussion will focus on one aspect of the duality contained within the Western approach to history. In this instance, the issue of Aboriginal nationhood will be taken as an example, in part because it is such a large umbrella issue that incorporates and/or affects many other issues, and in part because it is not well understood in the contemporary context.

Duality in the Western perspective of Aboriginal nationhood is illustrated in figure 2 of the model (appendix 1) by the broken line for Aboriginal society prior to contact. This broken line depicts the Western legal view that Aboriginal nations did not exist: although the peoples were present physically, they did not exhibit or possess the societal characteristics required by Western legal institutions for recognition as nations. Western military and economic forces, however, found it vital at times to accept Aboriginal peoples as nations. In this way, nationhood for Aboriginal society began to be designed, from intrinsically Western perspectives, with a duality to suit the variable purposes of the designers. Aboriginal peoples became nations by necessity or nations by choice but nations only at the behest of Western society.

That Aboriginal peoples as viewed by Western society could collectively possess and, at the same time, not possess the attributes of nationhood can be illustrated by the wording of the Royal Proclamation of 1763, where Indians are referred to as "Nations or Tribes with whom We are connected."[6] This wording suggests that from the perspective of Western society, Indians were at once nations and something less than nations (i.e., tribes). Similarly, as shown in the third stage (fig. 2), Aboriginal peoples as tribes could be displaced to a less-than-equal position without regard for existing concepts of nationhood, while at the same time being recognized as possessing the necessary status for the signing of treaties as nations to meet the legal requirements for the surrender to Western society of Aboriginal lands and rights.

From a Western perspective, Aboriginal nationhood features characteristics drawn from a broader if inaccurate view of Aboriginal peoples. Perhaps most significantly, the ambivalent duality intrinsic to the Western conception of Aboriginal nationhood—that it exists and does not exist—continues to influence contemporary approaches.

Aboriginal Perspective

Integrated into the composite RCAP model of societal interaction is the Aboriginal perspective of history. When shown in isolation, the Aboriginal perspective can be illustrated as two parallel lines, as viewed in figure 3 of appendix 1. In figure 3 a straight solid line through all four stages represents Aboriginal society, denoting the consistency of the Aboriginal perspective. The historical record for Aboriginal peoples begins with the understanding that, prior to contact, Aboriginal peoples possessed and exhibited their own attributes of civilized societies, as nations, albeit ones different from those of Europeans.

At the point of contact between the two societies, the line representing Western society is solid, indicating recognition by Aboriginal peoples of the histories and different sense of nationhood that Western society imported to the Americas. Despite the divergent conception of nationhood held by Western society, Aboriginal peoples respected the relative equality of Europeans as nations, as shown by the parallel position of the line for Western society after contact in relation to the line for Aboriginal society.

Based on this recognition of relative equality as nations, a relationship was established after contact between these two societies. The vertical line with arrows at each end symbolizes the nation-to-nation or equal relationship that was established at this time. Through subsequent historical stages, from the Aboriginal perspective, the fundamental nature of this societal relationship does not change. The relationship between Aboriginal society and Western society continues on the basis of relative equality, within the overall parameters and principles established by the recognition by both societies of both as nations. In this framework of relative equality as nations, the Aboriginal perspective recognizes that societal interaction will be changed, as a natural function of changing times and circumstances; however, it was understood that any agreement designed to account for such changes would take place within the parameters and principles of equality within the nation-to-nation relationship.

The negotiation of treaties provides an illustration of such agreements founded on the principle of relative equality in a nation-to-nation relationship. From the Aboriginal perspective, the signing of treaties was a recognition that changes in the nature of the societal interaction had occurred since contact. This illustration is depicted in the third stage of figure 3, where two vertical arrows meet equidistant between the two horizontal lines representing the two societies. The line, which is labelled "Treaties," is similar to the line in the second stage to reflect the egalitarian nation-to-nation relationship inherent in treaty making. The treaty process, as well as the documents themselves, is a recognition of changes in the societal relationship to be agreed upon by both societies. More importantly, they are a reaffirmation of the initial relationship established after contact between equal nations. Within this understanding, treaties for Aboriginal peoples represent and reinforce the relative equality of each nation.

As evident from this review of the Aboriginal perspective, the underlying understanding differs from that guiding the Western view of the historical record. To address the elements highlighted during the discussion of the Western perspective, the three key characteristics are absent from the Aboriginal interpretation. Not in any manner does the Aboriginal perspective perceive Aboriginal peoples as a single homogeneous group, a vanishing race, or a combination of simultaneous contrasts. Not only does this interpretation of the historical record recognize diversity among Aboriginal peoples and nations, it also accepts the diversity of non-Aboriginal or Western peoples. As distinct societies, Aboriginal peoples maintain the perspective that their identities, histories, knowledge, and other distinct cultural or societal attributes including nationhood are not disappearing. As for the conflicting dualities in Aboriginal society that are perceived by Western society, the Aboriginal perspective does not recognize them.

Aboriginal peoples consistently maintain their concept of their own nationhood that originated long before contact with Western society, as well as their view of the historical relationship with Western society as one between equal nations. These conceptions do not change. Consequently Aboriginal peoples regard legal instruments such as the Royal Proclamation and their treaties as between nations. The contrasting perspective of Western society, one that does not recognize the Aboriginal perspective, does not change the Aboriginal reality.

Reconciling the Differing Perspectives

Reconciling Aboriginal and Western perceptions, drawn as they are from differing original concepts and views of history, is challenging. Since contact, Western society has had little interest in Aboriginal concepts and perspectives. Instead, Western society produced an image of Aboriginal society in which the actual diversity among the peoples became singular and in which the evident persistence of these diverse cultures was believed to be temporary or replaceable by elements from Western society.

From the Western perspective, Aboriginal peoples as Indians collectively did and did not possess the fundamental characteristics of nationhood; regardless of individual circumstances, all people within Aboriginal society would eventually lose their powers of nationhood at the same time and in the same way. Any vestiges of aboriginality, including nationhood, would be protected until Indians vanished as a result of assimilation or the natural disintegration of their society. From the duality of the Western perspective, Aboriginal peoples were nations when necessary for Western society, for instance, in order to sign treaties required by Western nations; thus, nationhood for Aboriginal peoples but not as conceived by Aboriginal peoples existed in some forms with the understanding that it would be temporary. After assimilation, the era of Indian nations would be over.

With the eventual disappearance of Aboriginal peoples as a distinct entity there would be no need, from a Western perspective, to continue with such instruments as the Indian Act and treaties. Using the numbered treaties as illustrative examples, these legal instruments were viewed as temporary measures designed to accomplish a specific purpose. A primary purpose of these treaties was to displace Aboriginal peoples, physically and with respect to any residual rights of Aboriginal people to govern themselves or their lands. Thus Aboriginal people were viewed to have "given up" or "surrendered" all of their sovereign rights with the signing of the treaties. Similar to a contract, once the purpose of the treaty was fulfilled, the legal arrangement could be terminated by the only remaining party to the agreement: Western society.

From the Aboriginal perspective, Aboriginal nations, as conceived from creation and as developed after contact as a balanced relationship between nations equal in status, has continued through to the present. Neither the fundamental understanding of the concept nor the nature of this societal relationship has changed. The unchanging nature of this relationship is illustrated in the example of treaties. Aboriginal people do not view the signing of treaties in the same context of displacement. Accordingly treaties are not interpreted as placing Aboriginal peoples in a lesser than equal position in relation to Western society. Consequently the treaties are not interpreted as "giving away" or "surrendering" any of the rights, privileges, or jurisdiction of Aboriginal peoples to govern themselves or their lands. Contrary to the Western understanding, therefore, Aboriginal people view treaties as "sacred" agreements that will always stand the test of time, as they reinforce a sacred relationship established at creation that must be continued throughout time where Aboriginal and Western nations continue to share and coexist as equal nations.

These differing concepts are difficult to reconcile and underlie the differing approaches to most Aboriginal issues, including governance. The chances for success in negotiating and implementing an appropriate Aboriginal order of governance, one based on a shared understanding of history, could be enhanced if participants could agree on a similar conceptual approach to defining and delineating the issues. To move towards this conceptual approach, it is useful to review once again the theoretical model, which is a composite of Aboriginal and Western perspectives that the RCAP commissioners had to reconcile when producing their report and recommendations. It was offered by RCAP as a conceptual framework that may be acceptable to participants negotiating changes to the future relationship between the societies.

For this discussion, this composite model in figure 4 (appendix 1) can be seen to represent the differing concepts of nationhood and their respective approaches to governance. The Aboriginal perspective labelled A in the model maintains the spatial separation between two parallel societies to denote the persistence of the egalitarian nation-to-nation relationship; since this view is not widely recognized by Western society, this line is broken rather than solid. The Western perspective labelled "B" reflects the displacement of any vestiges of Aboriginal nationhood and its replacement with limited powers delegated by Western society.

This model of differing historical perspectives provides a common set of principles that can close much of the distance between differing interpretations of the past, much of which, as indicated, resulted from the historical perception of Aboriginal peoples. In the past, Aboriginal peoples were imagined to be a single group of Indians who were a vanishing race exhibiting a mixture of simultaneous conflicting characteristics. Clearly, a change of perception is required of the relationship between First Nations and the Canadian state in order to move beyond such fundamental misunderstandings.

Fundamental Change

The discussion now focuses on the fourth stage of the RCAP model (fig. 4), presenting first the Western, then the Aboriginal perspective on fundamental change to the contemporary societal relationship with Aboriginal people.

Western Perspective

From the Western perspective, any notions of fundamental change begin at the bottom line of the model, the place where Aboriginal people have been displaced to the margins of mainstream society. On the scale of displacement, listed on the line labelled "B," fundamental change begins with the mainstream of society delegating more administrative authority to Aboriginal society. The intent of these transfers is to elevate the situation of Aboriginal peoples, for example from 0 to 2 or 3 on the scale, thus decrease the degree of societal displacement, thus effect fundamental change in the relationship between Western and Aboriginal societies.

Aboriginal Perspective

From the Aboriginal perspective, the starting point for Aboriginal nationhood in the contemporary context remains as it has since contact, as represented by the dotted line in figure 4. The line for Aboriginal society, parallel to and at a consistent spatial separation from the line for Western society, represents the relative equality of Western and Aboriginal peoples as nations. The starting point therefore is to meet in the middle as societies, in positions of relative equality, to negotiate a mutually beneficial societal relationship.

The model illustrates the fact that this is not viewed as a "delegation" of power, of elevating Aboriginal society with increased administrative powers. Rather the process is viewed as being identical to the other nation-to-nation processes that established and affirmed equality historically, i.e., after contact and in the treaty making. From the Aboriginal perspective then, the fundamental nature of this societal relationship has not changed since contact.

The issue of how to reconcile these different historical perspectives pervades, to some degree, the resolution of most contemporary issues involving Aboriginal people and the Canadian state. From one perspective, that of majority/Western/Canadian society, Aboriginal peoples possess little, if any, residual powers and thus characteristics of nationhood. Thus fundamental change takes on the characteristics of administrative transfers. From the Aboriginal perspective, they continue to exist as nations and thus any fundamental change, as called for by the RCAP report, will not occur unless the Aboriginal understandings of history are recognized and incorporated into the process of equal nation-to-nation negotiations.

Conclusion

The RCAP final report broke new ground in a number of different and diverse areas. In the context of presenting the historical record, as a basis to interpret contemporary issues relating to Aboriginal peoples, the commissioners broke new ground and created another first: they were the first to utilize a model of historical societal interaction that has as its basis the traditional teachings of Aboriginal peoples in Canada. This convergence of different methodologies, historical interpretation, and understandings between Aboriginal and non-Aboriginal people, as viewed through the lens of a model of historical interpretation, can be a lasting legacy of the work by the commission.

Although the final report of the Royal Commission on Aboriginal People did not meet with a high level of implementation by the federal government, nor the provincial counterparts specifically charged with mandates that incorporate Aboriginal issues, the report does serve as an important reminder of how different perspectives can be combined to develop a more complete and thorough understanding of contemporary issues involving Aboriginal people in Canada. In this context perhaps the true legacy of the commission lies not in the final report itself, but in the process that was undertaken to produce the report.

In the process to develop the information that eventually went into the report, the Commission developed new and innovative methods to develop, collect, and synthesize information, to name but one area of innovation developed through the RCAP process. In the specific context of the historical record, the Commission used a visual representation of history. The visual characteristic of the historical model is a reflection of the oral tradition that is the basis for the model. As a report that investigates the nature of Aboriginal issues, the commission utilizes a historical model of societal interaction that is derived from the teachings, knowledge, and wisdom of Aboriginal peoples. Thus the interpretation of contemporary Aboriginal issues relies on the interpretation of ancient Aboriginal teachings, making the circle complete between the past and the present.

Notes

1 Canada. *Report of the Royal Commission on Aboriginal Peoples*, vol. 1 (Ottawa: Ministry of Supply and Services Canada, 1996), 31. (Hereinafter RCAP Report.)

2 This model, given its nature, has limitations that are discussed the RCAP Report (36–40), as well as in the source. The diagram here is reproduced from the RCAP Report, vol. 1, 36, as adapted from Mark Dockstator, "Towards an Understanding of Aboriginal Self-Government: A Proposed Theoretical Model and Illustrative Factual Analysis." DJur thesis (York University, 1993). The original model and its derivation are discussed in chapter 2, pages 11–23. The thesis also provides the basis for all variations of the model in this paper.

3 The term "imaginary Indian," found increasingly in recent literature, is applied here to this feature of the historical societal interaction; see especially Daniel Francis, *The Imaginary Indian* (Vancouver: Arsenal Pulp Press, 1992).

4 Francis, *The Imaginary Indian*, 23. Francis traces the evolution of this assumption through depictions of Aboriginal peoples in art and writings (e.g., *The Last of the Mohicans*) by non-Aboriginal peoples since contact and shows how these depictions have influenced policy and law makers.

5 For a discussion of this conflicting duality, see for example Francis, *The Imaginary Indian*, chapters 2 and 4.

6 The words *Indian Nations* in the Royal Proclamation are followed by the words *or Tribes*, which some commentators suggest may have been intended to reduce the standing of those nations. See, for a discussion of this issue, Clarence S. Bringham, ed., "British Royal Proclamations Relating to America," *Transactions and Collections of the American Antiquarian Society* 12 (1911): 212–18; David W. Elliot, *Aboriginal Peoples and the Law: Indian, Metis and Inuit Rights in Canada*, ed. Bradford W. Morse (Ottawa: Carleton University Press, 1985), 56; G.S. Lester, *The Territorial Rights of the Inuit of the Canadian Northwest Territories: A Legal Argument*, DJur Thesis (Toronto: York University, 1981); Brian Slattery, *The Land Rights of Indigenous Canadian Peoples as Affected by the Crown's Acquisition of Their Territories* (Saskatoon: University of Saskatchewan Native Law Centre, 1979) parts 1 and 2; and Jack Stagg, *Anglo-Indian Relations in North America to 1763 and an Analysis of the Royal Proclamation of 7 October 1763* (Ottawa: DIAND, 1981). For the Royal Proclamation and the wording of every version of the *Indian Act*, see S.H. Venne, ed., *Indian Acts and*

Amendments, 1868-1975, An Indexed Collection (Saskatoon: University of Saskatchewan Native Law Centre, 1981).

Bibliography

Bringham, Clarence S., ed. "British Royal Proclamations Relating to America." *Transactions and Collections of the American Antiquarian Society* 12 (1911): 212–18.

Canada. *Report of the Royal Commission on Aboriginal Peoples.* Vol. 1. Ottawa: Ministry of Supply and Services Canada, 1996.

Dockstator, Mark. "Towards an Understanding of Aboriginal Self-Government: A Proposed Theoretical Model and Illustrative Factual Analysis." DJur thesis, York University, 1993.

Elliot, David W. *Aboriginal Peoples and the Law: Indian, Metis and Inuit Rights in Canada.* Ed. Bradford W. Morse. Ottawa: Carleton University Press, 1985.

Francis, Daniel. *The Imaginary Indian.* Vancouver: Arsenal Pulp Press, 1992.

Lester, G.S. *The Territorial Rights of the Inuit of the Canadian Northwest Territories: A Legal Argument.* DJur thesis, York University, 1981.

Slattery, Brian. *The Land Rights of Indigenous Canadian Peoples as Affected by the Crown's Acquisition of Their Territories.* Saskatoon: University of Saskatchewan Native Law Centre, 1979.

Stagg, Jack. *Anglo-Indian Relations in North America to 1763 and an Analysis of the Royal Proclamation of 7 October 1763.* Ottawa: DIAND, 1981.

Venne, S.H., ed. *Indian Acts and Amendments, 1868-1975: An Indexed Collection.* Saskatoon: University of Saskatchewan Native Law Centre, 1981.

Appendix 1

FIGURE 1   Composite Model
Aboriginal and Western (Non-Aboriginal) Societal Interaction

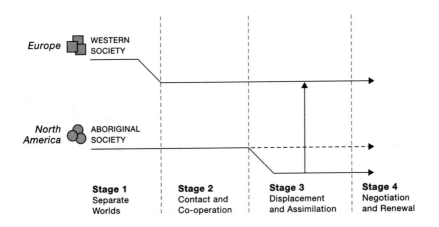

FIGURE 2   Western Perspective Isolated

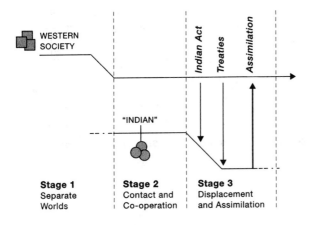

FIGURE 3   Aboriginal Perspective Isolated

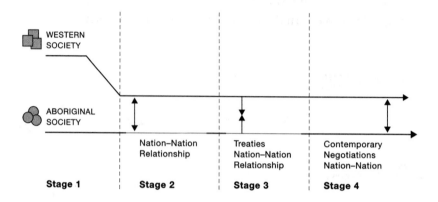

FIGURE 4   Two Different Perspectives of Fundamental Change

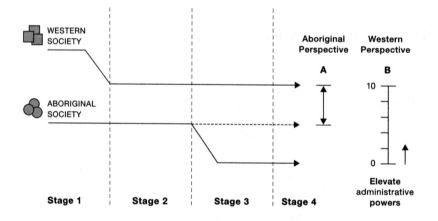

B Historical Representations

6

The Many Faces of Canada's History as It Relates to Aboriginal People

Olive Patricia Dickason

HISTORIES AND IDENTITIES, both national and personal, are closely entwined, not only with each other but also with the cultures from which they originate, and of which they are expressions. Both are not static but are rather flexible and dynamic and, in being so, accommodate and reflect the past as well as the present. Whether the parent society belongs to an oral or written tradition, the sense of identity is solidly based in the past, however that concept of time is conceived." This, of course, gives great importance to history, the record of where we are from, and how we got to where we are today.[1] To put it another way, we are making sense out of collective experiences. There are different ways of conceptualizing history, all of them connected with world views—that is, humans in their myriad relationships, with each other, with the world around them, and with the universe. In other words, history has many faces. This survey of mainly historical writing in Canada as it relates to Aboriginal peoples is not intended to be complete, which in any event would be impossible within the limits of this paper, but simply to illustrate certain trends that characterize the current scene, along with some background to put it in context.

As developed in the Western world, history is essentially a chronological and analytical narrative of "significant" human actions, based upon written documentation, particularly when derived from official sources. Its path is linear, and its overall direction is from the simple to the complex, as peoples work out their destinies within the limits of their time and place—the "arrow of change." Fundamental is the concept of time, framed by a beginning and an end. Although there are some individual exceptions, in general Western history reached its present form in nineteenth-century Europe, when it concentrated almost exclusively on public affairs, where the powerful and important dominated. It was a model that post-Confederation mainstream Canadian historians at first carefully followed, convinced as most of them were in that era that they were speaking for a society that had brought civilization to a land inhabited by Aboriginal "savages."

Aboriginal peoples took a different path: they traced their histories in myths that tell of their development as human beings through their relationship with the spiritual powers and with their land—place was of prime importance—as well as with all its varied forms of life. The Aboriginal conception of time as a web of interacting recurring cycles spanning the present, past, and future, did not give importance to chronology; rather, its mythic thought focused on how people related to the natural world that sustained them, to the human world that provided societal context, and to the spiritual world that gave meaning to it all. Important also were the traditions that prescribed the type of behaviour needed to keep these relationships in good order. Even when dealing with events that occurred within the range of human memory, the Aboriginal way was to embed them in myths or rituals that symbolized rather than reported them. Storytellers were performers rather than simply recounters of ancient tales; myths, like music, were designed to be heard. While principal themes were endlessly repeated, interpretations varied, so that the telling was never the same; far from exactly recounting memorized stories, each myth teller re-envisioned the tales afresh, even while retaining their substance. This meant that the myths were flexible in a way that eludes the literate tradition that fixes the word in print.[2] As Robert Bringhurst put it in his masterly study of Haida mythology and oral history, *A Story as Sharp as a Knife* (1999), mythic tales were never intended to be set in print, as they are "narrative music" to be "played by calling images into the mind with spoken words."[3] He likened the reading of myths that have been captured in writing as more like reading a painting. As well, Aboriginal cycles of rituals, by commemorating mythic beliefs and keeping alive memories of historic events, reinforced a sense of both identity and community solidarity. Other ways of recording important information

included the wampum belts of the eastern woodland Indians, the qui-
pus of the Peruvian Incas, and the petroglyphs and rock paintings scattered throughout the Americas. As with rituals, these records
symbolized rather than reported, which means that they cannot be
read literally, but must be interpreted. Myths, rituals, and by extension
the arts can, in an allegorical sense at least, be called the history books
of the First Peoples. For non-Aboriginal historians, trained in Western
methodologies, the connection between such symbolic recreations and
the actual events is not readily evident, if it can be recognized at all.

Different Paths, Similar Goals

That the gulf is wide between these two approaches is only too obvious. Yet, as just noted, their goals are similar; different methods do
not essentially alter their basic common purpose. But both begin by
reading the past, since reading comes before writing or drawing. Storytellers work by direct personal contact with small communities whose
members they most likely know, while mainstream historians for the
most part deal with more widespread communities through the
medium of print. Even though one is direct and personal, while the
other is once removed and impersonal, they both work to realize a
sense of identity and to reinforce community solidarity. Where the
Western historian seeks detachment and objectivity, for the Aboriginal
storyteller and his listeners the subjective experience is an integral
part of the story. Complementing this is the fact that the spoken word
can have a range of values that eludes transposition into print.

Today, of course, the written word predominates, for Aboriginals as
well as for non-Aboriginals, but that has not resulted in a common
approach to history, as the *Report of the Royal Commission on Aboriginal Peoples*, published in 1996, has made clear. As RCAP sees it,
where the literate world aims at a universal history, in the oral tradition a historical account depends on "who is telling it, the circumstances in which the account is told, and the interpretation the listener
gives to what has been heard."[4] In other words, it is in all aspects local,
even if it has been put into print. Pushing the point even further, RCAP
adds that each history is "characterized in part by how a people see
themselves, how they define their identity in relation to their envi-

ronment, and how they express their uniqueness as a people."[5] This
implies that there are as many histories as there are historians; in fact
more, if the listeners (or readers) are counted. As Julie Cruikshank
reported in "Oral Tradition and Oral History: Reviewing Some Issues,"
there are those who believe that "the contradictions in what constitutes
history—oral and written—cannot be resolved."[6]

On another plane, RCAP sees Western history as speaking to the
past, while Aboriginal history is seen as speaking to the present. There
is a fine distinction to be made here. RCAP explains its perspective by
saying that Western history views past events as one-time occurrences
from which consequences may or may not flow, while Aboriginal history sees events, even those originating in the distant past, as ongoing
processes.[7] One could note, however, that Western history is being
constantly reinterpreted in light of new knowledge and new questions
arising out of the new concerns of an ever-changing society. This
is true even when it deals with ancient times. Viewed from that perspective, all history is present history, as historian Benedetto Croce
observed. Thus the European view of time, instead of being described
as linear, with a beginning and an end, might better be described as a
spiral, but also with a beginning and an end.

Alternative Sources

A consequence of Western history's concentration on official documentation has been that so much has been left out. During the nineteenth and the first half of the twentieth centuries, it not only largely
ignored the greater part of its own societies, it totally excluded oral
societies, whose lack of writing was assumed to mean that they did not
have a history. Oral testimony was discounted as unreliable and not subject to proof. Only comparatively recently have historians been turning their attention to the broader issues involving the whole of their
societies, a move that has encouraged an interdisciplinary approach.
Although still according first rank to official documentary sources,
Western historians today are more willing to accept non-documentary
and oral evidence as historically valid.[8] This has meant drawing on the
resources of such varied fields as native studies, archaeology, anthropology, geography, law, linguistics, oral traditions, economics, and the

arts. Each provides insights that when pieced together with whatever documentary evidence exists helps to fill in the historical picture. Among other new directions, this movement has led historians to take another look at the roles of oral tribal societies in the development of Canada as we know it today, as Bruce Trigger has pointed out.[9]

A principal problem for this approach has been the development of critical techniques to evaluate information; crosschecking can be difficult, if possible at all.[10] This was illustrated by the Smithsonian Institution's 1981 multidisciplinary expedition to Kodlunarn Island in the Canadian Arctic to research Martin Frobisher's expeditions of 1576–78, with the aim of supplementing an already impressive body of contemporary documentation. While quickly establishing that the full story of the expeditions is broader and more varied than documentary sources alone indicate, problems were encountered with the stories the Inuit had to tell of those events, particularly evident where chronology was concerned. One of these was conflation, the blending of two or more events into one, although actually separated in time. Related problems were those of collapsing time, by which distant events were brought forward, and telescoping time, by which events that occurred in the recent past were put into the distant past. This, of course, reflected the traditional oral lack of concern with chronology. Sometimes there was outright contradiction. In one case, an informant changed his story. To balance this out, it needs to be remembered that written accounts also present problems. A major one is that published texts can be—and often are—changed from what was originally written, usually with the view of enhancing reader appeal. As with all evidence, whether written or unwritten, caution and care in assessment is the guiding principle.

Enter the Printing Press

The development of the printing press at the time of the voyages of discovery enabled Columbus's letter announcing his sensational news to be disseminated not only far more widely than would have been possible before, but also much faster. As well, it encouraged the rise of two new fashions in literature that to some extent helped to fill gaps in the official record: cosmographies and travel stories. The sixteenth century has become known as "the age of cosmographers," as geographers set themselves the task of describing not only the whole world and everything in it, but also the cosmos. Some of the most detailed early descriptions that we have of the Americas and its peoples are found in these cosmographies. At the popular level, travel tales took off during the period from the sixteenth to the eighteenth centuries, chronicling the experiences and impressions of those bold enough to venture into the strange worlds that were being revealed. The consequence was that a great deal of ink was spilled portraying Indians and Inuit, so different from any nations that Europeans had previously experienced. These accounts, personal and weighed down with cultural baggage as they are, reveal much to the historical researcher about the general level of knowledge and attitudes of their period. It is in these images that the prototypes of later popular stereotypes are found. Those stereotypes profoundly influenced attitudes and policies, leading to the nineteenth and early twentieth century "static and unchangeable" literary view of Indians as romantic figures of no historical significance. In this view, Aboriginal identities and histories were frozen in time. However, by that time, personal chronicles had been superseded by the more scientific explorers' accounts that continued to appear into the twentieth century.

In Canada, the myth that First Nations had no history[11] was compounded by the fact that early encounters with Europeans were poorly documented, as most visitors came over on their own initiative, attracted by the commercial potentialities of this new land. The principal exception was that of Jacques Cartier, whose three voyages, 1534–42, were under official auspices. Fishing, whaling, and later the fur trade dominated early contacts; if records were kept at all, they were for commercial reasons. Their poor survival rate reflects, at least in part, their low official importance. Official documentation for Canada did not get fully get under way until the mid-seventeenth century, when France formally took over the administration of the St. Lawrence colony.

Indians in Early Accounts

In contrast to the restricted historical view that developed during the nineteenth century, the earliest histories to deal with Canada—or New

France, as it was then—paid considerable attention to Indians, a situation that reflected their importance in the exploration of the country, in the fur trade, and as allies in the colonial wars. But, as Donald B. Smith noted in *Le Sauvage* (1974),[12] views were ambivalent to say the least, ranging from the "noble savage" of lawyer-historian Marc Lescarbot (ca. 1570-1642) to the "brutish, wild and stupid" people portrayed by the Récollet, Louis Hennepin (1626-1705). More realistic were the chronicles of entrepreneurs such as Nicolas Denys (1598-1688), whose two volumes on Acadia and its people were published 1672.[13] A three-volume work that aroused considerable interest at the time of its publication, 1703, and that has been classed by some as Canada's first history, chronicled the experiences of Louis-Armand de Lom d'Arce, Baron de Lahontan (1666-1713), who served as an officer with the colonial troops from 1683 to 1693. Its third volume includes his famous dialogues with the fictitious Adario, who is believed to have been modelled on the leading Huron chief, Kondiaronk (ca. 1649-1701).[14] Lahontan's purpose was more than just to present an Indian's view of what was happening in their lands, but to use the "Indian voice" (however that was conceived) to criticize European civilization. It would later become a favourite technique, although the views expressed were usually more European than Indian.

The first account to approach modern historical standards is *Histoire et description générale de la Nouvelle France* by Pierre-François-Xavier de Charlevoix (1682-1761), published in 1744.[15] It has been called "the first serious study of Canadian history."[16] Charlevoix, a Jesuit missionary and a scholar of the Enlightenment, was better informed and more open-minded in his approach to Indians than were later historians of the nineteenth and twentieth centuries. In Canada, the shift toward marginalizing Indians in its history began in the wake of the War of 1812-14, which had heralded the end of the colonial wars and consequently the usefulness of Indians as allies. This was complemented by the decline in importance of the fur trade, particularly during the second half of the nineteenth century. In the meantime, economic activities opened up in other areas at a dizzying rate. The experiences of one Indian community caught in this whirlwind of development are recalled by Annie York and put into ethnological and cultural contexts by Andrea Laforet in *Spuzzum: Fraser Canyon Histories, 1808-1939*.[17]

As the authors describe it, the village of Spuzzum "found itself in the path of virtually every commercial and province-building initiative undertaken in the southwestern interior of British Columbia" beginning with Simon Fraser's visit in 1808 and ending with the outbreak of the Second World War. Ironically, the effects of such activity were similar to what was happening throughout the land—the marginalization of Aboriginals. The fading of their political and economic importance was nowhere more evident than at Confederation, when Indians were neither consulted nor allowed a role.

Interdisciplinary Syntheses

It would be well after the Second World War before historians again began to pay serious attention to the role of Indians in Canadian national history. A spur was Harold Cardinal's angry *The Unjust Society* (1969),[18] expressing his outrage at the marginalization of the First Nations. Trigger's *Natives and Newcomers*, which appeared in 1985, was an early step toward giving Amerindians their due in the historical record.[19] A study of the first encounters of Natives and Europeans in Canada, it interweaves conventional history, historiography, archaeology, anthropology, and linguistics into a whole that graphically demonstrates the complexity of the situation. Trigger argues that all disciplines learn through accumulating and testing knowledge, and that it is the function of history to synthesize all pertinent contributions. His conclusion about first contacts in Canada—that Indians, far from reacting passively to the European invasion as so often portrayed, actually had been active and "resilient actors on the stage of history"—is a position that is generally accepted today.

A synthesis of a different order is Denys Delâge's *Bitter Feast* (1993), which originally appeared in French in 1985 as a prizewinning study, *Le Pays renversé*.[20] A sociologist by training and a historian by avocation, Delâge in this work examines the early seventeenth-century relationships between the Netherlands, France, and England on one side, with the League of Five Nations and Wendake (the Huron Confederacy) on the other. In Europe, the changing economic scene—as feudalism gave way to capitalism and industrialization—led to a search for markets and raw materials that extended across the Atlantic to reach the Americas, out of which arose the fur trade, among other commercial activities. As Delâge analyzes the scene, the benefits from becoming integrated into the world market were mixed as far as the two Iroquoian confederacies were concerned; in his view, their earlier economies had been better balanced than they became afterwards.

At about this same time, general histories were paying more attention to Indians, a good example of which is the two-volume work of R. Douglas Francis, Richard Jones, and Donald B. Smith, which appeared in 1988. The first volume is *Origins*, and the second, *Destinies*.[21] From there it was a comparatively small step to such works as J.R. Miller's *Skyscrapers Hide the Heavens*, which appeared in 1989,[22] leading to the sweeping synthesis, *The Cambridge History of the Native Peoples of the Americas*, of which the two-part first volume is devoted to North America. It is a collection of essays under the editorship of Trigger and Wilcomb E. Washburn, and appeared in 1996.[23]

Even missionary accounts, long a staple of the "colonialist" stance, have felt the effects of the winds of change. According to Mary McCarthy in *From the Great River to the Ends of the Earth* (1995),[24] the Oblates came to the Mackenzie River region with the goal of incorporating the Dene into Roman Catholicism on the basis that it was a universal religion to which all cultures could adapt without violating their individual integrity. This was to be achieved by the process of "inculturation," by which the Christian message assumes its own life within a culture without destroying it. In the case of the Dene, she argues, this was achievable because of the pre-existing common ground of Dene and Catholic beliefs. Such an approach is a far cry from the initial missionary goal in the Americas, which was cultural and spiritual replacement, pure and simple. The new spirit of accommodation inevitably recalls the difficulties of the Jesuits, who were suppressed by Rome in the late eighteenth century for advocating adaptation to local cultures in their Chinese missions. It was then called "syncretism." In any event, for the practical-minded Dene, Christianity presented an alternative route to spiritual power; when the Oblates arrived in the Mackenzie District, it was at their invitation.

Indians as Authors

In the meantime, although the words and views of Indians had been much reported, with few exceptions, it wasn't until the nineteenth century that they began to publish in their own right. Among the first were two Mississauga Ojibwas who were also Methodist ministers. Their publishing careers were oddly parallel: both published personal chronicles before launching into their histories. The first to appear in print was George Copway (Kahgegagahbowh, "He Who Stands Forever." 1818–1869) whose autobiography appeared in 1847, followed by his history in 1850,[25] which enjoyed considerable popular success. The diary of the Mississauga-Welsh Métis who had become an influential Methodist minister, Peter Jones (Kahkewaquonaby, "Sacred Feathers," 1802–1856) was published posthumously in 1860 under the title *Life and Journals,* and the following year his history appeared.[26] Both of these histories were republished during the 1970s, with Copway's appearing again in a 1997 edition by the University of Nebraska Press. The sweeping *History of the Ojibway People* by William W. Warren (1825–1853),[27] an Ojibwa speaker of mixed ancestry, tells his story in the European mode of the time, concentrating on wars and high politics, and even subscribing to the then-current myth of the vanishing Indian. For all that, he included his people's oral history as well, so that today his work is considered to be a valuable source for Ojibwa oral accounts. The Minnesota Historical Society Press republished it in 1984.

An Oblate missionary was one of those who encouraged the revival of interest in the writings of Native authors, which at first relied heavily on personal recollections, a trend that we have seen had been pioneered by Copway and Jones. Maurice Metayer translated and edited *I, Nuligak,* which appeared in 1966.[28] It is an Inuk's story of his life, beginning as a hunter in the traditional way, and ending with the increasing adoption of the white man's tools and ways of life. In 1973, two more or less autobiographical works caught immediate attention, one of which, Maria Campbell's *Halfbreed,*[29] became a national bestseller. Campbell's theme was expressed by one of her characters: "Because they killed Riel, they think they have killed us too, but some day, my girl, it will be different." And different it became as the Native voice began to be listened to. Campbell described the growing assertiveness: "People don't kowtow to the white civil servants on reserves and colonies any more."

The other work, Edward Ahenakew's posthumous *Voices of the Plains Cree* (1973)[30] poignantly evokes buffalo-hunting days through the recollections of Chief Thunderchild. In comparing those distant days with his world of the mid-twentieth century, Ahenakew, a Cree Anglican clergyman, found that not much of that proud, free time that had carried over into his day. The techniques of power within a complex technological society are a far cry from the personal freedoms in a hunting society unencumbered with the superstructure of a state organization. The task of trying to master these new skills within a short time was so formidable that a first reaction in some Plains Indian communities had been a tendency to retreat into the attitude expressed by the Cree word *keyam*—"What does it matter?" or "I don't care!" "Old Keyam" was the name Ahenakew gave to the book's semi-autobiographical figure that narrates the contemporary scene. That was not the attitude of another Cree author, Joseph F. Dion, whose *My Tribe the Crees* (1979) was also published posthumously.[31] A teacher and political activist during the time of the time of the 1885 troubles, he observed that some whites "liked to play jokes at the people's expense" even during times of difficulty. Noting that it "is always a difficult task to bring out the vanquished people's own account of any period of history," he pointed out that "only a very few of the more adventurous members took part at all in the rebellion." As he saw it, the history of the West would have been quite different if it had been otherwise.

The Indians' surrender was "a pathetic sight" as one by one, "warriors who had terrorized the country gave up their weapons … a pitiful assortment of firearms of every description, some tied with cord to prevent them from falling to pieces." The restrictions on the Indians that followed, particularly those that severely limited their farming, led to discouragement and eventually to the Indians simply giving up. In Dion's view, "The cattle business on the reserves died on that account."[32] The negative effects of the post-1885 restrictions on Natives have also been dealt with in detail by historian Sarah Carter in *Lost Harvests* (1990).[33] The picture she draws has been aptly described as one of "selectively applied administrative tyranny."[34]

On another plane, Anishnabe girlhood memories are recaptured in two languages by Maude Kegg in *Portage Lake* (1991),[35] English on the right-hand page, Anishinaabemowin on the facing page. These vignettes, personal and unpretentious as they are, recall Ojibway life as it was then. Another evocation of the Indian way of life, this time by a grand-

father, is that of Chief Dan George, *My Heart Soars* (1974).[36] As the
chief puts it, "My people's memory reaches into the beginning of all
things." A more academic approach was taken by the Dene Wodih Society for its compilation of traditional tales in Dene and English under
the title of *Wolverine Myths and Visions* (1990).[37] Nógha the wolverine and Nógha the prophet both have special significance for the Dene
of the far north. Coming to terms with Nógha the wolverine calls for
skill, finesse, and spiritual power, as does wresting a living from the
boreal forest; as one of the myths put it, wolverine's tracks go on and
on, back to the time before the arrival of people. Nógha was also the
name of a recent prophet of the Dene Dháa, a man so respected that
when a tea dance was held for him, everyone came. In a world changing as fast as that of today, a prophet can be a key figure.

Several compilations of elders' recollections appeared during the
nineties, led by George Blondin, a Dene elder who became concerned
that the traditional tales of his people were being forgotten. Raised in
the storytelling tradition, he saw it diminishing in the face of such dis-
tractions as television and video games. Blondin decided to capture
the tales in print in order to rescue them from oblivion; the result was
When the World Was New (1990),[38] the first of three compilations he
has published so far. His *Yamoria the Lawmaker* (1997)[39] recounts the
stories of a modern medicine man whose mission has been to help his
people retain the spirituality of their ancestors. In the same year that
Blondin began his series, Julie Cruikshank's *Life Lived Like a Story*
(1990)[40] appeared, in which three Yukon Native elders tell their stories.
The following year, 1991, two other such works were published: Dianne
Meili's *Those Who Know*,[41] and *The Old Man Told Us* by Ruth Holmes
Whitehead.[42] While the techniques of these latter three authors differ—Cruikshank's is that of the anthropologist, Meili's that of the jour-
nalist/historian, and Whitehead's that of the archivist—they all share
with Blondin the conviction of the importance of maintaining contact
with traditional beliefs and values. Scientific writers Peter Knudson
and David Suzuki carried this a step further when they went around the
world interviewing elders about their views on the relationships
between humans, animals, and the environment. The result is *Wisdom of the Elders* (1992).[43] Their search has convinced them that
answers to the world's ever-more-pressing need for a radically different

way of relating to our planet's support systems are to be found in Aboriginal knowledge, based as it is on profoundly intimate relationships with the land and its many forms of life.

The Two Realms of Culture and Nature

Robert Brightman challenged the notion that a society's productive modes tend to evolve toward the most efficient in his stimulating study, *Grateful Prey* (1993).[44] He believes that social considerations, rather than efficiency, are the key factor which, in the case of the Rock Cree of the boreal forest, concerned the harvesting of game and wild plants. They considered fish, a staple in their diet because it was their most reliable and easily available edible resource, to be an inferior food. Nor did language reflect animal utility when it came to naming species; frogs, which were neither eaten nor otherwise used by the Cree, were still named and categorized. In other words, cultures and languages have their own reasons for being, rather than simply reflecting either ecological factors or the use of resources. Nor is there a universal logic for resource management: European condemnation of the Cree lack of concern about food storage and consequent willingness to endure periods of hunger reflected arbitrary social values rather than economic "common sense."

The connection of Indian civilizations with nature was the theme of Georges Sioui, a Huron, in *For an Amerindian Autohistory* (1992).[45] The challenge for Indians, he says, is to "Amerindianize" (as he puts it) our technological society, that is, to restore its lost contact with the natural world. To this end, he called upon Indians to follow the examples of Jones and Copway, and write their own histories. A reviewer saw Sioui's message more confrontationally, as advocating "the recognition of oral tradition and storytelling as a means to deconstruct the so-called 'historical truths'" of mainstream histories.[46] Sioui, in a subsequent history of his own people, *Les Wendats* (1994),[47] developed the theme that they, by means of their deep connection with nature, had found a better way of life than has Western civilization, with all its technological sophistication. In the Maritimes, Mi'kmaq Daniel L. Paul was more overtly aggressive, as the title of his book indicates: *We Were Not the Savages* (1993).[48]

Taking Another Look at the Fur Trade

As the Indian voice was gaining an ever-widening audience, historians were moving away from regarding the fur trade as the realm of the amateur tale-spinner, and to agree that it had played an important role in Canada's early history, as Harold A. Innis had long previously demonstrated in *The Fur Trade in Canada*,[49] published originally in 1930 and subsequently revised and reprinted. A major stimulus for this new appreciation was Jennifer S.H. Brown's *Strangers in Blood*,[50] which appeared in 1980, and Sylvia Van Kirk's *Many Tender Ties*,[51] which came along three years later. Both of these studies examined a long overlooked aspect of Canada's social history, that of fur trade family relationships. To many, it was an eye-opener to learn that the trade had a social history worthy of the name. Standard histories had presented the fur trade as a male domain, whereas in actuality it had involved a considerable amount of female labour, from making clothes and equipment for hunters and trappers, to cleaning and drying pelts, preparing them for market. In other words, Indian and later Métis women played an essential role in what was Canada's principal economic activity for more than two centuries. Out of this situation arose a mixed-blood society that flourished and was influential as long as the fur trade remained dominant. However, pressures toward European mores grew with each succeeding generation. This shift in social values reached a critical point with the appearance of European women in the Canadian Northwest early in the nineteenth century. In spite of these pressures, Métis cultural values have persisted, and today the Métis are constitutionally recognized as an Aboriginal people, along with Indians and Inuit. In probing the courses of these events, Brown and Van Kirk enlarged and enriched the scope of Canada's history, exposing as they both did that its national roots are firmly planted in Indian as well as in European cultures.

Frits Pannekoek, in his *A Snug Little Flock* published in 1991,[52] picks up the tale with a partisan version of the social and political factionalism that shook the Métis community of Red River during the second half of the nineteenth century. Pannekoek narrows Red River's difficulties down to the antagonism between English Protestant and French Catholic mixed-bloods, an analysis that other historians, such as Gerald Friesen, find too restricted to adequately explain a complex situation, especially where Riel's resistance is concerned. Still others, such as Douglas Sprague in *Canada and the Métis* (1988),[53] have portrayed the Red River Métis as pawns in the game of national politics that led to the Northwest Rebellion of 1885. A more broadly based study of that conflagration is *Prairie Fire* by Bob Beal and Rod Macleod.[54] First appearing in 1984 and reissued ten years later, it graphically demonstrates the uprising's profound effects on the country's national politics, which have reverberated to this day. The movement to obtain a judicial pardon for Riel was supported by Maggie Siggins in her study of Riel that appeared in 1994.[55]

Problems with Justice, Education

In the realm of social history, it has long been recognized that Western justice has not served the Aboriginal community well. What has not been agreed upon is the alternative. Where the non-Aboriginal way treats crime as something to be punished, Aboriginal peoples view wrongdoing either as a misbehaviour, which requires guidance to be corrected, or as an illness, which requires healing. Aboriginals see the world as a web of multi-dimensional interacting relationships that inevitably affect each other, rippling across both space and time. No one acts in isolation: everyone is in that web where all things said and done have repercussions. Healing circles, instead of focusing on the misdeed itself, are concerned with the disharmony at its roots, and seek to re-establish harmony by encouraging offenders to genuinely acknowledge the harm they have done. Years of experience as a prosecutor in the Western justice system as applied in Aboriginal communities have convinced Rupert Ross of the validity of the Aboriginal approach, which he examines in *Returning to the Teachings* (1996).[56] The Aboriginal way emphasizes cooperative problem solving according to the particular circumstances and conditions of each case. Both slower and more all-embracing than the adversarial approach, it shows its greatest promise in small communities.

The more usual situation for Aboriginal offenders is to find themselves in the white man's court, as happened to Yvonne Johnson, who at the age of twenty-seven received a life sentence in 1991 for first-degree murder, the only woman in Canada serving for such a crime. A great-great-granddaughter of Big Bear, she collaborated with award-winning author Rudy Wiebe to tell her story in *Stolen Life* (1998),[57] which became a top-ranking best-seller. As Johnson describes it, she sought the collaboration of Wiebe to tell her story because even in prison it is possible to discover one's destiny, to find "the self you never knew you were." On a more traditional plane, she has been initiated to her spirit name, Medicine Bear Woman, under the guidance of her grandmother.

A particularly sensitive area is that of education, which illustrates with special clarity how difficult the process can be of translating ideals into the living patterns of society, especially when it is by imposition. Non-Native educators who imposed their ideas believed they were working for the "good" of Indians, and most of them were convinced they had a better appreciation of this than Indians themselves. If Canada's Aboriginal peoples suffered, as they did, over-attention must be included among the causes. The seventeenth-century astonishment of Indians that Europeans would take it upon themselves to instruct them in the arts of living has transformed over time into resentment at the official emphasis on assimilation. During the heyday of treaty signing, Indians were looking to education as their hope for the future, and it was at their insistence that provisions for schooling were included in the numbered treaties of the prairie West. Their idea was that school programs would be developed within the framework of a cultural partnership. Officialdom, of course, never seriously considered such a policy; Indian world views and cultural orientations were not taken into account as Western European models were imposed without question. The social dislocations and abuses that resulted have given rise to an enormous literature, most of it highly critical if not condemnatory, of which John S. Milloy's *A National Crime* (1999)[58] is an example. Providing, as it does, historical depth to the Indian residential school phenomenon, it follows J.R. Miller's *Shingwauk's Vision* (1996),[59] which is an encyclopedic cataloguing of the administrative misadventures that have made the schools infamous. Problems pervaded the entire system and eventually led to Indians taking over the operation of their reserve schools, a process that began when the Cree of Saddle Lake, Alberta, gained control of Blue Quills in 1970. That, too, has proved to be no simple road, but the movement is gaining momentum as challenges are worked out, sometimes painfully. Some of these are examined in a two-volume collection of essays entitled *Indian Education in Canada*, which appeared in 1986 and 1987.[60] Edited by Jean Barman, Yvonne Hébert, and Don McCaskill, these stimulating and informative essays examine the situation from a variety of perspectives. While observing that there are no panaceas, they testify to the vitality and originality with which Indians are attacking the problems. Indians have not lost their capacity for creative adaptability, which ensured their physical survival during the time of hunting and gathering, and today is operating to ensure their cultural survival within a technological context. In the meantime, the legacy of the residential schools has left a bitter aftermath: at the time of writing, about five thousand lawsuits involving more than eleven thousand complainants were pending as a consequence of that abusive exercise of assimilationist policies. Since the first claim was filed in 1988, settlements have been reached so far with 750 individuals.

Winds—or Breezes—of Change

When attitudes toward Aboriginal peoples began to shift worldwide after the Second World War, Canada went along with the current rather than being in the van. A sequence of events forebode change: at Montreal's Expo in 1967, celebrating Canada's Centennial as a confederation, Aboriginal peoples, with the aid of the Department of Indian Affairs, set up a pavilion that gave them their first opportunity to openly express their dissatisfaction with their lot on a national, not to say international, scale. The Canadian public, being generally uninformed about the indigenous situation, was taken by surprise, but not convinced enough to do much about it. It took the eruption of the Oka crisis in 1990 to jar them into realizing that Canadian history had far deeper roots than was being generally acknowledged, roots that extend beyond the days of first contact with Europeans. Earlier that summer of 1990, Elijah Harper, an OjiCree who at the time was a member of the Manitoba legislature, had withheld his vote from the ratification of the Meech Lake Accord, thereby killing it. Those last two events, happening so close together, finally aroused public awareness to the fact that there was more going on with the First Peoples than was generally realized.

This growing public interest was expressed in the daily headlines in the press as it rediscovered Aboriginal peoples. While this faded with the passing of the crisis, coverage of Indian news has continued at a much higher level than before. For just one example, Ingeborg Marshall's exhaustive study of the Beothuk[61] received an unprecedented full-page review in *The Evening Telegram* of St. John's, June 7, 1997. Bringhurst's study of Haida myths did even better—it was given a two-page centrefold spread in the *National Post*, July 6, 1999. Native newspapers, such as *Akwesasne Notes*, *Windspeaker*, and *Wawatay News*, are adding to the Aboriginal chorus. Of the books generated by the seventy-eight-day Oka crisis, one of the earliest was *People of the Pines*, by Geoffrey York and Loreen Pindera, which appeared the following year.[62] Both authors were journalists with extensive experience dealing with Aboriginal issues, and both had lived and reported from behind the Mohawk barricades during the final weeks of the standoff, as part of the corps of press, filmmakers, and observers who had flocked to the scene. York and Pindera gave truth to the saying that journalism is the first draft of history.

An immediate reaction to Oka was an upsurge in land claims, both new and longstanding, a spinoff that promises to continue for a long time and to change the administrative map of Canada. A recent count put the number at more than 3,300. David T. McNab, in *Circles of Time* (1999)[63] highlighted the 148-year-old resistance of the Teme-Augama Anishnabai (Deep Water People) to government, settler, and commercial pressures against their traditional lands around Ontario's Lake Temagami, as told from the Indian side. A court decision in 1984 denied Indian title to the contested lands, fuelling further resistance that culminated in blockades in 1988 and 1989, not to mention a series of court actions, the upshot of which has been to uphold the government's position. In the meantime, the people are not reconciled, clinging as strongly as ever to what they see as their Aboriginal rights. The Teme-Augama Anishnabai are far from being alone, as the book's eight chapters make clear, each detailing failed relationships between officialdom and Native peoples in various parts of Ontario. A classic example of a people who finally asserted themselves in the face of bureaucratic intransigence is recounted by Ila Bussidor and Üstün Bilgen-Reinart in *Night Spirits* (1997).[64] Alarmed at the reported decreasing numbers of caribou in northern Manitoba, and convinced that the caribou-dependent Sayisi Dene were a principal cause, the government arbitrarily rounded the people up in 1956 and airlifted them to the outskirts of Churchill, where they were left to fend for themselves. By 1973, one-third of the community had died, a result of alcoholism, violence, and living conditions that had gone from bad to terrible. At that point, the survivors took matters into their own hands and moved to Tadoule Lake, about 250 kilometres west of Churchill, where they are now in the painful process of revitalizing their community. As signers of Treaty Five in 1910, they have negotiated a land entitlement agreement with Ottawa for about nine thousand hectares, as well as for $580,000 for economic development. Even though their problems are far from being all solved, they are looking forward to a growing list of improvements in their situation.

Besides the land issues highlighted by Oka, the Bear Island case of the Teme-Augama Anishnabai, and the dislocation of the Sayisi Dene, self-government has come in for considerable attention. The Aboriginal position was expressed by Elijah Harper when he observed that self-government is not something that is given, but that is recognized. However, as Dan Smith pointed out in *The Seventh Fire* (1993),[65] while there is consensus that Aboriginal self-government is the goal, there the agreement ends. Not even the meaning of the term "self-government" has been generally agreed upon. With about a thousand Native communities across Canada, a figure that includes about 614 bands on reserves, many varying widely in their circumstances, there is no question of one solution serving all. The RCAP report sought to come to terms with this by recommending the merging of the communities and bands into between sixty and eighty nations. If the challenge is great, so is the opportunity; the Royal Commission had no illusions that the realization would be either easy or simple. As Frank Cassidy observed in 1991, self-government is an act of self-determination that cannot be imposed, as it comes from within; it has to be asserted and nurtured by those who will govern themselves.[66] Menno Boldt, in *Surviving as Indians* (1993),[67] agreed that Aboriginal peoples must be allowed to work out their own social and political problems within the framework of their own traditions. He argued that valuing the diversity of Aboriginal cultures for the knowledge they have to offer would benefit not only Canada, but the world. Highly critical of Ottawa, he blamed its administrative prac-tices for many of the Amerindians' problems. Ottawa bashing has been a popular way of dealing with these subjects.

On the level of contemporary politics, Ovide Mercredi, former national chief, Assembly of First Nations, argues for an equal partner-ship between First Nations and mainstream Canada to meet the chang-ing needs of our times. His book *In the Rapids* (1993),[68] produced in collaboration with Mary Ellen Turpel, now a judge with the Provincial Court of Saskatchewan, examines the problems involved in such an undertaking, which he backs with his own version of Canadian history. However, he makes a good point when he says part of the problem in Aboriginal–mainstream relations arises out of a profoundly divergent view of the nature of leadership and governance. In the parliamentary way, leaders take the initiative in making proposals, which are exam-ined by the rank and file and then voted on; the majority wins the day. In the Amerindian way, the process is reversed: the leader's role is to put into effect the wishes of the people, which have been hammered out previously in open discussions until a consensus has been reached. This points to another difference: the primacy of the individual in Western democracy, and that of the collective in Amerindian societies. In that light, Mercredi's vision of jointly navigating uncharted rapids calls for large measures of realism, mutual respect, and shared prepa-ration for what will be a demanding voyage. This, of course, is not a new challenge for Native leadership, as Janet Chute illustrated in *The Legacy of Shingwaukonse* (1998).[69] Shingwaukonse (1773-1854), an Ojibwa chief at Garden River near Sault Ste. Marie, fought hard for autonomy and cultural security in a period when assimilation was the official goal. While the pressures have since eased somewhat, the struggle still goes on. Gerald Alfred, a Mohawk who is a political science professor at the University of Victoria, argues that the basic goals of even the most radical forms of Native nationalism are oriented primarily toward pre-serving cultural distinctiveness and acquiring the level of governmen-tal autonomy necessary to achieve that goal. In *Heeding the Voices of Our Ancestors* (1995),[70] he attributes the persistence of Native identity in Canada to the longstanding pattern of negative interaction with the state; his *Peace, Power, Righteousness* (1999)[71] is a call to indigenous peoples to make self-determination a reality by returning to their traditions. Alfred has expressed his increasing militancy in this regard by changing his first name to the Mohawk "Taiaiake." Incidentally, as he points out, the Mohawks of Kahnawake have one of the highest per family annual incomes ($30,000 average) of Native communities anywhere in Canada.[72]

The Feminine Voice

Women's say in all this was recently expressed loudly and clearly in a collection of essays published under the title *Strong Women Stories*.[73] It consists of sixteen articles by Aboriginal women from a wide variety of walks of life, concluding with a wind-up piece from the pen of an Aboriginal man who is optimistic that the spiral of life will eventually see a restoration of the social balance that once existed in Aboriginal communities before the imposition of colonialism. In these essays, women tell their life stories, discuss the numerous challenges faced by Aboriginal women, and engage in such unexpected discourses as the role of art in political action—topics ranging from the routine to the offbeat. As Calvin Morrisseau observes in the book's cover blurb, these stories are a must read for those who wish "to open their minds and hearts to the world of Aboriginal people.... An opportunity for everyone to view life through a different filter, and essential reading for anyone who wishes to challenge the residual effects of assimilation."

In the Meantime, the Inuit

Inuit have also inspired an abundant literature. Baffin Islanders from Cape Dorset tell their own stories in *People from Our Side*[74] transcribed by Dorothy Eber and beautifully illustrated with photographs by Peter Pitseolak, first in 1975, and then in a new edition in 1993. Another autobiographical story is that of Minnie Aodla Freeman, who tells about survival in a white man's world in *Life among the Qallunaat* (1978).[75] It would be hard to imagine two more different worlds than the Arctic and a southern Canadian city; if there is one key to making the transition, it is a healthy sense of humour. A less sanguine note is struck by *Tammarniit (Mistakes)* by Frank James Tester and Peter Kulchyski (1994).[76] His is the unhappy story of the government's attempt to relocate Inuit, threatened by diminishing game, into sedentary communities where they were expected to adopt Western life ways. That the moves usually made matters worse does not seem surprising in hindsight. The most complete survey to date of the dramatic changes that have overtaken the Arctic is Marybelle Mitchell's *From Talking Chiefs to a Native Corporate Elite* (1996).[77] As Mitchell sees it, the Inuit have done remarkably well, which she attributes to their adaptability, which has always been a prime requirement for survival in the Arctic. The Royal Commission on Aboriginal Peoples agreed: in its view, the Inuit have made the most progress toward self-government of all of Canada's First Peoples. This was dramatically supported by the creation of Nunavut as a self-governing territory in 1999. It was a gesture toward correcting Sir John A. Macdonald's goal at Confederation, "to do away with the tribal system and assimilate the Indian people in all respects with the other inhabitants of the Dominion, as speedily as they are fit to change."

The message of Native history is clear: Canada's First Nations, far from just being interesting or romantic relics of a "savage" bygone age, are a vital part of the country's past, present, and future. This is becoming more and more evident as the nation's Aboriginal component becomes better understood by the general public, a process of self-discovery for which history is a major instrument. The many stories and many faces of that history ensure that the process will be a challenging one.

Notes

1 I have explored aspects of this topic in "Toward a Larger View of Canada's History: The Native Factor," in *Visions of the Heart*, eds. David Alan Long and Olive Patricia Dickason (Toronto: Harcourt Brace, 2000), 11–29; "Some Aspects of History, Aboriginal and Otherwise," *The Commission's View of History: Judgement on the Past, Relevance for the Future* (Montreal: McGill Institute for the Study of Canada, 1997), 9–12; and in "Tracking Down the History of Canada's First Nations," *Facsimile* 10 (November 1993): 2–4. Specific references to these works are not credited.
2 Olive Patricia Dickason, "Art and Amerindian Worldviews," *Earth, Water, Air and Fire*, ed. David T. McNab for Nin.Da.Waab.Jig. (Waterloo, ON: Wilfrid Laurier University Press, 1998), 22.
3 Robert Bringhurst, *A Story as Sharp as a Knife* (Vancouver: Douglas and McIntyre, 1999), 53.

4 Canada. *Report of the Royal Commission on Aboriginal Peoples*, 5 vols. (Ottawa: Minister of Supply and Services Canada, 1996), 1:32–36 (hereafter cited as RCAP).

5 RCAP, 33.

6 Julie Cruikshank, "Oral Tradition and Oral History: Reviewing Some Issues," *Canadian Historical Review* 75, 3 (September 1994): 410.

7 Cruikshank, "Oral Tradition," 33–34.

8 In law, also, oral history received an immense boost in December 1997, when the Supreme Court of Canada overturned the 1991 British Columbia court's rejection of the Gitksan and Wet'suwet'en claim to 58,000 square kilometres of land in *Delgamuukw v. British Columbia*. The grounds were that the BC court had not given due weight to the oral history upon which the claim had been based.

9 Bruce G. Trigger, "The Historians' Indian: Native Americans in Canadian Historical Writing from Charlevoix to the Present," *Canadian Historical Review* 67, 3 (1986): 315.

10 This section is from "Twenty-five Years of Progress in Doing Native History," a presentation I made at the annual conference of the Native History Study Group of the Canadian Historical Association at St. John's, Newfoundland, in 1997.

11 It was not just oral societies that were seen as not having a history. Lord Durham, in his famous report issued after the 1837–38 troubles, characterized Quebeckers as a people without a history or culture.

12 Donald B. Smith, *Le Sauvage: The Native People in Quebec Historical Writing on the Heroic Period (1534-1663) of New France*, History Division Paper 6 (Ottawa: National Museums of Canada, 1974), 4.

13 Nicolas Denys, *Description geographique et historique des Costes de l'Amerique Septentrionale, avec l'histoire naturelle du pais* (Paris: Louis Billaine, 1672). The second volume was entitled *Histoire naturelle des peuples, des animaux, des arbres et des plantes de l'Amérique Septentrionale, & de ses divers climats. Avec une description exacte de la pesche des molües, tant sur le Grand-Banc qu'à la Coste; & de tout ce qui s'y pratique de plus particulier*. In English, *The Description and Natural History of the Coasts of North America (Acadia)*, trans. William F. Ganong (Toronto: The Champlain Society, 1908). Latest reprint (New York: Greenwood Press, 1968).

14 Louis-Armand de Lom d'Arce, baron de Lahontan, *Supplément aux voyages du baron de Lahontan où l'on trouve des dialogues curieux entre l'auteur et un sauvage de bon sens qui a voyagé. L'on y voit aussi plusieurs observations faites par le même auteur dans ses voyages au Portugal, Espagne, en Hollande, et en Danemark, etc.* (La Haye: 1703).

15 Pierre-François-Xavier de Charlevoix, *Histoire et description générale de la Nouvelle France avec le journal historique d'un voyage fait par ordre du roi dans l'Amérique septentrionnale*, 3 vols. and 6 vols. (Paris: Nyon fils,

1744). In English, *History and General Description of New France by P.F.X. de Charlevoix*, trans. John Gilmary Shea. 6 vols. (New York: J.G. Shea, 1866–72). Latest reprint, Chicago, 1962.

16 Trigger, "The Historians' Indian." 316.

17 Andrea Laforet and Annie York, *Spuzzum: Fraser Canyon Histories, 1808–1939* (Vancouver: University of British Columbia Press in association with the Canadian Museum of Civilization, 1998).

18 Harold Cardinal, *The Unjust Society: The Tragedy of Canada's Indians* (Edmonton: Hurtig, 1969).

19 Bruce Trigger, *Natives and Newcomers: Canada's "Heroic Age" Reconsidered* (Montreal and Kingston: McGill-Queen's University Press, 1985).

20 Denys Delâge, *Bitter Feast: Amerindians and Europeans in Northeastern North America, 1600–64*, trans. Jane Brierly (Vancouver: University of British Columbia Press, 1993). In French, *Le pays renversé: Amérindiens et européens en Amérique du nord-ouest, 1600–1664* (Montréal: Boréal Express, 1985).

21 R. Douglas Francis, Richard Jones, and Donald B. Smith, *Origins: Canadian History to Confederation, and Destinies: Canadian History Since Confederation*, 3rd ed. (Toronto: Holt, Rinehart and Winston, 1988), 1992.

22 J.R. Miller, *Skyscrapers Hide the Heavens*, 2nd ed. (Toronto: University of Toronto Press, 1989), 1991.

23 Bruce G. Trigger and Wilcomb E. Washburn, eds., *Cambridge History of the Native Peoples of the Americas*, vol. 1 (Cambridge: Cambridge University Press, 1996).

24 Martha McCarthy, *From the Great River to the Ends of the Earth: Oblate Missions to the Dene, 1847–1921* (Edmonton: University of Alberta Press, 1995).

25 G. Copway [Kah-ge-ga-gah-bowh, chief of the Ojibway Nation], *The Traditional History and Characteristic Sketches of the Ojibway Nation* (London: Charles Gilpin, 1850).

26 Peter Jones [Kahkewaquonaby, Indian missionary], *History of the Ojebway Indians, with Especial References to Their Conversion to Christianity* (London: A.W. Bennett, 1861).

27 William W. Warren, *History of the Ojibway People* (St. Paul: Minnesota Historical Society, 1885).

28 Maurice Metayer, trans. and ed., *I, Nuligak* (Toronto: Peter Martin Associates, 1966).

29 Maria Campbell, *Halfbreed* (Toronto: McClelland and Stewart, 1973).

30 Edward Ahenakew, *Voices of the Plains Cree* (Toronto: McClelland and Stewart, 1973), reprinted 1995.

31 Joseph F. Dion, *My Tribe the Crees*, ed. and intro. Hugh A. Dempsey (Calgary: Glenbow Museum, 1979).

32 Ibid., 145.

33 Sarah Carter, *Lost Harvests: Prairie Indian Reserve Farmers and Government Policy* (Montreal and Kingston: McGill-Queen's University Press, 1990). See also her *Aboriginal People and Colonizers of Western Canada to 1900* (Toronto and Buffalo: University of Toronto Press, 1999).

34 F. Laurie Barron, "The Indian Pass System in the Canadian West, 1882–1935," *Canadian Forum* 13, 1 (1988): 39.

35 Maude Kegg, *Portage Lake: Memories of an Ojibwe Childhood*, ed. and transcribed by John D. Nichols (Edmonton: University of Alberta Press, 1991).

36 Chief Dan George and Helmut Hirnschall, *My Heart Soars* (Vancouver: Hancock House, 1974).

37 Pat Moore and Angela Wheelock, eds., *Wolverine Myths and Visions: Dene Traditions from Northern Alberta*, compiled by the Dene Wodih Society (Edmonton: University of Alberta Press, 1990).

38 George Blondin, *When the World Was New: Stories of the Sahtú Dene* (Yellowknife: Cutcrop, 1990).

39 George Blondin, *Yamoria the Lawmaker: Stories of the Dene* (Edmonton: NeWest Press, 1997).

40 Julie Cruikshank, *Life Lived Like a Story: Life Stories of Three Yukon Elders* (Vancouver: University of British Columbia Press, 1990).

41 Dianne Meili, *Those Who Know: Profiles of Alberta's Native Elders* (Edmonton: NeWest Press, 1991).

42 Ruth Holmes Whitehead, *The Old Man Told Us: Excerpts from Micmac History 1500–1950* (Halifax: Nimbus, 1991).

43 Peter Knudtson and David Suzuki, *Wisdom of the Elders* (Toronto: Stoddart, 1992).

44 Robert Brightman, *Grateful Prey: Rock Cree Human–Animal Relationships* (Berkeley: University of California Press, 1993).

45 Georges E. Sioui, *For an Amerindian Autohistory*, trans. Sheila Fischman (Montreal and Kingston: McGill-Queen's University Press, 1992). In French, *Pour une autohistoire amérindienne* (Montréal: Les Presses de l'Université Laval, 1989). It went through three printings before being translated into English.

46 Leah Dorion, in her review of Sioui's work in *The Journal of Indigenous Studies* 3, 2 (1997): 46. At the time she wrote the review, Ms. Dorion was curriculum officer at the Gabriel Dumont Institute.

47 Georges E. Sioui, *Les Wendats: Une civilisation méconnue* (Montréal: Les Presses de l'Université Laval, 1994).

48 Daniel N. Paul, *We Were Not the Savages: A Micmac Perspective on the Collision of European and Aboriginal Civilization* (Halifax: Nimbus, 1993).

49 Harold A. Innis, *The Fur Trade in Canada* (New Haven: Yale University Press, 1930), rev. ed., 1956, paperback edition, University of Toronto Press, 1962.

50 Jennifer S.H. Brown, *Strangers in Blood: Fur Trade Company Families in Indian Country* (Vancouver: University of British Columbia Press, 1980).

51 Sylvia Van Kirk, *Many Tender Ties: Women in Fur Trade Society 1670–1870* (Norman: University of Oklahoma Press, 1983), first published in 1980 by Watson and Dyer.

52 Frits Pannekoek, *A Snug Little Flock: The Social Origins of the Riel Resistance, 1869–70* (Winnipeg: Watson and Dwyer, 1991).

53 D.N. Sprague, *Canada and the Metis, 1869–1885* (Waterloo, ON: Wilfrid Laurier University Press, 1988).

54 Bob Beal and Rod Macleod, *Prairie Fire: The 1885 North-West Rebellion* (Edmonton: Hurtig, 1984), reprinted 1994.

55 Maggie Siggins, *Riel: A Life of Revolution* (Toronto: Harper Collins, 1994).

56 Rupert Ross, *Returning to the Teachings: Exploring Aboriginal Justice* (Toronto: Penguin, 1996); in an earlier work, *Dancing with a Ghost: Exploring Indian Reality* (Markham, ON: Octopus, 1992), Ross had examined how traditional Cree and Ojibwa world views often conflicted with the Canadian justice system.

57 Rudy Wiebe and Yvonne Johnson, *Stolen Life: The Journey of a Cree Woman* (Toronto: Alfred A. Knopf, 1998).

58 John Sheridan Milloy, *A National Crime: The Canadian Government and the Residential School System, 1879–1986* (Winnipeg: University of Manitoba, 1999).

59 J.R. Miller, *Shingwauk's Vision: A History of Native Residential Schools* (Toronto: University of Toronto Press, 1996).

60 Jean Barman, Yvonne Hébert, and Don McCaskill, eds., *Indian Education in Canada*, vol. 1, *The Legacy* (Vancouver: University of British Columbia Press, 1986); ibid., *The Challenge*, vol. 2 (Vancouver: University of British Columbia Press, 1987).

61 Ingeborg Marshall, *A History and Ethnography of the Beothuk* (Montreal and Kingston: McGill-Queen's University Press, 1996).

62 Geoffrey York and Loreen Pindera, *People of the Pines: The Warriors and Legacy of Oka* (Toronto: Little, Brown and Company, 1991).

63 David T. McNab, *Circles of Time: Aboriginal Land Rights and Resistance in Ontario* (Waterloo, ON: Wilfrid Laurier University Press, 1999).

64 Ila Bussidor and Üstün Bilgen-Reinart, *Night Spirits: The Story of the Relocation of the Sayisi Dene* (Winnipeg: University of Manitoba Press, 1997).

65 Dan Smith, *The Seventh Fire: The Struggle for Aboriginal Government* (Toronto: Key Porter, 1993).

66 Frank Cassidy, ed., *Aboriginal Self-Determination: Proceedings of a Conference Held September 30–October 3, 1990* (Toronto: Oolichan Books and the Institute for Research on Public Policy, 1991), 3, 15.

67 Menno Boldt, *Surviving as Indians: The Challenge of Self-Government* (Toronto: University of Toronto Press, 1993).

68 Ovide Mercredi and Mary Ellen Turpel, *In the Rapids: Navigating the Future of First Nations* (Toronto: Viking, 1993).

69 Janet E. Chute, *The Legacy of Shingwaukonse: A Century of Native Leadership* (Toronto: University of Toronto Press, 1998).

70 Gerald R. Alfred, *Heeding the Voices of Our Ancestors: Kahnawake Mohawk Politics and the Rise of Native Nationalism* (Toronto: Oxford University Press, 1995).

71 Taiaiake Alfred, *Peace, Power, Righteousness: An Indigenous Manifesto* (Toronto: Oxford University Press, 1999).

72 Alfred, *Heeding the Voices of Our Ancestors*, 2.

73 Kim Anderson and Bonita Lawrence, eds., *Strong Women Stories: Native Vision and Community Survival* (Toronto: Sumach Press, 2003).

74 Dorothy Eber, *People from Our Side: An Inuit Record of Seekooseelak—the Land of the People of Cape Dorset, Baffin Island* (Edmonton: Hurtig, 1973); the translation of Peter Pitseolak's manuscript is by Ann Hanson.

75 Minnie Aodla Freeman, *Life among the Qallunaat* (Edmonton: Hurtig, 1978).

76 Frank James Tester and Peter Kulchyski, *Tammarniit (Mistakes): Inuit Relocation in the Eastern Arctic 1939–63* (Vancouver: University of British Columbia Press, 1994).

77 Marybelle Mitchell, *From Talking Chiefs to a Native Corporate Elite: The Birth of Class and Nationalism among Canadian Inuit* (Montreal and Kingston: McGill-Queen's University Press, 1996).

Bibliography

Ahenakew, Edward. *Voices of the Plains Cree.* Toronto: McClelland and Stewart, 1973.

Alfred, Gerald R. *Heeding the Voices of Our Ancestors: Kahnawake Mohawk Politics and the Rise of Native Nationalism.* Toronto: Oxford University Press, 1995.

Alfred, Taiaiake. *Peace, Power, Righteousness: An Indigenous Manifesto.* Toronto: Oxford University Press, 1999.

Anderson, Kim, and Bonita Lawrence, eds. *Strong Women Stories: Native Vision and Community Survival.* Toronto: Sumach Press, 2003.

Barman, Jean, Yvonne Hébert, and Don McCaskill, eds. *Indian Education in Canada.* Vancouver: University of British Columbia Press, 1986.

Barron, F. Laurie. "The Indian Pass System in the Canadian West, 1882–1935." *Canadian Forum* 13, 1 (1988): 39.

Beal, Bob, and Rod MacLeod. *Prairie Fire: The 1885 North-West Rebellion.* Edmonton: Hurtig, 1984.

Blondin, George. *When the World Was New: Stories of the Sahtú Dene.* Yellowknife: Cutcrop, 1990.

————. *Yamoria the Lawmaker: Stories of the Dene*. Edmonton: NeWest Press, 1997.

Boldt, Menno. *Surviving as Indians: The Challenge of Self-Government*. Toronto: University of Toronto Press, 1993.

Brightman, Robert. *Grateful Prey: Rock Cree Human–Animal Relationships*. Berkeley: University of California Press, 1993.

Bringhurst, Robert. *A Story as Sharp as a Knife*. Vancouver: Douglas and McIntyre, 1999.

Brown, Jennifer S.H. *Strangers in Blood: Fur Trade Company Families in Indian Country*. Vancouver: University of British Columbia Press, 1980.

Bussidor, Ila, and Üstün Bilgen-Reinart. *Night Spirits: The Story of the Relocation of the Sayisi Dene*. Winnipeg: University of Manitoba Press, 1997.

Campbell, Maria. *Halfbreed*. Toronto: McClelland and Stewart, 1973.

Canada. *Report of the Royal Commission on Aboriginal Peoples*. 5 vols. Ottawa: Minister of Supply and Services Canada, 1996.

Cardinal, Harold. *The Unjust Society: The Tragedy of Canada's Indians*. Edmonton: Hurtig, 1969.

Carter, Sarah. *Lost Harvests: Prairie Indian Reserve Farmers and Government Policy*. Montreal and Kingston: McGill-Queen's University Press, 1990.

————. *Aboriginal People and Colonizers of Western Canada to 1900*. Toronto: University of Toronto Press, 1999.

Cassidy, Frank, ed. *Aboriginal Self-Determination*. Toronto: Oolichan Books and the Institute for Research on Public Policy, 1991.

Chute, Janet E. *The Legacy of Shingwaukonse: A Century of Native Leadership*. Toronto: University of Toronto Press, 1998.

Copway, G. *The Traditional History and Characteristic Sketches of the Ojibway Nation*. London: Charles Gilpin, 1850.

Cruickshank, Julie. *Life Lived Like a Story: Life Stories of Three Yukon Elders*. Vancouver: University of British Columbia Press, 1990.

————. "Oral Tradition and Oral History: Reviewing Some Issues." *Canadian Historical Review* 75, 3 (September 1994): 410.

Denys, Nicolas. *Description geographique et historique des Costes de l'Amerique Septentrionale, avec l'histoire naturelle du pais*. Paris: Louis Billaine, 1672.

————. *The Description and Natural History of the Coasts of North America (Acadia)*. Trans. by William F. Ganong. Toronto: The Champlain Society, 1908.

De Charlevoix, Pierre-Francois-Xavier. *Histoire et description générale de la Nouvelle France avec le journal historique d'un voyage fait par ordre du roi dans l'Amerique septentrionnale.* 3 vols. and 6 vols. Paris: Nyon Fils, 1744.

——— . *History and General Description of New France.* Trans. by John Gilmary Shea. 6 vols. New York: J.G. Shea, 1866–72.

Delâge, Denys. *Bitter Feast: Amerindians and Europeans in Northeastern North America, 1600–64.* Trans. by Jane Brierly. Vancouver: University of British Columbia Press, 1993.

Dickason, Olive Patricia. "Tracking Down the History of Canada's First Nations." *Facsimile* 10 (November 1993): 2–4.

———. "Some Aspects of History, Aboriginal and Otherwise." In *The Commission's View of History: Judgement on the Past, Relevance for the Future,* 9–12. Montreal: McGill Institute for the Study of Canada, 1997.

———. "Twenty-five Years of Progress in Doing Native History." Presentation at the annual conference of the Native History Study Group of the Canadian Historical Association, St. John's, Newfoundland, 1997.

———. "Art and Amerindian Worldviews." In *Earth, Water, Air, Fire.* Ed. David T. McNab for Nin.Da.Waab.Jig., 22. Waterloo, ON: Wilfrid Laurier University Press, 1998.

Dion, Joseph F. *My Tribe the Crees.* Ed. Hugh A. Dempsey. Calgary: Glenbow Museum, 1979.

Dorion, Leah. Review of the Work of George Sioui. *The Journal of Indigenous Studies* 3, 2 (1997): 46.

Eber, Dorothy. *People from Our Side: An Inuit Record of Seekooseelak—the Land of the People of Cape Dorset, Baffin Island.* Edmonton: Hurtig, 1973.

Francis, R. Douglas, Richard Jones, and Donald B. Smith. *Origins: Canadian History to Confederation.* Toronto: Holt, Rinehart, and Winston, 1988.

Freeman, Minne Aodla. *Life among the Qallunaat.* Edmonton: Hurtig, 1978.

George, Chief Dan, and Helmut Hirnschall, *My Heart Soars* (Vancouver: Hancock House, 1974).

Innis, Harold. *The Fur Trade in Canada.* New Haven: Yale University Press, 1930.

———. *Destinies: Canadian History since Confederation.* Toronto: Holt, Rinehart, and Winston, 1988.

Jones, Peter. *History of the Ojebway Indians, with Especial References to Their Conversion to Christianity*. London: A.W. Bennett, 1861.

Kegg, Maude, *Portage Lake: Memories of an Ojibwe Childhood*. Edited and transcribed by John D. Nichols (Edmonton: University of Alberta Press, 1991).

Knudtson, Peter, and David Suzuki. *Wisdom of the Elders*. Toronto: Stoddart, 1992.

Laforet, Andrea, and Annie York. *Spuzzum: Fraser Canyon Histories, 1808-1939*. Vancouver: University of British Columbia Press, 1998.

Lom d'Arce, Louis-Armand. *Supplément aux voyages du baron de Lahontan ou l'on trouve des dialogues curieux entre l'auteur et un sauvage de bon sens qui a voyagé. L'on y voit aussi plusieurs observations faites par le même auteur dans ses voyages au Portugal, Espagne, en Hollande, et en Danemark, etc.* La Haye: 1703.

Long, David Alan, and Olive Patricia Dickason, eds. "Toward a Larger View of Canada's History: The Native "Factor." In *Visions of the Heart*, 11-29. Toronto: Harcourt Brace, 2000.

Marshall, Ingeborg. *A History and Ethnography of the Beothuk*. Montreal and Kingston: McGill-Queen's University Press, 1996.

McCarthy, Martha. *From the Great River to the Ends of the Earth: Oblate Missions to the Dene, 1847-1921*. Edmonton: University of Alberta Press, 1995.

McNab, David T. *Circles of Time: Aboriginal Land Rights and Resistance in Ontario*. Waterloo, ON: Wilfrid Laurier University Press, 1999.

Meili, Dianne. *Those Who Know: Profiles of Alberta's Native Elders*. Edmonton: NeWest Press, 1991.

Mercredi, Ovide, and Mary Ellen Turpel. *In the Rapids: Navigating the Future of First Nations*. Toronto: Viking, 1993.

Metayer, Maurice, trans. and ed. *I, Nuligak*. Toronto: Peter Martin Associates, 1966.

Miller, J.R. *Shingwauk's Vision: A History of Native Residential Schools*. Toronto: University of Toronto Press, 1996.

——— . *Skyscrapers Hide the Heavens*. Toronto: University of Toronto Press, 1989.

Milloy, John Sheridan. *A National Crime: The Canadian Government and the Residential School System, 1879-1986*. Winnipeg: University of Manitoba, 1999.

Mitchell, Marybelle. *From Taking Chiefs to a Native Corporate Elite: The Birth of Class and Nationalism among Canadian Inuit*. Montreal and Kingston: McGill-Queen's University Press, 1996.

Moore, Pat, and Angela Wheelock, eds. *Wolverine Myths and Visions: Dene Traditions from Northern Alberta*. Edmonton: University of Alberta Press, 1990.

Pannekoek, Frits. *A Snug Little Flock: The Social Origins of the Riel Resistance, 1869-70*. Winnipeg: Watson and Dwyer, 1991.

Paul, Daniel N. *We Were Not the Savages: A Micmac Perspective on the Collision of European and Aboriginal Civilization*. Halifax: Nimbus, 1993.

Ross, Rupert. *Dancing with a Ghost: Exploring Indian Reality*. Markham, ON: Octopus, 1992.

———. *Returning to the Teachings: Exploring Aboriginal Justice*. Toronto: Penguin, 1996.

Siggins, Maggie. *Riel: A Life of Revolution*. Toronto: Harper Collins, 1994.

Sioui, George E. *For an Amerindian Autohistory*. Trans. by Sheila Fischmann. Montreal and Kingston: McGill-Queen's University Press, 1992.

———. *Les Wendats: Une civilisation méconnue*. Montréal: Les Presses de l'Université Laval, 1994.

Smith, Dan. *The Seventh Fire: The Struggle for Aboriginal Government*. Toronto: Key Porter, 1993.

Smith, Donald B. *Le Sauvage: The Native People in Quebec Historical Writing on the Heroic Period (1534-1663) of New France*, History Division Paper 6. Ottawa: National Museums of Canada, 1974.

Sprague, D.N. *Canada and the Metis, 1869-1885*. Waterloo, ON: Wilfrid Laurier University Press, 1988.

Tester, Frank James, and Peter Kulchyski. *Tammarniit (Mistakes): Inuit Relocation in the Eastern Artic 1939-63*. Vancouver: University of British Columbia Press, 1994.

Trigger, Bruce G. "The Historians' Indian: Native Americans in Canadian Historical Writing from Charlevoix to the Present." *Canadian Historical Review* 57, 3 (1986): 315.

———. *Natives and Newcomers: Canada's "Heroic Age" Reconsidered*. Montreal and Kingston: McGill-Queen's University Press, 1985.

Trigger, Bruce G., and Wilcomb E. Washburn, eds. *Cambridge History of the Native Peoples of the Americas*. Vol. 1. Cambridge: Cambridge University Press, 1996.

Van Kirk, Sylvia. *Many Tender Ties: Women in Fur Trade Society 1670-1870*. Norman: University of Oklahoma, 1983.

Warren, William W. *History of the Ojibway People*. St. Paul: Minnesota Historical Society, 1885.

Whitehead, Ruth Holmes. *The Old Man Told Us: Excerpts from Micmac History 1500–1950*. Halifax: Nimbus, 1991.

Wiebe, Rudy, and Yvonne Johnson. *Stolen Life: The Journey of a Cree Woman*. Toronto: Alfred A. Knopf, 1998.

York, Geoffrey, and Loreen Pindera. *People of the Pines: The Warriors and Legacy of Oka*. Toronto: Little, Brown, 1991.

7

The Whirlwind of History: Parallel Nineteenth-Century Perspectives on "Are They Savage?"[1]

Karl Hele

ABORIGINAL CONCEPTS OF HISTORY maintain that it is a fluid motion, bound by neither time nor space. A basic tool used to teach these conceptualizations is the medicine wheel; its centre remains fixed as the wheel turns, with history flowing around the circle. The teaching circle has allowed for the blending or placing of Western chronological concepts with those of the Aboriginal. Although it can be utilized to examine limited issues or interactions, in other words partial rotations, it fails to fully present the Aboriginal understanding of history of time. From the perspective of the circle, history is moving towards an era when Aboriginal and non-Aboriginal peoples will live in mutual respect and cooperation. While such hopes present us with a pleasant vision for the near future, the far future is troubling, for we must again move through a long period of disrespect and cultural destruction— the metaphor of simple circular motion is an inescapable cycle. Yet, as noted by the late Rodney Bobiwash, former director of the Native Canadian Centre, the true nature of Aboriginal perceptions of history is better explained as a whirlwind. Or, in the words of David McNab, "circles of time are ever-expanding and infinite."[2] I would add that such circles are also concentric and interlocking. The more complex understanding of Aboriginal conceptualizations allows not only an escape from circular determinism, but gives us the tools for comprehending the past within a new context. Simply, the past, present, and future reside together, yet they come before and after one another as the whirlwind spins history.

In 1843, two leading Methodist ministers to the Ojibwa of Canada West debated their understandings of Native history and society within the pages of the weekly Methodist newspaper *Christian Guardian*.[3] One, Thomas Hurlburt, a non-Native, concluded that the Indian was without Christianity and civilization, utterly debased, and a corrupting influence upon the white man. The other, Peter Jones or Kahkewaquonaby, a Mississauga Anishnabai convert, concluded that if the Indian was debased it was due to the influences of evil-minded whites. The debate occurred in four issues of the *Christian Guardian*, beginning on March 15 and running until May 24, wherein each man made his case until the editor, expressing some regret about having allowed the debate to appear on the pages of the paper, decided that although the issue was not settled, each view had been stated clearly. Apparently the debate elicited responses from readers and other interested parties that the editor felt he could not print, although he did not state why.[4] Nonetheless, the debate is symptomatic of a Euro-Canadian desire to place First Nations people within a framework to create understanding of the "other," regardless if this understanding mirrored reality or not, while ignoring the "other's" presentation of self.

Conflicting representation of the Aboriginal, as seen in the pages of the *Christian Guardian*, have existed since the first European landed in the New World. The argument between Jones and Hurlburt is interesting, for it occurred during a period of shifting policies and ideologies, as well as new roles for the First Nations within the emergent colonial state.[5] The meaning of *Indianness*, like all meanings, is "continually debated by different groups and individuals, each attempting to assert its own understandings, derived from its own assessments of interests."[6] It is these shifting explanations of interpretation and definition based upon the personal and societal that are seen in the 1843 debate between Hurlburt and Jones. Non-Native society was attempting to place First Nations within some context, which is continuously changing due to circumstance as well as shifting ideology, yet these new interpretations are based on past knowledge and experience. Both missionaries sought to present reality as they saw it, in hope that the reading public would adopt their vision. Essentially, the controversy in the *Guardian* highlights the shifting position of First Nations peoples in the post-War of 1812 world.

A "convenient shorthand" created as a method of understanding the complex and highly fluid nature of First Nation-Canadian relations has been developed by J.R. Miller and expanded upon by the *Royal Commission on Aboriginal Peoples* (RCAP) in 1996. J.R. Miller's 1989 text, *Skyscrapers Hide the Heavens*, first developed the idea that Indian–white relations within Canada can be divided into three stages.[7] More recently, RCAP has presented the Canadian public with a similar concept.[8] The commission, like Miller, maintains that the history of Indian–European relations is understandable in four essential stages: (1) separate worlds; (2) contact and co-operation; (3) displacement and assimilation; and, (4) negotiation and renewal.[9] The era of contact and co-operation between Europeans and First Nations, symbolized by the fur trade, is idealized by RCAP as the ultimate era for First Nation–European interaction and fellowship.[10] Additionally, RCAP authors argue that as the Canadian frontier moved west, the stages varied in length and intensity, depending on the date of contact for each Aboriginal group. For instance, the Iroquois passed through each stage over a longer period of time, covering approximately five hundred years, while the Inuit were confronted with the movement of these stages within a condensed period confined to the twentieth century. The commissioners, nonetheless, did attempt to establish a time frame within which each stage occurred; the first ended in AD 1500; the second ended in Ontario by 1830, and in British Columbia by 1870; the third in 1969; while the fourth is ongoing.[11] These linear demarcations of time, while useful to outline the progress of Canadian Indian policies, do not take into account the whirlwind. The various stages, as noted, do shift from east to west, but they do not remain constant within locales supposedly past. Simply put, the people of the Canadian west have passed through each stage numerous times, depending on situation, circumstance, and area, hence the circles of history narrow and expand across the Canadian landscape.

"Displacement and assimilation" or irrelevance—the third stage—is where the debate between the ministers is chronologically and spatially situated. It is characterized by increasing focus on the assimilation of the Anishnabai, or Ojibwa, into the dominant society through the process of Christianization and civilization. Beginning in 1830, with the shift from military administration to civil control and then to colonial administration of Indian Affairs by the end of the decade, the shift to displacement and assimilation was assured. The last request by the British-Canadian authorities of the First Nations to defend their North American claims occurred during the rebellions in Upper and Lower Canada.[12] As the population increased, contemporaries viewed the Aboriginal peoples as hindering the march of British civilization through their hoarding of land, which they, according to the colonizers, failed to utilize correctly through agricultural development. In Canada West the desire for land sparked a series of land surrenders that by mid-century had resulted in the loss of the southern portion of the colony, including the north shore of Lake Huron, excluding a few reserves restricted in threatened territory.[13] By mid-century, therefore, to many of the members of the expanding colonial-Canadian empire, Indians were degraded, uncivilized, and primitive individuals, in great need of Christian charity, guidance, and British civilization. The assimilative vision, under various guises, remained essentially unchanged until Native groups across Canada adamantly rejected the 1969 white paper, although it is rumoured that modern government policies are often based upon discredited proposals. In essence, First Nations were—to many Europeans, scholars, and the public alike—standing in the way of progress.

In spite of being neither smooth nor uncontested, the stages gradually shifted from co-operation to displacement and assimilation. Native minister Peter Jones, and non-Native Rev. Thomas Hurlburt, contested each other's personal authority to represent the Aboriginal person.[14] Furthermore, each man portrayed the other as having a distinct agenda inherent in his position and description of the Natives' nature. Both men's positions, nevertheless, do illustrate the contestation of changing ideologies about the "Indian." At stake was the delineation of First Nations roles as well as public perceptions of them within the future colonial-Canadian state and society.

Before analyzing the debate, it is fundamental to understand the two men involved, especially their careers prior to 1843. Peter Jones, acquiescing to his father's request, allowed himself to receive the Anglican sacrament of baptism. By his own admission, Jones felt no different at heart after he had become nominally a Christian. Three years later, while attending a camp meeting in 1823, he converted to Methodism.

While listening to a minister's sermon, Jones felt as if the minister were speaking to him directly, informing him of the sins he had committed. With the realization of his sins, Jones felt "very sorry in [his] heart," and began to pray to the Lord. It was only after a full night of prayer that God spoke to him, bringing "peace to [his] heart."[15] Jones's conversion narrative is fairly typical of the Methodist belief that an individual must have a profound sense of spiritual awakening before becoming a true Christian. Yet baptism did not necessarily indicate that a profound spiritual change had occurred. It demonstrated, however, that the individual had accepted the Christian God. In other words, divine intervention did not necessarily bring about baptism—man most often brought it about. Hence, anyone who had been baptized by another branch of Christianity (or remained unbaptized), without experiencing a recognized awakening, was a candidate for conversion to the Methodist faith.[16] In other words, the Methodists felt that experiential belief rather than scientific method assured the authenticity of conversions because "neither sacraments nor syllogisms can save a soul. It has been said that, 'as a matter of fact, no one was ever reasoned either into Christianity or out of it.' Every conversion is a miracle, the result of the direct, personal action of the Spirit of God upon the spirit of man."[17]

Peter Jones's father, Augustus, was a retired surveyor, and his mother, Tuhbenahneequay (Sarah Henry), was the daughter of a Mississauga chief. Until the age of fifteen, Jones lived among his Mississauga relations, at which time Augustus brought him to his Grand River estate. While living at the estate Jones learned the skills of animal husbandry and farming. Intending to further his education and perhaps work as a clerk in a trading establishment, Jones laboured for Archibald Russell, his sister's husband, making bricks all summer to earn the necessary tuition. He attended school for three months the following winter, and by the spring of 1823 felt he had enough education to enable him to work.[18] He never did become a clerk, because a Methodist camp meeting in Ancaster altered his goal.[19] Shortly after his conversion, Jones began to encourage the Mississauga to seek the Great Spirit through conversion to Christianity, convinced that the Methodist faith would save his people. Throughout the 1820s, Jones led the Mississauga of Rice Lake, the Ojibwa at Lake Simcoe, as well as many other Natives along the eastern shores of Lake Huron and the Muncey Mission, into the Methodist flock. During this period, Jones brought two men—Pahtaysagay (Peter Jacobs)[20] and Shahwundais (John Sunday),[21] who were to play a great role in proselytizing throughout the Great Lakes—into the Methodist congregation.[22] From 1829 to 1831 he toured the northeastern United States and Britain to bring attention to and raise financial support for the efforts of Methodist missionaries in spreading the Word of God among the Indians in Upper Canada. Eliza Fields, a pious English woman he met while on his travels in England, married Jones in 1833. Upon their arrival in the United States, the couple confronted racist assumptions about interracial marriage and even a threatened "rescue" of Eliza.[23] Undeterred, they proceeded to Upper Canada, where the Methodist church ordained Jones as a full minister.[24] Together they worked to bring those among whom they laboured to an advanced state of Christian spirituality and civilization. His proselytization tours during the 1830s took him to Sault Ste. Marie and the southeastern shores of Lake Superior, where he, along with Sunday, Jacobs, and other Native exhorters, met and influenced many Anishnabai. His desire to promote the civilization and Christianization of Natives led him to challenge policies that he felt were detrimental to their advancement. For example, he opposed the removal policy of Sir F.B. Head and other colonial governors' attempts to restrict Native freedom of religious worship. He also returned to England in an effort to preserve his people's land and identity.[25] Nevertheless, by the mid-1830s Jones experienced opposition to his role as leader of the Credit River community (Upper Canada) and his attempts to recast them as darker-complexioned Englishmen.[26] A claim to a portion of the Credit community's land, allegedly granted to Jones in 1805, was also being disputed by other local leaders. The internal strife in the village gradually eroded Jones's ability to function as a minister, and as a result the church transferred him to the Muncey mission in 1841, where he preached to the Ojibwa, Munsee Delaware, and Oneida. It was during Jones's labours at Muncey that his health began to noticeably deteriorate, eventually ending with his death in 1856.[27] In spite of declining health, he continued to bring more people to Christianity, and even his "noble" death served as an example to potential Christians.[28]

Thomas Hurlburt was born in 1808, six years after Peter Jones, in the township of Augusta. Although the details of his education and conversion to Methodism are unknown, his missionary career began in 1828. Hurlburt began his career among Native peoples as a teacher at the Muncey Mission, and within one year the church placed him in charge of it. Hurlburt was ordained while stationed among the Saugeen Ojibwa on Lake Huron from 1834 to 1837. After being transferred to the St. Clair Mission (Upper Canada) in 1837, he met James Evans[29] and began assisting him in the development of orthography for the Anishnabai language. In 1838 the two men were dispatched to the outposts of the Lake Superior Mission. Evans apparently doubted the sincerity of Hurlburt's desire to labour in the far north and felt that he preferred a posting to the southern United States.[30] Hurlburt decided to settle at Pic River, where he constructed a cabin and began to preach to the Anishnabai bands of Lake Superior who came to trade at the Hudson's Bay Company post. He remained at Pic River until approximately the spring of 1843 when he returned to Canada West. During his sojourn at the mission, Hurlburt had made few converts to Methodism.[31] Supposedly as a result of his wife's poor health, he left Canada West in 1844 to labour among the Native peoples removed to Missouri. After remaining seven years in the United States, he returned to British North America in 1851 to work once again as missionary to the Indians. Hurlburt, at some point prior to his death in 1873, learned to speak Anishnabai like a Native and was even referred to as an Indian with a white skin.[32] An approximate date when Hurlburt had become sufficiently fluent is not available, but his linguistic work indicates he was able to preach in Anishnabai before he left for the Pic River Mission. The need to function in near-isolation from English would have forced Hurlburt to become fluent or at least functional in Ojibwa. After spending approximately four decades working with the Anishnabai, Hurlburt was probably one of the few non-Native ministers who deserved recognition for his linguistic abilities.

Hurlburt, like Jones, believed the only way to save the First Nations was to teach them Christianity and civilization. As part of the conversion and civilization program, missionaries taught the Anishnabai reading, writing, and arithmetic, and instructed them in farming, animal husbandry, and handicrafts. Additionally, both espoused the view that the European family model, where the husband reigned supreme, must be recreated among the Indians. Furthermore, they sincerely felt that European Christianity was the highest form of civilization the world had yet seen. Hurlburt and Jones never doubted the ability of the Indians to become civilized Christians through the Gospel and education. But they did disagree on the fundamental nature of the Indian, as is evident in 1843.

Upon Hurlburt's return to civilization in the spring of 1843, he attended the annual meeting of the Toronto City Branch of the Missionary Society of the Wesleyan-Methodist Church. Here, Hurlburt commented on the condition of the people among whom he laboured, based upon his fourteen years of service and ability to speak their language fluently. He hoped, through his comments, to enlighten the committee and all present on the true condition of the Indians, especially those he encountered. He stated that

> the Indians, unchristianized, were destitute of fellow-feeling, were superstitiuos [*sic*], immoral, imbecile in mind, and degraded in social habits [and] that the Indians are cannibals, and that the intercourse of the White man does not corrupt the Indian, but that the Indian corrupts the White man, except in the case of ardent spirits.[33]

The *Christian Guardian* reported that Rev. Hurlburt certainly believed in the effects of the Gospel to elevate, civilize, and cast the Indian anew, although it admitted that some in attendance were shocked by the comments. In its summation of the meeting, the newspaper did not report whether or not anyone, including several experienced Native and non-Native missionaries present at the Methodist gathering, contested Hurlburt's words.

Rev. George Copway (Kahgegagahbowh)[34] and Rev. William Herkimer (Minowagiwan),[35] both Anishnabai-Mississauga and experienced labourers among the First Nations, failed to contest Hurlburt's statements, or their disagreement remained unreported. Instead, both Copway and Herkimer focused on the work the society had already completed among the Natives of Canada West. Reinforcing the opinion expressed by Hurlburt, and the underlying assumption of the society, Copway concurred that the Indian could indeed be elevated through the Gospel, for

> the white people were happy when they came to this country, the Indians were then wanderers from God. Now they can rejoice too,

and farm, and share the benefits of civilized life. Once they roved
in wickedness the streets of Toronto; now they could sing and
pray.[36]

Copway's remarks, as reported, even appear to lend credence to
the "unchristianized" and "superstitious" nature of the Indian in reference to his "offerings to various objects called gods—even to the
Devil."[37] Herkimer, building on and confirming Hurlburt's and Copway's speeches, moved the second resolution, which stated that despite
the "incalculable religious and civil advantages which have already
resulted ... such is the present spiritual destitution of new settlements
and Aboriginal tribes, as to require the continued and increased liber-
ality of an enlightened Christian community."[38] The meeting concluded by all appearances in confirmation with Hurlburt's typecasting
of Natives. Neither Herkimer nor Copway appears to have made reference to the notion of cannibalism among First Nations' people. Instead,
the reporter merely noted that some "fitting anecdotes were related."[39]

Rev. Jones, in reading the *Christian Guardian*, was much "startled
and astonished" by the "new and novel doctrine" presented by
Rev. Hurlburt and decided to come to the defence of his Native brothers' character.[40] Throughout the course of the debate, Jones and Hurlburt each contested the qualifications of the other to discuss the matter
at hand. They sought to discredit each other by convincing the reading
public that their opponent was unqualified and speaking not from
knowledge gained by personal experience, but from opinion assembled
in the heat of debate and formed through personal prejudice. Hurlburt
based his assumptions on his Western Christian education, notions of
spirituality, and knowledge of history. Jones's criticisms of Hurlburt's
comments, on the other hand, were a blending of Native and Christian interpretations, based upon his later Christian conversion and education, but primarily upon a nativistic understanding of spirituality
and history.[41]

Jones began the debate by first hinting that Hurlburt's portrayals
were imagined and were in fact "night-dreams," hence highly suspect.[42]
Jones implied that Hurlburt had imbibed Native culture more than
the people he was working among had imbibed non-Native culture.
Jones also insinuated that such dreams were those of the darkest kind,
perhaps revealing the malevolent side of Anishnabai culture, but not

the culture as a whole entity. Hurlburt's dreams or visitations, from Jones's perspective, could be seen as organic manifestations, not abstractions, visited upon the non-Native missionary by tricksters or malevolent entities. In other words, dreams contained many interpretations, and the representations that Hurlburt placed before Canadians, in Jones's opinion, were only one white man's opinion. From this perspective, Hurlburt's knowledge acquired through "night-dreams," while deserving consideration, allowed for others to present contradictory ones, in hopes of presenting non-Native society with the correct dream or presentation of Ojibwa society.

Jones continued his attack by alleging that Hurlburt had, instead of converting the Indian, become a *"white* Indian," converting entirely to all the "marvelous legends of the north (for Indians, you know, love to deal in the marvellous)." Furthermore, Jones suggested that Hurlburt had made a lucky escape from the cannibal Indians, from being entirely corrupted by the Indians, from losing all *fellow-feeling*, and from, eventually, joining the cannibals in feasting on human flesh. The sarcastic attack on Hurlburt's credibility concluded with Jones praising him for past labours, and calling him "a true friend to the Indian race." Jones further noted that Hurlburt had somehow "imbibed erroneous opinions" about the Indians, and in future he wished the Reverend would "be more cautious and guarded in treating subjects he does not fully understand."[43] To Jones, Hurlburt obviously failed to grasp the cultural meanings within which he was labouring.

Hurlburt responded with a letter to the editor that was published a week later. It defended his position against Jones's personal comments by reversing their argument. First, Hurlburt challenged Jones's assumed greater experience by claiming he had not travelled extensively "among his brethren where they are to be found in their pagan state." Jones claimed intimate knowledge of the Indian character, yet, according to his detractor, when he first went among the Indians they could not understand what he preached. Hence, the notion put forth by Jones that people must be cautious in speaking upon subjects they do not fully understand puzzled Hurlburt and, in his words, placed him "at a loss to ascertain upon what grounds he assumes the authority to warn others." The letter to the editor concluded with Hurlburt commenting, and quoting Jones, that "it is sincerely to be hoped that

Bro. J. will in future be more cautious and guarded in treating subjects he does not fully understand."[44]

In the remaining two letters to the editor, the two missionaries continued to discredit the other via the personal. For instance, Jones indicated it was he who first brought Christianity to many First Nations in Upper Canada/Canada West—such as those at the River Credit, Grape Island, Rice Lake, Lake Simcoe, Coldwater, Mud Lake, Balsam Lake, Munceytown, Saugeen, Walpole Island, Penetanguishene, and Sault Ste. Marie. He claimed to have worked, like Hurlburt, at more than three stations, saw hundreds of his fellows brought to the Lord, whether they understood him fully or not, and travelled the wilds of British North America by bad roads and canoes.[45] Hurlburt in turn noted that he too had visited Sault Ste. Marie, "whither, as I have witnessed, parties of pleasure frequently resort" and that during a trip across Lake Simcoe Jones did indeed travel by canoe, but a man older than himself paddled it.[46]

Both men asserted that their reality truly represented the people of whom they spoke. Instead, their interpretations were framed by their differing socio-cultural backgrounds, which deeply informed their conflicting understandings of history. Jones and Hurlburt based their opinions of the "three visions" within the experience of the personal, which led each of them to contest, probably much to the embarrassment of the missionary society, the qualifications of the other. To Jones, Hurlburt was dreaming very strange dreams, based upon "visions" he had at night, and was, quite possibly, a convert to the Indian superstitions—he had become the person corrupted through contact with the Indians. To Hurlburt, it was Jones who did not know what he was describing, and instead this strange dream was an "awful waking reality."[47] The incorporation of spirituality into the debate by Jones not only reflected his Native heritage but was also used to make Hurlburt aware that his "reality" was a misinterpretation, not a case of Native people lacking morality or virtue. Moreover, the idea that Hurlburt, the bringer of civilization, was in fact civilized by the "less-fortunate" hinted that Native culture was not totally lacking in all things. Hurlburt, reading the meaning of Jones's words, sought to bring the debate into a reality of the Western world, thereby denying the legitimacy of the Native viewpoint as well as the spiritual and cultural basis informing it.

Aside from the personal invective, Rev. Hurlburt's reality, as described at the Missionary Society of the Wesleyan-Methodist Church meeting in Toronto, presented the Anishnabai among whom he worked as ignoble savages, "superstitious," possibly cannibalistic, and definitely lacking in all aspects of brotherly love. Jones, upon reading the report, had first to overcome his astonishment at the accusations levelled against all Indians, especially non-Christians. Jones recovered his composure enough to classify Hurlburt's commentary into "three very strange dreams" or "night visions":

1st That the Indians, unchristianized, were *destitute* of *fellow-feeling*;
2nd that the Indians are *cannibals*;
3rd that the intercourse with the White man does not corrupt the Indian, but that the Indian corrupts the White man, except in the case of ardent spirits.[48]

It is within these three categories where we find the two images of the Indian—ignoble and noble savage—being contested. In breaking Hurlburt's speech into three categories Jones desired to present his arguments in a manner that a non-Native reader could easily follow, while interweaving points based upon his Native background.

The notion that the Indians were, as non-Christians, "destitute of fellow-feeling" was based on Hurlburt's twofold argument in response to Jones. Hurlburt's argument rested upon biblical affirmation that the barbarian races were "without natural affection."[49] To confirm the biblical declaration, he referred to his personal experiences from the Pic and Saugeen Missions. These examples consisted of Eurocentric interpretations of facts and culture. Hurlburt's first example presented the belief that Indians would appeal to traders and missionaries for help rather than their own brethren. These pleas arose, according to the missionary, because non-Natives were more willing to help a starving individual than their own relatives.[50] For instance, he noted that Mrs. Hurlburt spotted a young woman outside the mission house at Pic River, digging a frozen potato and quickly devouring it, despite the fact that her family was starving nearby. The mission family cared for her until the period of starvation, or scarcity, had passed. Another Indian, from the same area, apparently abandoned his family for a place where there was plenty of food and remained there until he received word that the danger was gone.[51] Even when the Indian decided to support his brethren, according to Hurlburt, his decision was based on potential gain, not the notion of Christian charity. The hunter, if successful, must divide his catch with all. This division of the game "[was] understood as a kind of trade—they expect to receive as much as gain."[52] Hence, Hurlburt concluded that giving merely represented an exchange of material wealth and not of goodwill.

Jones rested much of his argument against the assertion that the Indian could not be bereft of fellow feeling upon the notion of proverbial Indian hospitality, for the Indian would share his last morsel of food without compunction. In answer to the claim that the Indian would rather turn to the missionary or trader, Jones dismissed the lack of sympathy for starving relatives stressed by his brother member of the clergy. Instead, the reader was informed that the Indian often turned to the whites, "because the White man has the means, when his Indian brother is too often destitute,"[53] such as the case of the woman taken into Hurlburt's family. Jones revealed the stoicism of the Indian, commented upon by many, as a desired cultural trait. Specifically, warriors and chiefs did not show emotion publicly, for they saw it as a sign of weakness. They preferred instead to mourn in private.[54]

It is interesting that Jones did not directly comment on the nature or meaning of giving. He focused instead on "proverbial Indian hospitality," a stereotype readily understood by non-Natives familiar with missionary tales, as well as other popular forms of exploration literature and captivity narratives. Nonetheless, Hurlburt obviously witnessed the practice of gift exchange on many occasions, which led him to his crass, materialistic interpretations. The gift exchange within Anishnabai society "formally affirmed relationships of mutual trust and respect between people." Moreover, it was "practiced in all social relationships from the most intimate of the immediate family to the more public spheres."[55] Hence, giving within Native society was more social than economic. The custom of gift exchange functioned within the context of reciprocity, therefore giving was as much an obligation as was receiving.[56] Perhaps the "proverbial hospitality" referred to by Jones was merely his way of using a stereotype as a metaphor for a reality that many non-Natives could not grasp.

The remaining three examples of "lack of fellow feeling" included stories of barbarity Hurlburt heard while among the Ojibway of southern Canada West, specifically Saugeen and Munceytown. First, Hurlburt claimed that some unidentified Indians near Munceytown killed a lame young man who would never be an effective hunter. Later, in response to Jones's assertion of continuing dreams, Hurlburt stated that the murderers were a "wandering band Pottawattimies" who, when questioned by a Christian Indian about the location of the boy, stated, "They put him away."[57] The second example was of a man who refrained from killing his nephew for the murder of his dog, since he had already killed the nephew's father. The final and ultimate proof of the biblical assertion rested with a trader's story of an Indian who, while quite sober, killed one of his wives and used her flesh to bait his traps.[58]

Jones rejected out of hand the barbarity Hurlburt viewed as a sure sign of biblical rectitude. Jones freely confessed that "there are monsters in human shape to be found amongst the Indians." However, monsters were not confined to Native society, for they existed in "all other nations."[59] Instead of denying Hurlburt's tales of murder, Jones explained that they likely occurred while in a state of intoxication, and that whites also committed such horrible crimes. Finally, Jones hinted that perhaps Hurlburt imagined some of the examples, since they were related reader second-hand or were told to entertain and frighten an inexperienced missionary.[60] Unfortunately, Jones did not have the last word, for he was denied the opportunity to respond to Hurlburt's identification of the Potawatomis and the man who used his wife as bait. Assuredly, he would have answered both arguments as before by noting that such instances happen among whites, questioning the validity of hearsay and doubting the non-identification of the supposed Potawatomis.

Hurlburt and Jones hotly debated the second supposition, that Indians were cannibals, by using personal and public information to justify their positions. The reporter at the society's meeting did not elaborate on Hurlburt's initial comments. Instead he stated that the missionary, in describing "what he had seen and learned" of the Indian character, had some "startling" facts, particularly in relation to cannibalism.[61] These statements horrified Jones, who immediately responded to such an accusation by referring to his own inquiries into the question, after which he concluded that the Indians of the north and west were not cannibals. Sir George Simpson, head of the Hudson's Bay Company, as well as other men who frequented Indian country, apparently supported Jones's initial feelings on the subject.[62] All agreed that Indians viewed cannibalism with abhorrence, and a person known to have tasted human flesh was put to death as quickly as possible.[63] Furthermore, Jones noted that instances of cannibalism—the eating of human flesh for food, not ceremonial purposes—occurred, as among whites, during extreme dietary stress or starvation. His supporting example, based upon personal experience, was of a woman who fled the northwest after eating her husband out of extreme hunger and learning that the Indians in the northwest were going to put her to death for the crime. She now was seen as an "object of pity, and appeared as if an evil spirit haunted her, as she wandered about in the woods, hiding herself behind the trees and logs." Jones rejected supposed cannibalism, at least in the popular imagination of the western tribes. He patiently explained the ceremonial nature of the practice, where the heart was sliced and boiled, with each warrior taking a ladle in celebration for overcoming his enemies. The argument ended, first with a hint that perhaps the returned missionary had succumbed to believing in mythical "Weendegoos," and with a plea not to be "making them [the Anishnabai] out worse than they really are."[64] Again, Jones accused Hurlburt of consuming Ojibwa world views, thereby shading his own.

In responding to Jones, Hurlburt maintained that he was describing a "waking reality" and hence not unfairly representing the Indians. He asserted that the Indians were indeed cannibals, for they were so in Mexico and South America, and therefore "we might naturally suppose it would flow to the inferior surrounding tribes."[65] Hurlburt indirectly quoted another missionary, William Herkimer, as supporting his claim to the existence of cannibalism "among our own Indians." Moreover, the rejection of his personal experience rested upon the supposition that Jones had not travelled among the Indians in their pagan state, but had solely visited groups touched by civilization.[66] To Jones, the statement that northern Natives were cannibals because Mexican and South American Natives supposedly practised the custom, was simplistic and hence irrelevant. Simply put, Mexican and South American people were of no concern when describing local populations, since they did not live in British North America and came from a cultural background different from the Anishnabai under discussion.

The out-of-hand rejection of Hurlburt's cultural-transference argument forced him to use personal experience and "expert" evidence. Hurlburt cited two traders—Dougall Cameron and Thomas McMurray—as well as Rev. James Evans—a fellow Methodist missionary—to contest Jones's witness.[67] McMurray apparently related his experience with an Indian who had dreamed a cannibal presented him with a bowl of human flesh. Hence, the man believed he was destined to become a cannibal, and "being unsuccessful in his hunts, he killed one of his own children, then another, and so on, until there was but one boy left out of a large family."[68] The surviving boy eventually related the sad story to another group, thereby ending his father's crime. Hurlburt presented this incident as occurring more as a result of superstition than of dire necessity. Cameron told of an incident during the winter of 1841 on Lake Superior when a cannibal threatened his missionary son, James.[69] Evidently, the nephew, son, and father felt the threat to be legitimate, even though resentment and suspicion had led to it. Rev. James Evans and Dougall Cameron were further presented as witnesses to an incident where Cameron identified an old woman as a cannibal and accused her of killing and "eating up" a couple of his men.

Hurlburt used two Native ministers, Herkimer and Copway, to contest Jones's claim of legitimacy and knowledge based on ethnicity.[70] Copway's story, as related by Hurlburt, rejected ceremonial cannibalism as the sole reason for cannibalism. The tale described a band of Chippewas, who in victory cooked potatoes along with the flesh of the Sioux they had killed—"a common meal"—and took some home to friends and relatives for them to enjoy. Hurlburt then referred to Herkimer's experience as a missionary to confirm that the northern tribes indeed practised idol worship and human sacrifice. Apparently, Herkimer had "visited and preached to a tribe who had a great wooden image for a god." This tribe offered a child, and occasionally a man, twice yearly to the god's image and then ate the flesh. These two tales, and vague "other facts of the kind," convinced Hurlburt of the supposition that northern Indians did indeed have a tradition of human sacrifice and idol worship.[71]

Last, Hurlburt referred to an anecdote he heard at the Saugeen when in the company of a group of Christian converts. The story began when someone asked what human flesh tasted like and the respondent stated, "Like a bear or raccoon." One of the converts, Jacob Meticwaub, said he might have had it when travelling near Saginaw (Michigan). A group of Indians had offered him and his companions flesh that had neither skin nor bone and, quickly recollecting that these Indians were cannibals, they fled. Solomon Waupuhgas, another convert, narrated a story of when the Saugeen Anishnabai rescued a young boy and his mother from being eaten by a group of Indians living near Owen's Sound, Canada West. Supposedly it was their custom to eat the oldest child of a deceased man, and, once having done so, they were overcome with the desire to consume the remaining members of the family.[72]

As a result of the stories Hurlburt had heard, and biblical interpretation, he concluded that the Indians were cannibals in their primitive pagan state, unless he would "go far to invalidate all human testimony."[73] Hurlburt rejected Jones's hypothesis that white men occasionally consumed their fellows during times of starvation. Such occurrences, Hurlburt maintained, resulted only when the white men had been degraded thoroughly through contact with lesser civilizations. Instead, the pagan was presented as relishing the taste of flesh or easily succumbing to cannibalism, the result of lack of fellow feeling and Christian morals. Sadly, the editor of the *Christian Guardian* did not allow Jones to comment upon Hurlburt's stories, so one can only assume that they would have been placed in a context similar to that of his earlier arguments. Nonetheless, it must be remembered that often stories of cannibalism were simply misconstrued or taken out of context by the non-Native listener. These stories could simply be tales told for entertainment, refer to ceremonial incorporation of an enemy into oneself, or be metaphors for the practices and customs of adopting strangers into the group.

The final idea presented to the Christian reader was "that the intercourse with the White man does not corrupt the Indian, but that the Indian corrupts the White man, except in the case of ardent spirits."[74] According to Hurlburt, the prevalent notion that white men had corrupted Indians was not necessarily correct because "Truth is often found to be in an inverse ratio to the commonly received opinion."

Again, Hurlburt aligned facts to fit his scriptural interpretation. He believed that all Christian society contained influences based upon divine truths, therefore no matter how far the white man strayed from the virtuous path, he must always "refer to Christian principles," whereas "the pagan is dark, and has no such principles to refer to."[75] In confirmation of this view, Hurlburt mentioned the journals of Lewis and Clark, which apparently described Indians in their pristine condition and confirmed the utterly debased nature of their society.[76] As a result of his reading of Lewis and Clark, Hurlburt plainly asked, "How can those [First Nations] be corrupted among whom even incest, with other nameless crimes, are found to reign?"[77]

Jones answered the accusation, only once, in his initial response printed on April 12.[78] His reply rested upon the belief that white explorers, fur traders, and generally all Europeans, corrupted Indians through the introduction of "fire-water" and additional "vices." Jones claimed that the Indians in their natural state, before the Europeans, were more "honourable" and "inoffensive," "their words and promises" could be relied on, and "their women were more virtuous than...now." Several questions were rhetorically posed; first he asked, "Who taught the Indian to *swear*, which he could not do in his own language?" Hurlburt should have realized that the first words of English the Indian learned were those that took the Lord's name in vain. Similarly, Jones queried, "Who has taught the Indian to lie and cheat? Who has degraded the female character, and 'blanched their babies' faces?" Jones did not contest the superiority of the white man, but presented it instead in relation to the notion that the less civilized man will see all traits of the superior man as desirous and be unable to distinguish between those that are desirable and those that are not. After all, Jones charged, "How could it be otherwise than that the simple-minded Indians should receive and imitate the superior vices of his enlightened White visitor"?[79] Ironically, Jones rejected Hurlburt's supposition that the Natives of Canada West aped the vices of the "superior" Mexican and South American people, thereby dismissing the theory of cultural transference.

In contesting Hurlburt's vision of Native people, Jones distinguished between visions or dreams that were desirable and those that were not. He sought to teach the "enlightened White visitor," Hurlburt, and the *Christian Guardian*'s readership, about First Nations people and culture, thereby dispelling "simple-minded" opinions. To Peter Jones, the remarks made by Thomas Hurlburt would not only discourage future missionaries from working among people living in remote regions, but also damaged public opinion of Native populations. Hurlburt claimed he was not trying to discourage missionary work, but to inform people of the truth, to discourage romantic notions about "wild Indians." In Jones's own words, Hurlburt had "night visions" and appeared to have subscribed to the Indians' superstitions, whereas Hurlburt simply maintained that his "strange dream" was an "awful waking reality."[80] On the other hand, in all his responses to Hurlburt, Rev. Jones saw the "waking reality" as biased and of narrow vision, because he felt the worst specimen of any First Nation was no worse than his European counterpart. Thus, by implication, the non-Native and Native, prior to degradation, were equal or at least could be, once the Natives were redeemed from their debauchery through conversion to Christianity. The personal invective levelled at one another, in spite of the "objective truth" presented by the two men, likely discouraged potential candidates from entering the "wilds" of western British North America. Potential ministers may have had second thoughts about a life where two supposed "Brothers in the service of Christ" stooped to such levels. It definitely showed the pettiness and egos at play when attempting an objective description of the Indian based upon personal experience.

It is these two opposing images of Natives that informed public perceptions. The editor of the *Christian Guardian* apparently did not support Hurlburt's position, and perhaps the letters to the editor played a role in his transfer to the southern United States in 1844. Hurlburt's vision, nevertheless, did come to the fore in Canadian society and Indian policy. When the *Christian Guardian* printed Rev. Hurlburt's "Recollections of Missionary Life among the Indians" in August 1866, his opinions, which had not significantly changed since 1841, failed to arouse any debate or controversy.[81] Likewise, Eliza Jones began to notice in the 1830s that the Methodist Church kept her husband in subordinate positions, with some "treating him like an inferior."[82] The debate itself occurred during a period when the role and images of Indians in British North America were in flux—with negative and positive stereotypes competing for a place in society's consciousness. "It [the meaning of and place for the Indian] was generated and contested at every

level, in ways that were conscious and unconscious, formal and informal, carefully considered and spontaneous ... [with] many agents and
agencies ... anxious to shape responses favourable to their own projects."[83] Hence, Hurlburt's and Jones's contentious dream-visions illustrate a larger movement in colonial Canada to define and analyze the
"Indian" from the perspective of two "friends of the Indian"—one a
Euro-Canadian and the other a mixed-blood, self-identified Mississauga
Ojibwa.

One year later, a similar debate occurred on Walpole Island. Instead
of two Methodist ministers contesting the historical basis of the perceptions of the other, a Jesuit priest and two chiefs—Oshawana and
Petrokeshig—discussed differing religious traditions and interpretations.[84] While one debate focused on the perceptions of the "Indian" and
the second involved religion, both underlie the alternative interpretations of the past based on cultural perspective. Non-Natives argued
from their perspective of biblical rectitude and Western superiority.
The Anishnabai, while granting that Europeans had superior technology, held the opinion that Westerners did not have the sole interpretation of the world or the Aboriginal past. The Aboriginal interpretation
of the past was presented as equal to, if not greater than, that of the
European. For the non-Native, history represented progress, and European civilization represented its pinnacle. To the Anishnabai, history
was ever present; the tie to the past was immediate and personal, connected through the land, memory, and experience. Rev. Peter Jones
attempted to present to the readers of the *Christian Guardian* the Aboriginal conception of their society and past, whereas Rev. Thomas Hurlburt argued from a Western-biblical base to deny the validity of such
interpretations. The whirlwind of history left neither matter concluded;
the meaning of "Indianness" or Aboriginality remained "continually
debated by different groups and individuals, each attempting to assert
its own understandings, derived from its own assessments of interests."[85]

As the whirlwind of history spins, the debate about the inherent
value of Aboriginal concepts of history continues. A century and a half
after the Jones–Hurlburt exchange of letters, a Canadian court was
asked to decide the value and interpretation of Aboriginal history. Two
sets of lawyers representing competing interpretations of Canada's past

argued for and against the validity of Native knowledge and history. Unlike earlier debates where both sides failed to reach a conclusion, the Supreme Court of Canada ruled that oral traditions and the written word are to be given "equal weight." The decision, known as Delgamuukw, stands not only as a new beginning for Aboriginal claims but also for non-Aboriginal people as they strive to understand themselves in the North American perspective. Despite the conclusion reached, the whirlwind of history continues to shape the past, present, and future. Understanding and acceptance of Aboriginal concepts of history by non-Native society is still contested. Only through a greater understanding of their own societies, culture, and history will non-Aboriginal people begin to understand that Aboriginal cultures, languages, and history are as legitimate as their own. Nevertheless, the controversy generated by Delgamuukw highlights the continued debate about the significance and nature of Aboriginal history voiced earlier in the *Christian Guardian*.[86] Hurlburt's nightmarish vision of Indian life remains part of Euro-Canadian thought patterns. Indians and their history continue to be seen by many as interesting sidelines to a history of progress where Western civilization marks the pinnacle of achievement. Hurlburt's idea that Indian society was "nasty, brutish, and short" as well as bound by superstition remains popular today. Jones's response is remarkably similar to Aboriginal efforts to change the majority's opinion of the Native past and culture. Circumstances and times may have changed, but the whirlwind of history continues to stir up and bring old arguments to the fore. It is up to us, as Aboriginal people, to continue to present our conceptualizations of history to non-Natives, and contest the legitimacy of its simplistic linear or circular understandings. By taking into account that the whirlwind of history spins in ever expanding concentric and interlocking infinite circles of time that bind the past, present, and future, Jones and Hurlburt's debate about the nature of Indians endures. First Nations must continue to present their understanding of North American history to the newcomers, to avoid linear determinism in history and ethnic stereotyping of Indians based on an assumed Euro-American created past.

Notes

1 Originally presented at the Association of Canadian Studies Annual Conference, June 1998, Ottawa. Written with the support of the following grants and fellowships: MISC Fellowship, US–Canada Fulbright, R. Warren Research Fellowship, and the financial support of the Garden River FirstNation Education Unit.

2 David T. McNab, *Circles of Time: Aboriginal Land Rights and Resistance in Ontario* (Waterloo: Wilfrid Laurier University Press, 1999), 3. See also Dockstator (chap. 5), who similarly argues for the need to incorporate an Aboriginal perspective into historical interpretations, and Dickason (chap. 6).

3 Upon its establishment in 1829, the *Christian Guardian* (Toronto) (hereafter cited as *CG*), became the voice of the Canadian Methodists. In the early to mid-1800s, the paper's editorial slant under Egerton Ryerson became increasingly pro-Canadian Methodist, resulting in a verbal sparring with British Wesleyans. Despite the sectarian nature of its pages, the *CG* became, at least for a time, the largest circulating newspaper in British North America. Described by W. Meikle as a "bold and influential defender of Protestant Christian principles," and by Neil Semple as embodying "the principles of religious freedom and privilege," the journal also denounced religious favouritism. Furthermore, the *CG* presented itself as a loyal subject of Her Majesty that sought to uphold, promote, and forward—as well as being deeply committed to—the civilization of the Native population of Canada West. For more information see J.J. Talman, "The Newspapers of Upper Canada a Century Ago," *Canadian Historical Review* (March 1938); W. Meikle, *The Canadian Newspaper Directory or Advertisers Guide: Containing a Complete List of All the Newspapers in Canada—The Circulation of Each—and All Information in Reference Thereto* (Toronto: Blackburn's City Press, 1858), 16; Neil Semple, *The Lord's Dominion: The History of Canadian Methodism* (Montreal and Kingston: McGill-Queen's University Press, 1996), 76, 90, 92; and Goldwin French, *Parsons and Politics: The Role of the Wesleyan Methodists in Upper Canada and the Maritimes from 1780 to 1855* (Toronto: Ryerson Press, 1962), 115–18, 126, 221, 234.

4 "Editor's Comments," *CG*, 24 May 1843.

5 There is no single historical study that clearly illustrates the shifting policies, ideologies, and future roles involving First Nations. However, the following items taken together show the nature and extent of the uncertainty. John S. Milloy, "The Era of Civilization: British Policy for the Indians of Canada, 1830–1860," (PhD diss., University of Oxford, 1978); Robert J. Surtees, "Indian Land Cessions in Upper Canada, 1815–1830," in *As Long as the Sun Shines and Water Flows: A Reader in Canadian Native Studies*, ed. A.L. Getty and Antoine S. Lussier (Vancouver: University of British Columbia Press, 1983), 65–84; David T. McNab, "Herman Merivale and Colonial

Office Indian Policy in the Mid-Nineteenth Century," in *As Long as the Sun Shines and Water Flows*, 85-103; Rhonda Telford, "The Nefarious and Far-Ranging Interests of Indian Agent and Surveyor John William Keating, 1837-1869," *Papers of the Twenty-eighth Algonquian Conference* (Winnipeg: University of Manitoba, 1997), 372-402; John Leslie, "The Bagot Commission: Developing a Corporate Memory for the Indian Department," CHA *Historical Papers* (1982), 31; Robert J. Surtees, "Canadian Indian Policies," in *Handbook of North American Indians* (Washington, DC: Smithsonian Institution, 1988), 81-95; and Roger L. Nichols, *Indians in the United States and Canada* (Lincoln and London: University of Nebraska Press, 1998), 151-205. Dockstator, chapter 5 above.

6 Keith Walden, *Becoming Modern Toronto: The Industry Exhibition and the Shaping of Late Victorian Culture* (Toronto: University of Toronto Press, 1997), 5, generally, 4-6. Walden, while discussing a later period and different topic, presents a complex argument on the meaning of the Industrial Fair in Toronto that is salient to the Jones–Hurlburt debate. Walden's examination of the various meanings exhibited through Toronto's Annual Industrial Fair effectively shows how shifting ideologies and meanings influenced the position of the fair within the context of late nineteenth-century Ontario. It is the shifting of ideologies and contestation of meanings that are the focus of this paper.

7 J.R. Miller, *Sky Scrapers Hide the Heavens: A History of Indian-White Relations in Canada* (Toronto: University of Toronto Press, 1991).

8 Canada, *For Seven Generations. An Information Legacy of the Royal Commission on Aboriginal Peoples. Report of the Royal Commission on Aboriginal Peoples.* Vol. 1, *Looking Forward Looking Back* (Ottawa: Libraxus, 1997), see chapters 3 through 4, specifically pages 34-40 of the printed version. (Hereafter cited as RCAP, vol. 1.]

9 Ibid., vol. 1, 37-39.

10 Ibid., 34-35.

11 Ibid., 40; Dockstator, chapter 5 above.

12 In 1838, Captain George Ironside, a mixed-blood, led a force of about fifty Indians to repulse a patriot invasion that had landed at Windsor. Ironside, in response to apparent American complicity in the Upper and Lower Canadian Rebellions, proposed that the British government arm the Native population and an attack be made on Michilimackinac—essentially proposing to refight the War of 1812. The recriminations involved in suppressing the rebellions in the Canadas led one aggravated post commander, supposedly in a drunken rage, to fire on Sault Ste. Marie, Canada West. Additionally, Sir F.B. Head claimed in 1837 that the Americans had stockpiled arms along the Canadian border for the use of the rebels. By 1849 Ironside had risen to the post of Indian superintendent, replacing outgoing Superintendent Thomas G. Anderson. For more information see "s.s.m. Correspondence

Book, 1838–1839," B.194/b/13, Wm. Nourse to George Simpson, September 1, 1838, 34–35, Hudson's Bay Company Archives; Nourse to James Keith, November 24, 1838, 40; and Nourse to George Simpson, January 29, 1839, 49; Ged Martin, "Self-Defence: Francis Bond Head and Canada, 1841–1870," *Ontario History* 73, 1 (1981), 12–1, 4; Douglas Leighton, "George Ironside," *Canadian Dictionary of Biography*, vol. 9 (Toronto: University of Toronto Press, 1976), 407; and David T. McNab, "Who Is on Trial? Teme-Augama Anishnabai Land Rights and George Ironside, Junior: Re-Considering Oral Tradition," *The Canadian Journal of Native Studies* 18, 1 (1998): 119.

13 Surtees, "Indian Land Cessions," 65–84.

14 Donald B. Smith's biographical work on the Joneses briefly mentions the debate, wherein it is largely presented as a personal conflict. Donald B. Smith, *Sacred Feathers: The Reverend Peter Jones (Kahkewaquonaby) and the Mississauga Indians* (Toronto: University of Toronto Press, 1987), 186–87.

15 "Peter Jones's Speech, Delivered at the Anniversary of the Methodist Missionary Society, London, 2 May 2, 1831," CG, July 30, 1831.

16 Alan F. Segal's work titled *Paul the Convert: The Apostolate and the Apostasy of Saul the Pharisee* (New Haven: Yale University Press, 1990), 75, uses four points in his examination of the conversion of Paul that are pertinent to conversions generally and Jones specifically:

1. A convert is usually someone who identifies, at least retrospectively, a lack in the world, finding a remedy in the new reality promulgated by the new group.
2. The central aspect of the conversion is a decision to reconstruct reality.
3. The new group the subject enters supports that reality by its self-evident assumptions.
4. The talents and attitudes that the convert brings into the movement are greatly affected by the previous socialization, no matter how strongly the subject affirms the conversion of the denied past.

Jones fits items, 1, 2, and 4 of Segal's work. Jones viewed the Methodist faith as his people's saviour; he then sought to reconstruct the First Nations to whom he ministered in the image of non-Native civilization, casting them in the role of settled agriculturalists; and yet his efforts were deeply influenced by his own understandings of and upbringing within Aboriginal culture (specifically see his defence of the First Nations within this article and Smith's *Sacred Feathers*). For more information on differing views of conversion, see William Westfall, *Two Worlds: The Protestant Culture of Nineteenth Century Ontario* (Montreal: McGill-Queen's University Press, 1989); and Karl Hele, "'By the Rapids': The Anishinabeg–Missionary Encounter at Bawating (Sault Ste. Marie), c. 1821–1871" (PhD diss., McGill University, 2002), 296–97, 308, 433–58.

17 *CG*, November 27, 1889, reprinted from the *Christian Witness*.
18 Smith, *Sacred Feathers*, 50-51.
19 Donald B. Smith, "Jones, Peter," *Dictionary of Canadian Biography*, vol. 8, 439. (Hereafter cited as *DCB*.)
20 In May 1825 at the age of sixteen, Pahtaysagay walked into Belleville and requested an education. After being interviewed by several individuals, it was agreed that they would pay for his board while at school. He was given the name Peter Jacobs, according to Smith, for it was a phonetically rough approximation of his native name. Jacobs had a troubled youth: he lost both parents and three siblings through drink, and began to pray in English, in the belief that God could not understood his mother tongue. Pahtaysagay's heart remained unsettled until he met Peter Jones, who showed him that the Lord understood Ojibwa as well as English. Soon afterwards he became a convert. Like other early converts, Jacobs began to proselytize his own people. From 1838 to 1843, he served the Methodist along Lake Superior and in the Hudson's Bay Territory. From 1843 to his expulsion from the Methodist ministry in 1858, Jacobs worked in England raising money for missions, Canada West, and the Hudson's Bay Territory. In the year of his expulsion, he published an account of his adventures in Rupert's Land. According to his biography, Jacobs was reconverted in 1867, but "was constantly bedevilled by heavy drinking and sank into poverty and oblivion." G.S. French, "Pahtahsega," *DCB*, vol. 9, 660-601; Smith, *Sacred Feathers*, 90-93, 96, 151, 207; John Webster Grant, *Moon of Wintertime: Missionaries and the Indians of Canada in Encounter since 1534* (Toronto: University of Toronto Press, 1984), 92; Olive Patricia Dickason, *Canada's First Nations: A History of Founding Peoples from Earliest Times*, 3rd ed. (Toronto: Oxford University Press, 2002), 468, 43n; Edward S. Rogers, "Northern Algonkians and the Hudson's Bay Company, 1821-1890," *Aboriginal Ontario: Historical Perspectives on the First Nations*, ed. Edward S. Rogers and Donald B. Smith, *Ontario Historical Studies Series* (Toronto: Ontario Historical Studies Series and Dundurn Press, 1994), 329; George H. Cornish, *Handbook of Canadian Methodism* (Toronto: Methodist Book and Publishing Company, 1881), 38; and Peter Jacobs, *Journal of the Reverend P. Jacobs Indian Village Wesleyan Missionary, from Rice Lake to the Hudson's Bay Territory* (New York, published for the author, 1857).
21 Shahwundais, or John Sunday, served with the British in the War of 1812. In the mid-1820s he converted to Methodism and helped establish a model mission on Grape Island in the Bay of Quinte, to promote Christianity and agriculture among the Native people. With the encouragement of Peter Jones, Shahwundais became an itinerant among the Native people of Upper Canada and northern Michigan. In 1832 he became a ministerial candidate and was ordained four years later. Similar to other Native missionaries, Sunday visited England in an effort to raise awareness of Aboriginal issues and funds for missions. He continued to serve at various mission stations

until he was superannuated in 1867. G.S. French, Sunday's biographer, maintains that "for him, like many of his fellows, Christianity gave a new meaning to life and a measure of dignity and of material comfort, but it did not bring them fully into the white community or enable them effectively to adapt their own culture to new and changing social conditions." G.S. French, "Shahwundais," DCB, vol. 10, 647-48; Dickason, *Canada's First Nations*, 486, 43n; Grant, *Moon of Wintertime*, 241; and Smith, *Sacred Feathers*, 92-94, 98-99, 120, 164-66, 232.

22 Smith, "Jones, Peter," DCB, vol. 8, 440.

23 For more information about the relationship of Peter Jones and Eliza Fields, see Smith, *Sacred Feathers*; "Transatlantic Courtship of the Reverend Peter Jones," *Beaver*, outfit 308 (Summer 1977): 4-13; "Eliza and the Reverend Peter Jones," *Beaver*, outfit 308 (Autumn 1977): 40-46; "Peter and Eliza Jones: Their Last Years," *Beaver*, outfit 308 (Winter 1977): 16-23; and "The Life of George Copway or Kah-ge-ga-gah-bowh (1818-1869), and a Review of His Writings," *Journal of Canadian Studies*, 23, 3 (1988): 13.

24 Smith, "Jones, Peter," DCB, vol. 8, 441.

25 For more information about Sir F.B. Head, see D.B. Read, "Sir Francis Bond Head, Baronet, Lieutenant Governor," *Lieutenant-Governors of Upper Canada and Ontario, 1792-1899* (Toronto: William Briggs, 1900), 153-91; Martin, "Self-Defence: Francis Bond Head and Canada"; Ged Martin, "Sir Francis Bond Head: The Private Side of a Lieutenant Governor," *Ontario History* 73, 3 (1981): 145-70; and S.F. Wise, "Sir Francis Bond Head," DCB, vol. 10, 342-455.

26 F. Laurie Barron, "Alcoholism, Indians and the Anti-Drink Cause in the Protestant Indian Missions of Upper Canada, 1822-1850," in *As Long as the Sun Shines and Water Flows: A Reader in Canadian Native Studies*, ed. A.L. Getty and Antoine S. Lussier (Vancouver: University of British Columbia Press, 1983), 201, 21n.

27 Smith, "Jones, Peter," DCB, vol. 8, 441.

28 Deathbed narratives were useful tools to inspire the converted and unconverted alike. Stories surrounding the death of converts, non-converts, and missionaries were based loosely on actual events. The aim was to show that the Christian who died in the arms of Christ, no matter the circumstances, died happy and without regret, whereas those who steadfastly refused conversion often died full of apprehension and in the worst of circumstances. The description of Jones's death is likewise replete with the imagery of a Christian death and belief in the Lord's salvation (Smith, *Sacred Feathers*, 236-37). Horace Waller, as editor of the Livingstone diaries, modified the circumstances around the explorer's death to create a heroic Christian death. The creation of the myth surrounding the death of Livingstone is explored by Dorothy Helly, who claims that Livingstone very likely did not die while praying, for the position of his body suggested that he died alone in terrible pain. Another example, from Canada, is George M.

McDougall who froze to death on the Canadian plains. His son and editor of his biography claims his father died with Christ, for the body was supposedly found with arms across his chest and a peaceful look on his face. Even George Copway at the anniversary of the Toronto City Branch of the Missionary Society of the Wesleyan-Methodist Church (*CG*, March 15, 1843) drew "a contrast between the deaths of Christian and Pagan Indians." Additionally, Copway himself claimed to have been convinced by his mother to convert to Methodism on her deathbed. See Smith, "The Life of George Copway or Kah-ge-ga-gah-bowh," 8; and George Copway, *Life, History, and Travels* (Albany, NY: Weed and Parsons, 1847), 79; Horace Waller, *The Last Journals of David Livingstone*, vols. 1 and 2 (London: John Murray, 1874); Dorothy Helly, *Livingstone's Legacy: Horace Waller and Victorian Mythmaking* (Ohio: Ohio University Press, 1987); John McDougall, *George Millward McDougall: The Pioneer, Patriot and Missionary* (Toronto: William Briggs, 1888); and Dawn S. Barrett, "The Role of the Death-bed Narrative in the Conception Bay Revival of 1768–69," in *Historical Papers 1995 of the Canadian Society of Church History*, ed. Bruce L. Guenther (Toronto: Canadian Society for Church History, 1995): 55–68.

29 James Evans served the Methodist Church in Upper Canada, Lake Superior, and along Hudson Bay. He is most well known for his development of Cree syllabics, which is still in use today. Evans was recalled to England in 1846 to face rumours of improprieties, and eventually charges of sexual misconduct were levelled by the Natives of the Rossville community. A dispute with the Hudson's Bay Company also attributed to his recall. Evans was examined in England by the Wesleyan missionary society's secretaries and cleared of all allegations. He died suddenly of a heart attack, however, after attending a rally in Lincolnshire. It is rumoured that Evans had been poisoned by an unknown individual, possibly for his actions in the Bay. It is unclear, however, if poison was actually administered, or if an individual's "medicine power" brought about the death. Gerald M. Hutchinson, "Evans, James," *DCB*, vol. 7, 275–78; Fred Landon, "Letters of Rev. James Evans, Methodist Missionary, Written during His Journey to and Residence in the Lake Superior Region, 1838–39," *Ontario Historical Society* 28 (1932): 47–70; Grant, *Moon of Wintertime*, 101; Mrs. C.A. Chant, *James Evans: The Pioneer Missionary to the North American Indians* (Toronto: Woman's Methodist Society, n.d.); Lorne Pierce, *James Evans: The Ryerson Canadian History Reader* (Toronto: Ryerson Press, 1926); and Raymond Shirritt-Beaumont, "The Rossville Scandal, 1846: James Evans, the Cree, and a Mission on Trial" (MA thesis, University of Manitoba and of Winnipeg, 2001).

30 In 1841, Hurlburt wrote to J. Evans to inform him of his preference for a posting to the Mississippi Valley. Peter V. Krats, "'This Remote Field of Missionary Toil': Christianity at the Pic, Lake Superior to 1900," in *Historical Papers 1996: Canadian Society of Church History*, ed. Bruce L. Guenther (Toronto: Canadian Society for Church History,1996), 193–94.

31 "Lake Superior," *Cyclopedia of Methodism in Canada* (Toronto: Methodist Book and Publishing House, 1881), 341.

32 Erastus Hurlburt, "Thomas Hurlburt: Indian Missionary (1808–1873)," *Methodist Magazine*, 53 (photocopy), Bio file, Hurlburt Thomas (Rev.) (1808–1873), United Church Archives; Arthur C. Reynolds, "Hurlburt, Thomas" *DCB*, vol. 10, 372–73; and Krats, "This Remote Field," 194.

33 "The City Missionary Anniversary," *CG*, March 15, 1843, Rev. Thomas Hurlburt's speech on his experiences in the North-West, in moving the first resolution.

34 Kahgegagahbowh went through many incarnations. First he converted to Methodism and changed his name to George Copway. Copway then laboured to convert his fellows and eventually became the ideal redeemed Indian. From 1834 to 1843 Copway was stationed variously at Kewawenon, La Pointe, Illinois, Credit River, Wisconsin, Minnesota, Upper Canada, and the Saugeen Mission. Despite his talents, Copway became involved in an embezzlement scandal, served several weeks in jail, and was expelled from the Canadian conference of the Wesleyan Methodist Church. After his expulsion, Kahgegagahbowh utilized his identity as a Christianized Indian to successfully market books and lecture tours. According to Smith, Copway became an advocate of Indian rights, lobbying for the creation of an Indian territory in the United States, which coincidentally was named after himself. It was during this time that he became further alienated from his Aboriginal roots. He volunteered to convince the remaining Florida Seminoles to remove west of the Mississippi, desecrated Red Jackets' grave, abandoned his wife, and acted in Canada as a recruiting agent for the us federal army during the Civil War. He resurfaced in Detroit in 1867, advertising himself as healer, and travelled to Lake of Two Mountains one year later. In a last effort to recast himself, Kakikekapo, or Dr. Copway, sought to become a Catholic. The plan, however, was thwarted by his death several days after his baptism in 1869 as Joseph-Antoine.

The life of Kahgegagahbowh–George Copway–Kakikekapo–Joseph-Antoine can be characterized by his desire to become part of the dominant society. He rose to prominence occasionally, only to collapse into obscurity. Today Copway's publications have again found a place among Canadian and American readers, although Smith warns that historians must be careful when utilizing Copway as a historical source, for his writings contain numerous errors and half-truths. "Copway's real value lies," according to Smith, "in the man's life story and not in his writings." Smith, "The Life of George Copway," 5–38, specifically pages 5, 14, 16, 20, 23, 27–29; Donald B. Smith and A. Lavonne Brown Rouf, *Life, Letters and Speeches: George Copway (Kahgegahbowh)* (Lincoln: University of Nebraska Press, 1997); and Smith, "Kahgegagagahbowh," *DCB*, vol. 9, 419–21.

35 William Herkimer or Minowgiwan, after converting to Methodism, served the church throughout Upper Canada and along the shores of Lake Supe-

rior. He was one of the core group of Peter Jones's helpers at Credit River, because he was knowledgeable about farming. Both Herkimer and Jones sought the political, economic, and cultural independence of the Credit River Anishnabai. Despite this common desire, Minowgiwan and his brothers came to form the main opposition to Jones and his reforms. Essentially Jones represented "progressive reformers," a group that wanted to implement immediate and radical changes, while Herkimer navigated a moderate course. For instance, Minowgiwan and his brothers contested Jones's desire to alter traditional landholding practices and efforts to punish "ill-behaved" children. Herkimer also contested Jones's personal claim to 100 acres of land at the Credit, arguing that the property belonged to the entire nation. Finally, Herkimer's party refused to relocate to a new village site, which was supported by government authorities, thereby hindering Jones's efforts to effect many desired changes. Notwithstanding his conversion to Christianity, Minowgiwan aspired to retain his allegiance with the Aboriginal past while aiding his people in their adaptation to the future. Smith, "Jones, Peter," *DCB*, vol. 8, 439-43; *Sacred Feathers*, 80, 84, 155-58, 165; and Cornish, *Handbook of Canadian Methodism*, 33.

36 "The City Missionary Anniversary," *CG*, March 15, 1843. From Rev. George Copway's comments as reported.

37 Ibid.

38 Ibid. Quoted from the text of the second resolution, moved by Rev. William Herkimer.

39 "The City Missionary Anniversary," *CG*, March 15, 1843. From Rev. George Copway's comments as reported.

40 P. Jones (Kahkewaquonaby), letter to the editor, *CG*, 12 April 12, 1843.

41 Scholars dealing with First Nations seldom adequately address the issues surrounding the use of Western terminology to describe non-Western constructs. It is important to realize that by discussing Indigenous beliefs and conceptualizations while using English terminology, scholars risk misrepresenting Aboriginal thoughts and values. Scholars must be wary of translated concepts such as *God, spirit, vision, dream, and sacred*, for they are loaded with Western cultural assumptions. For a detailed discussion of these issues in a non-North American context, see Elizabeth Elbourne, "Early Khoisan Uses of Mission Christianity," *Kronos* 19 (November 1992): 12-13; James L. Cox, "Missionaries, the Phenomenology of Religion and 'Re-Presenting' Nineteenth-Century African Religion: A Case Study of Peter McKenzie's *Hail Orisha!*" *Journal of Religion in Africa* 31, 3 (2001): 336-53; and Paul Stuart Landau, "'Religion' and Christian Conversion in African History: A New Model," *Journal of Religious History* 23, 1 (February 1999): 8-30. For the applicability of the Africanists' thoughts on these issues to the North American context, see Hele, "'By the Rapids,'" 419-31.

42 P. Jones, letter to the editor, *CG*, April 12, 1843.

43 Ibid.

44 T. Hurlburt, letter to the editor, *CG*, April 19, 1843.

45 P. Jones, letter to the editor, *CG*, May 10, 1843.

46 T. Hurlburt, letter to the editor, *CG*, May 24, 1843.

47 T. Hurlburt, letter to the editor, *CG*, April 19, 1843. Dreams and visions are an important source of knowledge for the Anishnabai. While Jones and Hurlburt are using the two terms interchangeably, dreams and visions are different in the context of Anishnabai culture and thus subject to varying interpretations, understandings, and symbolic meaning. For a discussion of the importance of visions and dreams, Frances Densmore, *Chippewa Customs* (1929; repr., St. Paul: Minnesota Historical Society Press, 1979), 78–86; Christopher Vecsey, *Traditional Ojibwa Religion and Its Historical Changes* (Philadelphia: American Philosophical Society, 1986), 121–43; and Michael Angel, *Preserving the Sacred: Historical Perspectives on the Ojibwa Midewiwin* (Winnipeg: University of Manitoba Press, 2002), 27–28.

48 P. Jones (Kahkewaquonaby), letter to the editor, *CG*, April 12, 1843.

49 T. Hurlburt, letter to the editor, *CG*, April 19, 1843.

50 The term /starv-/, according to Mary Black-Rogers, is full of ambiguity and interpretation. In an 1986 study of Ojibwa usage of the term she concluded that it covers "a range of literal, technical, metaphorical, and ritual usages, governed by such situational formals ... belief systems and speaking conditions, degree of actual want, and crucial decisions between hunting and trapping." As such, the "contexts of usage" can be placed in three general categories, which are "Literal, Technical, and Manipulative." While the study is restricted to the placement of /starv-/ within the context of the fur trade, it is useful to understand similar ambiguities when referring to missionary–Native interactions. Aboriginal people cast the missionary in a role similar to, and already well established by, fur trade relationships. Hurlburt obviously believed that the people were literally starving, whereas technically, people were describing only scarcity of food, which had resulted in fewer furs, or they were attempting to manipulate the mission family, thereby receiving more supplies or assistance that would not have normally been forthcoming. M. Black-Rogers, "Varieties of 'Starving': Semantics and Survival in the Subarctic Fur Trade, 1750-1850," *Ethnohistory* 33, 4 (1986): 353–83.

51 T. Hurlburt, letter to the editor, *CG*, April 19, 1843; and May 24, 1843.

52 T. Hurlburt, letter to the editor, *CG*, April 19, 1843.

53 P. Jones, letter to the editor, *CG*, May 10, 1843.

54 P. Jones, letter to the editor, *CG*, April 12, 1843; and May 10, 1843.

55 Carolyn Podruchny, "'I have embraced the white man's religion': The Relations between the Peguis Band and the Church Missionary Society, 1820-1838," *Papers of the Twenty-sixth Algonquian Conference* (Winnipeg: University of Manitoba, 1995), 354.

56 Charles Cleland, *Rites of Conquest: The History and Culture of Michigan's Native Americans* (Ann Arbor: University of Michigan Press, 1995), 54–58.

57 These "wandering Pottawattomimies" were probably a band who had fled the United States rather than be removed west of Mississippi. Ottawa and Ojibwa, as well as the Potawatomi, fled across the Canadian border in search of a safe haven. Once in British North America, however, they were classed as foreign Indians and were "pushed" by Canadian authorities to return to their homes in the United States. For more information on a selection of these refugees, see James A. Clifton, *A Place of Refuge for All Time: Migration of the American Potawatomi into Upper Canada, 1830 to 1850*, National Museum of Man Mercury Series, Canadian Ethnology Service Paper No. 26 (Ottawa: National Museums of Canada, 1975); R. David Edmonds, *The Potawatomis: Keepers of the Fire* (Norman and London: University of Oklahoma Press, 1989); Rogers, "The Algonquian Farmers of Southern Ontario, 1830–1945," *Aboriginal Ontario: Historical Perspectives on the First Nations*, 122–23; Dickason, *Canada's First Nations*, 209; T. Hurlburt, letter to the editor, *CG*, April 19, 1843; P. Jones, letter to the editor, *CG*, May 10, 1843; and T. Hurlburt, letter to the editor, *CG*, May 24, 1843.

58 T. Hurlburt, letter to the editor, *CG*, April 19, 1843; and May 24, 1843.

59 P. Jones, letter to the editor, *CG*, April 12, 1843.

60 Ibid.; and May 10, 1843.

61 T. Hurlburt, "The City Missionary Anniversary," *CG*, March 15, 1843.

62 See John S. Gailbraith, "Simpson, Sir George," *DCB*, vol. 8, 812–18.

63 P. Jones, letter to the editor, *CG*, April 12, 1843; and May 10, 1843.

64 P. Jones, letter to the editor, *CG*, April 12, 1843. Windigos are the most terrifying creatures in Ojibwa oral tradition. Nevertheless, whether this figure is real or myth, the inherent fear of the windigo was and is pervasive in Ojibwa communities—the terror was and is real. The creatures are described most often as giant beings with an insatiable hunger for human flesh, hunting specifically during the long days of winter. The only aspiration of the windigo is to satisfy its all-consuming hunger, yet the more it eats the less satisfied it becomes, hence it is continually hungry. People were free from fear of the windigo only during the summer months because the creature did not like warm weather. The size and strength of the windigo made it impossible to kill with normal weapons—only the most powerful shaman might succeed. Moreover, any individual could become such a being either through possession or transformation. The windigo, however, is often presented as an evil spirit inhabiting the body of a human, although the physical manifestation of the form varied. In other words, the windigo could choose the shape it desired to appear in, whether human or animal. Anyone suspected of becoming a windigo would immediately be put to

death. Essentially, the windigo was a person who had become or was becoming a threat to society—an individual who physically or metaphorically consumed individuals. Basil Johnston, *The Manitous: The Spiritual World of the Ojibway* (Toronto: Key Porter, 1995), 221-25, 235-37; J.-Allen Burgesse, "Windigo," *Beaver* outfit 277 (1947): 4-5; Dickason, *Canada's First Nations*, 215; Herbert T. Schwarz, *Windigo and Other Tales of the Ojibways* (Toronto: McClelland and Stewart, n.d.), 11-12; and Alan D. McMillan, *Native Peoples and Cultures of Canada: An Anthropological Overview* (Toronto: Douglas and McIntyre, 1988), 98.

65 T. Hurlburt, letter to the editor, *CG*, April 19, 1843.

66 Ibid.

67 Dougal Cameron, the father of James, was a trader for the North West and Hudson's Bay Company who spent time at La Cloche, Lake Huron, and Michipicoton, Lake Superior. Sylvia Van Kirk, "Cameron, John Dugald," *DCB*, vol. 8, 121–22. I have chosen to use Jones's spelling of Dougal Cameron's name as seen in the *CG*. Hurlburt met Dougal Cameron at Cameron's posting to Michipicoton. According to Hurlburt, Thomas McMurray was a trader who had lived in the northwest for approximately fifty years. See Elizabeth Arthur's biography of Cuthbert Cumming, which indicates that T. McMurray served at the Hudson's Bay Company Pic River Post prior to 1841, *DCB*, vol. 8, 170.

68 T. Hurlburt, letter to the editor, *CG*, May 24, 1843.

69 James Cameron was a mixed-blood Baptist missionary in the Sault Ste. Marie area. His mother, known by her baptismal name of Mary, was an Ojibwa woman, from the Nipigon country (Ontario). Cameron travelled both the south and north shores of Lake Superior to preach to the Indians, and he founded the first Baptist Church in Sault Ste. Marie, Canada West, and Thunder Bay (then Fort William). Abel Bingham and Family Papers, Clarke Historical Library, Central Michigan University; James Cameron file, American Baptist Foreign Mission Society Correspondence, Indian Missions, Clarke Historical Library, Central Michigan University; and Van Kirk, "Cameron, John Dugald," 121.

70 Smith, "Kahgegagahbowh," *DCB*, 419–21.

71 T. Hurlburt, letter to the editor, *CG*, May 24, 1843.

72 Ibid.

73 Ibid.

74 P. Jones, letter to the editor, *CG*, April 12, 1843.

75 T. Hurlburt, letter to the editor, *CG*, April 19, 1843.

76 See Lewis Meriwether, *History of the Expedition under the Command of Lewis and Clark, to the Sources of the Missouri River, thence across the Rocky Mountains and down the Columbia River to the Pacific Ocean: Performed during the Years 1804-5-6 by Order of the Government of the United States* (New York: F.P. Harper, 1893); Albert Furtwangler, *Acts of*

Discovery: Visions of America in the Lewis and Clark Journals (Urbana: University of Illinois Press, 1993); and James P. Rhonda, *Lewis and Clark among the Indians* (Lincoln: University of Nebraska Press, 1984).

77   T. Hurlburt, letter to the editor, *CG*, May 24, 1843.

78   I would suggest that Jones did not respond to the accusation in his second response, printed on May 10, because of its heavy link with scriptural interpretation tied into the influence of Christian civilization upon the individual and collective membership. Jones, not as educated as Hurlburt, perhaps decided to limit his assertions to his immediate experience and those of people he knew and trusted, such as Sir George Simpson.

79   P. Jones, letter to the editor, *CG*, April 12, 1843.

80   T. Hurlburt, letter to the editor, *CG*, April 19, 1843.

81   Two years earlier Hurlburt made disparaging comments about the land and people of Walpole Island, which appeared on the pages of the *CG*. These comments, like those in 1866, appear to have passed uncontested. Despite a seven-year absence from Canadian missions, it is apparent that Hurlburt had not altered his opinions about Aboriginal society, culture, and spirituality. T. Hurlburt, *CG*, June 20, 1864, quoted in Dean Jacobs, "'We have but our hearts and the tradition of our old men': Understanding the Traditions and History of Bkejwanong," *Gin Das Winan Documenting Aboriginal History in Ontario: Occasional Papers of the Champlain Society*, no. 2, ed. David T. McNab and S. Dale Standen (Toronto: The Champlain Society, 1996), 9; and T. Hurlburt, "Recollections of Missionary Life among the Indians," *CG*, August 22, 1866; and August 29, 1866.

82   In the nineteenth century, Native ministers across Canada faced racial discrimination from their churches. In spite of stated policies advocating the creation of Native ministries, churches in Canada, as well as Africa, failed to act. The failure to advance Native ministers led South Africans in the nineteenth and early-twentieth centuries to create their own independent churches, but a similar movement in Canada did not occur. Donald B. Smith, *Sacred Feathers*, 151. For other examples see John Long, "Archdeacon Thomas Vincent of Moosonee and The Handicap of 'Métis' Racial Status," *Canadian Journal of Native Studies* 3, 1 (1983): 95-116; Winona Stevenson, "The Journals and Voices of a Church of England Native Catechist: Askenootow (Charles Pratt), 1851-1884," in *Reading beyond Words: Contexts for Native History*, ed. Jennifer S.H. Brown and Elizabeth Vibert (Peterborough: Broadview Press, 1996), 304-29. For more information on southern African churches see Jean Comaroff and John Comaroff, "Christianity and Colonialism in South Africa," *American Ethnologist* 13 (1986): 1-22; *Of Revelation and Revolution: Christianity, Colonialism, and Consciousness in South Africa*, vol. 1 (Chicago: University of Chicago Press, 1991); *Of Revelation and Revolution: The Dialectics of Modernity on a South African Frontier*, vol. 2 (Chicago: University of Chicago Press, 1997);

Jean Comaroff, *Body of Power Spirit of Resistance: The Culture and History of a South African People* (Chicago: University of Chicago, 1985); and Paul Stuart Landau, *The Realm of the Word: Language, Gender, and Christianity in a Southern African Kingdom* (Portsmouth, NH: Heinemaa, 1995).
83 Walden, *Becoming Modern in Toronto*, 6.
84 Denys Delâge and Helen Hornbeck Tanner, "The Ojibwa–Jesuit Debate at Walpole Island, 1844," *Ethnohistory* 41, 2 (1994): 295–321.
85 Walden, *Becoming Modern in Toronto*, 5. Debates surrounding the legitimacy of Native culture and belief, similar to those in 1843 and 1844, continued across Canada through the nineteenth and twentieth centuries.
86 *Delgamuukw v. British Columbia*, 1997.

Bibliography

Angel, Michael. *Preserving the Sacred: Historical Perspectives on the Ojibwa Midewiwin*. Winnipeg: University of Manitoba Press, 2002.

Barrett, Dawn S. "The Role of the Death-bed Narrative in the Conception Bay Revival of 1768-69." In *Historical Papers 1995: Canadian Society of Church History*. Ed. Bruce L. Guenther, 55–68. Toronto: Canadian Society for Church History, 1995.

Barron, F. Laurie. "Alcoholism, Indians and the Anti-Drink Cause in the Protestant Indian Missions of Upper Canada, 1822-1850." In *As Long as the Sun Shines and Water Flows: A Reader in Canadian Native Studies*. Ed. A.L. Getty and Antoine S. Lussier. Vancouver: University of British Columbia Press, 1983.

Black-Rogers, Mary. "Varieties of 'Starving': Semantics and Survival in the Subarctic Fur Trade, 1750-1850." *Ethnohistory* 33, 4 (1986): 353–83.

Burgesse, J. Allen. "Windigo." *Beaver* 308 (1947): 4–5.

Canada. *Report of the Royal Commission on Aboriginal Peoples*. Vol. 1. Ottawa: Libraxus, 1997.

Chant, Mrs. C.A. *James Evans: The Pioneer Missionary to the North American Indians*. Toronto: Women's Methodist Society, n.d.

Christian Guardian. "The City Missionary Anniversary." March 15, 1843.

Cleland, Charles. *Rites of Conquest: The History and Culture of Michigan's Native Americans*. Ann Arbor: University of Michigan Press, 1995.

Clifton, James A. *A Place of Refuge for All Time: Migration of the American Potowatomi into Upper Canada, 1830 to 1850*. Ottawa: National Museums of Canada, 1975.

Comaroff, Jean, and John Comaroff. *Body of Power Spirit of Resistance: The Culture and History of a South African People*. Chicago: University of Chicago Press, 1985.

———. "Christianity and Colonialism in South Africa." *American Ethnologist* 13 (1986): 1–22.

———. *Of Revelation and Revolution: Christianity, Colonialism, and Consciousness in South Africa.* Vol. 1. Chicago: University of Chicago Press, 1991.

———. *Of Revelation and Revolution: The Dialectics of Modernity on a South African Frontier.* Vol. 2. Chicago: University of Chicago Press, 1997.

Copway, George. *Life, History, and Travels.* Albany, NY: Weed and Parsons, 1847.

Cornish, George H. *Handbook of Canadian Methodism.* Toronto: Methodist Book and Publishing House, 1881.

Cox, James L. "Missionaries, the Phenomenology of Religion and 'Re-Presenting' Nineteenth-Century African Religion: A Case Study of Peter McKenzie's *Hail Orisha!*" *Journal of Religion in Africa* 31, 3 (2001): 336–53.

Delâge, Denys, and Helen Hornbeck Tanner. "The Ojibwa–Jesuit Debate at Walpole Island, 1844." *Ethnohistory* 41, 2 (1994): 295–321.

Densmore, Frances. *Chippewa Customs.* St. Paul: Minnesota Historical Society Press, 1979.

Dickason, Olive Patricia. *Canada's First Nations: A History of Founding Peoples from Earliest Times.* 3rd ed. Toronto: Oxford University Press, 2002.

Edmonds, R. David. *The Potawatomis: Keepers of the Fire.* Norman and London: University of Oklahoma Press, 1989.

Elbourne, Elizabeth. "Early Khoisan Uses of Mission Christianity." *Kronos* 19 (November 1992): 12–13.

French, Goldwin. *Parsons and Politics: The Role of the Wesleyan Methodists in Upper Canada and the Maritimes from 1780 to 1855.* Toronto: Ryerson Press, 1962.

French, G.S. "Pahtahsega." *Dictionary of Canadian Biography.* Vol. 11. Toronto: University of Toronto Press, 1966, 660–61.

———. "Shahwundais." *Dictionary of Canadian Biography.* Vol. 10. Toronto: University of Toronto Press, 1966, 647–78.

Furtwangler, Albert. *Acts of Discovery: Visions of America in the Lewis and Clark Journals.* Urbana: University of Illinois Press, 1993.

Gailbraith, John S. "Sir George Simpson." *Dictionary of Canadian Biography.* Vol. 8. Toronto: University of Toronto Press, 1966. 812–18.

Grant, John Webster. *Moon of Wintertime: Missionaries and the Indians of Canada in Encounter since 1534.* Toronto: University of Toronto Press, 1984.

Hele, Karl. "'By the Rapids': The Anishinabeg–Missionary Encounter at Bawating (Sault Ste. Marie), c. 1821-1871." PhD diss., McGill University, 2002.

Helly, Dorothy. *Livingstone's Legacy: Horace Waller and Victorian Mythmaking.* Columbus: Ohio University Press, 1987.

Hurlburt, T. Letter to the editor. *Christian Guardian.* April 19, 1843.

——. Letter to the editor. *Christian Guardian.* May 24, 1843.

——. "Recollections of Missionary Life among the Indians." *Christian Guardian.* August 22, 1866.

Hutchinson, Gerald M. "James Evans." *Dictionary of Canadian Biography.* Vol. 7. Toronto: University of Toronto Press, 1966. 275-78.

Jacobs, Dean. "'We have but our hearts and the tradition of our old men': Understanding the Traditions and History of Bkejwanong." In *Gin Das Winan Documenting Aboriginal History in Ontario: Occasional Papers of the Champlain Society.* Ed. David T. McNab and S. Dale Standen, 2. Toronto: The Champlain Society, 1996.

Jacobs, Peter. *Journal of the Reverend P. Jacobs Indian Village Wesleyan Missionary, from Rice Lake To the Hudson's Bay Territory.* New York: Published for the Author, 1857.

Johnston, Basil. *The Manitous: The Spiritual World of the Ojibway.* Toronto: Key Porter, 1995.

Jones, Peter. Letter to the editor. *Christian Guardian.* April 12, 1843.

——. Letter to the editor. *Christian Guardian.* May 10, 1843.

Krats, Peter V. "'This Remote Field of Missionary Toil': Christianity at the Pic, Lake Superior to 1900." *Historical Papers 1996: Canadian Society of Church History.* Ed. Bruce L. Guenther, 193-94. Toronto: Canadian Society for Church History, 1996.

"Lake Superior." *Cyclopedia of Methodism in Canada,* 341. Toronto: Methodist Book and Publishing House, 1881.

Landau, Paul Stuart. "'Religion' and Christian Conversion in African History: A New Model." *Journal of Religious History* 23, 1 (February 1999): 8-30.

——. *The Realm of the Word: Language, Gender, and Christianity in a Southern African Kingdom.* Portsmouth, NH: Heinemann, 1995.

Landon, Fred. "Letters of Rev. James Evans, Methodist Missionary, Written During His Journey to and Residence in the Lake Superior Region, 1838-9." *Ontario Historical Society* 28 (1932): 47-70.

Leighton, Douglas. "George Ironside." *Canadian Dictionary of Biography, 1861-1870.* Vol. 9. Toronto: University of Toronto Press, 1976, 407.

Leslie, John. "The Bagot Commission: Developing a Corporate Memory for the Indian Department." CHA Historical Papers, 1982, 31.

Long, John. "Archdeacon Thomas Vincent of Moosonee and the Handicap of 'Métis' Racial Status." Canadian Journal of Native Studies 3, 1 (1983): 95–116.

Martin, Ged. "Self-Defence: Francis Bond Head and Canada, 1841–1870." Ontario History 73, 1 (1981): 12–14.

———. "Sir Francis Bond Head: The Private Side of a Lieutenant Governor." Ontario History 73, 3 (1981): 145–70.

McDougall, John. George Millward McDougall: The Pioneer, Patriot and Missionary. Toronto: William Briggs, 1888.

McMillan, Alan D. Native Peoples and Cultures of Canada: An Anthropological Overview. Toronto: Douglas and McIntyre, 1988.

McNab, David T. Circles of Time: Aboriginal Land Rights and Resistance in Ontario. Waterloo, ON: Wilfrid Laurier University Press, 1999.

———. "Herman Merivale and Colonial Office Indian Policy in the Mid-Nineteenth Century." In As Long as the Sun Shines and Water Flows: A Reader in Canadian Native Studies. Ed. A.L. Getty and Antoine S. Lussier, 85–103. Vancouver: University of British Columbia Press, 1983.

———. "Who is on trial? Teme-Augama Anishnabai Land Rights and George Ironside, Junior: Reconsidering the Oral Tradition." The Canadian Journal of Native Studies 18, 1 (1998): 119.

Meikle, W. The Canadian Newspaper Directory or Advertisers Guide: Containing a Complete List of All the Newspapers in Canada—the Circulations of Each—and All Information in Reference Thereto. Toronto: Blackburn's City Press, 1858.

Meriweather, Lewis. History of the Expedition under the Command of Lewis and Clark, to the Sources of the Missouri River, thence across the Rocky Mountains and down the Columbia River to the Pacific Ocean: Performed during the Years 1804-5-6 by Order of the Government of the United States. New York: F.P. Harper, 1893.

Miller, J.R. Skyscrapers Hide the Heavens: A History of Indian–White Relations in Canada. Toronto: University of Toronto Press, 1991.

Milloy, John S. "The Era of Civilization: British Policy for the Indians of Canada, 1830–1860." PhD diss., University of Oxford, 1978.

Nichols, Roger L. Indians in the United States and Canada. Lincoln: University of Nebraska Press, 1998.

Pierce, Lorne. James Evans: The Ryerson Canadian History Reader. Toronto: Ryerson Press, 1926.

Podruchny, Carolyn. "'I have embraced the white man's religion': The Relations between the Peguis Band and the Church Missionary Society, 1820-1838." *Papers of the Twenty-sixth Algonquian Conference*. Winnipeg: University of Manitoba, 1995.

Read, D.B. "Sir Francis Bond Head, Baronet, Lieutenant Governor." *Lieutenant-Governors of Upper Canada and Ontario, 1792-1899*. Toronto: William Briggs, 1900, 153-91.

Reynolds, Arthur C. "Thomas Hurlburt." *Dictionary of Canadian Biography*. Vol. 10. Toronto: University of Toronto Press, 1966, 372-73.

Rhonda, James P. *Lewis and Clark among the Indians*. Lincoln: University of Nebraska Press, 1984.

Rogers, Edward S. "Northern Algonkians and the Hudson's Bay Company, 1821-1890." *Aboriginal Ontario: Historical Perspectives on the First Nations*. Ed. Edward S. Rogers and Donald B. Smith. Toronto: Ontario Historical Studies Series and Dundurn Press, 1994.

Schwartz, Herbert T. *Windigo and Other Tales of the Ojibways*. Toronto: McClelland and Stewart, n.d.

Segal, Alan F. *Paul the Convert: The Apostolate and the Apostasy of Saul the Pharisee*. New Haven: Yale University Press, 1990.

Semple, Neil. *The Lord's Dominion: The History of Canadian Methodism*. Montreal and Kingston: McGill-Queen's University Press, 1996.

Shirrit-Beaumont, Raymond. "The Rossville Scandal, 1846: James Evans, the Cree, and a Mission on Trial." MA thesis, University of Manitoba and Winnipeg, 2001.

Smith, Donald B. "Eliza and the Reverend Peter Jones." *Beaver* 308 (Summer 1977): 4-13.

———. "The Life of George Copway or Kah-ge-ga-gah-bowh (1818-1869), and a Review of His Writings." *Journal of Canadian Studies* 23, 3 (1988): 13.

———. "Kahgegagagahbowh." *Dictionary of Canadian Biography*. Vol. 9. Toronto: University of Toronto Press, 1996, 419-21.

———. "Peter and Eliza Jones: Their Last Years." *Beaver* 308 (Winter 1977): 16-23.

———. "Peter Jones." *Dictionary of Canadian Biography*. Vol. 8. Toronto: University of Toronto Press, 1966, 439.

———. *Sacred Feathers: The Reverend Peter Jones (Kahkewaquonaby) and the Mississauga Indians*. Toronto: University of Toronto Press, 1990.

————. "Transatlantic Courtship of the Reverend Peter Jones." *Beaver* 308 (Summer 1977): 4-13.

Smith, Donald B., and A. Lavonne Brown Ruoff. *Life, Letters and Speeches: George Copway (Kahgegahbowh).* Lincoln: University of Nebraska Press, 1997.

Stevenson, Winona. "The Journals and Voices of a Church of England Native Catechist: Askenootow (Charles Pratt), 1851–1884." In *Reading beyond Words: Contexts for Native History.* Ed. Jennifer S.H. Brown and Elizabeth Vibert, 304-29. Peterborough: Broadview Press, 1996.

Surtees, Robert J. "Canadian Indian Policies." *Handbook of North American Indians,* 81-95. Washington, DC: Smithsonian Institution, 1988.

————. "Indian Land Cessions in Upper Canada, 1815-1860." In *As Long as the Sun Shines and Water Flows: A Reader in Canadian Native Studies.* Ed. A.L. Getty and Antoine S. Lussier, 65-84. Vancouver: University of British Columbia Press, 1983.

TalmunTalman, J.J. "The Newspapers of Upper Canada a Century Ago." *Canadian Historical Review* (March 1938).

Telford, Rhonda. "The Nefarious and Far-Ranging Interests of Indian Agent and Surveyor John William Keating, 1837-1869." *Papers of the Twenty-eighth Algonquian Conference,* 372-402. Winnipeg: University of Manitoba, 1997.

Van Kirk, Sylvia. "John Dugald Cameron." *Dictionary of Canadian Biography.* Vol. 8. Toronto: University of Toronto Press, 1966, 121-22.

Vescey, Christopher. *Traditional Ojibwa Religion and Its Historical Changes.* Philadelphia: American Philosophical Society, 1986.

Waller, Horace. *The Last Journals of David Livingstone.* Vols. 1 and 2. London: John Murray, 1874.

Walden, Keith. *Becoming Modern Toronto: The Industry Exhibition and the Shaping of Late Victorian Culture.* Toronto: University of Toronto Press, 1997.

Westfall, William. *Two Worlds: The Protestant Culture of Nineteenth Century Ontario.* Montreal: McGill-Queen's University Press, 1989.

Wise, S.F. "Sir Francis Bond Head." *Dictionary of Canadian Biography.* Vol. 10. Toronto: University of Toronto Press, 1966, 342-45.

8

Reflections on the Social Relations of Indigenous Oral Histories[1]

Winona Wheeler

> Our annals, all happenings of human import, were stored in our song and dance rituals, our history differing in that it was not stored in books, but in the living memory. So, while the white people had much to teach us, we had much to teach them, and what a school could have been established upon that idea!
>
> —Luther Standing Bear, Lakota

RETURNING HOME TO SASKATCHEWAN from graduate studies in Berkeley required mental readjustments and spiritual recentring. At the wîkôhtowin ceremony that first summer, my mind drifted off to all the unfinished papers, unmarked exams, and phone messages waiting back at the office. Here it was, the beginning of the fall semester—could I really afford to spend twenty hours in the truck and twenty-four hours cooking and doing ceremony? Always so much to do. My poor command of Cree made it hard to follow the prayer songs, and I got tired of taxing my neighbours for translations. Very gently Maria leaned over and whispered "pê-atik nâtohta," *listen gently, softly, with care.* Reeled back in, I was calmed and refocused by the fires and the shadows of dancing feet, and I heard the songs again. They were talking to the spirits of the land, the animals, deceased relatives and ancestors, and they were asking for blessings, for guidance to help us live a good life. Wîtaskiwin, *to live together on the land in harmony.* Harmony and balance is a good thing to pray for, and my mind wandered off again—urban/bush, Cree/English, academic/nêhiyapwat, oral/written.

Wîhkôhtowin is a celebration of thanksgiving for life and renewal.
We feast and dance with our ancestors and other good spirits in thanks
for their sacrifices and teachings. Gazing into the fire that night I was
comforted, and I remembered why I am a historian and why I am here.
Nêhiyawîhckikêwin, *the Cree way/culture*, is an oral culture, a listening culture. We are a people to whom understanding and knowledge
comes by way of relationships—with the Creator, the past, the present,
the future, life around us, each other, and within ourselves. And, like
my ancestors, I am here on this earth to learn.

By no means am I an expert in Indigenous oral histories. By Cree
standards I am a fledgling, as my learning will take a lifetime and I
have only just begun. What I understand so far comes from many places.
It comes from being raised in a family that instilled in my generation
a strong Cree identity, connection to homeland, and appreciation for oral
traditions. It comes from living as a guest among many different Indigenous peoples, urban and rural, at home and abroad, and from close
friends and teachers. My understanding of the intersections between
Indigenous oral histories and Western historiography has also been as
influenced by critical and post-colonial theorists and ethno-historians,
as it has by our own Indigenous scholars and literary greats—Maria
Campbell, Gerald Vizenor, N. Scott Momaday, John Joseph Mathews,
Edward Ahenakew, Luther Standing Bear, and others—who have been
writing in the oral tradition for a very long time. They teach by "doing"
how oral traditions can inform our scholarship, and have paved the
way for people of my generation to return home, relearn, and find new
ways to write from our own places.

When our grandfather was alive, when he was here, he was
called Wapihesew (White Bird) that was his nickname. This is his
story that he told. Keep this story, do not forget this story. In the
future when you relate this story to your children you will keep
it alive a long time if you remember it. Before he would start a story
he used to pray first, then he would start his story. He gave thanks
for his life.

I am starting this story in the same fashion. I have finished my
prayer so that I will not relate this old story in a different way
than the way it is told. So I will also not slander the characters in

the story. [So] If I make a mistake the Great Spirit will make it right.

"Ah, grandchildren, I will tell you a story about myself.[2]

Memory is a beautiful gift. For those who grew up hearing stories about the distant past, the memories we hold of those times are more than mere mental exercises. Memories are also experienced at the somatic level and in the soul. To remember those times spent listening to old people tell histories at the kitchen table, on a road trip, or in the warm glow of a campfire, is to relive them. Memory, in the context of Indigenous oral traditions, is a resonance of senses—it evokes the relationship the listener had with the storyteller, and it evokes the emotional responses and the feeling of total absorption experienced at the time. The smells, nuances, facial expressions, body language, and range of audience response are as much a part of the memory of the story as the story itself. Very few historians recognize the deep effect that the oral transmission of knowledge has on the individual. Among them is Morris Berman, who tells us that "participation, or identification, is highly sensuous in nature, and it is a mode of knowing that cannot be intellectually refuted because of its immediate, visceral quality."[3]

For some time now, Indigenous and a handful of other scholars have stressed the importance of Indigenous oral history in the research, writing, and teaching of Indigenous histories. Studies galore have demonstrated that the exclusive dependence on documented records left by non-Indigenous people reinforces the colonialist notion that Western historical canons and conventions are superior—that their way of doing and writing history is the standard. and that Indigenous peoples have no intellectual traditions worth learning.[4] Slowly, historians are recognizing that Indigenous oral histories offer fresh insights and valuable information on significant historical events and outstanding personalities.[5] Following the lead of cutting-edge anthropology, ethnohistory, the oral history movement, and especially Native/Indian studies, they are becoming increasingly aware that the conventional, modern, academic, document-driven approach to studying the Indigenous past is passé at best, and elitist and colonialist at worst.[6]

Given the wealth of oral histories alive and well in Indian country throughout Canada, one would expect to find Indigenous voices in every book or article written on any aspect of the Indigenous past. To what degree, then, have all these new insights and the wealth of oral histories influenced historians writing Indigenous histories? A brief look at a few of the more recent and notable texts emerging in Saskatchewan is revealing.

J.R. Miller's historical biography of Chief Big Bear, published in the Canadian Biography Series of ECW Press, does not contain a single oral history interview, nor does it make reference to any oral history archival collections.[7] In light of a much earlier biography of Big Bear that was inspired by oral history, and considering that interviewing is one of the prescribed methods of modern biography (for subjects living and deceased), Miller's treatment of Big Bear is anemic.[8] From a Cree perspective, it is also disrespectful, given the substantial recorded (and archived) as well as living oral history on the life and times of this prominent and revered nêhiyaw leader.[9]

Miller's treatment of Mistahi Muskwa is surprising, considering that it was published the same year as *Shingwauk's Vision*, the most thorough and comprehensive study of Indian residential schools in Canada to date, and most noted for its good use of a wide range of Indigenous life histories and personal reminiscences.[10] Had Miller expended an iota of the energy seeking Native voices for *Big Bear* that he spent on *Shingwauk's Vision*, the resulting treatment would have been much more balanced.

The late F. Laurie Barron's study of the CCF's Native policies is recent history.[11] The events he focused on occurred during the lifetimes of thousands of Aboriginal peoples in this province, but their voices are barely detectable. *Walking in Indian Moccasins* makes great tribute to the "significant contribution ... made by the people who willingly participated in interviews recounting their personal experience and insights about the CCF," but there is little tangible evidence anywhere in the book to support the author's claim that the "views expressed by informants often shaped the content of the manuscript at critical points and provided a richness in detail unavailable in archival sources."[12] Barron did little beyond the confines of archives and classroom. Of the four Native "informants" praised in the acknowledgements, only two were cited in the text, for one sentence each.[13] Data from two additional Native informants, previously interviewed by his students, were also used a few times.[14] Given that many of us growing up in the 1960s and earlier heard stories from our grandfathers about Tommy Douglas (some of us have cousins named Tommy), it is disheartening that the man our grandfathers personally knew, argued with, strategized with, bartered with, ate with, and laughed with, barely peeks through.

Blair Stonechild and Bill Waiser's *Loyal till Death* is the only Indian–white relations history text from Saskatchewan that relied on oral histories of distant historical events for its primary thesis.[15] Two sets of oral history interviews were conducted. The first set was collected by Wilfred Tootoosis in 1984–85 for the Saskatchewan Indian Federated College and served as the basis for Stonechild's *Saskatchewan Indians and the Resistance of 1885: Two Case Studies.*[16] The second set of interviews was conducted by local research assistants from ten reserves in 1992–94. In the first project Stonechild participated in a few of the oral history interviews, and fully translated transcriptions were made. In the second project, neither Stonechild nor Waiser participated in the oral history recording except for their initial reserve visits to secure cooperation and endorsement from chief and/or council.[17] The instructions they gave to researchers in this instance were to provide one-page interview summaries.[18]

Some of the most substantial criticisms of *Loyal till Death* have already been addressed in Margaret L. Clarke's review article.[19] Clarke's primary criticism is that, despite its promise to provide an Indian view, it relies too heavily on published secondary sources.[20] This is most evident in their descriptions of spiritual and ceremonial occurrences. Instead of going to local elders for accounts on the Treaty Pipe ceremony or Thirst Dance, they relied on Euro-Canadian secondary authorities.[21] Clarke is also dismayed that they used only one-third of the oral histories collected in the second project, and that there is no analysis of the interviews, or the interview and oral data selection.[22] Clarke expresses disappointment that the "freshness and the use of first-person narrative" found in Stonechild's earlier work are sadly lacking here.[23] Because it is missing the emphases, nuances, and humanity inherent in the voices of Indigenous oral historians—the inside point of view—it reads like most other conventional histories.[24]

How did the Cree, Assiniboine, and Saulteaux voices disappear from this text? The authors offer some insight: "Although the oral history accounts were often lacking in specific detail and therefore of limited use, the interviews provided invaluable insight into Indian attitudes and motivation in 1885."[25] Had the historians actively participated in the interviews they might have heard details about events considered significant from the "Indian perspective" rather than the official record. They might have heard about the spiritual occurrences and the "inside the Indian camps" stories, some of which were so significant from the Indian point of view that the oral historians prayed before they related them on tape.[26] Back in 1984, John B. Tootoosis described the magnitude of the promises made at Treaty Six and how being bound to those promises affected Indian actions during 1885. Even brief mention of the treaty prompted John B. Tootoosis to exclaim, "I should have taken my pipe along with this. We should have a pipe here."[27] The voices disappeared in the written text because the authors did not hear them or they missed them.

While each of these studies is a valuable contribution to Indigenous history—historical biography, Native policy, Indian-white relations—they share varying degrees of the same problem: they treat and use Indigenous memories as they would any other documentary source, and in doing so, undervalued their potential. Miller in *Big Bear* simply ignores oral history; Barron gives it lip service; Stonechild and Waiser de-spiritualize/sanitize and distance themselves from it. While any number of factors could account for the choices these historians made, it is fair to say that most historians lack the understanding and skill to "do" Indigenous oral history within its own context. It is a methodological problem faced by many historians with no training in oral history methods, or more specifically, in traditional Indigenous oral history methods.

The tendency to treat oral history like any other documentary source comes from the conventional university training historians receive. Academic oral historians define that oral history as "a primary source material obtained by recording the spoken words—generally by means of planned, tape-recorded interviews—of persons deemed to harbor hitherto unavailable information worth preserving."[28] Oral historian William Moss speaks for most academics when he explains that once captured on tape, oral history becomes a document:

In a sense it is no longer alive but rather like a slice of tissue on a slide under the microscope of history. Like other documents, it is but a representation of a moment in time, an abstraction from the continuum of human experience, a suggestive benchmark.[29]

Such a perception is diametrically opposite how most Indigenous peoples relate to recorded voices. The fear that traditional knowledge and languages would be lost in this modern age of literacy, television, and socio-cultural alienation, prompted a series of elder workshops throughout the 1970s in Saskatchewan. From 1970 to 1978 approximately 414 elders from fifty-five Cree, Assiniboine, Saulteaux, Dakota, and Dene communities participated in workshops coordinated by the Saskatchewan Indian Cultural Centre.[30] At first many were hesitant and worried about recording their oral histories, sacred songs, and ceremonial information, but fear that all could be lost convinced them that recording might be the only way to retain them for future generations. As Cree/Assiniboine oral historian Tyrone Tootoosis explained, "They came to the conclusion that they would have to make some compromise and concession regarding the laws of access and the custom of traditional protocol."[31]

Cree elder Jim Kâ-Nîpitêhtêw shared his teachings about the Treaty Six Pipestem at one of these workshops, and expressed his thanks that the teachings were being recorded "so that our relatives might learn by hearing about it in this way... that the young might thereby remind each other."[32] Alex Bonais also agreed to record his stories, knowledge, and songs in the early 1970s because he also feared that all might be lost, and then "where will the people take their children?... Only the white man's world will remain." As Tyrone and I listened to this old man's lament on the cassette deck, a sudden surge of hope broke through. He moved closer, more directly into the microphone, and raising his gentle voice slightly, he called out, "In the future you youth try to educate each other with this information!"[33] Thirty-five years later that old man spoke directly to us.

Vivid images of the old man talking into the tape recorder with so much hope and faith in future generations were overwhelming. We felt his urgent plea and were humbled by his compassion—his voice and messages reached into the very depths of our hearts and souls. The voice on that tape was not dead to us, it was êpimatciw akitêmaka, *something that has a spirit, something that can give life.* It was left for us to build on, to draw strength from, to empower ourselves with, so our people would live on, so that it could live on and *not die.*

In the Cree world, everyone's personal, family, and regional histories interconnect and overlap; all are extensions of the past, and all are grounded in wahkôtowin, *kinship/relations.* According to Nêhiyawi-wîhtamawâkan, *Cree teaching, etymology,* we inherit relationships and obligations from and to the generations behind, among, and before us, to life on this earth as we know it, and to our homelands. Our histories are infused in our daily lives—they are lived experiences. So it is that the memories of our forefathers and foremothers become our own. And we are burdened with the obligation to keep them alive.

It is hard to avoid the language of essentialism, or even racialism some would charge, when trying to explain the nature of these generational memories. However, a few scholars of memory have found that "just as cultural memories may be imbedded in material artifacts, so too the memories of personal experiences leave permanent physical traces within our bodies."[34] Precisely how those traces are transmitted across the generations is hard to articulate. We carry inside us the stories we are personally given, but it is also true that we carry memories that we can't remember being given, and when we hear the voices of elders long gone on a tape, the body and spirit responds as if we were actually there, as if they were speaking directly to us. The only explanation I can give is wahkôtowin, *relations.*

So when historians have no relationship with the storyteller, or lack the lived experience, or have no personal investment in the histories they study, or do not understand the nature, quality, and role of Indigenous oral histories, it is no surprise that our oral histories become de-spiritualized, sanitized, amputated. The stories and teachings do not die when they are recorded on tape; rather, it is the way they are treated by historians that kills them. Undeniably, historians are most comfortable working in isolation with documents:

> Historians are literate people, *par excellence,* and for them the written word is paramount. It sets their standards and methods. It downgrades spoken words which are rendered utilitarian and flat compared to the concentrated meaning of text. The nuances and types of oral data are not seen.[35]

Perhaps this accounts for their apparent preference for transcripts over the experience of the actual tellings. Perhaps they believe that discursively transforming oral history into a document elevates its value and status. Then again, there is the ingrained precept that personal experiences, and above all personal relationships, undermine "psychic distance" and "scientific" objectivity. In addition to all that baggage, the "problem" historians confront when faced with embedded mystical or spiritual elements makes it perfectly clear how ill equipped conventionally trained historians are to work with Indigenous oral histories.

In most Indigenous societies there is little distinction between the physical and metaphysical realms, nor is there any fragmentation of knowledge into discipline-like categories. The tendency of conventional historians to "demythologize" oral histories to give it "greater validity" in the Western sense of history, "is a clear violation of its principles and practices."[36] Mainstream historians are not ignorant of the ethnocentrism inherent in the act of fragmenting Indigenous knowledge, but very few actually admit to the difficulties of transcending their own cultural norms. Richard White omitted significant supernatural events in Winnebago history because "I do not believe that the Winnebagos walked above the earth, nor that the prophet [Tenskwatawa (Shawnee)] turned his belt into a snake." White admits that in "making this narrative decision, I failed to convey a full Winnebago understanding of significant events.... It is precisely this kind of narrative conundrum that writing Native American history forces historians to face."[37]

From a mainstream perspective, once a story is shared and recorded, "facts" are extracted and the remaining "superfluous" data set aside. The bundle is plundered, the voice silenced, and bits are extracted to meet empirical academic needs. It is then that the story dies because the teachings, responsibilities, and shared experience inherent in the social relations of the story are absent, dismissed, or forgotten.

In the past few decades a handful of scholars acknowledge that "history," historical consciousness, even "significant events" are sociocultural constructs—that there are many more kinds and forms of "history" than the conventional/modernist template propagated in universities.[38] These few increasingly stress the need to "take seriously native theories of history as embedded in cosmology, in narratives, in rituals and ceremonies, and more generally in native philosophies and worldviews."[39] They have also agreed that historians' approaches, methods, values, and responsibilities derive from their own socio-cultural foundations, and these need to be seriously reconsidered. Anthropologist Julie Cruikshank came to understand that the elders she worked with had to provide "a kind of cultural scaffolding, the broad framework" that she needed to learn before she could even begin to ask intelligent questions about the past.[40] In a similar vein, Elizabeth Tonkins stresses that "Oralcy implies skilled production, and its messages are transmitted through artistic means. An oral testimony cannot be treated only as a repository of facts and errors of fact."[41]

Despite these and other new insights, few mainstream historians bother to go beyond the constructs of their academic training. Voicing the lament of most Native American scholars, Donald Grinde (Yamasee) explains, "Native Americans are painfully aware that our history is perhaps the only branch of the discipline in which one does not need a thorough knowledge of the language, culture, traditions, and philosophies of the people being studied."[42] How could one possibly study French or German social history, at the graduate level, without some working knowledge of their languages and cultures? History professors would consider such a proposition preposterous.

In Cree terms, education is understood as a lifelong process that emphasizes the whole person. It strives for spiritual, mental, and physical balance, and emotional well-being within the context of family and community. Unlike the Western pedagogical model, Cree education is relational. Solomon Ratt explains that in Cree terms, education does not come in compartmentalized institutional stages. Cree education, kiskinohamatowin, refers to a reciprocal and interactive teaching relationship between student and teacher, a "community activity."[43] Thus, seeking Cree knowledge requires an entirely different kind of relationship based on long-term commitment, reciprocity, and respect. Willie Ermine explains further that interpersonal relationships facilitate dialogue, an important "instrument in Aboriginal pedagogy and protocol."[44]

Given the current political climate, most scholars are careful to keep their skepticism and criticisms of Indigenous oral histories private, but the argument still whispered is that Indigenous oral histories do not stand up to the tests of academic scholarship, that they are hearsay or anecdotal, that they are useful only insofar as they provide insight into Indigenous attitudes and motives. Some historians rationalize that they do not want to be charged with appropriation, and others are content simply to know the past from their ivory towers. Let's face it, doing oral history the "Indian way" is hard work. Traipsing around Indian country, chauffeuring old people, picking berries, hauling wood, smoking meat, digging wild turnips, hoeing potatoes, or taking them to and from the grocery store or bingo is a lot of work. Our finely tuned grey matter has difficulty equating chopping wood with intellectual pursuits, because it is a totally different kind of pedagogy that requires us to learn a new way of learning. And why should we? Our academic training indoctrinates us into what Hayden White calls the "ironic perspective."[45] Consciously or unconsciously, many historians hold the elitist and ironic view that people generally lack the perspective in their own time to view their experiences as clearly as outside historians can see it in retrospect.

The study of kayâs âcimowina, *stories of long ago*, has taken me moose-hunting and taught me to clean and prepare such fine feast food delicacies as moose-nose and smoked-intestine soup. Traditional copyright teachings came in the wee hours of the morning over cold Tim Hortons coffee in a 4 x 4 truck heading down the Peace River highway. One of my teachers has a propensity for second-hand store shopping— entire days have been spent mining sale bins for gold. Once it took us almost two days to make a ten-hour road trip because we stopped at every second-hand store and garage sale along the highway. Cree education is based on interactive and reciprocal relations, and all knowledge comes with some degree of personal sacrifice.

A conventional historian has little responsibility to his sources other than to treat them with integrity and critically engage them with methods appropriate to their nature. While oral histories are also critically engaged with a range of appropriate methods, they require far more from the researcher than documents command. In the Cree world, our sources are our teachers, and the student–teacher relationship proscribes life-long obligations, responsibilities, respect, and trust.

The social relations between a teacher and student, more specifically the degree of commitment on the part of the student, determines
to a very large degree the quality and depth of knowledge the student
receives. Back in the early 1970s, Catherine Littlejohn promoted the use
of oral history in education curricula.[46] Applying conventional oral history techniques, she interviewed Mrs. Peemee—widow of Horse Child,
the youngest son of Big Bear. Ms. Littlejohn went to Mrs. Peemee for
the "Frog Lake Massacre" story, but instead of getting a narrative
account was referred to a version translated and published by Maria
Campbell in *Maclean's*.[47] While Mrs. Peemee elaborated on a few points,
she refused to tell the whole story since the published version told it
"as she wanted it told."[48] The researcher reasoned that Mrs. Peemee's
account was "shorter and in less detail" because it was "more personal
and apparently more painful to relate":

> Mrs. Peemee's traditionalism, her closeness to her husband and to
> the physical reminders of those troubled times—i.e., Cutknife
> Hill—may have kept the pain and sorrow more intimately with her.
> Therefore, in telling the story, Mrs. Peemee was concerned that her
> grandchild be present, for it was difficult to reveal the depths of her
> feelings to a stranger, especially one obviously outside her cul-
> tural background.[49]

The reader cannot ascertain whether Mrs. Peemee articulated these
reasons herself or whether they were conjecture. "Pain and sorrow"
may have been prohibiting factors behind Mrs. Peemee's reluctance to
retell the story, but Ms. Littlejohn also identified "that the researcher
must be accepted as from within the Cree worldview as well."[50] It may
have helped the researcher to understand the impact of history on
Poundmaker's people because it would have highlighted the depths of
distrust the people had for strangers. They were justifiably suspicious
of outsiders asking any questions about incidents associated with the
1885 resistance because both Poundmaker and Big Bear were wrongfully
incarcerated, a number of men were hanged, many more were incarcerated, and the federal government penalized the entire band by denying
them their treaty annuities and the right to select their own chief and
council until the 1920s. As old as Mrs. Peemee was, she directly experienced the retribution inflicted on her family and community for their

alleged role in the "massacre," and so, like other band members, she was extremely cautious of outsiders asking direct questions.

Maria Campbell, on the other hand, spent considerable time with Mrs. Peemee over a number of years during which strong and respectful student–teacher bonds were established. Maria chopped wood, carried water, drove Mrs. Peemee to town for shopping. In short, she was friend and apprentice. She not only received the full story—complete with biographical details on well- and lesser-known individuals, stories of spiritual occurrences, and humorous anecdotes—she and Mrs. Peemee collaboratively edited the story for publication; they agreed on an edited and somewhat softened version that respected Mrs. Peemee's caution and protected spiritual elements from outside judgments. Maria Campbell recalls that at no time did Mrs. Peemee express personal pain or sorrow when telling the stories: In fact, "she had a great sense of humor, laughing and talking the whole time."[51]

Two different research methods, two different results. Maria Campbell's research methods were grounded in nêhiyawîhcikêwin, *Cree ways/culture*. Clearly, conventional oral history interview methods do not meet Cree standards. Clearly there is a direct correlation between the depth and quality of knowledge a student acquires and the level of reciprocal trust and respect cultivated between the teacher and student. This is why the practice of racing into Indian country with tape recorder in hand and taking data meets with little success. This is also why historians who read interview summaries in distant offices are deaf to significant events from Indigenous perspectives.

Books or papers do not mediate the Cree relationship to the past. It is a lived experience embodied in everyday social interaction. The teaching and learning of history—historical study—is a social process based entirely on human relationships, and relations between human beings and the creation around them.

A conscientious historian, one who would take the time to learn about Cree ways of knowing (or Anishnabe, Nakoda, Dene, Metis, Dakota) would learn that there are many different kinds of stories in Cree oral traditions. They would learn that in Cree, as in Dakota and many other Indigenous worlds, there is no word for *history* in the Western sense.[52] They would learn that Cree histories consist of many different kinds of overlapping and related stories. That âtayôhkêwina are *sacred stories* of the mystical past when the earth was shaped, animal peoples conversed, and Wisakejac transformed the earth and its inhabitants through misadventure, mischief, and love into the world we presently know. Âtayôhkewina are the foundations of Cree spirituality/religion, philosophy, and world view, and contain the laws given to the people to live by. They would learn that âcimowina are *stories* of events that have come to pass since Wisakejac's corporeal beingness transformed into spirit presence, that there are many different kinds of overlapping and related kayâs âcimowina, *stories about long ago,* that are often infused with the sacred. Because in our traditions, experience and knowledge are not compartmentalized; they do not adhere to modernist fact/fiction, truth/myth binaries. Academic scholars would do well to take heed of Harvey Knight's caution:

> Because Indian oral tradition blends the material, spiritual, and philosophical together into one historical entity, it would be a clear violation of the culture from which it is derived if well-meaning scholars were to try to demythologize it, in order to give it greater validity in the Western sense of historiography. It would be equally unjust and inappropriate to place this history into the category of mythology or folklore, thereby stripping it of its significance as authentic historical documentation.[53]

Students of Cree history would also learn that some old and great stories handed down through the generations are formally governed by sacred protocols—for example, stories of the treaties and some stories concerning the 1885 resistance—while others are not, that personal life histories or reminiscences are not bound by the same rules of transmission as the sacred and historical narratives, but they may be infused with some of those elements. A conscientious historian would also learn how best to use the material his or her teacher gives because active engagement in the oral history teaches one to discern what the significant events are from an Indigenous perspective, what can and cannot become public knowledge, and what narrative style would be most appropriate for its textual transformation.

Academics also need to respect the fact that Cree copyright laws and protocols exist and need to be adhered to if trust is going to be established and maintained. One of the major tenets of Western erudition is the belief that all knowledge is knowable, that "knowledge is and should be essentially 'free' and open; this notion remains a corner-stone of many of the professional attitudes, training, and ethics maintained by scholarly societies."[54] In the Cree world, not all knowledge is unknowable. Some knowledge is kept in the family lines; other kinds have to be earned. While all knowledge is intended for community well-being and welfare, to acquire certain kinds one is obligated to adhere to the rules of its acquisition. Access to knowledge requires long-term commitment, apprenticeship, and payment in various forms. Maria Campbell earned the stories published in *Stories of the Road Allowance People* by being helper or servant to her teachers in addition to paying for them with "gifts of blankets, tobacco and even a prize Arabian stallion."[55] In some instances tobacco and a gift are all that is required, in other instances tobacco and a gift are the means to receive instruction on the appropriate protocol. Harold Cardinal and others refer to these rules as traditional copyright.[56]

Harold Cardinal explains that there are not many things in Cree life where the right of ownership—the concept of exclusive ownership—is recognized. The one area where it does apply is for stories and ceremonies. Maria Campbell explains further that while the English language has many words for various types of theft, some considered less horrendous or significant than others under law, in Cree there is only one word for *stealing*: kimotiwin. In Cree, any and all theft is considered unconscionable. To take a story and claim ownership without permission when it was only shared with you is stealing. Indigenous copyright systems are built on trust, and breach of that trust constitutes theft.[57]

Sadly, conventional copyright and intellectual property rights laws do not adequately protect Indigenous intellectual or "esoteric" knowledge from researchers.[58] This issue needs a more thorough treatment than space allows here. For now, it is vital to stress that signed consent forms do not mean that researchers have copyright over the stories. It means that the orator is willing to share them. Unlike Canadian copyright law, in the Cree world just because you acquired a set of cassette-recordings does not mean you own the content.

Since the issue of appropriation will be encountered by anyone doing oral history, it is vital that researchers become fully informed about their roles, responsibilities, and limits according to local standards and protocols.[59] Clearly, historians willing to engage in oral history research must take the time to learn how to learn. Learning how to learn from another people's point of view is not a revolutionary concept, but it is hard work. Learning in the oral tradition is not about racing into Indian country with tape recorder in hand and taking data. Neither is it about hiring locals to interview old people and supply transcripts for detached academic reflection in the isolated confines of distant offices. If historians take the time to question their motives and goals in doing historical research on the Indigenous past, great strides will be made.

When I think about the potential in my discipline—Native/Indian studies—for the development of a truly Indigenous oral traditions-based history, the voices of many long-gone old people fill my mind. They had dreams for us. They envisioned an education system where traditional knowledge and the "cunning of the white man" would be taught side-by-side. Neal McLeod accords that the biggest challenge in Indigenous studies today concerns "the transmission and translation of knowledge from traditional tribal environments to academic settings" as well as the "format and modes of articulation."[60] Like most scholars in the discipline, we see our tasks and our obligations differently from those in history, anthropology, and other disciplines. McLeod reminds us,

> The project of Indigenous Studies is an extension of collective memory which has existed since time immemorial … if we are to have genuine Indigenous Studies, we really need to use techniques of ways of knowing that stretch back deep within our tribal memories. The failure to utilize such techniques will amount, not to liberation through education, but rather assimilation through education.[61]

The challenge is not taken lightly. Luckily for us, our literary elders are in the forefront, guiding and encouraging us, with so much confidence in our abilities to meet the obligations we bear with mainstream tools. As Cree Metis elder Maria Campbell has noted,

> Our new storytellers have a big job. They must understand their sacred place and they must also understand the new language and use it to express their stories without losing the thoughts and images that are culturally unique to them. This new storyteller

must also be a translator of the old way, so that it will not be lost to a new generation. And all this must be done on paper, for that is the new way.[62]

Acknowledgements

Special thanks to Maria Campbell and Tyrone Tootoosis for all the teachings, guidance, and support they continue to give on this learning journey. I thank them also for reading and commenting on earlier drafts and for food and shelter.

Notes

1   This paper derives from research conducted for my PhD dissertation, "Decolonizing Tribal Histories" (University of California, Berkeley, 2000), portions of which were published in "The Social Relations of Oral History," *Saskatchewan History* 51, 1 (1999): 29-35, and "The Othering of Indigenous History," *Saskatchewan History* 50, 2 (1999): 24-27.

2   Andrew Kay, "An Old Cree Indian Named Old Worm (Amiskosese)," March 18, 1972 (audio tape). Kawakatoose (Poor Man) Oral History Project, Registration No. AH 71.67.1, Provincial Museum of Alberta.

3   Morris Berman, *Coming to Our Senses: Body and Spirit in the Hidden History of the West* (New York: Simon and Schuster, 1989), 112.

4   See, for example, Angela Cavender Wilson, "Power of the Spoken Word: Native Oral Traditions in American Indian History," in *Rethinking American Indian History*, ed. Donald Fixico, 101-16 (Albuquerque: University of New Mexico, 1997); and Angela Cavender Wilson, "American Indian History or Non-Indian Perceptions of American Indian History?" *American Indian Quarterly* 20, 1 (1996): 3-5; Devon A. Mihesuah, "Voices, Interpretations, and the 'New Indian History': Comment on the *AIQ* Special Issue on Writing about American Indians," *American Indian Quarterly* 20, 1 (1996): 91-105; Calvin Martin, *The American Indian and the Problem of History* (New York: Oxford University Press, 1987); Gordon M. Day, "Roger's Raid in Indian Tradition," *Historical New Hampshire* 17 (June 1962): 3-17; Julie Cruikshank, "Discovery of Gold on the Klondike: Perspectives from Oral Tradition," in *Reading beyond Words: Contexts for Native History*, ed. Jennifer S.H. Brown and Elizabeth Vibert (Peterborough: Broadview Press, 1996), 433-53.

5   See for example, Calvin Martin, "The Metaphysics of Writing Indian–White History," in *The American Indian and the Problem of History*, ed. Calvin Martin (New York: Oxford University Press, 1987), 6, 9; Ken S. Coates and Robin Fisher, eds., *Out of the Background: Readings on Canadian Native*

History, 2nd ed. (Toronto: Copp Clark, 1996), 3; Donald L. Fixico, ed., *Rethinking American Indian History* (Albuquerque: University of New Mexico Press, 1997), 7.

6 Martin, "The Metaphysics," 6, 9.

7 J.R. Miller, *Big Bear [Mistahimusqua]: A Biography* (Toronto: ECW Press, 1996).

8 Hugh Dempsey, *Big Bear: The End of Freedom* (Vancouver: Greystone, 1984).

9 Dr. Miller's biography would have been greatly enhanced had he consulted the oral history collections at the Saskatchewan Indian Federated College and the Saskatchewan Indian Cultural Centre. The work of his colleague, Dr. Bill Waiser, on the Indian involvement in 1885, with Blair Stonechild, also located oral history on Big Bear, which if not specifically helpful, could have steered Dr. Miller to living memories.

   Granted, Dr. Miller was writing for the general public rather than his academic peers, or, apparently, Aboriginal people. Miller's exclusion of Cree voices, and the fact that not a single Aboriginal person is mentioned in his acknowledgements, maintains colonialist intellectual hegemony and promotes the notion that Cree people have no historical traditions worth consulting. A tone of condescension is also evident in his narrative: "Big Bear, of course, showed little or no awareness ..." (25), "Big Bear would have hated ..." (120). How does he know? This lack of Indigenous voice is especially offensive when coupled with Miller's literary strategy. He uses the voice of an extradiegetic omniscient narrator who tells the story in the third person, uses commentorial discourse, and is not accountable for his information. Through "psycho-narration," he implies personal knowledge of Big Bear and suggests the power to reach into his mind to know his thoughts and feelings, all of which is offensive to those who know the oral histories of Big Bear's life. For a more thorough description of this literary strategy, see Wallace Martin, *Recent Theories of Narrative* (Ithaca: Cornell University Press, 1991).

10 J.R. Miller, *Shingwauk's Vision: A History of Native Residential Schools* (Toronto: University of Toronto Press, 1996). Dr. Miller clearly expended considerable energies in search of Native voices, which he collected through interviews (conducted by himself and research assistants) and from attending conferences. He also searched out oral history collections.

11 F. Laurie Barron, *Walking in Indian Moccasins: The Native Policies of Tommy Douglas and the CCF* (Vancouver: University of British Columbia Press, 1997).

12 Barron, *Walking in Indian Moccasins*, xi–xii.

13 Ibid., 105n39; 132n148.

14 "Respondent A, Interviewed on James Smith Reserve as Part of a Native Studies 404.6 course project, March 1987," Ibid., 217n40; and two apparently

separate interviews with John B. Tootoosis, one conducted by Murray Dobbin, November 9, 1977, housed in the SAB Oral History Project 21, Ibid., 68n39; the other (Ibid., 131n146) cited in James M. Pitsula, "The Saskatchewan CCF Government and Treaty Indians, 1944-64," *Canadian Historical Review* 75, 1 (1989): 34n56, n58. Ibid., 234.

15 Blair Stonechild and Bill Waiser, *Loyal till Death: Indians and the North-West Rebellion* (Calgary: Fifth House, 1997).

16 Blair Stonechild, *Saskatchewan Indians and the Resistance of 1885: Two Case Studies* (Regina: Saskatchewan Education, 1986).

17 Stonechild and Waiser, *Loyal*, viii.

18 Tyrone Tootoosis, personal communication, August 1999.

19 Margaret L. Clarke, "Review Article," *Prairie Forum* 23, 2 (1998): 267-73.

20 Clarke, "Review Article," 270.

21 Why go to Euro-Canadian secondary "authorities" for matters of Cree spirituality when living elders could give "authentic" accounts, and when a more thorough account, for example of the Calumet Dance has been written by Joseph Dion? (See Joseph F. Dion, *My Tribe the Crees*, ed. Hugh Dempsey [Calgary: Glenbow, 1993, reprint.]) See Stonechild and Waiser, *Loyal*, 269n18, 292n50. While David G. Mandelbaum gives a brief description of the Pipestem Bundle Dance on pages 210-11 in *The Plains Cree: An Ethnographic, Historical and Comparative Study* (Regina: Canadian Plains Research Centre, 1979), Joseph Dion's account on pages 52-53 describes it in relation to peace talks between nations. Katherine Pettipas's description of the Thirst Dance can be found on pages 56-61 in *Severing the Ties that Bind: Government Repression of Indigenous Religious Ceremonies on the Prairies* (Winnipeg: University of Manitoba Press, 1994), which is based almost entirely on published anthropological accounts except for snippets from Able Watetch, *Payepot and His People* (Saskatoon: Modern Press, 1959) and Edward Ahenakew, *Voices of the Plains Cree*, ed. Ruth Buck (Toronto: McClelland and Stewart, 1973).

22 Clarke, "Review Article," 268, 271-72.

23 Ibid., 267.

24 Oral historians are increasingly turning their attention to how oral histories, especially cross-cultural ones, can and perhaps should be represented in textual form. For example see Peter Burke, "History of Events and the Revival of Narrative," in *New Perspectives on Historical Writing* (University Park: Pennsylvania University Press, 1992); Raphael Samuel, "Perils of the Transcript," in *The Oral History Reader*, ed. Robert Perks and Alistair Thomson (London: Routledge, 1998); Ruth Finnegan, *Oral Traditions and the Verbal Arts: A Guide to Research Practices* (London: Routledge, 1992); Dennis Tedlock, *The Spoken Word and the Art of Interpretation* (Philadelphia: University of Pennsylvania Press, 1983).

25 Stonechild and Waiser, *Loyal*, 264.

26 Tootoosis, personal communication, 1999.

27 Saskatchewan Indian Federated College, 1885 Indian Oral History Project. John B. Tootoosis, Poundmaker First Nations, interviewed by A. Blair Stonechild and Wilfred Tootoosis. Cutknife, Saskatchewan, 30 November 1984 (transcript).

28 Louis M. Star, "Oral History," *Encyclopedia of Library and Information Science* (New York: Marcel Dekker, 1978), 440.

29 William Moss, "Oral History: What Is It and Where Did It Come From?" in *The Past Meets the Present*, ed. David Strickland and Rebecca Sharpless (New York: University Press of America, 1988), 10.

30 Tyrone Tootoosis, "Our Legacy: Ka ke pesi nakatamakiawiyak," *Eagle Feather News* 1, 10 (1999), 21.

31 Ibid.

32 Jim Kâ-Nîpitêhtêw quoted in Freda Ahenakew and H.C. Wolfart, eds., *Ana kâ-pimwêwêhahk okakêskihkêmowina: The Counselling Speeches of Jim Kâ-Nîpitêhtêw* (Winnipeg: University of Manitoba Press, 1998), 105, 65.

33 Alex Bonais, Plains Cree, Little Pine First Nation. Interviewed by Wilfred Tootoosis, Poundmaker First Nations, ca. 1974. Audiotape in possession of Tyrone Wilfred Tootoosis.

34 Patricia Fara and Karalyn Patterson, eds., "Introduction," in *Memory* (New York: Cambridge University Press, 1998), 3.

35 Gwyn Prins, "Oral History," in *New Perspectives on Historical Writing*, ed. Peter Burke (University Park: Pennsylvania University Press, 1992), 118.

36 Harvey Knight, "Preface," in Alexander Wolfe, *Earth Elder Stories: The Pinayzitt Path* (Saskatoon: Fifth House, 1988), ix.

37 Richard White, "Using the Past: History and Native American Studies," in *Studying Native America: Problems and Prospects*, ed. Russell Thornton (Madison: University of Wisconsin Press, 1998), 227, 228.

38 See for example, Renato Rosaldo, *Ilongot Headhunting 1883-1974: A Study in Society and History* (Stanford: Stanford University Press, 1980), 54-55; Marshall Sahlins, "Other Times, Other Customs: The Anthropology of History," *American Anthropologist* 85 (1983), 517; Kirsten Hastrup, ed., *Other Histories* (New York: Routledge, 1992).

39 Raymond D. Fogelson, "The Ethnohistory of Events and Nonevents," *Ethnohistory* 36, 2 (1989): 134-35.

40 Julie Cruikshank, *The Social Life of Stories: Narrative and Knowledge in the Yukon Territory* (Lincoln: University of Nebraska Press, 1998), 27.

41 Quoted in Mary Chamberlain and Paul Thompson, eds., "Introduction: Genre and Narrative in Life Stories," in *Narrative and Genre* (London: Routledge, 1998), 10.

42 Donald A. Grinde Jr., "Teaching American Indian History: A Native American Voice," *Perspectives: American Historical Society Newsletter* 32, 6 (1994): 1.

43 Solomon Ratt, Testimony, *Office of the Treaty Commissioner Mock Trial* (14 September 1992), video.

44 Willie Ermine, "Pedagogy from the Ethos: An Interview with Elder Ermine on Language," in *As We See ... Aboriginal Pedagogy*, ed. Lenore A. Stiffarm (Saskatoon: University of Saskatchewan Extension Press, 1998), 10.

45 For a discussion on Hayden White's theory that modern historians are "locked within an ironic perspective" see Lloyd S. Kramer, "Literature, Criticism, and Historical Imagination: The Literary Challenges of Hayden White and Dominick LaCapra," in *The New Cultural History*, ed. Lynn Hunt (Berkeley: University of California Press, 1989), 104.

46 Catherine Isabel Littlejohn, "The Indian Oral Tradition: A Model for Teachers," M.Ed. Thesis: University of Saskatchewan College of Education, 1975).

47 Maria Campbell, "She Who Knows the Truth of Big Bear: History Calls Him Traitor, but History Sometimes Lies," *Maclean's* 88, 9 (1975), 46.

48 Ibid.

49 Ibid., 56.

50 Ibid., 58.

51 Maria Campbell, personal communication, August 1999.

52 See for example, Angela Cavender-Wilson, "Ehanna Woyakapi: History and the Language of Dakota Narration," paper presented at the Western History Association Conference, Sacramento, CA, October 15, 1998, 4.

53 Knight, "Preface," ix.

54 James D. Nason, "Native American Intellectual Property Rights: Issues in the Control of Esoteric Knowledge," in *Borrowed Power: Essays on Cultural Appropriation*, ed. Bruce Ziff and Pratima V. Rao (New Bunswick, NJ: Rutgers University Press, 1997), 245.

55 Maria Campbell, *Stories of the Road Allowance People* (Penticton: Theytus, 1995), 2.

56 Harold Cardinal, personal communication, August 1997.

57 Alexander Wolf, "Introduction," in *Earth Elder Stories: The Pinayzitt Path* (Saskatoon: Fifth House, 1988), xv.

58 *Esoteric knowledge* is defined as "traditional, valued knowledge that is intended for and is to be used by the specially initiated or trained and that is most often owned or held in trust and treated as private property or secret by an individual, by a group within the community (such as a clan or society), or by the community as a whole." Nason, "Intellectual Property Rights," 242. See also, Gordon Christie, "Aboriginal Rights, Aboriginal Culture, and Protection," *Osgoode Hall Law Journal* 36, 3 (1998): 447–84; Jill Jarvis-Tonus, "Legal Issues Regarding Oral Histories," *Canadian Oral History Association Journal* 12 (1992): 18–24.

59 See for example, Bruce Ziff and Pratima V. Rao, eds., *Borrowed Power: Essays on Cultural Appropriation* (New Bunswick, NJ: Rutgers University Press, 1997).

60 Neal McLeod, "What is *indigenous* about Indigenous Studies?" *SIFC Magazine* (1998–99), 52.
61 Ibid.
62 Maria Campbell, "Introduction," *Acimoona* (Saskatoon: Fifth House, 1985), n.p.

Bibliography

Ahenakew, Edward. *Voices of the Plains Cree*. Regina: Canadian Plains Research Centre Reprint, 1995.

Ahenakew, Freda, and H.C. Wolfart, eds. *Ana kâ-pimwêwêhahk okakêskihkêmowina: The Counselling Speeches of Jim Kâ-Nîpitêhtêw*. Winnipeg: University of Manitoba Press, 1998.

Barron, F. Laurie. *Walking in Indian Moccasins: The Native Policies of Tommy Douglas and the CCF*. Vancouver: University of British Columbia Press, 1997.

Berman, Morris. *Coming to Our Senses: Body and Spirit in the Hidden History of the West*. New York: Simon and Schuster, 1989.

Burke, Peter. "History of Events and the Revival of Narrative." In *New Perspectives on Historical Writing*. Ed. Peter Burke, 233–48. University Park: Pennsylvania State University Press, 1991.

Campbell, Maria, ed. *Acimoona*. Saskatoon: Fifth House, 1985.

——— . "She Who Knows the Truth of Big Bear: History Calls Him Traitor, but History Sometimes Lies." *Maclean's* 88, 9 (1975): 46–51.

——— . *Stories of the Road Allowance People*. Penticton: Theytus, 1995.

Cavender Wilson, Angela. "American Indian History or Non-Indian Perceptions of American Indian History?" *American Indian Quarterly* 20, 1 (1996): 3–5.

——— . "Ehanna Woyakapi: History and the Language of Dakota Narration." Paper presented at the Western History Association Conference, Sacramento, CA, October 15, 1998.

——— . "Power of the Spoken Word: Native Oral Traditions in American Indian History." In *Rethinking American Indian History*. Ed. Donald Fixico, 101–16. Albuquerque: University of New Mexico, 1997.

Chamberlain, Mary, and Paul Thompson, eds. *Narrative and Genre*. London: Routledge, 1998.

Christie, Gordon. "Aboriginal Rights, Aboriginal Culture, and Protection." *Osgoode Hall Law Journal* 36, 3 (1998): 447–84.

Clarke, Margaret L. "Review Article." *Prairie Forum* 23, 2 (1998): 267–73.

Coates, Ken S., and Robin Fisher, eds. *Out of the Background: Readings on Canadian Native History*. 2nd ed. Toronto: Copp Clark, 1996.

Cruikshank, Julie. "Discovery of Gold on the Klondike: Perspectives from Oral Tradition." In *Reading beyond Words: Contexts for Native History*. Ed. Jennifer S.H. Brown and Elizabeth Vibert, 433–53. Peterborough: Broadview Press, 1996.

————. *The Social Life of Stories: Narrative and Knowledge in the Yukon Territory*. Lincoln: University of Nebraska Press, 1998.

Day, Gordon M. "Roger's Raid in Indian Tradition." *Historical New Hampshire* 17 (June 1962): 3–17.

Dion, Joseph F. *My Tribe the Crees*. Ed. Hugh Dempsey. Calgary: Glenbow, 1993 reprint.

Dempsey, Hugh. *Big Bear: The End of Freedom*. Vancouver: Greystone Books, 1984.

Ermine, Willie. "Pedagogy from the Ethos: An Interview with Elder Ermine on Language." In *As We See… Aboriginal Pedagogy*. Ed. Lenore A. Stiffarm, 9–28. Saskatoon: University of Saskatchewan Extension Press, 1998.

Fara, Patricia, and Karalyn Patterson, eds. *Memory*. New York: Cambridge University Press, 1998.

Finnegan, Ruth. *Oral Traditions and the Verbal Arts: A Guide to Research Practices*. London: Routledge, 1992.

Fixico, Donald L., ed. *Rethinking American Indian History*. Albuquerque: University of New Mexico Press, 1997.

Fogelson, Raymond D. "The Ethnohistory of Events and Nonevents." *Ethnohistory* 36, 2 (1989): 133–47.

Grinde Jr., Donald A. "Teaching American Indian History: A Native American Voice." *Perspectives: American Historical Society Newsletter* 32, 6 (1994): 11–16.

Hastrup, Kirsten, ed. *Other Histories*. New York: Routledge, 1992.

Jarvis-Tonus, Jill. "Legal Issues Regarding Oral Histories." *Canadian Oral History Association Journal* 12 (1992): 18–24.

Kawakatoose (Poor Man) Oral History Project, Registration AH71.67.1. Andrew Kay, 18 March 1972 (audio tape).

Kay, Andrew. "An Old Cree Indian Named Old Worm (Amiskosese)." Provincial Museum of Alberta.

Knight, Harvey. "Preface." In *Earth Elder Stories: The Pinayzitt Path*, by Alexander Wolfe. Saskatoon: Fifth House, 1988.

Kramer, Lloyd S. "Literature, Criticism, and Historical Imagination: The Literary Challenge of Hayden White and Dominick LaCapra." In *The New Cultural History*. Ed. Lynn Hunt, 97–128. Berkeley: University of California Press, 1989.

Littlejohn, Catherine I. "The Indian Oral Tradition: A Model for Teachers." MA thesis, University of Saskatchewan, 1975.

Mandelbaum, David G. *The Plains Cree: An Ethnographic, Historical and Comparative Study.* Regina: Canadian Plains Research Centre, 1979.

Martin, Calvin. "The Metaphysics of Writing Indian-White History." In *The American Indian and the Problem of History.* Ed. Calvin Martin, 27-34. New York: Oxford University Press, 1987.

Martin, Wallace. *Recent Theories of Narrative.* Ithaca: Cornell University Press, 1991.

McLeod, Neal. "What is *indigenous* about Indigenous Studies?" *SIFC Magazine* (1998-99): 52-53.

Mihesuah, Devon A. "Voices, Interpretations, and the 'New Indian History': Comment on the *AIQ* Special Issue on Writing about American Indians." *American Indian Quarterly* 20, 1 (1996): 91-105.

Miller, J.R. *Big Bear [Mistahimusqua]: A Biography.* Toronto: ECW Press, 1996.

——— . *Shingwauk's Vision: A History of Native Residential Schools.* Toronto: University of Toronto Press, 1996.

Moss, William. "Oral History: What Is It and Where Did It Come From?" In *The Past Meets the Present.* Ed. David Strickland and Rebecca Sharpless, 5-14. New York: University Press of America, 1988.

Nason, James D. "Native American Intellectual Property Rights: Issues in the Control of Esoteric Knowledge." In *Borrowed Power: Essays on Cultural Appropriation.* Ed. Bruce Ziff and Pratima V. Rao, 237-54. New Bunswick, NJ: Rutgers University Press, 1997.

Pettipas, Katherine. *Severing the Ties that Bind: Government Repression of Indigenous Religious Ceremonies on the Prairies.* Winnipeg: University of Manitoba Press, 1994.

Prins, Gwyn. "Oral History." In *New Perspectives on Historical Writing.* Ed. Peter Burke, 114-39. University Park, PA: Pennsylvania State University Press, 1991.

Ratt, Solomon. Testimony. *Office of the Treaty Commissioner Mock Trial* (September 14, 1992). Film.

Rosaldo, Renato. *Ilongot Headhunting 1883-1974: A Study in Society and History.* Stanford: Stanford University Press, 1980.

Sahlins, Marshall. "Other Times, Other Customs: The Anthropology of History," *American Anthropologist* 85 (1983): 517-44.

Samuel, Raphael. "Perils of the Transcript." In *The Oral History Reader.* Ed. Robert Perks and Alistair Thomson. London: Routledge, 1998.

Standing Bear, Luther. *Land of the Spotted Eagle.* 1933. Press reprint. Lincoln: University of Nebraska 1978.

Star, Louis M. "Oral History," 440. *Encyclopedia of Library and Information Science.* New York: Marcel Dekker, 1978.

Stonechild, Blair. *Saskatchewan Indians and the Resistance of 1885: Two Case Studies.* Regina: Saskatchewan Education, 1986.

Stonechild, Blair, and Bill Waiser. *Loyal till Death: Indians and the North-West Rebellion.* Calgary: Fifth House, 1997.

Tedlock, Dennis. *The Spoken Word and the Art of Interpretation.* Philadelphia: University of Pennsylvania Press, 1983.

Tootoosis, John B. Interview by A. Blair Stonechild and Wilfred Tootoosis. Cutknife, Saskatchewan, November 30, 1984 (transcript). Indian Oral History Project. Saskatchewan Indian Federated College, 1885.

Tootoosis, Tyrone. "Our Legacy: Ka ke pesi nakatamakiawiyak." *Eagle Feather News* 1, 10 (1998-1999): 21.

Watetch, Able. *Payepot and His People.* Saskatoon: Modern Press, 1959.

Wheeler, Winona. "The Othering of Indigenous History." *Saskatchewan History* 50, 2 (1999): 24-27.

——— . "Decolonizing Tribal Histories." PhD diss., University of California, 2000.

———. "The Social Relations of Oral History." *Saskatchewan History* 51, 1 (1999): 29-35.

White, Richard. "Using the Past: History and Native American Studies." In *Studying Native American: Problems and Prospects.* Ed. Russell Thorton, 217-43. Madison: University of Wisconsin Press, 1998.

Wolfe, Alexander. *Earth Elder Stories: The Pinayzitt Path.* Saskatoon: Fifth House, 1988.

Ziff, Bruce, and Pratima V. Rao, eds. *Borrowed Power: Essays on Cultural Appropriation.* New Brunswick, NJ: Rutgers University Press, 1997.

9

Scientists and Evolving Perceptions of Indigenous Knowledge in Northern Canada

Stephen Bocking

SOMETHING OLD HAS BECOME SOMETHING new in the political and scientific landscapes of northern Canada. As recently as 1970 virtually no government agency, and few scientists, gave more than token acknowledgement to indigenous knowledge.[1] Now, however, it is being applied in wildlife management by territorial and other resource agencies, its use is required in assessing the impacts of new developments, and it is gaining an increasing presence in northern scientific research.[2] Territorial governments and land claims regions are recognizing, gathering, and preserving indigenous knowledge, while scientists across a range of disciplines are examining how they can draw on it, in a variety of ways, in their research.

This recognition of indigenous knowledge might be considered inevitable. After all, it represents the accumulation of wisdom over hundreds or thousands of years, its validity attested to by the long-term survival of people and cultures in an often harsh environment. But until relatively recently it was dismissed by governments and scientists alike. It was viewed as anecdotal and non-quantitative, not amenable to testing under controlled conditions, often based more on myth and folklore than on empirical evidence, and a poor basis for general scientific theory. In short, it corresponded poorly to conventional ideas of reliable scientific evidence.

This paper examines changes in scientists' perceptions of indigenous knowledge, and how these changes fit within the history of northern politics and science. As will become evident, these perceptions have been shaped by the political context of research and environmental management, by evolving scientific ideas, by scientists' changing ideas about northern research, and by their views of the North itself, as, for example, a homeland, or a resource hinterland. While norms for scientific practice have influenced scientists' attitudes, so have more immediate concerns about the assertion of their own credibility and authority as experts. These concerns, in turn, have been influenced by scientists' changing roles within the political, economic, and social contexts of northern Canada.

These developments in northern Canada must also be placed within a larger context. Over the last three decades, experience, changing attitudes, and changing politics have led to a radical revision, in much of the world, in the status of indigenous people and their knowledge. The superiority of Western knowledge and forms of development has been questioned; the value of local knowledge, particularly in agriculture and resource management, has been recognized; and, especially, indigenous people themselves have asserted their rights to self-determination. These developments have been reflected in work by institutions and initiatives ranging from UNESCO, to the American Association for the Advancement of Science, to the Arctic Environmental Protection Strategy. These have also led to continuing controversies over access and control of resources, and the ownership of intellectual property. Thus, while much of the story of northern indigenous knowledge relates to matters specific to the North, such as land claims, they must also be placed within this global context.

Understanding changing attitudes towards indigenous knowledge is in itself an important aspect of understanding the history and politics of science in northern Canada. However, it also provides an opportunity to consider more general themes in the history and sociology of science. Some of these themes include how attitudes towards knowledge relate to efforts to assert disciplinary boundaries and disciplinary authority, as well as the evolution of ideas about the nature of science—from objective knowledge to a way of knowing that is embedded in specific political and institutional contexts. It also provides an opportunity to consider how changing local conditions relate to global trends: while indigenous knowledge is usually specific to a particular local context, and the political significance of this knowledge is tied to local conditions, advocacy of the value of this knowledge, as well as protection of its status as intellectual property, is also embedded within a global movement for indigenous rights and activism.

Exploration and Natural History

Perhaps the most persistent image of colonial history is that of imperial superiority: the assumption of explorers, missionaries, colonial scientists, and administrators that it was their task to use their more advanced attitudes and knowledge to "civilize" the more primitive colonies. There was little sense of an exchange: the colonists had, it was believed, little to learn from the colonized. However, this general image has been partly belied by historical experience in Oceania, Asia, and Africa, where European scientists learned a great deal from colonized peoples.[3] And neither does it describe adequately what occurred in northern Canada. Early European and North American explorers and traders in the Arctic often attached great value to indigenous knowledge, as a source of knowledge and a means of survival. Explorers used Natives as guides, drawing on their skills, and using their geographic knowledge to prepare maps, often retaining Native names of landscape features. Fur traders relied on Natives to find beaver and other species, with the fur industry in large part dependent on Native inventions and skills.[4] Thus, indigenous knowledge played a crucial, if often unacknowledged, role in northern exploration and trading.

Even in the twentieth century, some scientists drew on indigenous knowledge to enhance their understanding of the northern landscape. In 1929 J. Dewey Soper, an experienced northern naturalist, discovered the breeding grounds of the blue goose on Southampton Island. This, one of his most noteworthy achievements, was achieved, in part, by tracking down Inuit reports.[5] Similarly, A.E. Porsild, while studying the Mackenzie Delta in 1927 and 1928 and again between 1931 and 1935, gathered information from Native trappers, compiled Inuit names of delta mammals, and recorded their knowledge of delta muskrats and fish, and of the abundance and distribution of moose, caribou, and mountain sheep.[6]

That Soper, Porsild, and other naturalists used indigenous knowledge during the early twentieth century reflected, in part, the similarities between how they and Native peoples lived, worked, and understood the northern environment. They travelled by canoes and dogsled. They focused on detailed study of a specific area (in Soper's case, Baffin Island; in Porsild's case, the Mackenzie Delta), making primarily qualitative rather than quantitative observations. These features of their scientific work paralleled the place-based, non-quantitative knowledge held by Natives. In effect, scientists like Soper and Porsild saw themselves as something like mediators: drawing on indigenous knowledge and interpreting its accuracy and significance in terms of the taxonomic or geographical categories of contemporary science. These scientists' combination—between the 1920s and early 1940s—of indigenous knowledge and scientific knowledge, also reflected a transition: between the period of exploration, when there was no sustained government presence in the North, and the extension of Canadian government administration. Completion of this transition by the late 1940s would see the near-complete removal of indigenous knowledge from the northern intellectual landscape.

Post-war Science and Politics

The Second World War marked a watershed in northern science and government. Wartime projects, such as the construction of the Alaska highway, the CANOL pipeline, and airfields greatly enhanced the North's accessibility. Governments suddenly recognized the region's strategic importance, given its circumpolar location between North America and the Soviet Union. The influence of a small number of Canadian and American government officials, scientists, and other individuals, including Raleigh Parkin, Trevor Lloyd, Maxwell Dunbar, Arnold Heeney, Brooke Claxton, and others, who sought to convince their governments of the need for a stronger presence in the North, was also important. Their influence was reflected in the creation of the Arctic Institute of North America in 1944, as a private organization to finance and publicize northern research.[7]

During the 1950s and 1960s Canadian interest in the North continued to increase, with road and airport construction, subsidies for resource development, and expansion of social programs into northern communities. These initiatives reflected both the desire to develop northern resources to supply southern markets, and a sense of responsibility for the well-being of northern peoples. Twenty years after the war, the Canadian government had a significant permanent presence in the North, furthering its goal of integrating the North into the Canadian economy and nation.

In this effort science played a major role. Studies of natural resources were especially important, including minerals, water, fish, and wildlife. The Canadian Wildlife Service was of particular importance to environmental and ecological research. During the 1950s and early 1960s, through studies of caribou, polar bear, muskox, and other species, the Wildlife Service became the most active biological research agency in the North.[8] Non-governmental agencies also played an important role, especially the Arctic Institute.

In the 1960s the federal government also increased its support for northern ecological research by universities. As a result, many universities established centres or programs for northern research, including the Boreal Institute at the University of Alberta, and the Institute for Northern Studies of the University of Saskatchewan. The federal government also set up other programs to support northern research, such as the Polar Continental Shelf Project, beginning in 1958, and the Inuvik Research Centre, which opened in 1964. These encouraged scientific activity by providing logistical support and research facilities, thereby making northern science less expensive. As a result of such programs, and the availability of air travel, scientists travelled north in increasing numbers.

In this post-war era, scientists sought to break away from past approaches. New tools, and especially the airplane, enabled a new approach to the northern environment. The "view from above" provided by aircraft was the key to scientists' new-found ability to extend their perspective over large areas of the North, breaking with the previous reliance on ground study, when canoes or dog teams had been the only available modes of transport.

The support provided by the Polar Continental Shelf Project, including aircraft and research laboratories, meant that scientists no longer needed to live amongst Natives, or learn their techniques for travel and survival or, indeed, have any real contact with them. And as scientists took to the air and to their laboratories, indigenous knowledge largely disappeared from northern science. Instead, it was commonly dismissed as subjective and partial, inadequate in comparison to the more extensive and objective knowledge possible through the new methods. For example, in 1955 Kenneth Hare, leader of a geographic research team at McGill University, argued that for the study of large-scale patterns of vegetation, aerial survey was clearly superior to the previous reliance on field-notes based on river travel, usually assisted by Native guides.[9]

New approaches to research, and an accompanying dismissal of indigenous knowledge, were especially apparent in wildlife science. During the 1950s and 1960s Canadian Wildlife Service researchers sought to develop an approach to managing wildlife, including control over hunting, that would be based on scientific, quantitative knowledge. They did so, in large part, by emphasizing large-scale survey of wildlife populations, and by identifying the factors influencing the dynamics of these populations. As part of an effort to impose science-based management on northern hunters, they denied the existence of Native methods of resource management, as well as the knowledge that was part of these methods.

One statement of this perspective appeared in 1968, in the form of a monograph on the barren-ground caribou written by John Kelsall, an experienced caribou biologist. A compendium of knowledge accumulated over fifteen years of research, it was also a statement of attitudes towards indigenous knowledge. While Kelsall mentioned indigenous knowledge only a few times, when he did so he tended to dismiss as unreliable Native claims regarding caribou ecology or behaviour. For example, he noted that Natives had observed that caribou drive moose before them during their migration to winter ranges, and that caribou sometimes remained in forested areas during the summer. He then explained that these observations were contrary to those made by scientists, and likely reflected confusion between woodland and barren-ground caribou. He also described how when caribou gathered near Lake Athabasca in 1956–57, the apparently huge population misled residents into believing that caribou were in little danger from hunting: "The fact that this was the only such body of animals on the entire range bore little weight with residents."[10] Thus, he suggested, Natives had a limited perception of caribou abundance, because they lacked the wide-ranging synoptic view provided by aerial surveys.

More generally, Kelsall, like other scientists, portrayed Native hunting as wasteful: marked by careless slaughter, wounding without killing, and the use of only certain parts of the caribou, leaving other parts to waste. Such practices reinforced perceptions of Native wildlife harvesting as primitive, and contrary to "rational" resource use. They also indicated, according to Kelsall, heedless ignorance of the status of a limited resource, and he quoted with approval A.H. Lawrie's 1948 claim that "with no abstract ideas of conservation to restrain him and with apparently limitless numbers of caribou migrating through his country, [the Eskimo] takes what he can with reckless prodigality."[11] Once, according to Kelsall, Natives' capacity to kill wildlife had been limited by the size of their own population, and by primitive technology. But with a growing Native population and the widespread use of rifles, these checks on exploitation had been removed, making scientific management essential.

The need for controls on Native hunting was also justified with anecdotal accounts of waste. Such waste, Kelsall argued, endangered not only caribou populations, but Natives themselves, who, he noted, failed to demonstrate even elementary caution, planning, and foresight. While settlers had soon learned not to put their trust in the uncertain availability of caribou, "many natives have found it difficult, or impossible, to practise this basic rule in Northern survival."[12] The consequence, he argued, was that as recently as 1957–58 Natives had starved to death when the caribou had failed to appear.

Throughout the 1960s and early 1970s, caribou scientists accorded little recognition to Native knowledge.[13] Native hunters, they argued, had little capacity for conservation, or even awareness of the need for conservation. Instead, faced with highly variable wildlife populations, hunters were opportunistic, killing wildlife wherever encountered. No restraint could evolve under conditions in which survival depended on a variable food source, and hence conservation and sustained yield were foreign concepts to Native hunters.[14] Even as recently as 1981 scientists repeated the claim that Native hunting had once been limited only by primitive technology and low populations, and that rifles and snow machines had destabilized the balance between hunters and wildlife.[15]

During the 1970s, when (as I discuss below) Natives asserted more forcefully a role in northern wildlife management, wildlife scientists responded by arguing that while better communication and cooperation would help, science-based management had to maintain a primary role. Science was the only reliable source of knowledge about wildlife populations, and the only rational basis for managing hunting, and "science is not a part of the Indian or Inuit tradition."[16] Opposition to scientists' prescriptions suggested confusion, a reluctance to face the facts, and a need for more education. Scientists' and managers' resistance to Native perspectives was reflected in disputes in the late 1970s over the relative significance of the effects of hunting, wolves, and exploration activity on the Beverly-Kaminuriak caribou herds.[17]

There were many reasons why wildlife biologists resisted acknowledging the existence or utility of indigenous knowledge. These can be best understood in terms of the various identities that these scientists maintained: as scientists, as wildlife biologists, and as part of the state-based administration of northern Canada.

As scientists, their assumptions about the nature of reliable knowledge encouraged them to see indigenous knowledge as anecdotal, non-quantitative, subjective, and poorly amenable to experimental test—in short, as unscientific. Indigenous knowledge was also seen as inseparable from the immediate context of hunting, and hence contrary to the ultimate objective of science, of developing theoretical generalizations true in every context.

As wildlife biologists, their attitudes were influenced by theoretical and practical commitments. Their understanding of wildlife populations, to a large extent based on wildlife science as developed in southern Canada and the United States, emphasized demography (births, growth, and deaths), physiological factors influencing the health of populations, and range ecology. Observations of behaviour, or of relative changes in the status of local populations, or of the possibility of long-term cycles in populations, were viewed as irrelevant. The theoretical commitments implied by reliance on large-scale, synoptic overviews of wildlife populations, as provided by aerial surveys, also rendered irrelevant place-based indigenous knowledge.

In addition, two principles of wildlife management contradicted indigenous perspectives, rendering them invisible to biologists. One was that each resource user acts as an individual, potentially in competition with other individuals. The other was the distinction between the manager and the managed: resource users could not police themselves, but had to be regulated by an expert outside authority. Both principles were contrary to the view of resource harvesting as inseparable from the life and culture of the community.

Finally, the scientists' immediate context, within state-based northern administration, influenced their attitudes towards indigenous knowledge. By the late 1950s the fur trade had collapsed, and the federal government had concluded that the traditional Native economy was no longer viable. Instead, the future was said to lie in oil, minerals, and other resources demanded by southern markets. Wage employment would be the future for northern Natives.[18] In this new resource frontier, hunting, and knowledge tied to hunting, was seen as primitive and outdated—a vestigial remnant of former cultures, awaiting assimilation under the banner of progress and integration into the dominant culture. Consistent with this assumption, studies of the economic basis of northern communities tended to dismiss the significance of country food, while the frontier was portrayed as an empty wilderness, not a land extensively used and understood. Such a wilderness could be viewed as a resource, awaiting exploitation in the interests of the southern economy, or, alternatively, as a pristine landscape, awaiting appreciation by southern nature-lovers seeking a unique recreational and aesthetic experience. Denial of Native knowledge of the land reached an extreme expression in the relocation of many northern Natives, ostensibly to sites where more wildlife was available.[19] Nor were Native people viewed as potential contributors to the northern scientific agenda. None attended the First National Northern Research Conference in October 1967.[20]

Scientists' Use of Indigenous Knowledge

Nevertheless, within this context of marginalization, some scientists did draw on indigenous knowledge. One example is William O. Pruitt, a distinguished wildlife ecologist. In his research he used many Inuit terms to designate different types of snow. Describing the subarctic Indians and Eskimos as the "wisest instructors" on the nature of snow, he argued that their terms enabled far more precise description than was possible with English words.[21] His use of these terms supported his ambition to demonstrate the ecological significance of snow, and, more generally, to oppose the inappropriate application in the North of concepts and techniques developed in temperate regions. Instead, he sought to develop a distinctive, northern perspective on ecological science, to be known as "boreal ecology."[22] Thus, for Pruitt, indigenous knowledge, once removed from its cultural context, could contribute to northern ecology, and particularly to the development of boreal ecology as a distinct scientific specialty.

A few wildlife scientists also used indigenous knowledge. For example, polar bear researchers applied indigenous knowledge to describing bear behaviour and denning habits, and as an aid in locating dens.[23] Scientists also used Inuit observations of ringed seal behaviour. In 1975 Thomas Smith and Ian Stirling discussed Inuit words and ideas regarding seal lairs and behaviour, noted that this knowledge can be corroborated by scientific observations, and acknowledged that their Inuit assistant "still knows more about the breeding habitat of the ringed seal than we do."[24]

Scientists studying landscape history also drew on indigenous knowledge for insights. Julie Cruikshank has noted several examples, including a geographer who used Inuit testimonies as records of isostatic rebound, a glaciologist who reconstructed events surrounding the emptying of a glacier-dammed lake in the Yukon, and a dendroclimatologist who reconstructed past climates in northern Canada using Yukon traditions of a very cold summer.[25] These illustrate how scientists found value in using oral traditions as clues to an otherwise missing historical record.

These examples also illustrate how indigenous knowledge has been drawn on by scientists when it has contributed to their scientific goals, by supplying knowledge or observations not available through conventional research. They also suggest that scientists seeking to develop ideas particular to the North have been more receptive to indigenous knowledge. In contrast, researchers within disciplinary frameworks defined outside the North (such as wildlife biology), have often been less receptive to indigenous knowledge.

The Case of Anthropology

For several decades anthropologists have pursued a distinct perspective on other cultures, manifested in efforts to validate aspects of these cultures, including knowledge of nature, that had been deprecated by the dominant culture. This pattern has also been evident in northern Canada, where the most complex perceptions of northern indigenous knowledge have been those of anthropologists. There is an extensive history of such perceptions, an early and notable signpost of which was Franz Boas's recording of Inuit geographic knowledge, using maps, in his *The Central Eskimo*, based on his stay on Baffin Island in 1883–84.[26]

Anthropologists' perceptions of Native knowledge continued to develop during the twentieth century, with several, including Diamond Jenness, remarking on Native adaptability and inventiveness, as essential to survival in the harsh northern environment.[27] However, admiration for survival skills and for technology (weapons, clothing, and housing) usually did not extend to direct mention of knowledge of the environment, or to exploration of a capacity to adapt to changing conditions. Instead, anthropologists tended to adopt a static perspective, viewing indigenous knowledge as resistant to change, and accessible primarily in terms of material technology or oral traditions, amenable to collection and interpretation in terms of successive stages of cultural development.[28] Knowledge that could not be seen, touched, or expressed in words received much less attention.

Implicit in anthropologists' perspectives was the assumption that traditional knowledge was destined to be lost, as a result of the transition from Native to modern lifestyles. Between the 1940s and late 1960s much northern anthropology, including that sponsored by the federal government through the Northern Coordination and Research Centre, focused on understanding the transition to a modern, wage-based economy, and on providing advice to administrators and policy makers to facilitate this transition.[29]

However, in the 1950s anthropologists elsewhere began to develop ideas that would lead to greater interest in indigenous knowledge. In particular, they developed more awareness of how societies perceive, adapt, and relate ecologically to their environment. This was the perspective provided by cultural ecology, a field created by Julian Steward and his colleagues, which emphasized the reciprocal links between culture and environment, and placed adaptation at the centre of anthropological inquiry. Since then, ethnoscience (the study of conceptions of the world held by a people or culture) and human ecology (including study of adaptive responses to the environment) have become among the most active fields engaged in study of indigenous knowledge. In numerous fields, including agriculture, pharmacology, and botany, indigenous perspectives have been closely studied. Anthropologists also drew on ecology to construct the subfield of ethnoecology. A parallel development has been the emergence of "cognitive anthropology." Instead of fitting cultures within a pre-arranged, ethnocentric historical narrative of primitive to modern, anthropologists now seek to understand them on their own terms. Researchers in anthropology and human ecology attempt to view indigenous knowledge as part of comprehensive, holistic perspectives, embedded in complex social systems of resource use, choice, and decision making that are central to the adaptation of societies to their environment.

These trends have led many anthropologists to view indigenous knowledge, embedded in a distinctive world-view and system of ethics and actions, as part of the defining subject matter of their discipline.[30] They have also tended to develop a view of themselves as mediators, or cultural translators, between modern states and indigenous populations.

While developing an awareness of indigenous knowledge, anthropologists have also imposed a particular perspective on it. This has sometimes included a resistance to viewing it as able to change and learn. Indigenous knowledge has been contrasted with conventional science: the former closed, subject to only minor change, the latter open and able to change. Anthropologists have often insisted on this dichotomy between closed and open ways of viewing the world.[31] A second aspect of anthropologists' perspective on indigenous knowledge has been the emphasis on those components most readily recorded and passed to other parties—the hard data generated by ethnobotany and related fields. Such a perspective relies on the assumption that indigenous knowledge is empirical knowledge, rather than a way of learning about the world, transmitted not only through words, but through tacit, informed experience and practical demonstration, as well as symbols, myths, and rites.[32]

These anthropological perspectives were eventually applied to the study of northern people and their environment. A significant early work was Richard Nelson's *Hunters of the Northern Ice* (1969) (based on field work conducted in Alaska in 1964 and 1965), since described as a seminal study of Inuit knowledge and adaptation to the Arctic environment.[33] That same year, Eleanor Leacock drew attention to indigenous knowledge, noting the "prodigious knowledge" of elders, and interpreting this in terms of the availability of a variety of choices for hunting.[34]

By the late 1960s other northern researchers were applying ecological concepts to anthropology. On the Belcher Islands, Milton Freeman studied Inuit perceptions and knowledge of the environment, and how they used this knowledge in decisions about settlement and hunting. Questioning whether there can be an objective basis for evaluating the relations between Natives and wildlife (an assumption central to science-based wildlife management), he described how hunters' decisions reflected not only the actual abundance of wildlife, but their availability, as influenced by social structures, knowledge, and other aspects of culture.[35] In other research, Freeman emphasized the value of Native knowledge as a source of information on various species, regarding, for example, eider duck wintering areas, and muskox population dynamics. He also described how maps of Southampton Island demonstrated the superiority of Native knowledge of the ecology of the island over that provided by science. Freeman's work in the 1960s marked the beginning of a long and influential career in northern anthropology.

The early 1970s saw the emergence of indigenous knowledge as an active area of study in northern anthropology. Henry Lewis described the importance of fire to Native strategies for adaptation to the northern boreal forest.[36] Harvey Feit worked with the Quebec Cree, describing their knowledge of wildlife populations and other ecological phenomena, such as the importance of snow to moose behaviour, and placing this knowledge within their overall view of the world, in which animals, winds, and other aspects of nature are seen as "like persons," causality is personal, and hunting success is influenced by the hunter's previous behaviour. Feit also described how the Cree regulated their harvests by rotational hunting.[37] Julie Cruikshank's studies of the biographies and stories of elderly Athapaskan women demonstrated the importance of landscape, flora, and fauna to their knowledge; she also found a remarkable persistence and conservatism in these accounts, thereby making them more attractive to scientists and historians.[38] In British Columbia, Robin Ridington described the technical content of Native oral traditions and argued that such information serves as a critical adaptive resource for hunters. Ridington also explained how hunters and gatherers view the world as imbued with human qualities of will and purpose: that there are common understandings between hunters and game, with each knowing the other before they meet; how hunters seek to think like animals, to predict their behaviour; they study the life cycles of plants and animals, internalize detailed information about topography, seasonal changes, and mineral resources, and plan their movements in relation to this information; and that they organize and express their knowledge through dreams, songs, and stories.[39] Fikret Berkes described how subarctic fishers adapt to unpredictable fluctuations in environmental conditions and rely on both knowledge about the environment and cooperation in harvesting.[40] In the following decades Berkes would study many aspects of indigenous knowledge and community-based resource practices, in Canada and elsewhere. Finally, in northeastern British Columbia Hugh Brody described how Natives had developed particular cultures and social systems that drew on environmental knowledge and skills, particularly for hunting.[41]

Thus, northern anthropologists began in the 1970s to identify the significance of Native knowledge: its role in hunting and survival, and its place within overall world views. Their work reflected many of the intellectual currents that had begun to emerge in anthropology during the 1950s: an interest in adaptation, in understanding human–environment relations from the perspective of the people themselves, and in research methods that involved listening and participating in activities and experiences. As an active outpost of the anthropology discipline, northern Canada became a site for exploring and applying ideas developed within cultural ecology, ethnoscience, and other branches of anthropology.[42] In exploring Native perceptions and relations to the environment, northern anthropologists, like their colleagues elsewhere, also asserted a role as cultural translators, demonstrating the value of indigenous knowledge, as a baseline or supplement to conventional science; and, increasingly, as a resource for Native land claims.

By the late 1970s a diversity of views on indigenous knowledge were evident within the northern scientific community. While some anthropologists were devoting considerable study to it (as an alternative source of information about the northern environment, or as an entire world view, incorporating social and spiritual as well as empirical dimensions), wildlife biologists (like other scientists) still tended to dismiss any forms of knowledge that had not been generated by the scientific community. This diversity reflected the barriers between disciplines within the scientific community, and the absence of any single "scientific" perspective on indigenous knowledge.

During the 1970s, however, some of these barriers began to break down, and a wider awareness of indigenous knowledge outside anthropology developed. In this, the evolving politics of northern science played a major role.

Environmental and Land Claims Controversies

Northern environmental politics were reshaped by the intensive search for oil and gas that began after the discovery of petroleum in Alaska in 1968. Large-scale efforts in environmental science accompanied this exploration activity, initially by the private sector, and, by the early 1970s, by the federal government. To adhere to land-use and environmental assessment requirements for proposed production and pipeline facilities, oil and gas companies financed dozens of studies of the northern environment. The federal government conducted its own studies, increasingly through direct cooperation with the private sector. However, this research effort usually failed to acknowledge indigenous knowledge. In part, this reflected the overall ideology of northern development: the image of the North as an empty resource frontier was antithetical to the notion of an already occupied and appreciated homeland. More specifically, northern environmental research (like wildlife science) was conducted primarily by university or government scientists (or, increasingly, by consultants), trained in the south, writing for southern audiences, and addressing southern theoretical and practical concerns.

By the early 1970s the impacts of industry on northern ecosystems had also become the focus of national controversy. In this controversy, however, issues tended to be framed in terms of southern scientific concepts. Ecologists advocating environmental protection used ecological theory to support their arguments, and especially the view that relatively simple northern ecosystems were especially fragile and susceptible to damage. This invocation of the authority of science in environmental controversies tended to marginalize other forms of knowledge, and particularly indigenous knowledge. The environmental concerns of southerners contributed to this marginalization. Southerners tended to see the North as a "largely undisturbed" or "almost untouched" wilderness of wild rivers and free-roaming caribou; such views could not readily acknowledge forms of knowledge grounded in using, not preserving, the land.

Northern Native Self-Determination

A third development, and the most significant in terms of scientists' attitudes towards indigenous knowledge, was the increasing weight of Natives in northern politics, expressed through demands for greater self-determination. By the early 1970s Native organizations had begun building the basis for land claims. Because an effective negotiating position required establishing that certain lands had long been occupied by Natives, there arose a demand for anthropologists to do studies of land use and occupancy. In Quebec, negotiations for the James Bay Agreement required documentation of Native land use and knowledge, drawing on information provided by hunters, trappers, and other land users, as well as assessment of the impact of the James Bay power project on Native ways of life.[43] This research drew on anthropologists' experience in the James Bay region, gained through McGill University's Cree Developmental Change Project, established in 1964.[44] In the Northwest Territories the Inuit Land Use and Occupancy Study, initiated in 1973 and directed by Milton Freeman, also used map biographies and other techniques to document land use.[45] Such techniques served not so much to accurately represent the cultural dimensions of Native knowledge, but as a means of translating this knowledge into a format suited to the requirements of land claims negotiations.

Land use and occupancy studies showed (to the surprise of some) that northern land and waters remained of crucial importance to Native communities, as a basis for both material well-being and cultural strength.[46] More generally, land use research, harvest studies, and anthropological accounts of indigenous knowledge challenged the strictly biological perspective on renewable resources and impacts of industrialization that had provided the basis for decision making. This research also had an impact on anthropology. It introduced some anthropologists (including Hugh Brody, who participated in the Inuit land use study) to the study of Native knowledge, influencing their future careers. It also enabled anthropologists to reach a larger audience, beyond their own discipline, and encouraged them to assert a role as intermediaries between Native communities and the rest of society, introducing the concept of "advocacy anthropology": scientists working for the rights of Native peoples.[47] However, Native distrust of researchers, and a desire to speak directly, without mediation, to the dominant society has generated active resistance to this role, posing new challenges and uncertainties for anthropologists.[48]

Other events and developments in the North have also influenced perspectives on indigenous knowledge. Justice Thomas Berger's Mackenzie Valley Pipeline Inquiry (1974-1977) focused national attention on Natives and their land. Travelling to virtually every community within the region, listening to all who wished to speak about the proposed pipeline or any other aspect of the North, and then stressing the significance of Native knowledge in his recommendations, Berger brought this knowledge to a much wider audience.[49] At the same time, while his report raised awareness of the value of indigenous knowledge, scientists' reaction, particularly to his discussion of the impacts of development and the future role of renewable resources in the northern economy, exposed a continuing skepticism.[50]

In the 1970s another factor began to influence attitudes towards indigenous knowledge, albeit indirectly. The expansion of research during this decade led to resentment among northerners, as scientists often failed to establish any real connection with, or provide any benefits to, northern communities. Scientists would fly in, take measurements, and fly out, without explaining to those living nearby what they were up to. Such methods gained the pejorative label of "helicopter science." Science also shared in increasingly negative attitudes towards federal agencies. In particular, the Department of Indian Affairs and Northern Development lost credibility because of its centralized structure, its failure to consult, and its encouragement of development regardless of impacts on communities or the environment. This loss of credibility affected science, because science came to be seen as simply a tool of government—an instrument of outside authority, unaccountable to northerners.

In response, territorial governments and northern communities asserted a stronger role in influencing scientific research, through guidelines, licences, and other measures.[51] New agencies appeared, such as the Science Institute of the Northwest Territories (now the Aurora Institute), as well as, eventually, processes within land claims settlement areas for review of applications for research licences. Beyond reporting and employment requirements, communities began to insist that their own knowledge be incorporated into research. Thus, scientists increasingly found that to obtain permission to do northern research, they had to demonstrate some awareness of Native knowledge.

Evolving Attitudes towards Science

During the 1970s and 1980s attitudes towards indigenous knowledge were influenced not only by political developments, but by changing views on northern science itself. For the first time, indigenous knowledge was compared directly against the predictions of science. Often the encounter led to diminished confidence in science and more credibility for indigenous knowledge.

One such encounter involved the Beverly/Kaminuriak caribou herd. In the late 1970s biologists claimed that the herd had been severely depleted and was now in "crisis." In contrast, Inuit argued that the population was actually much larger. When in 1982 more extensive surveys were conducted, the Inuit position was confirmed by new, higher population estimates.[52] This experience shook biologists' confidence and made them more open to the possibility that factors other than hunting or wolves (such as population cycles) could influence caribou populations.[53] Since then, the long-term accumulation of indigenous knowledge of caribou (by, for example, Michael Ferguson, who has collected Inuit knowledge on Baffin Island since 1983), has increased the credibility of this knowledge among wildlife biologists, helping to shift their attitude from one of denial, to acknowledgement, to acceptance.[54] Closer working relationships within cooperative resource management institutions such as the Beverly-Kaminuriak Caribou Management Board have also encouraged biologists to recognize the value of hunters' knowledge.[55]

Similar episodes, such as one in which Inuit hunters provided far more accurate estimates of bowhead whale populations than did scientists, have also been influential.[56] Much of the Inuit success in estimating whale populations reflected a better understanding of whale behaviour: where they travel, and when. This is a reflection of how Native knowledge of whales, caribou, muskox, and other species has, historically, drawn much more than has science on observations of behaviour. Biologists have often failed to incorporate behaviour into their understanding of population dynamics, and in fact Native knowledge was seen as less credible because of its emphasis on behaviour. Once, on the other hand, biologists were forced by empirical success to include behaviour in their understanding of wildlife, this removed another impediment to their acceptance of indigenous knowledge. Empirical success also encouraged biologists to be receptive to other results generated by indigenous knowledge, such as the possibility that caribou herds are not geographical but biological units, lacking close ties to specific calving grounds.[57] Overall, indigenous knowledge has provided, for scientists, an increasingly significant alternative to accepted views of how nature works. Most convincing was its empirical success, particularly when accompanied by awareness of the uncertainties embedded within their own science. As Fred Roots, one of the most experienced Canadian Arctic experts of the last fifty years noted in 1981, "It is a truism to say that one of the most underutilized sources of information in many vital areas of Arctic development is the accumulated practical knowledge that the Inuit possess.... Southerners who have worked or studied in the Arctic for many years and know it well are those most conscious of the soundness and depth of traditional knowledge."[58]

However, there have been limits to how far biologists would go in accepting indigenous knowledge. In particular, a distinction was often drawn between the knowledge required to find and kill game, and that required to ensure its sustainable use. While scientists readily accepted the former, they were more reluctant to acknowledge the latter: hunters may accumulate large amounts of empirical data, and possess a finely honed instinct of how, say, caribou will behave in certain situations, but that did not mean this knowledge could be integrated into a management strategy. These views of scientists were affected by their own contexts, especially characteristics of their research sites. For example, the eastern Cree, with small family-owned territories and restricted ranges, were seen as possessing the strongest evidence of self-regulation.[59] Accounts of their regulatory practices provided in the 1970s by Feit and Berkes undoubtedly encouraged wider acceptance of this evidence.

Beyond northern Canada, developments in other areas of environmental science also influenced how scientists would view indigenous knowledge. For example, in the 1970s scientists seeking a more effective connection between science and management—which could incorporate an acknowledgement of the incompleteness of scientific knowledge and of the possibility of "surprises"—developed the concept of adaptive management.[60] Its principle of a close, supportive relationship between science and management has been interpreted by some scientists as consistent with indigenous knowledge, because it breaks down the distinction, basic to conventional resource management, between learning about a resource, and using it. Interest in indigenous knowledge has also been generated by a desire for critiques of, and alternatives to, Western science. Fritjof Capra, for example, has suggested that indigenous knowledge contains an "intuitive wisdom" about the world. In effect, critiques of science, or even of modern society, have been projected onto indigenous knowledge, now designated as a source of new environmental attitudes for Western society, creating the phenomenon, examined by Shepard Krech, of the "ecological Indian."[61] The tendency of Western society to sometimes make uncritical assumptions about the environmental wisdom of Native peoples is epitomized by the acceptance of exaggerated versions of Chief Seattle's speech regarding respect for nature.[62] The status of indigenous knowledge is as much a political as a scientific matter, involving not just questions of reliability and commensurability, but of power and authority. This is one reason why it can be so contentious. This was evident in the early 1990s when the environmental assessment process for BHP's diamond mine in the Northwest Territories mandated "full and equal consideration" of indigenous knowledge alongside scientific knowledge. A variety of difficulties ensued, including the short period of time available for collecting data, the ambiguous meaning of "full and equal," given the absence of standards for indigenous knowledge, and the Dene's desire to maintain control over their intellectual property. These challenges, in turn, provoked debate on the value of indigenous knowledge. Albert Howard and Frances Widdowson began this debate, claiming that traditional knowledge is a threat to environmental assessment, because it relies on a spiritual rather than a scientific perspective on nature. While several respondents demonstrated convincingly that Howard and Widdowson's claims were based on a misunderstanding of both conventional science and indigenous knowledge, the episode demonstrated that re-negotiating the status of indigenous knowledge remains a major political challenge in northern Canada.[63]

Conclusions

Indigenous knowledge and science in northern Canada share a long and complex history. From initial reliance by scientists on it for survival and as an adjunct to natural history observations, indigenous knowledge was then eclipsed, rendered near-invisible by a scientific community intent on developing modern, capital-intensive research. More recently, scientists have become increasingly aware of the value of indigenous knowledge. But this awareness has tended to reflect the concerns and priorities of the scientists themselves, such as the disciplinary evolution of anthropology, or the ambition to develop the distinctive discipline of boreal ecology, or the need for empirical data on wildlife populations.

Scientists' perceptions of indigenous knowledge have also been influenced by wider developments. Especially important has been the increasing political weight of Natives in northern politics (particularly through land claims settlements) and accompanying requirements for greater attention to indigenous knowledge, in a variety of contexts. Changing views of the North, and its place in Canada, have also been significant: as an "empty" resource frontier, a "pristine" wilderness, or a Native homeland.

Another factor in changing attitudes towards indigenous knowledge has been changing attitudes towards science. This has been stimulated, in part, by practical experience in environmental and other controversies, in which scientific knowledge has been seen to be something other than simply objective knowledge of nature: as, rather, the product of negotiations between scientists, and their patrons and other interests. Many historians and sociologists of science have also demonstrated how science is a complex amalgam of practical skills, technical devices, theory, and social strategies intimately tied to its wider political, social, and institutional contexts.[64]

One implication of this account for contemporary discussion of the relation between science and indigenous knowledge is that it is necessary to revise the view of "science" as a unitary category. Science is heterogeneous, exhibiting a range of attitudes towards indigenous knowledge, reflecting diverse disciplinary perspectives and political and managerial contexts. While some scientists have tended to dismiss it, others have applied it to their own purposes, and a few have studied it within its cultural context. And while "science" and "indigenous knowledge" have often been described in isolation, over the last century their histories have become interwoven. Particularly in the last two decades, science in northern Canada—both its practice and its empirical content—has been increasingly influenced by indigenous knowledge.

This heterogeneity obviously reflects significant differences between the perspectives of scientists, such as wildlife biologists, who evaluated indigenous knowledge as being of no value, and the perspectives of those who have seen it as important and useful. There are, however, common elements.

First, strategies of rejection and of acceptance of indigenous knowledge both illustrate ways in which scientists define the boundary between their knowledge and other ways of understanding the world. This process of definition, sometimes referred to as "boundary work," constitutes a major way by which scientists assert their authority as sources of reliable knowledge.[65] Those seeking to dismiss indigenous knowledge draw this boundary so as to exclude all forms of it from science, often by noting its anecdotal nature, its incompleteness, or its inaccuracy (as evaluated by comparison with scientific knowledge), or by emphasizing its spiritual dimensions. In contrast, scientists accepting of indigenous knowledge tend to emphasize those aspects, such as taxonomic classifications or behavioural information, that can be most readily understood in scientific terms. In effect, they redraw the boundary between science and non-science to include those aspects of indigenous knowledge that have meaning within the scientific tradition, while excluding other aspects, such as spiritual values, that do not.

These strategies of boundary work illustrate something else that is shared by those who rejected, and those who accepted, indigenous knowledge: the asymmetrical relationship between science and indigenous knowledge, in which the latter is evaluated in terms of criteria established by the former, particularly empirical accuracy (that is, fidelity to the results provided by scientists).[66] This asymmetry is closely tied to current controversies about the application of indigenous knowledge in contexts other than those in which it originated.[67] Just as scientists tend to recognize only those aspects of indigenous knowledge that can be understood in terms of their own disciplines, so too do environmental management agencies prefer to draw on those aspects that can be expressed using the familiar tools of management (such as geographic information systems), while institutions of national and international environmental governance seek to apply indigenous knowledge on scales far larger than the local level at which they originated, and pharmaceutical firms recognize only those aspects of indigenous knowledge that are relevant to identifying medicinal plants with commercial possibilities. In a variety of ways, indigenous knowledge has been routinely reshaped, reified, and detached from its contexts to meet the requirements of dominant institutions.

Notes

1 Many terms are used to refer to the knowledge of Native peoples: *indigenous knowledge, naturalized knowledge systems, traditional ecological knowledge*, and so on. As one of the more widely used terms, *indigenous knowledge*, will be used in this paper. Its use does not imply a particular position in the debates over the relative merits of these terms.

2 Discussions of indigenous knowledge in northern Canada from various social science perspectives include Fikret Berkes, "Indigenous Knowledge and Resource Management Systems in the Canadian Subarctic," in *Link-*

ing Social and Ecological Systems: Management Practices and Social Mechanisms for Building Resistance, ed. Fikret Berkes and Carl Folke (Cambridge: Cambridge University Press, 1998), 98–128; F. Duerden and R.G. Kuhn, "Scale, Context, and Application of Traditional Knowledge of the Canadian North," *Polar Record* 34 (1998): 31–38; M.G. Stevenson, "Indigenous Knowledge in Environmental Assessment," *Arctic* 49, 3 (1996): 278–91; Peter J. Usher, "Traditional Ecological Knowledge in Environmental Assessment and Management," *Arctic* 53, 2 (2000): 183–93; George Wenzel, "Traditional Ecological Knowledge and Inuit Reflections on TEK Research and Ethics," *Arctic* 52, 2 (1999): 113–24.

3 Richard H. Grove, *Green Imperialism: Colonial Expansion, Tropical Island Edens and the Origins of Environmentalism, 1600–1860* (Cambridge: Cambridge University Press, 1995).

4 Julie Cruikshank, "Oral Tradition and Scientific Research: Approaches to Knowledge in the North," *Social Science in the North: Communicating Northern Values*, 3–23 (Ottawa: ACUNS, Occ. Stud. 9, 1984); W.L. Morton, "The 'North' in Canadian Historiography, *Royal Society Canada, Trans.* Series 4, vol. 8 (1970): 31–40; Berkes, "Indigenous Knowledge."

5 C. Bart, "On the Wing to the Arctic: Canada's Lesser Snow Geese," *Nature Canada* 6, 3 (1977): 33–38.

6 A.E. Porsild, "Mammals of the Mackenzie Delta," *Canadian Field-Naturalist* 59 (1945): 4–22.

7 Shelagh D. Grant, *Sovereignty or Security? Government Policy in the Canadian North 1936–1950* (Vancouver: University of British Columbia Press, 1988).

8 John P. Kelsall, *The Migratory Barren-Ground Caribou of Canada* (Ottawa: CWS, 1968); Charles R. Harington, "Polar Bear Study: East Coast of Baffin Island, 1961," *Arctic Circular* 15, 2 (1962): 21–24.

9 Frederick K. Hare, "Mapping of Physiography and Vegetation in Labrador-Ungava: A Review of Reconnaissance Methods," *Canadian Geography* 5 (1955): 17–28.

10 Kelsall, *Migratory Barren-Ground Caribou*, 147.

11 Ibid., 209.

12 Ibid., 17.

13 D.C. Thomas, "Population Estimates and Distribution of Barren-Ground Caribou in Mackenzie District, Northwest Territories, Saskatchewan, and Alberta—March to May, 1967," *CWS Report No. 9*, 1969; F.L. Miller and E. Broughton, "Calf Mortality on the Calving Ground of Kaminuriak Caribou, during 1970" (Ottawa: Canadian Wildlife Service, 1974).

14 D.M. Dickinson and T.B. Herman, *Management of Some Terrestrial Mammals in the Northwest Territories for Sustained Yields* (NWT Science Advisory Board, 1979); George W. Calef, *The Population Status of Caribou in the Northwest Territories.* (NWT Wildlife Service, 1979); Lorraine Allison, "Cari-

bou: Management of a Vital Resource," *Northern Perspectives* 6, 3 (1978): 5–8.

15 A.H. Macpherson, "Commentary: Wildlife Conservation and Canada's North." *Arctic* 34, 2 (1981): 103–107; John B. Theberge, "Commentary: Conservation in the North; An Ecological Perspective," *Arctic* 34, 4 (1981): 281–85; George W. Calef, *Caribou and the Barren-lands*, (Ottawa/Willowdale: CARC/Firefly Books, 1981).

16 N.M. Simmons, D.C. Heard, and G.W. Calef, "Kaminuriak Caribou Herd: Interjurisdictional Management Problems," *North American Wildlife and Natural Resources Conference* 44th, March 24–28, 1979.

17 Milton M.R. Freeman, "Traditional Land Users as a Legitimate Source of Environmental Expertise," in *The Canadian National Parks: Today and Tomorrow Conference II: Ten Years Later*, ed. James Nelson, et al., vol. 1 (Waterloo: University of Waterloo, 1979).

18 David Judd, "Canada's Northern Policy: Retrospect and Prospect," *Polar Record* 14 (1969): 593–602.

19 James Smith and Ernest S. Burch, "Chipewyan and Inuit in the Central Canadian Subarctic, 1613–1977," *Arctic Anthropology* 16, 2 (1977): 76–101; Frank J. Tester and Peter Kulchyski, *Tammarniit (Mistakes): Inuit Relocation in the Eastern Arctic, 1939–63* (Vancouver: University of British Columbia Press, 1994); Alan R. Marcus, *Relocating Eden: The Image and Politics of Inuit Exile in the Canadian Arctic* (Hanover: University Press of New England, 1995).

20 Walter O. Kupsch, ed., *Proceedings, First National Northern Research Conference, Saskatoon, October 30, 31, 1967* (Saskatoon: University of Saskatchewan, 1968).

21 Quoted in William O. Pruitt, "Life in the Snow," *Nature Canada* 4, 4 (1975): 40–44.

22 William O. Pruitt, *Boreal Ecology* (London: Edward Arnold, 1978).

23 Charles R. Harington, "Denning Habits of the Polar Bear (*Ursus maritimus Phipps*)," *CWS Report* 5 (1968); R.H. Russell, "The Food Habits of Polar Bears of James Bay and Southwest Hudson Bay in Summer and Autumn," *Arctic* 28 (1975): 117–29; Charles Jonkel, "The Present Status of the Polar Bear in the James Bay and Belcher Islands Area," *CWS Occasional Paper* 26 (1976).

24 Thomas G. Smith and I. Stirling, "The Breeding Habitat of the Ringed Seal (*Phoca hispida*): The Birth Lair and Associated Structures," *Canadian Journal of Zoology* 53 (1975): 1297–1305.

25 Julie Cruikshank, "Legend and Landscape: Convergence of Oral and Scientific Traditions in the Yukon Territory," *Arctic Anthropology* 18, 2 (1981): 67–93.

26 Franz Boas, *The Central Eskimo: Sixth Annual Report of the Bureau of American Ethnology for the Years 1884–1885* (Washington, DC: Smithsonian Institution, 1888), 399–669.

27 D. Jenness, "The Canadian Eskimo," in *The Unbelievable Land*, ed. I. Norman Smith (Ottawa: Queen's Printer, 1964), 6–14. Jim Lotz, "Social Science Research and Northern Development," *Arctic* 21, 4 (1968): 291–94.

28 Asen Balikci, "Ethnography and Theory in the Canadian Arctic," *Études/Inuit/Studies* 13, 2 (1989): 103–11.

29 Victor F. Valentine, "Anthropology," *The Unbelievable Land*, ed. I.N. Smith (Ottawa: Queen's Printer), 45–48; Charles C. Hughes, "History of Ethnology after 1945," *Handbook of North American Indians*, ed. David Damas (Washington: Smithsonian Institution, 1984), 5:23–26.

30 Ralph D. Grillo, "Discourses of Development: The View from Anthropology," in *Discourses of Development: Anthropological Perspectives*, eds. Ralph D. Grillo and R.L. Stirrat (Oxford: Berg, 1997), 1–33; Paul Sillitoe, "The Development of Indigenous Knowledge: A New Applied Anthropology," *Current Anthropology* 39, 2 (1998): 223–52.

31 Arun Agrawal, "Dismantling the Divide between Indigenous and Scientific Knowledge," *Development and Change* 26 (1995): 413–39.

32 Sillitoe, "Development of Indigenous Knowledge."

33 Richard K. Nelson, *Hunters of the Northern Ice* (Chicago: University of Chicago Press, 1969); Wenzel, "Traditional Ecological Knowledge."

34 E. Leacock, "The Montagnais–Naskapi Band," in *Contributions to Anthropology: Band Societies*, ed. David Damas (Ottawa: National Museum, Bulletin 228, 1969).

35 Milton M.R. Freeman, "An Ecological Study of Mobility and Settlement Patterns among the Belcher Island Eskimo," *Arctic* 20, 3 (1967): 154–75.

36 Henry T. Lewis, "Maskuta: The Ecology of Indian Fires in Northern Alberta," *Western Canadian Journal of Anthropology* 7 (1977): 15–52.

37 Harvey A. Feit, "The Ethno-Ecology of the Waswanipi Cree; or How Hunters Can Manage Their Resources," in *Cultural Ecology: Readings on Canadian Indians and Eskimos*, ed. Bruce Cox (Toronto: McClelland and Stewart, 1973), 115–25; Harvey A. Feit, "Self-Management and State-Management: Forms of Knowing and Managing Northern Wildlife," in *Traditional Knowledge and Renewable Resource Management in Northern Regions*, ed. Milton M.R. Freeman and Ludwig N. Carbyn (Edmonton: Boreal Institute for Northern Studies, 1988), 72–91.

38 Cruikshank, "Legend and Landscape."

39 Robin Ridington, "Technology, World View, and Adaptive Strategy in a Northern Hunting Society," *Canadian Review of Sociology and Anthropology* 19, 4 (1982): 469–81.

40 Fikret Berkes, "Fishery Resource Use in a Subarctic Indian Community," *Human Ecology* 5, 4 (1977): 289–307.

41 Hugh Brody, *Maps and Dreams: Indians and the British Columbia Frontier* (Vancouver: Douglas and McIntyre, 1981).

42 Balikci, "Ethnography and Theory"; Wenzel, "Traditional Ecological Knowledge."

43 IRRC/AINA, *Circumpolar Aboriginal People and Co-Management Practice: Current Issues in Co-Management and Environmental Assessment* (Calgary: AINA, 1996); Ernest S. Burch, "The Ethnography of Northern North America: A Guide to Recent Research," *Arctic Anthropology* 16, 1 (1979): 62–146.

44 Edward J. Hedican, *Applied Anthropology in Canada: Understanding Aboriginal Issues* (Toronto: University of Toronto Press, 1995).

45 Milton M.R. Freeman, et al., *Inuit Land Use and Occupancy Project* (Ottawa, 1976).

46 Brody, *Maps and Dreams.*

47 George Wenzel, *Animal Rights, Human Rights: Ecology, Economy and Ideology in the Canadian Arctic* (Toronto: University of Toronto Press, 1991).

48 Michael Asch, "Indigenous Self-determination and Applied Anthropology in Canada: Finding a Place to Stand," *Anthropologica* 43 (2001): 201–20.

49 Thomas R. Berger, *Northern Frontier, Northern Homeland: The Report of the Mackenzie Valley Pipeline Inquiry* (Ottawa, 1977); Paul Sabin, "Voices from the Hydrocarbon Frontier: Canada's Mackenzie Valley Pipeline Inquiry (1974-1977)," *Environmental History Review* 19, 1 (1995): 17–48.

50 Lawrence C. Bliss, "The Report of the Mackenzie Valley Pipeline Inquiry, Volume 2: An Environmental Critique," *Musk-Ox* 21 (1978): 28–33, 34–38.

51 Association of Canadian Universities for Northern Studies, "Ethical Principles for the Conduct of Research in the North."

52 Milton M.R. Freeman, "Graphs and Gaffs: A Cautionary Tale in the Common-Property Resources Debate," in *Common Property Resources: Ecology and Community-Based Sustainable Development*, ed. Fikret Berkes (London: Belhaven Press, 1989), 92–109.

53 E. Tennenhouse, *Caribou Protection Measures for the Beverly and Kaminuriak Caribou Herds* (NWT. Department of Renewable Resources, 1968); Roderick Riewe and L. Gamble, "The Inuit and Wildlife Management Today," in *Traditional Knowledge and Renewable Resource Management in Northern Regions*, ed. Milton M.R. Freeman and Ludwig N. Carbyn (Edmonton: Boreal Institute for Northern Studies, 1988), 31–37.

54 M.A. Ferguson, R.G. Williamson, and F. Messier, "Inuit Knowledge of Long-term Changes in a Population of Arctic Tundra Caribou," *Arctic* 51, 3 (1998): 201–19.

55 Peter Cizek, "The Beverly-Kaminuriak Caribou Management Board: A Case Study of Aboriginal Participation in Resource Management" (Ottawa: Canadian Arctic Resources Committee, 1990).

56 "Breaking the Ice," CBC *Ideas*, September 21, 1995.

57 Ferguson, et al., "Inuit Knowledge."

58 Quoted in Milton M.R. Freeman, "Ethnoscience, Prevailing Science, and Arctic Co-operation," *Canadian Papers in Peace Studies* 3 (1992): 90.

59 Peter J. Usher, "Indigenous Management Systems and the Conservation of Wildlife in the Canadian North," *Alternatives* 14, 1 (1987): 3–9.
60 Carl Walters, *Adaptive Management of Renewable Resources* (New York: Macmillan, 1986).
61 Shepard Krech, *The Ecological Indian: Myth and History* (New York: W.W. Norton, 1999).
62 Fikret Berkes, *Sacred Ecology: Traditional Ecological Knowledge and Resource Management* (Philadelphia: Taylor and Francis, 1999), 147–48.
63 A. Howard and F. Widdowson, "Traditional Knowledge Threatens Environmental Assessment," *Policy Options* 17, 9 (1996): 34–36; Stevenson, "Indigenous Knowledge"; Fikret Berkes and T. Henley, "Co-Management and Traditional Knowledge: Threat or Opportunity?" *Policy Options* 18, 2 (1997): 29–31.
64 Bruno Latour, *Pandora's Hope: Essays on the Reality of Science Studies* (Cambridge: Harvard University Press, 1999).
65 Thomas F. Gieryn, *Cultural Boundaries of Science: Credibility on the Line* (Chicago: University of Chicago Press, 1999).
66 Michael T. Bravo, "The Accuracy of Ethnoscience: A Study of Inuit Cartography and Cross-Cultural Commensurability," *Manchester Papers in Social Anthropology* 2 (1996).
67 Julie Cruickshank, *The Social Life of Stories: Narrative and Knowledge in the Yukon Territory* (Lincoln: University of Nebraska Press, 1998).

Bibliography

Agrawal, Arun. "Dismantling the Divide between Indigenous and Scientific Knowledge." *Development and Change* 26 (1995): 413–39.

Allison, Lorraine. "Caribou: Management of a Vital Resource." *Northern Perspectives* 6, 3 (1978): 5–8.

Asch, Michael. "Indigenous Self-determination and Applied Anthropology in Canada: Finding a Place to Stand." *Anthropologica* 43 (2001): 201–20.

Association of Canadian Universities for Northern Studies, "Ethical Principles for the Conduct of Research in the North."

Balikci, Asen. "Ethnography and Theory in the Canadian Arctic." *Études/Inuit/Studies* 13, 2 (1989): 103–11.

Bart, C. "On the Wing to the Arctic: Canada's Lesser Snow Geese." *Nature Canada* 6, 3 (1977): 33–38.

Berger, Thomas R. *Northern Frontier, Northern Homeland: The Report of the Mackenzie Valley Pipeline Inquiry.* Ottawa, 1977.

Berkes, Fikret. "Fishery Resource Use in a Subarctic Indian Community." *Human Ecology* 5, 4 (1977): 289–307.

——— . "Indigenous Knowledge and Resource Management Systems in the Canadian Subarctic." In *Linking Social and Ecological Systems: Management Practices and Social Mechanisms for Building Resistance.* Ed. Fikret Berkes and Carl Folke, 98–128. Cambridge: Cambridge University Press, 1998.

——— . *Sacred Ecology: Traditional Ecological Knowledge and Resource Management.* Philadelphia: Taylor and Francis, 1999.

Berkes, Fikret, and T. Henley. "Co-Management and Traditional Knowledge: Threat or Opportunity?" *Policy Options* 18, 2 (1997): 29–31.

Bliss, Lawrence C. "The Report of the Mackenzie Valley Pipeline Inquiry, Volume 2: An Environmental Critique," *Musk-Ox* 21 (1978): 28–33, 34–38.

Boas, Franz. *The Central Eskimo: Sixth Annual Report of the Bureau of American Ethnology for the Years 1884–1885.* Washington, DC: Smithsonian Institution, 1888, 399–669.

Bocking, Stephen. *Ecologists and Environmental Politics: A History of Contemporary Ecology.* New Haven: Yale University Press, 1997.

Bravo, Michael T. "The Accuracy of Ethnoscience: A Study of Inuit Cartography and Cross-Cultural Commensurability." *Manchester Papers in Social Anthropology* 2 (1996).

"Breaking the Ice," CBC *Ideas*, September 21, 1995.

Brody, Hugh. *Maps and Dreams: Indians and the British Columbia Frontier.* Vancouver: Douglas and McIntyre, 1981.

Burch, Ernest S. "The Ethnography of Northern North America: A Guide to Recent Research." *Arctic Anthropology* 16, 1 (1979): 62–146.

Calef, George W. *Caribou and the Barren-lands.* Ottawa/Willowdale: CARC/Firefly, 1981.

——— . *The Population Status of Caribou in the Northwest Territories.* NWT Wildlife Service, 1979.

Cizek, Peter. "The Beverly-Kaminuriak Caribou Management Board: A Case Study of Aboriginal Participation in Resource Management." Ottawa: Canadian Arctic Resources Committee, 1990.

Cruikshank, Julie. "Legend and Landscape: Convergence of Oral and Scientific Traditions in the Yukon Territory." *Arctic Anthropology* 18, 2 (1981): 67–93.

——— . "Oral Tradition and Scientific Research: Approaches to Knowledge in the North." *Social Science in the North: Communicating Northern Values*, 3–23. Ottawa: ACUNS, Occ. Stud. 9, 1984.

——— . *The Social Life of Stories: Narrative and Knowledge in the Yukon Territory.* Lincoln: University of Nebraska Press, 1998.

Dickinson, D.M., and T.B. Herman. *Management of Some Terrestrial Mammals in the Northwest Territories for Sustained Yields.* NWT Science Advisory Board, 1979.

Duerden, F., and R.G. Kuhn. "Scale, Context, and Application of Traditional Knowledge of the Canadian North." *Polar Record* 34 (1998): 31–38.

"Ethical Principles for the Conduct of Research in the North." Association of Canadian Universities for Northern Studies Occasional Publication, 7, 1982.

Feit, Harvey A. "The Ethno-Ecology of the Waswanipi Cree; or How Hunters Can Manage Their Resources." In *Cultural Ecology: Readings on Canadian Indians and Eskimos.* Ed. Bruce Cox, 115–25. Toronto: McClelland and Stewart, 1973.

——— . "Self-Management and State-Management: Forms of Knowing and Managing Northern Wildlife." In *Traditional Knowledge and Renewable Resource Management in Northern Regions.* Ed. Milton M.R. Freeman and Ludwig N. Carbyn, 72–91. Edmonton: Boreal Institute for Northern Studies, 1988.

Ferguson, M.A., R.G. Williamson, and F. Messier. "Inuit Knowledge of Long-term Changes in a Population of Arctic Tundra Caribou." *Arctic* 51, 3 (1998): 201–19.

Freeman, Milton M.R. "An Ecological Study of Mobility and Settlement Patterns among the Belcher Island Eskimo." *Arctic* 20, 3 (1967): 154–75.

——— . "Ethnoscience, Prevailing Science, and Arctic Co-operation." *Canadian Papers in Peace Studies* 3 (1992): 79–93.

——— . "Graphs and Gaffs: A Cautionary Tale in the Common-Property Resources Debate." In *Common Property Resources: Ecology and Community-Based Sustainable Development.* Ed. Fikret Berkes, 92–109. London: Belhaven Press, 1989.

——— , et al. *Inuit Land Use and Occupancy Project.* Ottawa, 1976.

——— . "Traditional Land Users as a Legitimate Source of Environmental Expertise." In *The Canadian National Parks: Today and Tomorrow Conference II; Ten Years Later.* Vol. 1. Ed. James Nelson, et al., 345–61. Waterloo: University of Waterloo Press, 1979.

Gieryn, Thomas F. *Cultural Boundaries of Science: Credibility on the Line.* Chicago: University of Chicago Press, 1999.

Grant, Shelagh D. *Sovereignty or Security? Government Policy in the Canadian North 1936–1950.* Vancouver: University of British Columbia Press, 1988.

Grillo, Ralph D. "Discourses of Development: The View from Anthropology." In *Discourses of Development: Anthropological Perspectives.* Ed. Ralph D. Grillo and R.L. Stirrat, 1–33. Oxford: Berg, 1997.

Grove, Richard H. *Green Imperialism: Colonial Expansion, Tropical Island Edens and the Origins of Environmentalism, 1600–1860.* Cambridge: Cambridge University Press, 1995.

Hare, Frederick K. "Mapping of Physiography and Vegetation in Labrador-Ungava: A Review of Reconnaissance Methods." *Canadian Geography* 5 (1955): 17–28.

Harington, Charles R. "Denning Habits of the Polar Bear (Ursus maritimus Phipps)." *cws Report* 5 (1968).

———. "Polar Bear Study: East Coast of Baffin Island, 1961." *Arctic Circular* 15, 2 (1962): 21–24.

Hedican, Edward J. *Applied Anthropology in Canada: Understanding Aboriginal Issues.* Toronto: University of Toronto Press, 1995.

Howard, A., and F. Widdowson. "Traditional Knowledge Threatens Environmental Assessment." *Policy Options* 17, 9 (1996): 34–36.

Hughes, Charles C. "History of Ethnology after 1945." In *Handbook of North American Indians.* Vol. 5. Ed. David Damas, 23–26. Washington, DC: Smithsonian Institution, 1984.

IRRC/AINA. *Circumpolar Aboriginal People and Co-Management Practice: Current Issues in Co-Management and Environmental Assessment.* Calgary: AINA, 1996.

Jenness, D. "The Canadian Eskimo." In *The Unbelievable Land.* Ed. I. Norman Smith, 6–14. Ottawa: Queen's Printer, 1964.

Jonkel, Charles, et al. "The Present Status of the Polar Bear in the James Bay and Belcher Islands Area." *cws Occasional Paper* 26 (1976).

Judd, David. "Canada's Northern Policy: Retrospect and Prospect." *Polar Record* 14 (1969): 593–602.

Kelsall, John P. *The Migratory Barren-Ground Caribou of Canada.* Ottawa: cws, 1968.

Krech, Shepard. *The Ecological Indian: Myth and History.* New York: W.W. Norton, 1999.

Kupsch, Walter O., ed. *Proceedings, First National Northern Research Conference, Saskatoon, October 30, 31, 1967.* Saskatoon: University of Saskatchewan Press, 1968.

Latour, Bruno. *Pandora's Hope: Essays on the Reality of Science Studies.* Cambridge: Harvard University Press, 1999.

Leacock, E. "The Montagnais–Naskapi Band." In *Contributions to Anthropology: Band Societies.* Ed. David Damas. Ottawa: National Museum, Bulletin 228, 1969.

Lewis, Henry T. "Maskuta: The Ecology of Indian Fires in Northern Alberta." *Western Canadian Journal of Anthropology* 7 (1977): 15–52.

Lotz, Jim. "Social Science Research and Northern Development." *Arctic* 21, 4 (1968): 291–94.

Macpherson, A.H. "Commentary: Wildlife Conservation and Canada's North." *Arctic* 34, 2 (1981): 103–107.

Marcus, Alan R. *Relocating Eden: The Image and Politics of Inuit Exile in the Canadian Arctic.* Hanover: University Press of New England, 1995.

Miller, F.L., and E. Broughton. "Calf Mortality on the Calving Ground of Kaminuriak Caribou, during 1970." Ottawa: Canadian Wildlife Service, 1974.

Morton, W.L. "The 'North' in Canadian Historiography." *Royal Society Canada, Trans.* Series 4, vol. 8 (1970): 31–40.

Nelson, Richard K. *Hunters of the Northern Ice.* Chicago: University of Chicago Press, 1969.

Porsild, A.E. "Mammals of the Mackenzie Delta." *Canadian Field-Naturalist* 59 (1945): 4–22.

Pruitt, William O. *Boreal Ecology.* London: Edward Arnold, 1978.

——— . "Life in the Snow." *Nature Canada* 4, 4 (1975): 40–44.

Ridington, Robin. "Technology, World View, and Adaptive Strategy in a Northern Hunting Society." *Canadian Review of Sociology and Anthropology* 19, 4 (1982): 469–81.

Riewe, Roderick, and L. Gamble. "The Inuit and Wildlife Management Today." In *Traditional Knowledge and Renewable Resource Management in Northern Regions.* Ed. Milton M.R. Freeman and Ludwig N. Carbyn, 31–37. Edmonton: Boreal Institute for Northern Studies, 1988.

Russell, R.H. "The Food Habits of Polar Bears of James Bay and Southwest Hudson Bay in Summer and Autumn." *Arctic* 28 (1975): 117–29.

Sabin, Paul. "Voices from the Hydrocarbon Frontier: Canada's Mackenzie Valley Pipeline Inquiry (1974-1977)." *Environmental History Review* 19, 1 (1995): 17–48.

Sillitoe, Paul. "The Development of Indigenous Knowledge: A New Applied Anthropology." *Current Anthropology* 39, 2 (1998): 223–52.

Simmons, N.M., D.C. Heard, and G.W. Calef. "Kaminuriak Caribou Herd: Interjurisdictional Management Problems." *North American Wildlife and Natural Resources Conference* 44th. March 24-28, 1979.

Smith, James, and Ernest S. Burch. "Chipewyan and Inuit in the Central Canadian Subarctic, 1613-1977." *Arctic Anthropology* 16, 2 (1977): 76–101.

Smith, Thomas G., and I. Stirling. "The Breeding Habitat of the Ringed Seal (Phoca hispida): The Birth Lair and Associated Structures." *Canadian Journal of Zoology* 53 (1975): 1297-1305.

Stevenson, M.G. "Indigenous Knowledge in Environmental Assessment." *Arctic* 49, 3 (1996): 278-91.

Tennenhouse, E. *Caribou Protection Measures for the Beverly and Kaminuriak Caribou Herds.* NWT. Department of Renewable Resources, 1968.

Tester, Frank J., and Peter Kulchyski. *Tammarniit (Mistakes): Inuit Relocation in the Eastern Arctic, 1939-63.* Vancouver: University of British Columbia Press, 1994.

Theberge, John B. "Commentary: Conservation in the North; An Ecological Perspective." *Arctic* 34, 4 (1981): 281-85.

Thomas, D.C. "Population Estimates and Distribution of Barren-Ground Caribou in Mackenzie District, Northwest Territories, Saskatchewan, and Alberta—March to May, 1967." CWS Report No. 9, 1969.

Usher, Peter J. "Indigenous Management Systems and the Conservation of Wildlife in the Canadian North." *Alternatives* 14, 1 (1987): 3-9.

———. "Traditional Ecological Knowledge in Environmental Assessment and Management." *Arctic* 53, 2 (2000): 183-93.

Valentine, Victor F. "Anthropology." In *The Unbelievable Land.* Ed. I.N. Smith, 45-48. Ottawa: Queen's Printer.

Walters, Carl. *Adaptive Management of Renewable Resources.* New York: Macmillan, 1986.

Wenzel, George. *Animal Rights, Human Rights: Ecology, Economy and Ideology in the Canadian Arctic.* Toronto: University of Toronto Press, 1991.

———. "Traditional Ecological Knowledge and Inuit Reflections on TEK Research and Ethics." *Arctic* 52, 2 (1999): 113-24.

10

Mi'gmaq Lives: Aboriginal Identity in Newfoundland

Dennis Bartels and *Alice Bartels*

ANTHROPOLOGIST FREDERICK BARTH argues that cultural, physical, national, or linguistic differences do not automatically generate boundaries between ethnic or racial groups. Rather, such differences are used in particular contexts to construct boundaries based on self-ascription and ascription-by-others.[1] Buckley and Kenney, following Barth, suggest that "identity, whether ethnic or otherwise, is a social construct and is negotiated during social interaction."[2] In some contexts, negotiation or assertion of ethnic identity may be advantageous, obligatory, or even necessary for survival. In such cases, people of mixed descent or with claims to multiple ethnicities may emphasize one side of their descent or ethnicity while ignoring or minimizing others. Sometimes this is required by state policy. For example, in the former USSR, the nationality of every Soviet citizen was entered on his or her internal passport. Nationality was determined by parentage and was identical in many cases to ethnicity. Census records of nationality were, however, based on self-ascription. In cases of mixed nationality, individuals, at age sixteen, had to choose the nationality of their mother or father. For example, a girl whose mother was Evenk and whose father was Ukrainian could have chosen Evenk or Ukrainian for her passport nationality. But the same girl, if she had been born and brought up in Moscow, might have regarded herself as Russian, or, more specifically, as a Muscovite. Thus, she might have described herself as Russian to a census-taker.

State policy is also a factor in the construction of ethnic boundaries in Sweden. Hugh Beach writes, "According to [Swedish] state policy, the

Saami (but only certain Saami) are permitted to practice reindeer herding in order to maintain their distinctive culture. This distinctive culture is then simplistically equated with reindeer herding, and should a Saami herder come to receive the greater part of his or her income from a non-herding source, that person is to be deprived of the herding privilege.[4] Swedish state policy thus links Saami ethnicity to herding, irrespective of criteria of self-ascription. In 1993, there were about 900 officially recognized Saami who practised herding on ancestral Saami lands. At the same time, about 8000 Saami who lived on ancestral lands did not have official status as herders.[5] The majority of Saami lived in Stockholm.[6]

In Canada, as in Sweden, state policy is a factor in the construction of certain ethnic boundaries. The Indian Act confers Indian status on members of bands composed mainly of people whose Aboriginal ancestors signed treaties with the British Crown. Status is also conferred upon members of bands that signed treaties with the Canadian federal government. Until 1985, women lost Indian status when they married non-status men, while non-status women who married men with Indian status gained status. The revised Indian Act of 1985 allowed women (and their children) to retain status irrespective of the status of their husbands. The revised Indian Act also empowered bands to define criteria for band membership.[7] These criteria are based mainly, but not exclusively, on lineal descent from Aboriginal ancestors. Some non-status people of Aboriginal descent are classified legally as Métis[8] or Inuit. There are, however, many people who regard themselves as Indian, part Indian, Inuit, or Métis, and who are so regarded by others, who do not fall into any of the legal categories mentioned above. Like status Indians, Métis, and Inuit, they are often distinguished by physical appearance and/or Aboriginal descent.

Possession of Indian status confers certain economic advantages. Status Indians are exempt from federal and provincial taxes. As well, bands administer government-funded programs that sometimes provide housing, vocational training, or other benefits for band members. At the same time, Indians suffer more than any other group in Canada from unemployment, poverty, family violence, substance abuse, suicide, incarceration, and low levels of education. Indians are sometimes stereotyped as lazy, violent, or alcoholic, and thus undeserving of government support. These stereotypes often underlie discriminatory practices. Thus, Indians without status may suffer from stigmatization and discrimination without receiving any of the benefits that status confers.

The historical interplay between the benefits and burdens of "being Indian" provides the context for the resurgence of Mi'gmaq identity in Newfoundland. Up to the late 1970s, many people of mixed descent in Newfoundland attempted to hide their Mi'gmaq ancestry and publicly identified themselves as English or Irish Newfoundlanders. Amid widespread stigmatization and discrimination, European identity trumped Indian identity. Their Mi'gmaq roots were present, but eclipsed by other identities that were more acceptable in the dominant culture. With the rise of "Indian politics" in the 1980s, this situation began to change. Mi'gmaq identity began to trump others. It is now not uncommon for people to seek to discover their Mi'gmaq ancestry and to negotiate Mi'gmaq identity. This paper explores the ongoing process in which people in western Newfoundland are "becoming Indians."

Until recently, Newfoundland Mi'gmaq were excluded from maps that purported to show traditional territories of Canadian Aboriginal peoples. The Beothuk were the only indigenous group shown on the island of Newfoundland.[9] This view was consistent with the Newfoundland folk belief, reinforced by many historical works, that the Beothuk became extinct in the nineteenth century. In a 1968 history textbook that was widely used in Newfoundland schools, Leslie Harris, former president of Memorial University of Newfoundland, wrote, "For several hundred years [after the Vikings left Newfoundland] the Eskimos and the Beothucks were the only inhabitants of Newfoundland."[10] According to *Native Rights in Canada*, by Cumming and Mickenberg, "In 1829 the last of the Beothuk Indians died."[11] Hope Maclean is more tentative: "The last known Beothuk, a woman named Shananditt [Shanaditti], died in 1829."[12]

While the Beothuk were sometimes portrayed by nineteenth-century Newfoundland writers as thieving, treacherous, and savage, they were later characterized as a "shy, brave people" in a Newfoundland school textbook by Frances Briffet that was widely used during the 1950s and 1960s.[13] Richard Budgell cites further instances where Beothuk are portrayed as "noble savages" by Newfoundland writers.[14] Several writers have claimed that the Beothuk were partial descendants of the Vikings who briefly lived on Newfoundland's Northern Peninsula around 1000 CE.[15] In 1837, a prominent Newfoundland magistrate claimed that the Beothuk were descended from the tribe of Oguskhan, a Tartar ruler who conquered much of Asia around 875 BCE.[16]

Newfoundlanders were, of course, aware that there were Mi'gmaq people living in Newfoundland, but they were not acknowledged as Aboriginal. Aboriginality was exclusively reserved for the "extinct" Beothuk. When Newfoundland joined Canada in 1949, the federal and provincial governments failed to recognize the existence of Aboriginal peoples.[17] In 1987, the Progressive Conservative premier of Newfoundland and Labrador, Brian Peckford, referred to Mi'gmaq as one of the groups who, like the Irish and English, immigrated to Newfoundland in the eighteenth century.[18] This view was recently reaffirmed in a decision of the Newfoundland Supreme Court according to which the province has jurisdiction over hunting and fishing on traditional Mi'gmaq lands adjoining the Miawpukek (Conne River) First Nation.[19]

The Beothuk are widely acknowledged by Newfoundlanders as the earliest known inhabitants of the island, and therefore Aboriginal. The question of their origins is seldom addressed outside academic circles. Sixteenth-, seventeenth-, and eighteenth-century settler populations from England and Ireland, as well as Mi'gmaq from Nova Scotia, are seen as the founders of Newfoundland society, and are distinguished from more recent immigrants, such as the Lebanese, who have been in Newfoundland for three or four generations. Current Mi'gmaq claims to Aboriginality contradict important parts of this picture.

Until recently, it was widely believed that French colonial authorities in the seventeenth and eighteenth centuries, and perhaps earlier, invited Cape Breton Mi'gmaq to Newfoundland and paid a bounty for every Beothuk that the Mi'gmaq killed. This set of beliefs has been characterized as the Micmac Mercenary Myth, or MMM.[20] The first edition of Briffett's textbook contained a tentative version of the MMM: "Over in Nova Scotia there was a tribe of Indians known as Micmacs. These were allies of the French and had been armed by them with guns. Some of these Micmacs settled on the banks of the Conne River in Bay D'Espoir not far from the French colony of Plaisance. Some say that the French had offered a reward for every Beothuk destroyed. Whatever the motive, the Micmacs did murder the Beothuks."[21] It is widely acknowledged that certain English settlers, notably a few members of the Peyton family in central Newfoundland, murdered many Beothuk.[22] European diseases may also have been a factor in the demise of the Beothuk.[23]

The belief that the Mi'gmaq were relative newcomers to Newfoundland, and that they were historically tainted with the murder of the Beothuk, was an important part of an ethnic boundary that, from the mid-nineteenth century to the late twentieth century, separated "savage/uncivilized" Mi'gmaq from "civilized" Newfoundlanders of English or Irish descent, and from the "extinct/noble" Beothuk. Richard Budgell suggests, "Describing the Micmac as later arrivals to Newfoundland, i.e., imported by the French, allows Newfoundlanders to deny the aboriginality of Micmacs, which is still largely the policy of the Newfoundland government."[24] Dorothy Anger writes,

> The word "Micmac" was often accompanied by "dirty," "thieving" or "lazy." After over fifty years of being looked down on, it is surprising only that the Micmac heritage did not die completely in Bay St. George.... If insult was not meant by the term Micmac, most people took it as a simple statement of fact. With such ambiguity surrounding it, Micmac identity was kept private by most people, remaining alive only within family circles.[25]

In some cases, Roman Catholic records of Mi'gmaq baptisms included the word *savage*. Fr. Stanley St. Croix, who served the parish—which included the Bay d'Espoir Mi'gmaq community of Conne River from 1916 to 1946—forbade the use of the Mi'gmaq language in the Conne River school. (The last fluent Mi'gmaq speaker in Newfoundland died at Conne River in the 1980s). St. Croix also ordered young couples seeing each other over three months to marry. A plan by the Conne River chief and band council to build a church at Conne River was opposed by St. Croix, who wished Conne River Mi'gmaq to attend the church at neighbouring St. Alban's. As a result of this dispute, St. Croix used his spiritual authority to exile the chief and to abolish the band council.[26] But Mi'gmaq were not always characterized by clergy as "uncivilized." In 1835, the Anglican archdeacon Edward Wix described the Mi'gmaq of Bay St. George as "of equal, if not higher, moral character than the Europeans with whom they associated."[27]

Individuals of French-Mi'gmaq descent on Newfoundland's west coast were distinguished in Newfoundland dialect by the epithet *jackatar*. The *Dictionary of Newfoundland English has the following entry for jackatar*: "A Newfoundlander of mixed French and Micmac Indian descent; the speech of such a person. 1857 Lind MS Diary 23 May [I] went to see a poor man who has been very ill for 7 months, he & all his family belong to a much despised & neglected race called 'Jackatars,' they speak an impure dialect of French & Indian, RC's [Roman Catholics] and of almost lawless habits."[28] Downer suggests that *jackatar* is derived from *Jacques à Terre*, a phrase used to characterize French naval deserters who jumped ship at Bay St. George.[29] This view is consistent with reports by Mi'gmaq informants in Flat Bay. In the mid-1970s, *jackatar* was a pejorative term, connoting laziness, dishonesty, and promiscuity. Calling someone a jackatar was extremely provocative.

Mi'gmaq culture in Newfoundland was not significantly different from that of many rural Newfoundlanders. Dorothy Anger attributes this to adoption of Mi'gmaq woods-based subsistence activities by non-Mi'gmaq.[30] She writes that Mi'gmaq were generally poor, "but non-aboriginal people shared that poverty level and lifestyle (even kinship), making demarcation of ethnic identity difficult."[31] Anger's analysis of ethnic boundaries between Mi'gmaq and non-Mi'gmaq in different parts of Newfoundland is worth quoting at length:

> In central Newfoundland, the traditional skills of Micmac men were invaluable for finding routes and transporting supplies in to railway construction and mining camps.... They were respected community members because their abilities were vital to development. And they were respected as Micmacs. As a way of "fitting in," they spoke English and passed only that language on to their children. They kept the family history, as Micmacs, alive, if not the traditions and beliefs. But they, and their non-Micmac neighbours, encouraged adaptation of their children to the majority, non-Micmac way of life. For the younger generation, (those elderly now) Micmac heritage was somewhat separate from Micmac identity.
>
> On the west coast, there were few industries which needed Micmac skills....

Few took part in the main economic activities of the region. Indeed their subsistence, woods-based activities were somewhat of a nuisance to the main economy....

In order to avoid the stigma of "dirty Indian" or "jackatar" many denied their heritage and, trying to help their children, did not pass on any knowledge of their ancestry. In Bay St. George, the most valued status was "English," then "French," with "Indian" at the bottom....

The west coast town [of Corner Brook] is the point at which the two Micmac geographical groups meet in an urban environment. A paper town, it was built by east coast Irish and English who went to find work. The English and Anglo-Newfoundland executives formed the upper social echelon. Mill workers, office staff, and loggers scrabbled for their place in the hierarchy. The central Newfoundland Micmacs found their place in the lower end of the respectability scale. The "Frenchies," Micmacs from Bay St. George, did not take part in the paper industry, and were marginalized by all other sectors of the Corner Brook society. They eked out an existence based on subsistence activities, legal and illegal. Their part of town [Crow Gulch] was avoided by "respectable" people....

The genealogies of the two groups in Corner Brook show no difference in degree of "Micmacness," indeed show extensive intermarriage, but the differences in social standing—within the Corner Brook Micmac population—points to the importance of value to the community in defining the expression, and social value, of ethnic identity.[32]

In the early 1970s, Newfoundland Mi'gmaq became politically organized.[33] In 1981, the Federation of Newfoundland Indians (FNI) and the Conne River Band Council demanded "recognition" for Newfoundland Mi'gmaq under the Indian Act, and filed a comprehensive land claim for the southwestern third of the island of Newfoundland. Today, this claim includes all of Newfoundland except the Avalon Peninsula. According to Mi'gmaq folklore and the Mi'gmaq land claim, Newfoundland was, from time immemorial, Ktaqamkuk, part of the Unamakik (The Foggy Lands) district of a Mi'gmaq confederacy, or Mi'kma'ki.[34] Mi'kma'ki also included New Brunswick, Cape Breton, Nova Scotia, the Magdalen Islands, the Gaspé Peninsula, and part of northeastern Maine.

Mi'kma'ki roughly corresponds to what the archaeologist Charles Martijn has called "An Eastern Micmac Domain of Islands."[35] Prior to the inclusion of Newfoundland in Canada, the Mi'gmaq Grand Council recognized Ktaqamkuk [Newfoundland] as a "special district" of Mi'kma'ki.[36] Interestingly, Robert M. Levitt excludes Newfoundland from Mi'kma'ki: "As far as we know, they and their direct ancestors (Mi'gmaq) have lived in what is now Mi'kma'kik (except Newfoundland) for at least the past 30,000 years."[37] No reasons for this exclusion are given.

Many Newfoundlanders and, most notably, the Progressive Conservative government of Newfoundland and Labrador, did not take Mi'gmaq claims to land and status seriously at first, possibly because their claims contradicted the view that the ancestors of Newfoundland Mi'gmaq were relatively recent arrivals who had killed the Beothuk. An initial attempt by the government of Newfoundland and Labrador to refute the Mi'gmaq land claim argued that Mi'gmaq had not permanently resided in Newfoundland prior to a particular date, which seemed to vary between establishment of English sovereignty and European contact in the 1500s.[38] The government refutation of the Mi'gmaq land claim has been challenged by a great deal of recent scholarship. For example, if "assertion of English sovereignty" is interpreted to mean nothing more than French cession of Newfoundland to the British Crown according to the Treaty of Utrecht in 1713, then it is clear from seventeenth- and eighteenth-century French records that Mi'gmaq used Newfoundland long before that, probably because of the excellent quality of Newfoundland beaver pelts for the fur trade.[39] It has also been pointed out that a lack of permanent Mi'gmaq settlements in pre-contact Newfoundland does not necessarily invalidate a claim to Aboriginal rights and lands in light of the "nomadic nature of aboriginal land tenure" as defined by Canadian courts.[40] This consideration seemed to be absent from the recent Newfoundland Supreme Court decision that denied Mi'gmaq jurisdiction over hunting and fishing on lands adjoining the Miawpukek (Conne River) First Nation.[41]

Ingeborg Marshall acknowledges that in pre-contact times, "Micmac may have visited the south coast [of Newfoundland] to trap or fish."[42] She also writes that there are no "reliable documents which would prove that the Micmacs crossed the Cabot Strait during the first

150 years of European contact."[43] In the *Atlas of Newfoundland and Labrador*, the map of "Early Aboriginal Migrations" to Newfoundland is restricted to Maritime Archaic, Paleo Eskimo, Recent Indian, and Beothuk.[44] Charles Martijn, however, refers to archaeological evidence from the Magdalen Islands showing that prehistoric voyages took place between them and Cape Breton over a period of several millennia, and across a similar distance from the mainland. "Some of the lithic remains found on the Magdalen Islands are made from a gray silicious shale whose geological source may be on Ingonish Island, just off the northeast coast of Cape Breton. Quite evidently then, the Micmac and their ancestors must have developed considerable navigational skills and they undoubtably possessed a great store of knowledge about tides, currents, winds, and weather patterns.... That the capacity for traversing the Cabot Strait existed in ancient times cannot be contested."[45]

Professor William Newbigging's examination of French records from sixteenth-century Plaisance revealed no evidence that the French brought or invited Mi'gmaq to Newfoundland, or that French colonial authorities paid Mi'gmaq to kill Beothuk.[46] Nevertheless, the MMM is still influential. It appears in the entry on the Beothuk by Barrie Reynolds in volume 15 of the *Handbook of North American Indians*,[47] and in Carl Waldman's *Encyclopedia of Native American Tribes*.[48] In the *Atlas des Indiens d'Amérique du Nord*, Gilbert Legay writes, "*Alliés des français, ils [the Mi'gmaq] retarderent l'implantation des anglais en Nouvelle-Écosse et au Nouveau-Brunswick, après avoir aider a l'élimination des Béothuks de Terre Neuve en 1706.*"[49] Thus, the MMM is still a potent weapon for opponents of Mi'gmaq claims to land and Aboriginal status. In 1987, the government of Newfoundland and Labrador declared that it would not participate in land claims negotiations unless Aboriginal groups could "meet the fundamental criteria of aboriginal use and occupancy of the land, from time immemorial, prior to European discovery and the establishment of sovereign jurisdiction."[50]

Archaeology plays an important role in controversy surrounding Newfoundland Mi'gmaq claims. According to Marshall,

> It is generally accepted that around 50 BC, a second Indian population migrated across the Strait of Belle Isle to western Newfoundland. Called Recent Indians to distinguish them from the [earlier] Maritime Archaic tradition, they are grouped archaeolog-

ically into three complexes according to the distinctive tools and other remains of these populations: the "Cow Head," "Beaches," and "Little Passage" complexes.[51]

Even if some burial sites can be positively identified as Beothuk,[52] this does not mean that other pre-contact sites were not Mi'gmaq. So far, however, there are no definitive criteria for distinguishing Recent Indian sites as Mi'gmaq. Even a total absence of pre-contact Mi'gmaq sites would not necessarily mean that Mi'gmaq had not used and occupied Newfoundland from "time immemorial." M.G. Wetzel, one of the founders of the FNI, writes,

> Ironically no prehistoric sites that can be positively identified as Mi'kmaw have been found in Nova Scotia to date (personal communication from Mr. Steve Davis, Prof. of Archaeology, St. Mary's University, Halifax). Yet the absence of such sites in Nova Scotia has not been used to deny the aboriginality of the Mi'kmaw people living there. This unique argument is only being developed [with regard to Mi'gmaw in Newfoundland].[53]

If, as Mi'gmaq folklore suggests, Newfoundland was part of a pre-contact Mi'gmaq confederacy, this may have implications for scholarly claims about Mi'gmaq-Beothuk hostility.[54] Presumably, the Mi'gmaq confederacy, like the seventeenth-century Huron and Iroquois confederacies, lacked state organization.[55] Thus, there was no centralized political authority that could order disparate Mi'gmaq groups in Newfoundland to make war on the Beothuk.[56] While hostility may have erupted at times between particular groups of Beothuk and Mi'gmaq,[57] this does not mean that all Newfoundland Mi'gmaq became permanently hostile to all Beothuk, or vice versa. The assumption of such generalized hostility may arise from a projection of contemporary state organization onto pre-contact Aboriginal peoples.

Mi'gmaq folklore provides an account of the end of the Beothuk that differs radically from the MMM. When their numbers decreased in the nineteenth century, the remaining Beothuk married into other groups, such as the Innu of Labrador, Cape Breton Mi'gmaq, and Newfoundland Mi'gmaq. Several Mi'gmaq in Newfoundland and Cape Breton claim partial Beothuk descent.[58] This is relevant to Ingeborg Marshall's claim that "the Beothuk were the direct cultural and genetic [our emphasis] descendants of the Little Passage Indians."[59] Marshall does not cite

DNA analysis to support her claim. Presumably such analysis would require procurement of an "authentic" sample of Beothuk DNA and matching it with DNA from the remains of Little Passage Indians. If "authentic" Beothuk DNA could be found, it could also be matched with the DNA of living individuals who claim partial Beothuk descent. If such a match could be made, it would mean that the demise of the Beothuks should be characterized as ethnocide, not genocide.[60]

In 1983, the Mi'gmaq struggle for recognition and land took an unexpected turn when a provincial government archivist found records of the negotiations regarding the incorporation of Newfoundland and Labrador into Canada that referred unequivocally to a Mi'gmaq reservation at Conne River. It was thus clear that the Newfoundland and Canadian governments had recognized the Aboriginal status of Conne River Mi'gmaq prior to the incorporation of Newfoundland into Canada in 1949. With this evidence, the Conne River Mi'gmaq pressed home their claim to Aboriginal status. They acquired Indian status upon being declared a band in 1984 by the governor-in-council under Section 2(1)(c) of the Indian Act. In 1986–87, a 2.6-square-kilometre reserve at Conne River was created. This reserve is now the Miawpukek First Nation.

The Miawpukek First Nation has attempted to revive Mi'gmaq language and culture. The Mi'gmaq language is now taught to elementary school students who also perform traditional songs and dances. A sweat lodge has been constructed. There is a commercial outlet for traditional clothing and craft items in the building that houses the band offices. Miawpukek has hosted several powwows. These activities are rhetorical in the sense that they publicly demonstrate and demarcate Mi'gmaq ethnicity. They also involve a proprietary/curatorial role that protects Miawpukek culture from appropriation by outsiders.[61]

During the 1980s, political conflict in Miawpukek centred on the issue of whether the *saquamow* ("wise man," or chief) was to be periodically elected or elected for life. This issue was partially resolved by allowing a ceremonial chief, who served for life, to coexist with a periodically elected political chief. The ceremonial chief is, in effect, a curator of Miawpukek cultural traditions, and represents these traditions to the outside world.

An infusion of federal funds has brought relative prosperity to Miawpukek. A sewage system and new homes have been constructed, and a fish-farming enterprise has been started. Miawpukek's school, St. Anne's, is well equipped with computers and has a community exercise facility. Miawpukek students are eligible for post-secondary education funding under federal positive action programs. And, like all members of First Nations in Canada, members of the Miawpukek First Nation are exempt from federal and provincial taxes. In Newfoundland and Labrador, Canada's poorest province, these are tangible benefits. It is not surprising that members of Mi'gmaq bands outside Miawpukek would like to benefit in similar ways. Without recognition under the Indian Act, FNI bands have received some federal funding. For example, the Corner Brook Band has used federal funds from Human Resources and Development Canada to buy houses in Corner Brook, which are rented to band members.

The Federation of Newfoundland Indians, which represents Mi'gmaq bands outside Miawpukek, claims that John Munro, federal minister of Indian and Northern Affairs from 1981 to 1984, promised in 1982 to recognize the Conne River Band first, with recognition of other bands to follow.[62] But this promise was broken. Mi'gmaq bands at St. Alban's, Glenwood, Gander Bay, Exploits, Stephenville Crossing, St. George's, Port au Port, Flat Bay, Corner Brook, Benoit's Cove, and Bartlett's Harbour have not been recognized under the Indian Act, even though their members claim the same ancestry as members of the Miawpukek First Nation. Thus, over 4,000 members of the Federation of Newfoundland Indians have not gained Indian status.

In early 1989, the FNI began a legal action seeking Indian status under the equality provision of the Charter of Rights and Freedoms (section 15). They claim that FNI members and the people of Conne River were not treated equally. The FNI also argues that, by failing to recognize the Indian status of FNI members and bands, the Crown has failed to honour its fiduciary obligations to protect the interests of Aboriginal people. In 1990, the federal government agreed to negotiate the FNI case out of court, and the FNI suspended legal proceedings. In early 1992, however, the federal cabinet rejected a proposal by Minister of Indian and Northern Affairs Siddon to recognize FNI bands. Attempted resolution of this dispute has alternated between negotiations and legal proceedings. In October 1997, a report prepared for the Canadian Human Rights Commission by Noel Lyon recommended that the federal government meet FNI demands by granting self-government outside the Indian Act to FNI bands. Many FNI members, however, believe that the federal government will undertake registration of FNI members under the Indian Act. According to this view, registration will proceed either as a result of an FNI legal victory or because the federal government wishes to avoid the possibility of a legal defeat.

FNI band councils have defined criteria for band membership in accordance with the Indian Act.[63] These criteria are generally based on demonstrated descent from Mi'gmaq ancestors. For example, the Corner Brook Band requires demonstration of lineal descent from a Mi'gmaq ancestor within four generations.[64] The band council decides whose ancestors were Mi'gmaq. There is widespread agreement that certain families were Mi'gmaq.[65] But in other cases, some band members claim that a particular ancestor was Mi'gmaq, and the band council disagrees.

Stigmatization led some Mi'gmaq in Corner Brook to hide their ancestry from their children, who then spent many years unconsciously "passing" as "respectable" non-Mi'gmaq. The resurgence of Mi'gmaq identity that accompanied the rise of FNI political activity allowed some of these people to discover their roots. For example, in Ottawa, around 1996, we met an old friend from Corner Brook who had lived outside of Newfoundland for many years. She was unaware of FNI political activity and was surprised to learn some of the names of the band councillors in Corner Brook and Benoit's Cove. "I'm related to these people and they're no more Indian than I am," she exclaimed. Then she paused, realizing that she, too, was Mi'gmaq. In September 1997, the Corner Brook Band Council urged its members to "begin or further [research on] family genealogy." Band members were told that genealogical knowledge would be "critical" for expected registration of band members under the Indian Act. In light of these circumstances, some band members who did not possess genealogical data attempted to buy or trade it from others. We are unaware of any other instance in Canada of such commoditization of genealogical data in anticipation of registration.

In spring 1999, the Flat Bay Band announced its intention to seek registration under the Indian Act, independent of other FNI bands.[66] According to Indian and Northern Affairs, a criterion for registration under the Indian Act is continuous maintenance of a distinctive Aboriginal community. Members of the band believe that Flat Bay clearly meets this criterion. If registration proceeds, the Flat Bay Band will seek self-government without creation of a reserve. It will be interesting to see whether other FNI bands emulate the Flat Bay strategy. FNI members whom we interviewed are interested in tracing their Mi'gmaq roots irrespective of any material benefits that might accrue from gaining Indian status. But if they are entitled to such benefits, they will not refuse them.

For many Newfoundland Mi'gmaq, Aboriginal identity was once a shameful secret. It is now proudly proclaimed. This transformation is reflected in the stories we heard from three members of the Corner Brook Band, and from Mr. Calvin White, chief of the Flat Bay Band. Their stories illustrate the evolution of Mi'gmaq identity and shed light on anthropological theories of Aboriginality, "indigenousness," identity, and ethnicity.

Mi'gmaq Lives

J

The following account is based on three interviews that were conducted in November 1997, January 1998, and January 2000. All taped interviews were transcribed by the late Joanne Greenlee, to whom we are greatly indebted.

J was born in Corner Brook, Newfoundland, in 1945. He went to high school in Corner Brook, and graduated from St. Francis Xavier University in Cape Breton, Nova Scotia. He studied in Toronto for the Roman Catholic priesthood, but decided not to be ordained. Instead, he returned to Newfoundland and married a nurse from Argentia, Newfoundland. They have two grown daughters. For many years, J worked in Corner Brook as an employment counsellor for Human Resources and Development Canada (HRDC).

J had cousins named Prosper who claimed to be Mi'gmaq, so J suspected that he had Mi'gmaq ancestors. But when he asked relatives about this, they never answered directly. At his wedding, one of his uncles jokingly told J's bride that she had married a "jackatar."

J administered HRDC programs for Mi'gmaq bands in Corner Brook and Benoit's Cove. Around 1993, he asked Marie Newman, chief of the Corner Brook Band, whether he had Mi'gmaq ancestry. "[She] looked at me and smiled and laughed, and she said, 'Sure, you're a Native person. We've known that for years.'" She was surprised that J didn't know. She said that Gerard Webb, the late chief of the Federation of Newfoundland Indians, once said, "You know, that J, he's an Aboriginal person and won't admit it." After he discovered his Mi'gmaq ancestry, J wanted to talk to Gerard about the discovery. Sadly, Gerard died before J could do so.

After discovery of his Mi'gmaq ancestors, J joined the Corner Brook Band and began serious research on his genealogy. One of J's ancestors was John Prosper (Prospère) Companion (Compagnon). According to local oral history, JPC was a crew member on a French ship in the early nineteenth century. He fought with another crew member and, believing that he had killed his opponent, jumped ship near Little Port, Newfoundland.[67] He later moved to Woods Island, then to Frenchman's Cove. In order to conceal his identity from the French authorities, he used his middle name, Prosper. He later learned that the man he thought he had killed had survived. JPC was literate and became a Catholic lay deacon. He kept records of births and marriages, but these were, unfortunately, destroyed.

Over the course of his life, JPC had three wives, all Aboriginal. One of his wives was from the Blanchard family, the sole inhabitants of the north shore of the Bay of Islands in the 1780s. Some of the Blanchards were Beothuk. According to J, "It only makes sense that when the Beothuk were being hunted [by English settlers] in eastern and central Newfoundland, they took to their heels and came to the west coast. The English fishermen and settlers weren't here then. The French were along this shore in western Newfoundland, and, for whatever reason, the French historically seem to have had a much better rapport with the Aboriginal people than the English ever did."

J said that as he was growing up, it was widely believed that the French had brought the Mi'gmaq to Newfoundland to kill the Beothuk. He thinks that this may have been "disinformation" to absolve white people of guilt for killing the Beothuk. "If you invent a lie that's big enough, people will believe it."

J believes that he is descended from JPC and his first wife, but isn't sure. He said, "Depending on which marriage, or possibly the stage of [JPC's] life, you became a Companion or a Prosper." There are families of Prospers and Companions all along the Bay of Islands. "My grand-mother, Mary Minnie Prosper, always used to go down to Halfway Point to see her cousin, Hodge Companion." J's closest relatives used the name Companion.

J's great-grandfather was William Henry Prosper, and his great-grandmother was Margaret Ida Pike. She was of Innu descent. Her family lived in the area of Red Bay and Pinware in southern Labrador. William Henry Prosper owned a fishing schooner, which he sailed from Bonne Bay to Forteau, Labrador, in the summer. J's grandmother, Mary Minnie Prosper, was a cook on the schooner and in charge of her five younger brothers.

In 1998, J discovered that his maternal great-grandmother was Jenny Benoit, a well-known midwife.

A distant cousin of J's had a Mi'gmaq grandmother who told a younger relative never to reveal his Mi'gmaq ancestry because a bounty of two dollars was paid for killing any Aboriginal person, Beothuk or Mi'gmaq. This led people to hide knowledge of their Mi'gmaq ances-try, especially in light of what happened to the Beothuk. In some lines of J's family, the knowledge of Mi'gmaq ancestry was passed down, but never revealed to outsiders.

French-speaking people, especially Mi'gmaq, were looked down upon by English-speakers on Newfoundland's west coast. French was not taught in schools, and authorities provided no resources for French education.[68] Roman Catholic clergy, themselves Irish, often anglicized French names—for example, LeBlanc became White, and Lejeune became Young. A priest in Bay St. George identified certain Mi'gmaq individuals as *sauvage* in church records. J thinks this wasn't necessar-ily intended as a racist slur because the priest was known to be sym-pathetic to the Mi'gmaq.

J does not think that Mi'gmaq were refused jobs because of their ethnicity at the Corner Brook paper mill, established in 1924, because the demand for labour was so great. He worked there during summers, and other workers were Mi'gmaq. [Members of the Corner Brook Band Council claim that there was discrimination, and that this led some Mi'gmaq people to hide their ancestry.][69]

J has collaborated on genealogical research with his cousin K, who is also interested in tracing her Aboriginal roots. They found that Catholic priests were sometime reluctant to allow access to genealogical records in their churches, possibly because they believed that records of adoptions or "illegitimate" births should not be publicly accessible. There are, however, copies of all church records of births and deaths in the archives of Newfoundland, housed in the Colonial Building in St. John's. These records are open to the public.

After J learned about his ancestry he told his siblings and got some "wonderful" responses. J's niece, a PhD candidate in microbiology at Queen's University, Kingston, Ontario, told him that she tested herself for Aboriginal genetic material and found it. J hopes that genetic testing will be increasingly used to trace ancestry. He said, "I've had a lifetime of front-stage, back-stage with aboriginal ancestry.... [In] the Bay of Islands, Bonne Bay, Bay St. George, there's so much intermarriage of white and Aboriginal people that we're all related. It's really kind of funny and scary. There are a few of these revelations that some [people] would just as soon keep secret."

In 1998–99, interviews with an old woman revealed Mi'gmaq connections on both sides of J's family. This filled a major gap in the genealogical research carried out by J and his cousin K.

K

The following account is based on three interviews conducted in January 1998, February 1998, and February 2000:

K (née Prosper) was born in Corner Brook, Newfoundland, in 1956. She went to a Protestant[70] high school in Corner Brook and worked in different clerical jobs connected with medicine. Since 1996, she has been a secretary at the O'Connell Long Term Care Centre, which is part of the Western Memorial Regional Hospital in Corner Brook. K and her husband were married in 1975. They have two sons.

K was always interested in genealogy and suspected that she may have been partly Native. She started serious genealogical research in 1988 and discovered that she was descended on her mother's side from the Hawkins family of Labrador. Her mother's family was English, but there were Inuit among them. Her great-grandfather was a cooper by trade, and most of the Coopers were Native.

K's father, Stanley Prosper, who died in 1986, looked Native. His family had "skeletons in the closet." Many of his family were Native, and he said that his great-great-grandfather's name was Companion, later changed to Prosper. K recently found out that her great-great-grandfather had a brother in Nova Scotia who was a Mi'gmaq.

One of K's father's ancestors was from the Blanchard family, the sole inhabitants of the Bay of Islands around 1780. Some of the Blanchards were Beothuk. K believes that her father's great-great-grandfather changed his name from Companion to Prosper because of the Indian tradition of giving a child the first name of the father.

K believes that she is of partial Beothuk descent. People laugh when she mentions this because it is widely believed that Shanaditti was the last Beothuk. But K is convinced that not all the Beothuk died. They fled from central Newfoundland to escape persecution. She believes that DNA testing would confirm her claim that she is of partial Beothuk descent.

James Prosper, a sea officer, was K's grandfather. He drowned in the sinking of the *Caribou*.[71] K has a photo of him, and he looks "very Native." K's great-grandfather, William Prosper, was Roman Catholic, but became an Anglican after he married Margaret Ida Pike who was a member of the Church of England. According to "Indian custom," he moved with her family to Bonne Bay, Newfoundland. Ruth Holmes Whitehead[72] confirmed that Prosper was a Mi'gmaq name, and sent K a photo of William Prosper, K's great-grandfather.

K's husband is descended from the André family, which is recognized as Mi'gmaq in Newfoundland and Nova Scotia. They lived on André's Island in Notre Dame Bay.

K grew up thinking that she was unrelated to the other Prospers in Corner Brook who were Roman Catholic. She had relatives who belonged to the Orange Lodge, and some of them disapproved of her marrying a Catholic. She said that this is no longer an issue, nor is being an Indian.

William Prosper's mother—that is, K's great-great-grandmother— was Jenny (Geneviève or Genova) Benoit, a well-known midwife on the Northern Peninsula of Newfoundland. She made her own medicines from herbs that she gathered at St. John's Island. K has recently discovered that Jenny Benoit had a sister in Conne River, now the Miawpukek First Nation. With assistance from relatives in Nova Scotia, K has completed tracing her descent from the Companions of Benoit's Cove, and discovered that the Brakes were the third family of John Prospère Compagnon (see above). She has also received assistance with her genealogical research from another relative, Murray Leggo, who was a teacher for many years in Port-aux-Port, Newfoundland. Mr. Leggo is now a resident of the Veterans' Unit at the O'Connell Centre where K works.

K is a member of the Corner Brook Mi'gmaq Band, and she has registered her sons and her sister's children with the band.

Recently, K obtained application forms for Indian status, and she may apply "directly" for registration to Indian and Northern Affairs Canada. She shares ancestors with members of the Miawpukek First Nation, and with members of Mi'gmaq First Nations in Nova Scotia.

Discovery of her Indian identity has strengthened K's love of Newfoundland. She also loves living in Corner Brook, and would leave only if the alternative was going on welfare. She is interested in her Native ancestry irrespective of any material gain that might result from it. She doesn't think that there will be any.

L

The following account is based on three interviews that were conducted in April 1997, March 1998, and February 2000.

L was born in 1940, in Sandy Point, St. George's, Newfoundland. He grew up in Corner Brook, and went through the Roman Catholic school system. He taught for five years at a vocational school in Corner Brook, but was mostly self-employed. Since 1988, he has taught carpentry at a college in Corner Brook.

William Olssen, L's grandfather, was from Oslo, Norway. Around 1878, when he was twenty-five years old, Olssen and several other Norwegians were stranded near Sandy Point, after their ship was wrecked. In 1882, he married a Mi'gmaq girl, Mary Jane Lejeune (anglicized as Young), and ran a carpentry business that produced large, ornamental parts of church interiors. Mary Jane Lejeune's father was Alexander Young, and his mother was Elizabeth Camus (anglicized as Cammie).

L was adopted by Peter Cammie at the age of two and moved to Corner Brook. L's biological father also lived in Corner Brook and was on good terms with L's adoptive parents. Peter Cammie was unaware that L was also descended from a member of the Cammie/Camus family (see above). L was elated when he discovered his Camus ancestry. "When my father adopted me," L said, "he was actually adopting a blood relative." Unfortunately, L discovered his Camus ancestry after Peter Cammie died. But L was able to reveal his discovery to his Cammie cousins.

Peter Cammie sometimes said, "Our name was Camus, and I liked it. I don't know why they changed it to Cammie." The Camus family left Sandy Point in 1820 and settled in Arichat, Nova Scotia. Many of their descendants live in Cheticamp. One of the Camus daughters, Marie, married Jim Webb, and they returned to Newfoundland. They were the founders of a prominent Mi'gmaq family in the Corner Brook area. Matilda Camus, also from Nova Scotia, married Gus Vincent. They returned to Newfoundland with their son, Joe.

Peter Cammie claimed French descent, but never told L that he was also Indian. Twenty years ago, few people on Newfoundland's west coast admitted Indian ancestry. French-Indian people were sometimes ostracized. Consequently, French-Indian people intermarried. People often didn't know who their grandparents were. This has changed only recently.

L feels that he inherited a knack for carpentry and crafts from his Norwegian grandfather and from his Mi'gmaq ancestors. At fifteen, he began to make a living by selling hunting knives, moccasins, and snowshoes that he made.

Ollie, L's brother, died of cancer in 1995. At the funeral, L met Mr. Brake, a relative from Humbermouth, Corner Brook, who was unaware that L was Ollie's brother. Mr. Brake was of partial Mi'gmaq descent, so L realized that he also had Mi'gmaq ancestors. He then began to seriously pursue genealogical research. Mr. Brake encouraged L's research, and they kept in touch. L has also obtained genealogical information from Allen Stride, a relative of partial Mi'gmaq descent who lives in Ottawa, and from a woman who lives in South Brook, Newfoundland, who is related to L through the Vincent family.

L discovered that one of his ancestors was Henri L'Officiel (anglicized as Fishell), who came to Quebec from France and married an

Aboriginal woman. They sailed down the St. Lawrence and were ship-wrecked near Sandy Point. They had three children: George, Marie, and Anne. L's biological, paternal great-great-grandfather, Jean René Charles Camus, married Marie L'Officiel in 1792. Anne married François Benoit in 1790. He was the first of the Benoits in Sandy Point. Alexander Lejeune, L's great-grandfather (see above) married a Benoit. L also discovered that his adoptive father's mother may have been Innu, from Battle Harbour, Labrador.

Like J and K (see above), L believes that the Beothuk came to Labrador and western Newfoundland in order to avoid persecution by English settlers. L believes that one of John Prospère Compagnon's wives was Beothuk, and that Mi'gmaq and Beothuk may have lived together in Bay St. George's. William Prosper, one of the children of JPC's first marriage, lived in Nova Scotia, and knew many Beothuk customs.

L's cousin, Bernard, believes that the Cammie/Camus family may be related to the French author and philosopher Albert Camus. After Albert Camus's death, French people visited the Bay St. George area to find relatives of the late author.

Before he learned of his Mi'gmaq ancestry, L wasn't sure whether having an adoptive parent of Mi'gmaq descent would entitle him to membership in the Corner Brook Band. But the band executive accepted him because his adoptive father was of Mi'gmaq descent. The band now knows that L also has biological Mi'gmaq ancestors. Some people say that L isn't an Indian because he doesn't "look like an Indian." "It doesn't make any difference," L says. "Down in Conne River [Miaw-pukek], they're all fair-skinned and everything else, but they've still got Indian blood." L often talks to local people who don't know that they have Mi'gmaq ancestors, but he doesn't tell them unless they ask him directly.

L can't predict whether FNI band members will get status under the Indian Act. He believes that more people will claim Mi'gmaq descent if there is a prospect of financial benefit: "Everything comes down to dollars and cents, I think." He would like to see FNI bands get official status, irrespective of financial benefits, so that valuable aspects of Mi'gmaq culture can be revived. L intends to pursue his genealogical research whether or not it leads to registration under the Indian Act. He has begun research on his Norwegian ancestry.

The following account is based on conversations and meetings that have taken place over the last twenty-five years.

Calvin White was born in 1943, in Flat Bay, Newfoundland, and is chief of the Flat Bay Mi'gmaq Band. He received an elementary school education, and, like his parents, pursued a traditional Mi'gmaq way of life based on hunting and fishing. In 1964 he married Frances, a teacher in Flat Bay who was originally from the east coast of Newfoundland. When she first came to teach in the Bay St. George area, Frances was unaware of the nature and history of local inter-ethnic relations.

Calvin and Frances White have four sons and two daughters, all of whom are active in Mi'gmaq politics. One daughter was acting chief of the Flat Bay Band and now practises law in Gander, Newfoundland. One of her clients is the Miawpukek First Nation. The other daughter is a band councillor at Flat Bay. One son is an actor in Halifax, whose professional activity focuses on Mi'gmaq culture. He was recently part of an all-Aboriginal cast of *Drunks and Children Don't Lie*, a stage production taken on the road and performed for First Nations communities in Nova Scotia.

In the early 1970s, Mr. White worked for four years as a heavy-equipment operator at a gypsum mine in the Bay St. George area. During the 1990s, he was a literacy instructor. He is currently an outfitter and hunting guide.

Mr. White was one of the founders of the Federation of Newfoundland Indians and the Flat Bay Band. At different times he has served as FNI president and chief negotiator. Frances White has supported his political activity and maintained their household during her husband's frequent absences on FNI business.

Mr. White's Aboriginal identity was never in doubt. Both his parents were Mi'gmaq, and his mother was from the Brake family. They took pride in their Aboriginal ancestry and way of life.

Flat Bay was—and remains—an area of high unemployment. Mr. White became involved in politics partly in order to improve economic conditions there. Because he had a good job, he was one of the few who had time and money to pursue political activity. The television production of Alex Haley's *Roots* led him to focus his political activity on reviving Mi'gmaq culture and identity. He did not want his descendants to read about the Mi'gmaq as an extinct culture; preservation and revival of Mi'gmaq culture was a goal worth fighting for. But without support from the community, he could not have persisted. He was motivated, in part, by encouragement from elderly Mi'gmaq people.

The criterion for membership in the Flat Bay Band is demonstration of lineal descent from a Mi'gmaq ancestor within four generations. The Band Council believes that this should entitle Flat Bay Band members to recognition as status Indians under the Indian Act. In 2000, samples of documentation required for band membership were submitted to seven federal government ministers by the Flat Bay Band. The chief of the Assembly of First Nations and the chief of the Mi'gmaq Grand Council have pledged support for the Flat Bay Band's attempt to gain status.

Beginning in the 1980s, the Flat Bay Band received federal and provincial funding for vocational training and other programs. Mr. White was instrumental in opening these programs to non-Mi'gmaq in Flat Bay. "We didn't want to isolate people," he said. "Our forefathers opened their arms to Europeans. Who were we to turn them away?" Consequently, most (but not all) non-Mi'gmaq people in Flat Bay support the band's attempt to gain recognition and self-government under the Indian Act.

Mi'gmaq Lives and Theories of Ethnicity and Identity

These accounts illustrate several theoretical aspects of ethnicity and identity. Dorothy Anger remarks that, until recently, "Indian" was the least-valued identity in the Bay St. George area.[73] But when Calvin White was growing up, his Mi'gmaq identity was never in doubt. Not only did he learn traditional bush skills from his older family members, but as part of a visible minority it was impossible for him or his older relatives to deny their Mi'gmaq roots. His employment as a skilled worker in the 1970s perhaps indicates a relaxation of the exclusion of Indians from local industries. In contrast, it seems likely that J, K, and L's Mi'gmaq ancestry was hidden or disguised by their older relatives in order to avoid such exclusion. As well, their physical appearance allowed them to pass as non-Indian, and to avoid the stigma attached to "jackatars."

Richard Jenkins writes, "Significant in the processes whereby people acquire the identities with which they are labeled is the capacity of authoritatively applied identities effectively to constitute or impinge upon individual experience. This is a question of whose definition of a situation counts (put crudely, power)."[74] Political activists such as Calvin White managed to replace local pejorative definitions of Indian with the state-sanctioned concept of First Nation citizen. The possibility that Mi'gmaq identity could be a source of pride rather than shame was exemplified by the Conne River Band's successful attempt to obtain the advantages of "status" for its members in 1984.

J's case illustrates several aspects of what Barth has called self-ascription and ascription-by-others.[75] J did not regard himself as Mi'gmaq before 1993 because he was unaware of his Mi'gmaq ancestry. The chief of the Corner Brook Band Council, however, saw J as an Indian who was unwilling to acknowledge his Mi'gmaq ancestry. But self-ascription and ascription-by-others began to coincide after J discovered and publicly acknowledged his Mi'gmaq roots. At the same time, it seems likely that most non-Mi'gmaq people in Corner Brook still regard J as white.

The stories of J, K, and L clearly show that there was a distinction in Corner Brook between those who could pass as non-Mi'gmaq (unknowingly or otherwise), and those who, for reasons such as physical appearance, could not. Until recently, the latter were stigmatized. Do they consider themselves "more Indian" than people such as J, K, and L who were not subject to stigmatization? Perhaps. But this issue is beyond the scope of our current research. In any case, the federal government does not recognize degrees of Indianness.

J, K, and L are all of European-Mi'gmaq descent. J and K also have Inuit and perhaps Beothuk ancestors. They could all claim multiple ethnic identities. But the emphasis on Mi'gmaq ancestry that has emerged with the possibility of registration under the Indian Act has meant that many people of mixed descent have assumed an exclusive public or social identity as Mi'gmaq. Indian identity trumps others, at least for now. At the same time, J, K, and L retain mixed personal identities. For example, K's discovery of her Aboriginal ancestry has strengthened her identity as a Newfoundlander. L's public assertion of Mi'gmaq identity has not lessened his curiosity about his Norwegian ancestry. And we once heard Calvin White and other Mi'gmaq in Flat Bay discuss the ways in which their French ancestors came to Bay St. George. As Jenkins remarks, "Social identity is a practical accomplishment, a process.... Individual and collective social identities can be understood using one model, of the dialectical interplay of processes of internal and external definition."[76]

Appendix

The following notice was published in the Stephenville *Georgian* on April 20, 1999, as well as in the Corner Brook *Western Star.*

Flat Bay Indian Band Council
NOTIFICATION

Persons living outside the community of Flat Bay who were former residents or who have direct ties to families in the Flat Bay area.

The Flat Bay Indian Band Council is undergoing a registration process and if any of those people are interested or wish to be included in that process they are advised to notify the Flat Bay Council in writing and provide them with any documentation which they have to support their inclusion.

Send letters to

P.O. Box 375, St. George's, NF AON 1ZO

According to an article in the April 20, 1999, issue of the *Georgian,* the "vast majority" of Newfoundland Mi'gmaq were identified as Indian in the census of 1945. Calvin White, chief of the Flat Bay Band, was quoted as follows: "Basically, all that anyone has to do in the current registration process is to show they were identified in that census, or their parents or grandparents were. Birth certificates are often sufficient as supporting documentation."

Notes

1 See Frederick Barth, *Ethnic Groups and Boundaries,* ed. Frederick Barth (Boston: Little Brown, 1969); chapter 10 of Richard Jenkins, *Social Identity* (London and New York: Routledge, 1996); and Martin Sokefield, "Debating Self, Identity, and Culture in Anthropology," *Current Anthropology* 40, 4, (1999): 414–47.

2 See Anthony D. Buckley and Mary Catherine Kenny, *Negotiating Identity: Rhetoric, Metaphor, and Social Drama in Northern Ireland* (Washington, DC: Smithsonian Institution Press, 1995); Sandra Wallman, "Ethnicity and the Boundary Process in Context," in *Theories of Race and Ethnic Relations*, ed. J. Rex and D. Mason (Cambridge: Cambridge University Press, 1986), 26.

3 Jenkins, *Social Identity*, 26.

4 Hugh Beach, *A Year in Lapland* (Washington, DC: Smithsonian Institution Press, 1993), 218.

5 Ibid.

6 Personal communication with Hugh Beach, 1995.

7 Indian and Northern Affairs Canada. *Indian Band Membership: An Information Booklet Concerning New Indian Band Membership Laws and Preparation of Indian Band Membership Codes* (Ottawa: Indian and Northern Affairs Canada, 1985).

8 Métis are descendants of Aboriginals and Europeans who lived mainly in Saskatchewan, Alberta, the Red River region of Manitoba, and Ontario.

9 For example, see Harold Driver, *Indians of North America*, 2nd ed., rev. (Chicago: University of Chicago Press, 1969); Peter A. Cumming and Neil H. Mickenberg, eds. *Native Rights in Canada*, 2nd ed. (Toronto: Indian-Eskimo Association of Canada, 1972); and Hope MacLean, *Indians, Inuit and Métis of Canada* (Toronto: Gage, 1982).

10 Leslie Harris, *Newfoundland and Labrador* (Don Mills, ON: J.M. Dent, 1968).

11 Cumming and Mickenberg, *Native Rights*, 93.

12 MacLean, *Indians*.

13 See Frances Briffett, *The Story of Newfoundland and Labrador* (Don Mills, ON: J.M. Dent, 1954), 22; quoted in Richard Budgell, "The Beothuks and the Newfoundland Mind," *Newfoundland Studies* 8, 1 (1992): 16-17.

14 Budgell, "Beothuks," 17-18.

15 Ibid., 19.

16 James P. Howley, *The Beothucks, or Red Indians: The Aboriginal Inhabitants of Newfoundland* (Coles Canadiana Collection, 1980), 252-55.

17 Edward Tompkins, "Pencilled Out: Newfoundland and Labrador's Native People and Canadian Confederation," Unpublished ms., 1988.

18 *Western Star*, Corner Brook, NL, December 10, 1987.

19 *Globe and Mail*, July 21, 2003.

20 Dennis Bartels, "Time Immemorial? A Research Note on Micmacs in Newfoundland," *Newfoundland Quarterly* 75, 3 (1979): 6-9.

21 Briffet, *Story of Newfoundland*; quoted in Michael G. Wetzel, *Decolonizing Ktaqmkuk Mi'kmaw History*, LLM thesis, Dalhousie University, 1995.

22 Leslie Upton, "The Extermination of the Beothucks of Newfoundland," *Canadian Historical Review* 58, 2 (1977): 133-53.

23 Ingeborg Marshall, "Disease as a Factor in the Demise of the Beothuck Indians," in *Change & Continuity: A Reader on Pre-Confederation Canada*, ed. Carol Wilton (Whitby, ON: McGraw-Hill Ryerson, 1991), 138-49; see also Ralph Pastore, "The Collapse of the Beothuk World," *Acadiensis* 19, 1 (1989): 52-71.

24 Budgell, "The Beothuks," 23.

25 Dorothy Anger, *Nowa'mkisk (Where the Sand Blows): Vignettes of Bay St. George Micmacs* (Port au Port East, NL: Bay St. George Regional Indian Band, 1988), x.

26 Doug Jackson, *On the Country: the Micmac of Newfoundland* (St. John's: H. Cuff, 1993), 163-64.

27 Quoted in Donovan Downer, *Tubulent Tides: A Social History of Sandy Point* (Portugal Cove, NL: ESP Press, 1997), 81.

28 George M. Story, W.J. Kirwin, and J.D.A. Widdowson, eds., *Dictionary of Newfoundland English* (Toronto: University of Toronto Press, 1982), 272.

29 Downer, *Turbulent Tides*, 20.

30 Dorothy Anger, "Situational Ethics: Meanings of Micmac Identity in Newfoundland," presented at the conference of the Canadian Anthropology Society, City, June 1997, 1.

31 Ibid., 4.

32 Ibid., 57.

33 See Dorothy Anger, "The Micmacs of Newfoundland: A Resurgent Culture," *Culture* 1, 1 (1981): 78-81.

34 Wetzel, *Decolonizing*, 77.

35 Charles Martijn, "An Eastern Micmac Domain of Islands," *Actes Vingtième Congrès des Algonquinistes*, ed. William Cowan (Ottawa: Carleton University Press, 1989).

36 Adrian Tanner and Sakej Henderson, "Aboriginal Land Claims in the Atlantic Provinces," in *Aboriginal Land Claims in Canada*, ed. Ken Coates (Toronto: Copp Clark Pitman, 1992) 147.

37 Robert M. Levitt, *Micmac of the East Coast* (Markham, ON: Fitzhenry and Whiteside, 1993), 4.

38 Government of Newfoundland and Labrador, *Assessment and Analysis of the Micmac Land Claim in Newfoundland* (St. John's: Government of Newfoundland and Labrador, 1982), 93, 115.

39 See Commodore Grayson, Royal Navy, to the Lords of Trade and Plantations, 1701, Colonial Office, 1942, 180; Dennis Bartels, "Newfoundland Micmac Claims to Land and Status," *Native Studies Review* 7, 2 (1991): 43-51.

40 Tanner and Henderson, "Aboriginal Land Claims," 147–48.

41 *Globe and Mail*, 21 July 2003.

42 Ingeborg Marshall, *The History and Ethnography of the Beothuck*. Montreal: McGill-Queen's University Press, 1996, 14.

43 Ibid., 54.

44 Gary E. McManus, et al., *Atlas of Newfoundland and Labrador* (St. John's: Breakwater, 1991), pl. 7.1.

45 Martijn, "Eastern Micmac Domain," 212–23; also Charles Martijn, "Review of *A History and Ethnography of the Beothuk*, by I. Marshall," *Newfoundland Studies* 12, 1 (1999): 105–31.

46 Unpublished ms. cited in Wetzel, *Decolonizing*, 164.

47 Barrie Reynolds, "Beothuk," in *Handbook of North American Indians, Northeast*, vol. 15, ed. Bruce Trigger (Washington, DC: Smithsonian Institution, 1978), 101.

48 Carl Waldman, *Encyclopedia of North American Tribes* (New York and Oxford: Facts on File, 1988), 30.

49 Gilbert Legay, *Atlas des Indiens d'Amérique du Nord* (Paris: Casterman, 1993), 20.

50 Quoted in Carolyn Dittburner, Katherine Graham, and Frances Abele, "Public Policy and Aboriginal Peoples 1965-1992," vol. 1 (Ottawa: Royal Commission on Aboriginal Peoples, 1996), 103.

51 Marshall, *History and Ethnography*, 13.

52 Ibid., 566–567n.

53 Wetzel, *Decolonizing*, 283n.

54 Ingeborg Marshall, "Beothuk and Micmac: Re-examining Relationships," *Acadiensis* 17, 2 (1988).

55 See Bruce Trigger, *The Huron Farmers of the North*, 2nd ed. (New York: Harcourt Brace Jovanovich, 1990), 80–96.

56 Wetzel, *Decolonizing*, 76–82.

57 Jackson, *On the Country*, 42.

58 Bartels, "Newfoundland Micmac Claims"; John Mitchell, "All Gone Widden: Was Shawnawdithit Right? A Speculative Approach," *Newfoundland Quarterly* 93, 1 (1999): 39–41.

59 Marshall, *History and Ethnography*, 13.

60 See Mitchell, "All Gone Widden," 40.

61 Buckley and Kenny, *Negotiating Identity*, 9–12.

62 Noel Lyon, *The Mikmaqs of Newfoundland: A Report Prepared for the Canadian Human Rights Commission* (Ottawa: Canadian Human Rights Commission, 1997), 5–6.

63 Indian and Northern Affairs Canada, *Indian Band Membership*, 1985.

64 Personal Communication, Corner Brook Band Council, 1997.

65 See Frank Speck, *Beothuk and Micmac* (New York: Museum of the American Indian—Heye Foundation, 1922); Jackson, *On the Country*, 125-27.

66 See Appendix.

67 According to another version of this story, JPC was in a bread line during hard times in St. Malo, France. He got into a fight with another man in the line, and, believing he had killed his opponent, escaped on a fishing boat, which took him to Newfoundland.

68 Seasonal access to fishing grounds and coastal areas of a vast stretch of the northeast and west coasts of Newfoundland was granted to migratory French fishers by two eighteenth-century treaties. French access to these areas ended only in 1904. See J. Smallwood, et al., eds., "The French Shore," in *Encyclopedia of Newfoundland and Labrador*, vol. 2 (St. John's: Newfoundland Book Publishers, 1984), 407-15 .

69 Personal communication, Corner Brook Band Council, 1997.

70 Until 1998, the education system in Newfoundland and Labrador was controlled by major Christian denominations. Catholics and Protestants went to separate schools, and teachers who did not belong to the denominations that administered the schools were excluded from teaching positions. Special provision for continued denominational control of education was made when Newfoundland-Labrador joined Canada in 1949.

71 The s.s. *Caribou* regularly carried passengers and freight across the Cabot Strait from Port-aux-Basques, Newfoundland, to North Sydney, Nova Scotia. The *Caribou* was torpedoed by a German submarine, *U-69*, in October 1942. One hundred and thirty-seven passengers and crew members of the *Caribou* lost their lives.

72 Ruth Holmes Whitehead is a well-known anthropologist who specializes in Mi'gmaq culture and history. She is the author of several books on the Mi'gmaq, including *The Old Man Told Us* (Halifax: Nimbus Press, 1991).

73 Anger, "Situational ethnics," 5-7.

74 Jenkins, *Social Identity*, 22-23.

75 Barth, *Ethnic Groups*, 1969; Buckley and Kenny, *Negotiating Identity*.

76 Jenkins, *Social Identity*, 25.

Bibliography

Anger, Dorothy. "The Micmacs of Newfoundland: A Resurgent Culture." *Culture* 1, 1 (1981): 78-81.

——— . *No*waímkiskº (Where the Sand Blows): Vignettes of Bay St. Georges Micmacs*. Port au Port East, NL: Bay St. George Regional Indian Band, 1988.

——— . "Situational Ethnics: Meanings of Micmac Identity in Newfoundland." Presented at the conference of the Canadian Anthropology Society, City, June 1997.

Bartels, Dennis. "Newfoundland Micmac Claims to Land and Status." *Native Studies Review* 7, 2 (1991): 43–51.

——— . "Time Immemorial? A Research Note on Micmacs in Newfoundland." *Newfoundland Quarterly* 75, 3 (1979): 6–9.

Barth, Frederik. "Introduction." In *Ethnic Groups and Boundaries.* Ed. Frederik Barth. Boston: Little Brown, 1969.

Beach, Hugh. *A Year in Lapland.* Washington, DC: Smithsonian Institution Press, 1993.

Briffett, Frances. *The Story of Newfoundland and Labrador.* Don Mills, ON: J.M. Dent, 1949.

——— . *The Story of Newfoundland and Labrador.* Don Mills, ON: J.M. Dent, 1954.

Buckley, Anthony D., and Mary Catherine Kenny. *Negotiating Identity: Rhetoric, Metaphor, and Social Drama in Northern Ireland.* Washington, DC: Smithsonian Institution Press, 1995.

Budgell, Richard. "The Beothuks and the Newfoundland Mind." *Newfoundland Studies* 8, 1 (1992): 15–33.

Cumming, Peter A., and Neil H. Mickenberg, eds. *Native Rights in Canada.* 2nd ed. Toronto: Indian-Eskimo Association of Canada in association with General Publishing, 1972.

Dittburner, Carolyn, Katherine Graham, and Frances Abele. "Public Policy and Aboriginal Peoples 1965–1992." Vol. 1. Ottawa: Royal Commission on Aboriginal Peoples, 1996.

Downer, Donovan. *Turbulent Tides: A Social History of Sandy Point.* Portugal Cove, NL: ESP Press, 1997.

Driver, Harold. *Indians of North America.* 2nd ed., rev. Chicago: University of Chicago Press, 1969.

Government of Newfoundland and Labrador. *Assessment and Analysis of the Micmac Land Claim in Newfoundland.* St. John's: Government of Newfoundland and Labrador, 1982.

Harris, Leslie. *Newfoundland and Labrador.* Don Mills, ON: J.M. Dent, 1968.

Howley, James P. *The Beothucks, or Red Indians: The Aboriginal Inhabitants of Newfoundland.* Coles Canadiana Collection, 1980.

Indian and Northern Affairs Canada. *Indian Band Membership: An Information Booklet Concerning New Indian Band Membership Laws and Preparation of Indian Band Membership Codes.* Ottawa: Indian and Northern Affairs Canada, 1985.

Jackson, Doug. *On the Country: The Micmac of Newfoundland.* St. John's: H. Cuff, 1993.

Jenkins, Richard. *Social Identity.* London and New York: Routledge, 1996.

Legay, Gilbert. *Atlas des Indiens d'Amérique du Nord.* Paris: Casterman, 1993.

Levitt, Robert M. *Micmac of the East Coast.* Markham, ON: Fitzhenry and Whiteside, 1993.

Lyon, Noel. *The Mikmaqs of Newfoundland: A Report Prepared for the Canadian Human Rights Commission.* Ottawa: Canadian Human Rights Commission, 1997.

MacLean, Hope. *Indians, Inuit, and Métis of Canada.* Toronto: Gage, 1982.

Marshall, Ingeborg. "Beothuk and Micmac: Re-examining Relationships." *Acadiensis* 17, 2 (1988): 52–82.

——— . "Disease as a Factor in the Demise of the Beothuck Indians." In *Change & Continuity: A Reader on Pre-Confederation Canada.* Ed. Carol Wilton, 138–49. Whitby, ON: McGraw-Hill Ryerson, 1991.

——— . *The History and Ethnography of the Beothuk.* Montreal: McGill-Queen's University Press, 1996.

Martijn, Charles. "An Eastern Micmac Domain of Islands." In *Actes Vingtième Congrès des Algonquinistes.* Ed. William Cowan, 208–31. Ottawa: Carleton University Press, 1989.

——— . "Review of *A History and Ethnography of the Beothuk*, by I. Marshall." *Newfoundland Studies* 12, 1 and 2 (1999): 105–31.

Martijn, Charles, ed. *Les Micmacs et la Mer.* Montréal: Recherches amérindiennes au Québec, 1986.

McManus, Gary E., et al. *Atlas of Newfoundland and Labrador.* St. John's: Breakwater, 1991.

Mitchell, John. "All Gone Widden ('asleep'/died): Was Shawnawdithit Right? A Speculative Approach." *Newfoundland Quarterly* 93, 1 (1999): 39–41.

Pastore, Ralph. "The Collapse of the Beothuk World." *Acadiensis* 19, 1 (1989): 52–71.

Reynolds, Barrie. "Beothuk." In *Handbook of North American Indians, Northeast.* Vol. 15. Ed. Bruce Trigger, 101–108. Washington, DC: Smithsonian Institution, 1978.

Smallwood, J., et al., eds. "The French Shore." In *Encyclopedia of Newfoundland and Labrador.* Vol. 2. St. John's: Newfoundland Book Publishers, 1984, 407–15.

Sokefeld, Martin. "Debating Self, Identity, and Culture in Anthropology." *Current Anthropology* 40, 4 (1999): 417–47.

Speck, Frank. *Beothuk and Micmac.* New York: Museum of the American Indian–Heye Foundation, 1922.

Story, George M., W.J. Kirwin, and J.D.A. Widdowson, eds. *Dictionary of Newfoundland English.* Toronto: University of Toronto Press, 1982.

Tanner, Adrian, and Sakej Henderson. "Aboriginal Land Claims in the Atlantic Provinces." In *Aboriginal Land Claims in Canada.* Ed. Ken Coates, 131–49. Toronto: Copp Clark Pitman, 1992.

Tompkins, Edward. "Pencilled Out: Newfoundland and Labrador's Native People and Canadian Confederation." Unpublished ms., 1988.

Trigger, Bruce. *The Huron Farmers of the North.* 2nd ed. New York: Harcourt Brace Jovanovich, 1990.

Upton, Leslie. "The Extermination of the Beothucks of Newfoundland." *Canadian Historical Review* 58, 2 (1977): 133–53.

Waldman, Carl. *Encyclopedia of Native American Tribes.* New York and Oxford: Facts on File, 1988.

Wallman, Sandra. "Ethnicity and the Boundary Process in Context." In *Theories of Race and Ethnic Relations.* Ed. J. Rex and D. Mason, 226–345. Cambridge: Cambridge University Press, 1986.

Wetzel, Michael G. *Decolonizing Ktaqmkuk Mi'kmaw History.* LLM thesis, Dalhousie University, 1995.

Whitehead, Ruth Holmes. *The Old Man Told Us. Halifax*: Nimbus, 1991.

C Literary and Cinematic Representations

11

"Show me the money": Representation of Aboriginal People in East-German Indian Films

Ute Lischke and *David T. McNab*

In *Jerry Maguire*, THE AFRICAN-AMERICAN football hero Rod Tidwell has a most amusing scene with his white agent, Jerry Maguire, played by Tom Cruise. Maguire has seemingly forsaken the American dream of making the most money he can by exploiting people, at least until he is fired because he told the truth. All he has left is one fading football player, Tidwell, played hilariously by Cuba Gooding Jr. In response to Maguire's entreaties to stay on as his last meal ticket, Gooding screams at Maguire, "Show me the money! *Show me the money!*" Maguire shouts back, "Show *me* the money!" The lesson is not lost. Actions speak louder than words, or money itself.

There is a similar theme in the *Indianerfilme*, produced at the DEFA (*Deutsche Film Aktiengesellschaft*, the state-run film studio of the former East Germany) in the late twentieth century. The "hero" is the Yugoslav star Gojko Mitic. In the end, money is made while the land is exploited for the white man's dollars.

Between 1966 and 1983, during the Cold War, the East German state produced films about the American West. In all, fourteen *Indianerfilme* were created at the DEFA studio in co-production with studios in Yugoslavia, the Soviet Union, Bulgaria, Romania, and Cuba. In these filmic representations, the Indians were the heroes—not the villains— and the Americans, English, and French were the imperialists and the bad guys, playing to the political rhetoric and propaganda of Communism in the Cold War.[1] Only since 1996 have these Indian films from the "Wild" East become available in North America and have been marketed as the "true history" and representations of Native lives in North America.[2] However, what these films purport to portray as a factual, historical representation of Natives in North America is not, in fact, the "true history," since Aboriginal people have their own independent history as well as their own world views and spirituality that contradict this celluloid representation.

These Indian films tell us more about the politics and culture of former East Germany and Germans in the late twentieth century than they do about Native people in North America. When the Berlin Wall fell in 1989 (a period referred to in Germany as the *Wende*), East Germans were known to West Germans as wild, uncultivated people in much the same manner in which "Indians" used to be viewed as part of the Wild West. So there is a historical correspondence in the DEFA Indian films between how the "Indians" were stereotyped in the nineteenth and twentieth centuries and how East Germans were represented in the rest of Europe, particularly in West Germany. After the *Wende*, of course, for West German capitalists the former East became an opportunity for speculation and investment. Western capitalist "cowboys" wanted to conquer the "Wild East." Speculators soon discovered, however, a Wild East that had been so devastated by pollution that it became exceedingly difficult to exploit without spending millions of Deutschmarks. Still today, the former East is economically depressed with high unemployment, a polluted landscape, and a large migration of young people to the West in search of jobs. East Germans and reunification continue to be blamed for a very depressed economy in the reunited Germany. After reunification, and without state-supported funding, the DEFA was closed down and its writers, producers, directors, actors, and everyone else associated with it became unemployed. And there were no more *Indianerfilme*, or westerns, from the Wild East.[3]

For almost two centuries, "Indians" have fascinated Europeans, particularly the Germans.[4] Humorist Drew Hayden Taylor, who refers to himself as a "blue-eyed Ojibway," made the following observation about Germans:

> I waved good-bye to Turtle Island as my girlfriend and I left its familiar shores and flew out over the Atlantic. We were on our way to a country that is widely known to Aboriginal people across

North America as a land curious, intrigued, and downright infatuated with us Injuns—a place known as Germany. It was ... my third [trip] to that fabled land where beads, fluff, feather, and leather are always in fashion—even for those who look more German than Native. Nobody really knows why.

Some theorize it's because of a turn-of-the-century writer named Karl May who wrote several books romanticizing the North American Indians. Others believe it's because Germans were once tribal themselves, never fully conquered by even the mighty Roman Empire. Or perhaps it's our connection to a wilderness that is practically non-existent in Europe.[5]

Hayden Taylor is one of many "Indians" who have visited Europe over the course of hundreds of years. It has been suggested that as early as 1620, almost two thousand "Indians" had crossed the Atlantic to Europe, many of them involuntarily.[6] They were succeeded by many more who later became part of travelling circuses, for example the German Circus Sarrasani's Wild West Show and the American Buffalo Bill's Wild West Show, all of which helped to introduce the image of the noble savage, the exotic "other," to the German psyche. Some "Indians" were even born in Europe on such tours.[7]

These shows clearly influenced the German writer Karl May (1832–1912), who subsequently published numerous travelogues and accounts of "American Indians" in the vein of James Fenimore Cooper, before ever having set foot in North America, and became one of the most popular authors in Germany and Eastern Europe. Using the first-person narrative in his best-known works in an attempt to create authenticity of place, he saw his characters such as Winnetou and his sidekick Old Shatterhand become household names in Germany.[8] Beginning in 1962, Harald Reinl successfully adapted these popular Karl May novels for film in West Germany. To this day, re-enactments of May's novels still take place in enormous outdoor amphitheatres all over Germany and Eastern Europe. Germany's fascination with the "other" persists today, not only in watching and identifying with "Indians" but also in "playing Indian," as attested by the re-enactment camps set up across Eastern Germany and the former Czechoslovakia, where men and women gather to dress up as Indians, live in tepees, and engage in beading and quill work.

The Germans were also imperialists in the nineteenth and twentieth centuries, especially in southern Africa and, of course, in Europe itself. Their treatment and representation of Indigenous peoples as the "other,"[9] while different from English imperialism,[10] was also shaped, in part, by their own colonial encounters and experiences. Sabine Hake concluded, in her thoughtful analysis of German films of the Third Reich, that

> racism, exoticism, nationalism, and antisemitism define the terms under which the binaries of colonial discourse—culture vs. nature, mind vs. body, male vs. female—are collapsed into an ongoing triangulation of desire. Defeated on the field of colonial politics, the Germans in their films appropriated the colonial through a double movement: the instrumentalizing of established colonial narratives in a continuation of war by other means and the pursuit of an attraction that allowed them to encounter themselves in the natives.[11]

And this is precisely the imperial rationale that remained in Germany from its empire, to be resurrected in the 1960s in the East German Indian films.

In the early 1960s the DEFA was in financial straits and began to investigate making alternative films that would bring in cash at the box office. Discussions were begun about a series of films dealing with North American Indians. DEFA officials had watched the runaway success of the Karl May films in West Germany; East Germans would frequently travel to Prague to see them.[12] What the DEFA wanted, in contrast to the Karl May films, was a product that would be historically authentic, yet carry a message that would be appropriate for the socialist state. The Indians, struggling to survive imperialist and capitalist forces, would reflect the proletarian ideal of hard work and cooperation. Ideologically, these films were positioned as anti-imperialistic, entertaining, yet didactic, emphasizing historical events about the conquest of North America and the genocide of Indians. Genocide, technological advances, and profit joined forces under capitalism. The struggle against such evil forces in a socialist state gave legitimacy to the German Democratic Republic. Inherent contradictions within the films were levelled and harmonized by the DEFA, and the result was a product that appealed to all age groups. The *Indianerfilme* became politically correct mass entertainment that was a box office success both in East Germany and in many Eastern European countries. Most importantly, these films kept the studio in the black.[13] Ironically, the objective of the DEFA Indian films was purely commercial, and the films were made in order to keep the corporation solvent. However, as the films themselves reveal, any attempt to lend accuracy or authenticity to them was quite secondary.

The representation of Indians was seemingly subordinated to a European based knowledge system and served as propaganda. The films show war and not the Aboriginal objectives of peace.[14] The depiction of Native people was no more than a caricature of Indians as "noble savages." Given the insularity of the Communist countries during the Cold War, the studio had no access to the Wild West in the United States. Instead, the DEFA looked for locations in Eastern Europe to represent the American West. And that is the most serious weakness of the Indian films: the American West was a real place that could not be commercialized and made to be authentic or accurate. Cinematically, the appropriation of the Wild West in the Wild East failed miserably. To get beyond these caricatures, we need to understand something about the multi-dimensional character of Aboriginal world views, their places and the spirituality they embody, which are never portrayed in westerns of any kind. For an alternative, a different approach was taken in the CBC movie *Big Bear*,[15] which was written, produced, and acted by Aboriginal people. It was the antithesis of the western.

The best-selling Native American writer Louise Erdrich has provided some indication of this approach in *The Last Report on the Miracles at Little No Horse*. *Last Report* opens with a statement by Nanapush about the framework of Creation: "Nindinawemaganidok. There are four layers above the earth and four layers below. Sometimes in our dreams and creations we pass through the layers, which are also space and time. In saying the word nindinawemaganidok, or my relatives, we speak of everything that has existed in time, the known and the unknown, the unseen, the obvious, all that lived before or is living now in the worlds above and below."[16]

There are spiritual journeys in some of the DEFA Indian films that appear to represent spirituality, such as in *The Sons of Great Bear*,[17] which was the first DEFA Indian film, and in *Tecumseh*.[18] Indian people and places have had a profound impact on Europeans, and these two films are, ironically, powerful witnesses to the presence of spirituality in their histories and its impact on Europeans. Central to this world view is the complexity of Aboriginal oral traditions as well as the notion of time. It is against this framework that one must judge the early Hollywood westerns as well as the westerns from the GDR, otherwise one will mistake apparent authenticity for accuracy. But what is missing from these DEFA films is an understanding of Aboriginal oral traditions—their stories told in their ways, something that cannot be captured in books or on film.

Alberto Manguel has observed that "a society can exist—many do exist—without writing, but no society can exist without reading and that even "in societies that set down a record of their passing, reading precedes writing; the would-be writer must be able to recognize and decipher the social system of signs before setting them down on the page."[19] Similarly, in order to understand Aboriginal oral traditions, it is necessary to learn how to read the names and the clans and understand their cultures before one can comprehend their ideas of time and history. They are symbolized by beads, which, like Grandfather Sun, are circular. To provide but one example, Erdrich has also commented on the importance and relationship of beading to the circularity of time and the fact that all stories are interconnected. In *The Antelope Wife*, Klaus Shawano, the Chippewa trader, observed that his "stories have stories. My beadwork is made by relatives and friends whose tales branch off in an ever more complicated set of barriers."[20] Here the presence of Native spirituality is present not only in the concept of time, but also in the making of things, the beadwork.[21]

The Aboriginal notion of history begins with the sun. Each day the sun rises, travels its course, and sets in the west. So, too, is the life of human beings. It is in this way that history exists for Aboriginal people. The sun is also represented by the metaphor and shape of the drum. The sound of the drum is the heartbeat of Mother Earth as we walk her each day, through the seasons of our lives. It is both very simple and profoundly complex, far more complicated than the linear notions of time and history inherent in, and part of, European-based knowledge systems, the theoretical perspectives that they have engendered, and the colonialism that has resulted.[22]

This idea of circles of time is common to all indigenous peoples, including the Ojibwa. In the mid-nineteenth century, in his writings, Kahgegagahbowh (George Copway) described the concept succinctly: "The Ojibwas, as well as many others, acknowledged that there was but one Great Spirit, who made the world; they gave him the name of good or benevolent; kesha is benevolent, monedoo is spirit; Ke-sha-mon-e-doo. They supposed he lived in the heavens; but the most of the time he was in the *Sun*. They said it was from him they received all that was good through life. And that he seldom needs the offering of his Red children, for he was seldom angry."[23] The sun, the sustainer of life, is also a metaphor for time. Aboriginal peoples' ideas of time and history are circular in form and substance as well as parallel in structure. And it was Copway who made a huge splash in Germany when he attended an international peace conference there in the mid-nineteenth century.[24]

When the DEFA began making its first *Indianerfilm*, it was at least initially obsessed with historical authenticity, in order to tap into the markets for all things "Indian." *The Sons of Great Bear* had launched the DEFA's most successful series of films in one genre by attracting more than 10 million enthusiastic viewers. The studio deliberately distanced itself from the genre of the Hollywood western, as well as West Germany's adaptation of Karl May, by using the label *Indianerfilm*. Like its West German counterpart, its focus was on the Indian, not the cowboy, adopting the Native American point of view; nevertheless, the film is advertised on its video jacket as a "Western from the East," but "based on actual historical events."

The Sons of Great Bear is based on a 1951 novel by Liselotte Welskopf-Henrich (1901–1979), a fact that purportedly gives credence to the film's foundation on historical truth. Welskopf-Henrich was a professor of history at Humboldt University, and a novelist known in East Germany for her youth books as well as her trilogy based on *Die Söhne der großen Bärin* (1951).

In an interview in *Junge Welt*, Welskopf-Henrich emphasized that *The Sons of Great Bear* was different from similar films made in the West, not only because it intended to portray the "Indian problem" realistically, but it was also made from the "Indian point of view." She argued that her forty years in studying Indian history, as well as a trip to Canada and the United States where she visited with the Lakota, provided her with enough experience to write an authentic and historically accurate novel.[25] A fanatic about details, Welskopf-Henrich worked as an advisor on the film until she resigned when some horses resisted being ridden without a saddle. She allowed no compromises. "Indians" rode their horses bareback.[26]

Gojko Mitic, a Yugoslavian physical education student with an attractive, muscular physique, became an instant audience hit as the handsome hunk in the starring role in all of the films. He plays the part of the stoic Indian chief and to this day he continues to promote these films in Germany, Eastern Europe, and North America, frequently appearing with his stallion at film festivals and suburban malls throughout Germany. All the films reveal the Native struggle against the greed of white settlers, broken treaties, corruption, and imperialism. Although most critics agree that the productions lack quality, the plots are predictable, and much of the acting is poor, the hero is clearly Mitic, who drew audience sympathy and always won the day.

In *The Sons of Great Bear* Mitic plays the role of the Dakota-Sioux (Lakota) chief Tokei-ihto who must avenge the death of his father Mattotaupa, killed by his white brother "Red Fox" when he refuses to reveal the location of the cave that contains the gold. The geography is muddled. The plot is rather predictable: an army colonel breaks the treaty, Indians are relocated to a reservation, and white settlers are greedy for gold. It is Tokei-ihto who leads his people out of the forced reservation back to freedom. The film opens with Tokei-ihot's arrival at the saloon where he attempts to rescue his father from the demons of firewater, and concludes with settlement of the tribe on rich agricultural land across the Missouri River, where, Tokei-ihto declares, they will settle on "this fertile ground, to raise tame buffalo, to forge iron and make ploughs," bringing home the DEFA message of finding a new way to a worker and collective farming state. But this is not "Indian" land, much less "Indian" philosophy.

The scenes of the film are romantic, filled with "wild Indians." There is the stark setting of the fort and its tavern, the cabaret scenes of heavy brandy-drinkers and one sexy barmaid, and then the lush setting of the "Indian" settlement with its peaceful teepees, women working, and children playing. Then there is the wagon train, hurriedly making its way toward the fort. Within the fort, the army is intent on opening new gold mines in the sacred Black Hills of the Lakota. The railway is behind schedule; work must proceed quickly so that the mine can open. The "Indians" must be moved from the land immediately. The Lakota must be on their new reservation by January 31, 1876. The problem is, Tokei-ihto is resisting because of the murder of his father. And he wants to preserve his land on the prairies. The army is afraid that Tokei-ihto may join up with Toshunka Witko's rebels. In the fort, treaties are meant to be broken. Outside the fort, the "Indians" fight for their people and their honour.

Two years pass. Tokei-ihto and Toshunka Witko talk of joining forces. The "Indians" attack the wagon train. Rapid action shots criss-cross, showing general confusion, but end with a wagon wheel left spinning in the foreground, a metaphor for the medicine wheel, the wheel of life. Tokai-ihto crouches behind the wheel. Once again, he has won the day. The soldiers are left to return to the fort by foot, demoralized. Tokai-ihto returns to the fort and delivers Major Samuel Smith's daughter, Kate, to her father. He wishes to smoke a peace pipe to discuss justice and peace. The ungrateful major arrogantly denies this request for peace.

When Tokai-ihot returns to his camp, there is a much different atmosphere. Unlike the sparse and desert-like surroundings of the fort, the Lakota live in a peaceful, romanticized place; the trail is beautiful, lined with trees and bushes. There is the sparkling river. The women and children gather, stylized, in formation. The warriors ride back into camp across the river. Children play in the water as a warrior waters his horse. When Red Fox arrives, the mood changes. Wolfchief of the Delaware acknowledges that the fire of his tribe has gone out on their new reservation. There are no more warriors and they cannot escape the "white flood."

Tokai-ihto must talk to Major Smith. The music swells as the warriors depart across the river. The army has decided that the gold in the Black Hills determines the new boundaries of the reservation, not the treaty. It has become a matter of honour versus the interest and greed of the white people. An army escort forces the Lakota tribe to the new reservation. The trail is long and mournful, evoking the trail of tears. The expedition is funereal, and at the end there is nothing but rocky land. No fertile soil, just devastation and death. Adam Adamson advises Tokai-ihto to flee to Canada. The Lakotas seem to have been conquered. But Tokai-ihto wants to lead the tribe out of the reservation and return to the mountains of the Great Mother Bear. With a drum, a prayer is offered to the totem of the great bear. Since he is the son of the "drunk" man who revealed the secret of the gold, Tokai-ihto must go to the mountains for a vision. But before that can happen, a white man has entered the sacred cave, followed by two brave young warriors who want to save Tokai-ihto. Confronted by the bear (spirit), the white man shoots the bear. The bear kills the white man before she dies. However, the Bear Spirit is female and cannot die. Tokai-ihto and the young warriors rescue the bear cub before they make their way across the river to find their new way in a different place. But Aboriginal people do not leave their places. And even if forced out, they always return home. The world of the spirits brings them back. There this improbable linear narrative ends. Aboriginal spirits and the spirit world are not understood and are interpreted for the political propaganda of the former East. Once again, this film exploits the "Indians."

Tecumseh is based on historical records, and perhaps for this reason appears to be less exploitive of "Indians."[27] Like the *Sons of Great Bear*, *Tecumseh* purports to be an authentic historical film. But one asks, whose history? Who's telling? John Sugden, in his modern study of Tecumseh, has written that this film was "as bad as its only widescreen American counterpart, *Brave Warrior* (1952), in which Jay Silverheels [aka Harry Smith from the Six Nations] better known as television's Tonto strove to bring Tecumseh to life from a lame script."[28] Yet it is a much better film than, for example, *The Sons of Great Bear.* The "good guys" do not win this time. The film ends dramatically with the death of Tecumseh on the battlefield at Longwoods near Moraviantown, southwest of present-day London, Ontario. But here again, the point is missed. Like Mother Bear, the spirits cannot be killed.

Chingachgook, The Great Snake,[29] is based on historical fiction so the issue is not its authenticity or even whether it loosely follows (as it does) James Fenimore Cooper's novel *The Deerslayer.* The protagonist, Chingachgook, the last of the Mohicans, fights for the Delaware (Lenape) against the Wyandot (Huron) and is respected for his great courage. The setting is North America in the 1740s. The French and the

English imperialists are fighting each other for "ownership" of the territories of the Aboriginal nations in northeastern North America. Using a blatant divide-and-conquer strategy, the French and the English imperialists attempt, with varying degrees of success, to exploit the Aboriginal nations, to take their land and fight and exterminate one another. In this film the Wyandot Nation supports the French, and the Delaware support the English. Chingachgook has been adopted by the Delaware because he saved the life of their chief. In return, he is to marry the chief's beautiful daughter Wah-ta!-Wah. But the Wyandot, in turn, kidnap her, during an attack on the Delaware. There is no doubt that Chingachgook, along with his friend Deerslayer, will set out to free Wah-ta!-Wah from the Wyandot.

Setting out on parallel paths, Chingachgook and Deerslayer are to meet at Glimmerglas, a mountain lake modelled on Lake Otsego, adjacent to present-day Cooperstown, where Cooper lived. Both the Wyandot and the Delaware frequented this place, a traditional hunting ground, during the summer months, in peaceful times. Intercut with images of this quiet place are scenes from a nearby English fort where Warley, a cynical and barbaric English captain, is giving his orders. He tells Thornton, his young officer, "The Crown needs land, power, riches. We must work hard. We pay the Delaware, and the Wyandot are in the pay of the French. Thus, we have no choice but to fight, on both sides, to the last Indian! In this way we will not only conquer our European enemy, but will also exterminate the natives of this land."

When the Deerslayer arrives at the designated meeting place, he finds his old acquaintance, the trapper Harry Hurry, who is meeting the white hunter Tom Hutter, a former pirate, and his daughter Judith.[30] The Hutters reside in a water castle on the lake. They have no intention of helping an "Indian" rescue his kidnapped woman, and this they forcefully tell the Deerslayer. On the contrary, they are intent on hunting—hunting Indians—and scalping as many men, women, and children as possible in return for money.[31] Hutter states, "In camp there are plenty of sleeping scalps. That means big money, head money. Women and children, large and small scalps—the colony is paying." Just as Chingachgook is trying to rescue Wah-ta!-Wah, the Wyandot, along with the fleeing Wah-ta!-Wah, capture Hutter and Hurry. The Deerslayer and Chingachgook are able to free them by offering "sacred" gifts—a two-tailed animal and two miniature ivory elephants that Hutter obtained illegally on hunts in Africa. The exchange of prisoners is almost complete, when Hurry fires after the Wyandot. The Wyandot return and scalp Hutter. Hurry subsequently flees to the English fort. He convinces Warley to go after easy money by sending in the English army to attack, murder, and scalp the peaceful Wyandot summer camp. Hurry leads the English army to the Huron campsite, where they massacre and then scalp men, women, and children. After this horrific event, Chingachgook tries to bring about peace between the Wyandot and the Delaware. The young Wyandot chief, Arrowhead, rejects this proposal, and in a hand-to-hand fight, Chingachgook kills him. The dream of peace between the Wyandot and the Delaware is shattered.

The film opens and closes with images of water and fire. It shows the potential for peace and treaties in the meeting grounds of northeastern North America. It shows powerful images of water and fire, and the way of the two-row wampum belt, and presents messages as well. For example, the Deerslayer rejects Judith, who is in love with him, because he refuses to live in the fort under the protection of the English who have massacred his friends. Judith then sets her father's water castle ablaze and follows Warley to the English fort and embraces the garrison mentality of the European imperialists. The message is one of both racism and sexism.[32]

Apaches is one of the more sophisticated of the DEFA films. Gojko Mitic represents Ulzana, a "real (although minor) war/raid leader of the Chiricahua known for his daring.[33] This is surprising, since neither the director, Kolditz, nor Mitic visited North America before the screenplay for *Apaches* was written. Mitic visited the United States for the first time after the fall of the Berlin Wall. Before then, he had never ever seen an "Indian."

Apaches is set in 1846 in present-day southeastern New Mexico. Unlike other DEFA Indian films, this one is historically accurate, yet it is a film and a narrative from a European perspective. It is without Aboriginal history or oral traditions—a wild western from the East made for late-twentieth-century propaganda. The Apaches are portrayed as role models for the East German regime. They are simply grafted onto the German myth of the noble savage, which had been propounded by Karl May and his successors.

The plot is straightforward and simple. The theme is mining and mineral exploitation, the conquest of the land, and the extermination of the Apaches. Since this film, like the others, was written and shot during the Cold War, the Americans are the "bad guys" and the "Apaches" are the good guys. But in spite of the Apaches winning this round of the conflict, the primary point of this film was political propaganda, to show good socialist citizens how bad the Americans really were in their dealing with Aboriginal people. However, in the process, the representation of Aboriginal people was once again subordinated to the political framework and ideology of Europe in the late twentieth century. A noble savage is still a savage, the white man is still stoic, this time in adversity and defeat.

The film opens with the Apaches confronting a wagon, which is carrying weapons and ammunition, and mining "cowboys" who have come to take over the enterprise from the Mexicans. Their leader, Johnson, an American sociologist, is bent on getting the copper and silver from the Apache lands and collecting the bounty for killing and scalping every last one of them: $100 for each man, $50 for each woman, and $25 for each child. Perhaps this profession has more in common with the big-game hunter striving to exploit and dominate nature and the natural world than we think. In another form, it is a concomitant of what John MacKenzie has called the European "Empire of Nature."[34] The Apaches are hunted as if they were animals. Johnson is particularly shown as pure evil in a Christian sense. Yet Johnson is bested by our Apache hero, who uses medicine power to shape shift and disappear, much to the consternation of Johnson and his fellow Americans. This is an intriguing element in the film: the Apaches—or at least the male warriors—are, for the most part, not at all stoic. They are very intelligent and show a great deal of moxie as warriors, in spite of the stereotype of the noble savage.

The Mexicans, also conquerors, are portrayed as a gentler sort. Historically, they were not, of course. It is they who work the copper mines for the American mining company. They have accomplished this so far by the use of collaboration—a peace treaty between the Mexicans and the Apaches. This approach has apparently been of great economic benefit for the Mexicans and the Apaches, at least until the Americans arrive. In fact, the Apaches have received nothing substantive from the profits taken from their lands by the Mexicans in this one-sided agreement.

It is Treaty Day and the Americans have arrived at Santa Rita. The Apaches come to town and receive their presents. The Mexican leader discovers the plans of the Americans and refuses to co-operate. But they have no weapons and seem powerless to act. When the Apaches gather to receive their presents in the town square, the Americans roll up a cannon, open fire, and finish this nasty job with their repeating rifles. Men, women, and children are massacred; only a few escape, including Ulzana. The Americans are the savages, taking the scalps of the Apaches for bounty. The Apaches resist, seeking revenge, since they outnumber both the Mexicans and the Americans. They catch up to the Americans and destroy their wagon and some of their small force, and recapture the scalps of their people. Johnson is captured, taken to the Apache village, and made out to be a fool.

Throughout, Apache women are shown as either meek homemakers serving their men like slaves, or "Indian" princesses. This is the usual inaccurate representation of Aboriginal women as passive and obedient, reflecting what German women should be and not what Aboriginal women really were (and are) like. These films make no attempt to be authentic, being more concerned with accuracy or inaccuracy. To this extent, *Apaches* demonstrates racism and gender bias, still exploitive, using caricatures of Aboriginal people.

Ulzana then takes Johnson into town and ties him over a well, without water or food, and leaves him in the sun to die. When the frightened Mexicans flee, the Apaches raid their wagon train. The Mexicans run out of water and start killing themselves out of fear. The American army arrive to find the town deserted and Johnson barely alive. They cut him down, give him water, and then leave him, saying that he is tough—the archetypal stoic white man. They have their orders to wage war on the Mexicans first, to drive them out of the country, then deal with the Apaches.

Throughout the film, one theme is that this land belongs to the Apaches, although the Mexicans are occupying it and the Americans are stealing it. The film is disjointed and episodic: stories within stories loosely tied together by the theme of American greed and the exploitation and the adventures of our hero Ulzana. Johnson and his friends finally arrive at their mining camp. They capture Ulzana, who, having discovered that Johnson escaped his certain death, has set out once again to seek revenge. They tie our hero to a tree and whip him viciously, each taking a turn as they laugh. The stoic Indian never flinches. Then the Apache brothers arrive, free their warrior, and then surround the little garrison. Johnson sends for help that never arrives. The American commander has his orders, and it is the Mexicans who are their initial and primary target; Johnson can wait until later. The Apaches attack and finally use flaming arrows to drive the Americans from their cabin into the open and pick them off one by one. Getting his revenge, Ulzana kills Johnson in a blazing inferno in their cabin. The Apaches have won this battle and ride off triumphantly into their territory. There the film ends, with the good guys smarter and braver, winning yet again.

In spite of the ending—in which the "Indians" win—the audience is left with the message that the evil American empire will inevitably return to conquer the Apaches and their lands; the Americans are the bad guys and the "Indians" the good guys. It is clear that the Apaches and their history are subordinated to both American history in the late nineteenth century and European history in the late twentieth century. The result was different and yet similar in *Jerry Maguire*: "Show me the money," Jerry Maguire was told. The representations of Aboriginal people were again subordinated to the Euro-American story and propaganda, to misogyny and racist caricatures. However, despite the Yugoslav hunk playing Ulzana, the latter was a real Apache hero. Unlike some of the other DEFA films, here many of the historical details are accurate. There is some blending and mixing of the mid- and late-nineteenth-century history of the relationships among the Apaches, Mexicans, and Americans. But in the end, this film does nothing to alter the European view that, in spite of winning one war, the Americans will inevitably conquer the Apaches. The DEFA's purpose is to show how bad the Americans really were (and are) in the nineteenth and twentieth centuries. The Apaches are "real," but they exist as celluloid "Indians," as noble savages, and part of the propaganda of the late-twentieth-century Cold War. So is there any real difference in the representation of the Indian in this western from the wild East? Perhaps superficially, but in the end it comes down to the time-worn issue: "Show me the money."

John M. MacKenzie has persuasively demonstrated, in his *Propaganda and Empire*, the "pervasiveness of imperialism as an ideological cluster in this process, and the extraordinary staying-power of some of the components of that cluster in the twentieth century."[35] Clearly German imperialism—strongly rooted in the nineteenth century, aided and abetted by the literature of Karl May (itself a branch of popular culture)—retained a powerful hold upon German popular culture, especially about the "other," in particular about "Indians" in North America. The DEFA westerns are a notable example of this pervasive German imperial imagination. They are still very popular in Germany, and since their release in 1996, they have also become, rather ironically, a commercial cultural export to the United States.

The DEFA "Indian" films served the propaganda of the East German state during the Cold War, where peace is illusory and war becomes an end in itself. The French, English, and American imperialists/capitalists are the bad guys and the "Indians" the good guys. There are no German imperialists in these DEFA films—although real ones existed, of course. But there are cross-dressing German imperialists "disguised" in this and other DEFA films, as the English or American imperialists, speaking with East German dialects.[36] But in spite of the role reversal, with the "Indians" as the "good guys and gals," has anything really changed?

The DEFA purpose was to show how bad the imperialists/capitalists really were and still are. The stereotypical "Indians" in the DEFA films as "good" but "wild" Indians, "noble savages," was part of the propaganda and simply another way of appropriating culture. But are the "Indians" in these westerns from the East different in any way? Superficially, perhaps yes, but it comes down to the issue of exploitation of "Indians" as stereotypes and caricatures either "good" or "bad." The issue is not authenticity but accuracy and appropriation. The multiple and fluid identities of Aboriginal people as human beings are never really identified or explored in these East German films.[37] These films remain as inaccurate representations of Aboriginal peoples in North and South America and they tell us more about German imperialism and Eastern-European Communism in the late twentieth century.

Notes

1 Gerd Gemünden, "Between Karl May and Karl Marx: The DEFA Indiannerfilme," in *Germans & Indians: Fantasies, Encounters, Projections*, ed.
   Colin G. Calloway, Gerd Gemünden, and Susanne Zantop (Lincoln: University of Nebraska Press, 2002), 243–58.

2 For example, ICESTORM International Inc., which markets the DEFA films,
   sent us the following e-mail message on August 14, 2001:
   Starting in September, the Goethe Institut Inter Nationes in Los Ange-
   les will present the DEFA KINDER MATINEE. This series of eight DEFA children's films is supported by the DEFA Foundation in Berlin, Germany, and
   ICESTORM International in Northampton, Massachusetts. In addition to
   the DEFA KINDER MATINEE film screenings, there will be drawing contests
   and quizzes about the films, as well as educational workshops and handouts.
   The Berlin based film distribution company PROGRESS (www.progress
   film.de) and the Northampton based companies Interlink Publishing
   (www.interlink books.com) and ICESTORM International (www.icestorm
   video.com) will provide books and videos as prizes. Initial screening schedule: Sunday, September 23, 2001 Die goldene Gans (Siegfried Hartmann,
   1964) Sunday, October 21, 2001 Der Drache Daniel (Hans Kratzert, 1990),
   Sunday, December 2, 2001 Chingachgook, Die Grosse Schlange (Richard
   Groshopp, 1967). Please note that this program and these films will be in
   German only, unless otherwise noted. Look for more detailed information
   in September and a complete schedule of the 2001/2002 DEFA KINDER MATI-
   NEE on the web at <www .goethe.de/uk/los/enpfilm.htm#ex9>. We hope
   you enjoy this exceptional film program!

3 This section is based on the authors' joint experiences while residing in and
   visiting both West and East Germany, 1972–74 and 1989–2003.

4 Colin G. Calloway, Gerd Gemünden, and Susanne Zantop, eds., *Germans &
   Indians: Fantasies, Encounters, Projections* (Lincoln: University of Nebraska Press, 2002).

5 Drew Hayden Taylor, *Further Adventures of a Blue-Eyed Ojibway: Funny,
   You Don't Look Like One Too/Two* (Penticton: Theytus Books, 1999), 5.

6 Bernd Peyer, "A Nineteenth Century Ojibwa Conquers Germany," in *Ger-
   mans & Indians, Fantasies, Encounters, Projections*, ed. Colin G. Calloway,
   Gerd Gemünden, and Susanne Zantop (Lincoln: University of Nebraska
   Press, 2002), 143.

7 Charlotte Black Elk stated that she was born in Paris "on tour" of the last
   Buffalo Bill Wild Wrest Show in 1947: "Re-figuring the Ecological Indian,"
   panel discussion at the American Heritage Center, University of Wyoming,
   Laramie, Wyoming, April 26, 2002.

8 Nina Berman, "Orientalism, Imperialism, and Nationalism: Karl May's
   Orientzklus," in *The Imperialist Imagination, German Colonialism and Its*

Legacy, ed. Sara Friedrichsmeyer, Sara Lennox, and Susanne Zantop (Ann Arbor: University of Michigan Press, 1998), 51-68.

9 On the "other" see Edward W. Said, *Orientalism* (New York: Pantheon, 1978); *Culture and Imperialism* (London: Chatto and Windus, 1993). For a critique of Said see John M. MacKenzie, *Orientalism, History, Theory and the Arts* (Manchester: Manchester University Press, 1995).

10 See for example, John M. MacKenzie, ed., "Introduction," in *Imperialism and Popular Culture* (Manchester: Manchester University Press, 1986), 1-16, and on film by Jeffrey Richards, "Boy's Own Empire: Feature Films and Imperialism in the 1930s," 140-64.

11 Sabine Hake, "Mapping the Native Body: On Africa and the Colonial Film in the Third Reich," in *The Imperialist Imagination, German Colonialism and Its Legacy*, ed. Sara Friedrichsmeyer, Sara Lennox, and Susanne Zantop (Ann Arbor: University of Michigan Press, 1998), 187.

12 Gemünden, "Between Karl May and Karl Marx," 399.

13 Frank-Burkhard Habel, *Gojke Mitic, Mustangs, Marterpfähle. Die DEFA-Indianerfilme. Das grosse Buch für Fans.* (Berlin: Schwarzkopf and Schwarzkopf, 1977), 6-12.

14 Ute Lischke and David T. McNab, Introduction to *Blockades and Resistance* (Waterloo, ON: Wilfrid Laurier University Press, 2003), 1-12.

15 *Big Bear*, directed by Douglas Cardinal (Canadian Broadcasting Corporation, 1999).

16 Louise Erdrich, *The Last Report on the Miracles at Little No Horse* (New York: HarperCollins, 2001), i.

17 *The Sons of Great Bear*, directed by Josef Mach (DEFA, 1966, film).

18 *Tecumseh*, directed by Hans Kratzert (DEFA, 1972, film).

19 Alberto Manguel, *A History of Reading* (Toronto: Alfred A. Knopf Canada, 1996), 1-2.

20 Louise Erdrich, *The Antelope Wife* (New York: Harper Flamingo, 1998), 27.

21 Gerald Hausman, *Turtle Island Alphabet: A Lexicon of Native American Symbols and Culture* (New York: St. Martin's Press, 1992), 8-9.

22 David T. McNab, *Circles of Time: Aboriginal Land Rights and Resistance in Ontario* (Waterloo, ON: Wilfrid Laurier University Press, 1999), 1.

23 Ruoff, A. LaVonne Brown, and Donald B. Smith, eds. *Life, Letters & Speeches, George Copway (Kahgegagahbowh)* (Lincoln: University of Nebraska Press, 1997) (1850), 8.

24 Peyer, "A Nineteenth Century Ojibwa," 141-67.

25 Habel, *Gojke Mitic, Mustangs, Marterpfähle*, 22.

26 Ibid., 11.

27 Tecumseh, a Shawnee prophet from the spirit world, was born in Shawnee Territory, present-day Ohio, in March 1768. His clan was the celestial panther and his name literally meant "I Cross the Sky" or Shooting Star. He died at the Battle of the Longwoods on October 5, 1813. He has been recog-

nized as one of the greatest heroes in both Canadian and American history. Today, for Indian people, his career still represents the "dream of a brotherhood of tribes capable of resisting white expansion, and who tried to replace intertribal indifference and conflict with unity and common purpose." That dream, that vision, has not died and will be fulfilled. His life is a message sent from the Creator to the Indian Nations. Tecumseh's life, then, is both history and prophecy.

28 John Sugden, *Tecumseh: A Life* (New York: Henry Holt), 394–95.
29 *Chingachgook, The Great Snake*, directed by Richard Groschopp (1967).
30 In the novel, Judith is adopted and also has a sister named Hetty. This aspect of Cooper's more complicated plot is not in the DEFA film.
31 John M. MacKenzie, *The Empire of Nature, Hunting, Conservation and British Imperialism* (Manchester: Manchester University Press, 1988), 25–54.
32 Hake, "Mapping the Native Body," 187. One of the very first movies I (McNab) ever saw was at the drive-in theatre in Breslau, near Kitchener, Ontario, near the Grand River, a place of the Mississauga, in 1952. It was a Hollywood western called *Broken Arrow*. I recall it was about Cochise, the Apache warrior, who was played by the Jewish actor Jeff Chandler. In spite of the fact that no Aboriginal people were in the film, and representation of Aboriginal people left much to be desired, it was a level above the ordinary Hollywood western, showing the Apaches as real people, as human beings. Cochise was the hero. And the Indians won. The DEFA film *Apaches* brought back memories of Cochise and my first film.
33 Personal communication with Hadziin M., a Mescalero Apache, August 18, 2000.
34 MacKenzie, *The Empire of Nature*, 7.
35 John M. MacKenzie, *Propaganda and Empire* (Manchester: Manchester University Press, 1984), 2.
36 We would like to thank Professor Charmaine Eddy, chair, Women's Studies Program, Trent University, for drawing this interpretation to our attention at the faculty seminar at St. Lawrence University on October 12, 2001.
37 See Ute Lischke, "An Introduction to Louise Erdrich's *The Antelope Wife*," in *Germans & Indians: Fantasies, Encounters, Projections*, ed. Colin G. Calloway, Gerd Gemünden, and Susanne Zantop (Lincoln: University of Nebraska Press, 2002), 281–86.

Bibliography

Apaches. Directed by Gottfried Kolditz. DEFA, 1973. Film.
Berman, Nina. "Orientalism, Imperialism, and Nationalism: Karl May's *Orientzklus.*" In *The Imperialist Imagination, German Colonialism and Its Legacy*. Ed. Sara Friedrichsmeyer, Sara Lennox, and

Susanne Zantop, 51–68. Ann Arbor: University of Michigan Press, 1998.

Big Bear. Directed by Douglas Cardinal. Canadian Broadcasting Corporation, 1999.

Calloway, Colin G., Gerd Gemünden, and Susanne Zantop, eds. *Germans & Indians: Fantasies, Encounters, Projections.* Lincoln: University of Nebraska Press, 2002.

Chingachgook, The Great Snake. Directed by Richard Groschopp. (1967).

Erdrich, Louise. *The Antelope Wife.* New York: Harper Flamingo, 1998.

——— . *The Last Report on the Miracles at Little No Horse.* New York: HarperCollins, 2001.

Gemünden, Gerd. "Between Karl May and Karl Marx: The DEFA Indiannerfilme." In *Germans & Indians: Fantasies, Encounters, Projections.* Ed. Colin G. Calloway, Gerd Gemünden, and Susanne Zantop, 243–58. Lincoln: University of Nebraska Press, 2002.

Habel, Frank-Burkhard. *Gojke Mitic, Mustangs, Marterpfähle. Die DEFA-Indianerfilme. Das grosse Buch für Fans.* Berlin: Schwarzkopf and Schwarzkopf, 1977.

Hake, Sabine. "Mapping the Native Body: On Africa and the Colonial Film in the Third Reich." In *The Imperialist Imagination, German Colonialism and Its Legacy.* Ed. Sara Friedrichsmeyer, Sara Lennox, and Susanne Zantop. Ann Arbor: University of Michigan Press, 1998.

Hausman, Gerald. *Turtle Island Alphabet: A Lexicon of Native American Symbols and Culture.* New York: St. Martin's Press, 1992.

Hayden Taylor, Drew. *Further Adventures of a Blue-Eyed Ojibway: Funny, You Don't Look Like One Too/Two.* Penticton: Theytus Books, 1999.

Kreis, Karl Markus. "Indians Playing, Indians Praying, Native Americans in Wild West Shows and Catholic Missions." In *Germans and Indians: Fantasies, Encounters, Projections.* Ed. Colin Calloway, Gerd Gemünden, and Susanne Zantop, 195–21. Lincoln: University of Nebraska Press, 2002.

Hodgins, Bruce W., Ute Lischke, and David T. McNab, eds. *Blockades and Resistance: Studies in Actions of Peace and the Temagami Blockades of 1988–89.* Waterloo, ON: Wilfrid Laurier University Press, 2003.

Jerry Maguire. Directed by Cameron Crowe. TriStar, 1997. Film.

Lischke, Ute. "An Introduction to Louise Erdrich's *The Antelope Wife.*" In *Germans & Indians: Fantasies, Encounters, Projections.* Ed. Colin G. Calloway, Gerd Gemünden, and Susanne Zantop, 281–86. Lincoln: University of Nebraska Press, 2002.

MacKenzie, John M. *The Empire of Nature, Hunting, Conservation and British Imperialism.* Manchester: Manchester University Press, 1988.

————. *Imperialism and Popular Culture.* Ed. John M. MacKenzie. Manchester: Manchester University Press, 1986.

————. *Orientalism, History, Theory and the Arts.* Manchester: Manchester University Press, 1995.

————. *Propaganda and Empire.* Manchester: Manchester University Press, 1984.

Manguel, Alberto. *A History of Reading.* Toronto: Alfred A. Knopf Canada, 1996.

McNab, David T. *Circles of Time: Aboriginal Land Rights and Resistance in Ontario.* Waterloo, ON: Wilfrid Laurier University Press, 1999.

Peyer, Bernd. "A Nineteenth Century Ojibwa Conquers Germany." In *Germans and Indians, Fantasies, Encounters, Projections.* Ed. Colin G. Calloway, Gerd Gemünden, and Susanne Zantop, 141-67. Lincoln: University of Nebraska Press, 2002.

Ruoff, A. LaVonne Brown, and Donald B. Smith, eds. *Life, Letters & Speeches, George Copway (Kahgegagahbowh).* Lincoln: University of Nebraska Press, 1997 (1850).

Said, Edward W. *Culture and Imperialism.* London: Chatto and Windus, 1993.

————. *Orientalism.* New York: Vintage Books, 1994 (1978).

Sugden, John. *Tecumseh: A Life.* New York: Henry Holt, 1997.

The Sons of Great Bear. Directed by Josef Mach. DEFA, 1966. Film.

Tecumseh. Directed by Hans Kratzert. DEFA, 1972. Film.

12

Kwakwa̲ka̲'wakw on Film

Kathryn Bunn-Marcuse

DRAMA AND PERFORMANCE ARE CENTRAL to Kwakwa̲ka̲'wakw ceremonies and traditions. Since the early twentieth century, filmmakers
have tried to capture this drama in their footage.[1] The films of Edward
Curtis, Franz Boas, Robert Gardner, and the U'mista Cultural Society
all feature the potlatch and its dramatic dances. Not surprisingly, all of
these films reflect the viewpoints of their makers and the times. The
films by Curtis and Boas (*In the Land of the Head-Hunters*, rereleased
as *In the Land of the War Canoes*, 1914; *A Documentary on the Kwakiutl*, 1930) are firmly rooted in the salvage ethnography of the early
twentieth century. Robert Gardner attempted to capture a more complete picture of Kwakwa̲ka̲'wakw life in the 1950s (*Blunden Harbour and
Dances of the Kwakiutl*, 1951) but still omitted any presentation of
contemporary cultural struggles. By looking at these films and comparing them to two films produced by the U'mista Cultural Society, one
may discover some of the devices used by the white filmmakers and
how they have been reappropriated by Kwakwa̲ka̲'wakw filmmakers to
re-present or represent their culture through their own creative lens.
This paper concludes that the modern U'mista films (*Potlatch… A
Strict Law Bids Us Dance*, 1975, and *Box of Treasures*, 1983) reclaim
and reinterpret ceremonial imagery from the earlier films as part of a
larger Native-directed effort to document their own history.

These films are connected by more than just their general subject
matter; many of them build on thematic and visual precedents set by
the earlier films, which include the presentation of certain events as

central to the Kwakwa̱ka'wakw character, and most important, the use of song and dance.

In the Land of the Head-Hunters

In 1911, Edward Sheriff Curtis decided to make a film about the Kwak-wa̱ka'wakw. His film—and his photographs—portrayed Native people in a pictorialist manner: not as they appeared at the time but as their parents and grandparents had appeared. He was familiar with the area and had produced hundreds of photographs of Northwest Coast peoples. Curtis carried with him a number of props and wigs in order to trans-form twentieth-century Native people into his romantic ideal of a glorious Native past. The film *In the Land of the Head-Hunters*, re-leased in 1914 and lost shortly thereafter, featured Kwa-gulth people from Fort Rupert and 'Nak'waxdáxw people from Blunden Harbour in an exotic Hollywood melodrama. The film disappeared from circulation until 1947 when a print of the film was donated to the Chicago Field Museum.[2] When George Quimby left the Field Museum to come to the Burke Museum in Seattle, he brought copies of the footage with him. In 1973, Quimby and Holm restored and re-edited the film. They removed damaged footage and created a sound track of dialogue and songs recorded by three of the original actors in the film and eight oth-ers who were relatives of the original actors.[3]

Brian Winston notes three elements that are key to current inter-est in the film: the use of Kwakwa̱ka'wakw actors, footage of Native cer-emonials that give the film its ethnographic value, and Curtis's recognition of the desires of a non-Native audience for a melodramatic framework.[4] In considering Curtis's contribution to ethnographic film-making, Winston correctly leaves out consideration of the new sound-track and footage added during Holm and Quimby's reconstruction of the film in 1973. However, rather than denouncing the "anthropolog-ically accurate soundtrack" as Winston does, it should be considered as consistent with Curtis's published goals for the film: the prospectus of the Continental Film Company—a company established by Curtis and a few Seattle businessmen—explains in Curtis's own words his approach to filmmaking.

The questions might be raised as to whether the documentary material would not lack the thrilling interest of the fake picture. It is the opinion of Mr. Curtis that the real life of the Indian contains the parallel emotions to furnish all necessary plots and give the pictures all the heart interest needed. In this respect it is as important that we take into consideration the Indian's mental processes as it is to picture his unique costume.... In making such pictures, the greatest care must be exercised that the thought conveyed be true to the subject, that the ceremony be correctly rendered, and above all, that the costumes be correct.[5]

In order to accomplish the correct rendering of costume, ceremony, and "the Indian's mental processes," Curtis needed a Native assistant. When Curtis arrived in Victoria in 1911 intending to make a film, George Hunt's reputation marked him as the man for Curtis to hire. *In the Land of the Head-Hunters* was the first of four films in which "Hunt would play a major facilitating role."[6] In the three years prior to the actual shooting of the film (which took place in the summer of 1914), Hunt was employed in various capacities: in 1911–12, he worked with Curtis's assistant William Myers, recording history and customs for volume 10 of the *North American Indian*, providing the ethnographic foundation for the film; in 1913–14 Hunt collected and commissioned props for the film and took photos of possible filming sites.[7] The collection included old ceremonial costumes and masks as well as pieces commissioned specifically for the film. Hunt commissioned twenty-one masks in addition to numerous blankets, capes, robes, and neck rings made of cedar bark.[8] He hired a number of women from Fort Rupert, including many from his own family.[9] Many of the actors and actresses (each of whom received fifty cents a day for non-principal roles) were related to Hunt, including his son Stanley, who plays the leading role in the film. This was suitable to Curtis because they were attractive, talented, and respectful of directions given by Hunt.[10] According to both Bill Holm and Gloria Cranmer Webster, the actors enjoyed participating in the project. Not only was it a lot of fun but there was most likely a pleasing irony that Curtis was paying them to do things for which they would otherwise go to jail under Canadian law.[11] The film's use of pieces similar to those that Hunt collected for other museums suggests Hunt was free to make decisions according to his own experience. In addition to pieces that Hunt commissioned or bought for the film, Hunt provided pieces owned by his family to use during the filming.

Aside from gathering all of the props for the film, Hunt acted as hiring chief, bookkeeper, and assistant director. Holm and Quimby assert that Hunt not only furnished Curtis with information that became the basis of the movie but also provided much of the text and served as interpreter for information received from other sources.[12] Still photos taken during the filming by photographer Edmund Schwinke illuminate Hunt's role on the set: two photos show Curtis behind the camera and Hunt equipped with a megaphone, directing the action (fig. 1).[13] According to Curtis, it was impossible to hire an actor to wear a mask that was not his hereditary prerogative. Hunt's knowledge of the actors and their hereditary rights was crucial to Curtis's record of the masks and dances.[14] Only a Native person with knowledge about traditional ceremonies and lifestyle could have captured the scenes that Curtis was determined to record. *In the Land of the Head-Hunters* certainly contains fanciful moments of artistic licence—the name of the film is a good example—but one can only imagine what the final outcome would have been had Curtis not benefited from Hunt's expertise.[15]

The product of their collaboration caught the eye of the film critics of the time, who had high praise for *In the Land of the Head-Hunters*. In *The Art of the Moving Picture* (1915) Vachel Lindsay wrote, "This work of a lifetime, a supreme art achievement, shows the native as a figure in bronze."[16] New York film critic W. Stephen Bush penned the most telling commentary on the film's brief success:

> Mr. Curtis conceived this wonderful study in ethnology as an epic. It fully deserves the name. Indeed, it seemed to me that there was a most striking resemblance all through the film between the musical epics of Richard Wagner and the theme and treatment of this Indian epic. The fire dance, the vigil journey with its command of silence and chastity, the whole character of the hero were most strangely reminiscent of Parsifal and the Ring of the Nibelungs.[17]

The comparison of the critics' reviews with Curtis's published aims illuminate the success that the film had on its release and its continued

FIGURE I: George Hunt with megaphone in hand and Edward Curtis standing behind the camera on the set of *In the Land of the Head-Hunters*. [Photo by Edmund Schwinke. Courtesy of the Burke Museum of Natural History and Culture, Seattle, Washington.]

use (since its rerelease) in an educational context. The popular (albeit short-lived) success of the film in its Seattle and New York showings was due in large part to the romantic melodrama that Curtis invented. It had all the essential markers of a native "Other" that were expected at the time: head-hunting, warfare, and ceremony with elaborate ritual costume, combined with a familiar Western narrative of a villain, a hero, and his love. Conversely, today the dramatic storyline is largely ignored by audiences who excuse Curtis's romantic tendencies by praising the film's ethnographic value. Its current popularity is due to the accuracy (and drama) of the masks and costumes that appear in the film—a result of Curtis's desire for "documentary material" and George Hunt's ability to produce that material for the camera.

The Curtis film was the first film of Aboriginal people on the Northwest Coast. Primarily dramatic rather than anthropological, it contains all the issues that later ethnographic filmmakers would have to deal with: "problems of authenticity, of historical reconstruction, and of the means by which one is to present ethnographic information within a narrative frame."[18] Although the narrative of the film was popular with audiences in 1915, Curtis's contemporary renown is

FIGURE 2: The appearance of all the masks in the house before the ceremony was called *gílsgumlihla* or *húkhsumlihla*. [Photo by Edmund Schwinke, taken during the filming of *In the Land of the Head-Hunters*. Courtesy of the Burke Museum of Natural History and Culture, Seattle, Washington.]

through those scenes that are constantly shown in museums and class-rooms, particularly those depicting dancing and canoes (fig. 2). The inter-title before the dance scene is perhaps the most "ethnographic" moment in the film, and like all the inter-titles in the present version, was written by Bill Holm. It describes the power of the Winter Cere-monials: "The killing of enemies brings on the Winter Ceremonial power of the warriors. The ceremony of First-Appearance-of-Masks-in-the-House is following by the performance of the masked dances." The following portion of the film is frequently shown in anthropology and art history classes in order to present masks in use, although it is not offered in an ethnographically accurate ceremonial context. The scene of all the masks dancing in a circle was not a traditional activ-ity and was apparently directed by Curtis so as to enhance the specta-cle. Holm's informants called the appearance of all the masks simultaneously before the start of the ceremony *gilsgumlihla*, while both Boas and Curtis described the ritual as *húkhsumlihla* when it occurred at the start of the Winter Ceremonial (fig. 2).[19]

One canoe scene is an icon of Curtis's work on the Northwest Coast (fig. 3). The presentation of the Thunderbird in the prow of one

FIGURE 3: Canoe scene with Thunderbird, Grizzly Bear, and Wasp dancers taken during the filming of *In the Land of the Head-Hunters*. [Photo by Edmund Schwinke. Courtesy of the Burke Museum of Natural History and Culture, Seattle, Washington.]

of three war canoes is used as the film's introductory image (in the Holm and Quimby restoration) and is later incorporated into what is certainly the most quoted scene of this film, and perhaps one of the most famous filmic moments of Northwest Coast culture, appearing in numerous museum exhibits in the past few decades (fig. 3).[20] Although Curtis was interested in including moments of Kwakwa̲ka'wakw ceremonialism and wanted to be relatively truthful in the images of their material culture (although privileging his own conception of a dramatic moment over the Native one), his main objective was a successful combination of entertainment and ethnography.

Franz Boas's Documentary

In 1886 Franz Boas arrived on the Northwest Coast, where he began his lifelong association with the Kwakwa̲ka'wakw. In 1888, Boas met George Hunt, who was working in Victoria as a court interpreter. When Boas returned to the coast as an assistant ethnologist for the Chicago Field Museum in 1891, he met up again with Hunt.[21] From Boas's first visit on the coast until his last in 1930, Boas and Hunt worked together to produce an encyclopedic catalogue of Kwakwa̲ka'wakw material culture. On Boas's last trip to the coast, he brought with him a 16mm camera and wax cylinders for sound recording. The sound and film footage were never intended to produce a synchronous sound production—both were merely records of the type of movement and music associated with the individual dances. Franziska Boas, Franz Boas's daughter, told Holm that her father's intention was to record the dance sequences for a study of dance.[22] The material collected was divided into three categories: technologies, games, and dance. The film footage consisted of short sequences—twenty seconds to several minutes—of various activities, such as "Woodworking," "Weaving Baskets," "Stick Game," "Hamatsa Dance," and "Feather Dance."

Boas never created a film from the 1930 footage. The editing and film production was completed in 1973 by Bill Holm.[23] The footage, such as it was, was given to Dr. Erna Gunther at the Burke Museum by Franziska Boas.[24] According to Holm, the sequences were already in place, and he contributed to the film through the extensive notes he compiled to go along with the film, explaining in detail what was happening in each scene, rather than substantial changes in the appearance of the footage.[25] Holm's production is consistent with Boas's approach to the compilation of information. The film echoes Boas's written notes, which provided detailed descriptions (recordings) of various kinds of technologies and activities. When the film was made, Boas knew almost nothing about the technical side of filming. It was not intended as a complete filmic ethnography and—if finished by Boas— would probably have served as an aid to field notes.[26] Holm writes, "Boas saw the advantages of film in recording specific actions that were difficult to describe verbally. His 1930 film must be seen from this point of view and not as film ethnography in any complete sense." Holm says that he had the clear idea that Boas never intended this footage to be a "film."[27]

Boas and Hunt were both in their seventies when the film was made in the winter of 1930–31. The film was shot at Fort Rupert, and the opening scenes show the village along the shores of Beaver Harbour. The first reel consists of technology and games. Here we see woodworking, spinning, and weaving, as well as children's games and the actions of official speakers. The second reel records a variety of dances.

Boas was aware of the limitations of lighting and film length, and instead of trying to obtain a complete record of the dances, he hoped to record segments that (together with his extensive notes) could constitute a study of Kwakiutl dance.[28] He wrote to Ruth Benedict that he wanted to compile "adequate material for a real study" of dance.[29] The film footage was intended to provide a visual accompaniment to the extensive notes that Boas had taken on earlier trips to the coast.

Rosalind Morris looks at Boas's film in *New Worlds from Fragments: Film, Ethnography, and the Representation of Northwest Coast Cultures.* She examines ethnographic film on the Northwest Coast, exploring how the techniques of individual filmmakers relate to broader questions of film and literary theory, history, and anthropology. Among the films that Morris examines are three of the films in my study: *A Documentary on the Kwakiutl, Blunden Harbour, and Box of Treasures.* Morris's highly theorized observations often provide a counterpoint to my observations on the use of certain types of visual imagery and as such will be included where they can provide a more theoretical interpretation of the films under consideration.

Morris seems greatly concerned with the lack of context or interpretation for the images in Boas's film.

> Without an expository narration or additional footage, it becomes impossible to interpret what might be the particular significance of any of these images. Decontextualization in this manner becomes a mode of objectification in the sense that the subjective and objective dimensions of practice are rent apart; the image becomes something akin to the (collectible) material artifact and need no longer be interpreted with reference to any Native meaning system. Instead, it is incorporated into the meaning system of its viewer and possessor.[30]

She suggests that this lack of context leaves the viewer to come up with his or her own interpretations; accordingly, Morris provides her own interpretation of the scenes and their significance.[31] She blames Holm and Boas for collaborating in the production of a film in which the "participants' perception is excluded from the interpretive frame provided for the viewer by Boas' own camera work and Holm's subsequent editing."[32] Her final condemnation of the film posits Holm and Boas as universalists, assigning "global significations":

Ingenuity and economy of technique, bounty of resources, diversity of ceremonial forms and rites, and, finally, the ultimate barbarism of cannibalism. These qualities or essences, which Boas and Holm manage to diffuse almost imperceptibly amid the mere cataloging of culture, are not neutral, of course, but form the conceptual latticework of a normative ethical system. Included within that system is a vision of the Native as Adamic, as originary. This is the image of the savage as custodian of the paradisical garden, where labor is neither onerous nor constant, and where leisure can be pursued energetically.[33]

All of Morris's commentary ignores a key aspect of the film: unlike many of the earlier films made on the coast, it was never intended for the general cinema. Rather, it was intended purely as research footage, compiled and presented in the way it is now presented, as a visual record accompanied by detailed written texts. The field-note nature of the footage is apparent at once: dogs and cats wonder in and out of the frame; the sound-recording device is placed next to the singer in the dance scenes; and Julia Averkieva, Boas's assistant, slips in to wind the recorder during the "Paddle Dance" scene. The text that Holm compiled to accompany the film was based on interviews with the participants and on Boas's notes.[34] The text is, in fact, informed by the very "participants' perception" that Morris feels is excluded. It seems that Morris deliberately ignores Holm's text, even though she poses the question of "what kind of meanings can be assigned *with* and without reference to extrafilmic sources" (my emphasis). The only information that Morris includes from "extrafilmic" sources is what appears in Browne's summary, rather than from information in Holm's notes.[35]

Nevertheless, the textual component of the film is an integral part of the presentation. Think of it as an early multimedia production: to consider the film alone without the text is to examine something that is less than the whole. If Morris wants simply to approach Boas's footage, then she must acknowledge that Boas never created a "film," and begin her analysis from there. If Morris managed to view the film without the text—they are supposed to be kept together at the institutions that have the film—that is certainly not the fault of either the original filmmaker or the editor.[36]

However, not all of Morris's criticisms of the film seem so unwarranted. She justly notes that Boas's film—and his ethnologies—ignore many of the present realities of Fort Rupert in the early twentieth century.[37] Like those of Curtis, Boas's material collections and his visual images try to capture or reestablish an imaginary culture untouched by Euro-Canadian influences. This romanticized view is seen in the presentation of old technologies, old political forms ("Chiefs Boasting"), and shamanic healing practices. The conspicuous absence of new forms of technology, medicine, or political power serves to enhance this fictionalized viewpoint. However, Morris includes in her criticism the performance of "rites of a ceremony no longer in practice" on a staged set. Although she admits that using "extinction" to describe these ceremonies is extreme (since they "had been performed less than a decade before"), she is not aware that despite government persecution, many Kwakwa̲ka'wakw—including the families of those individuals seen in the film—actively participated in these ceremonies.[38] As with all of the films in this study, Boas focused most of his attention on images of dances from these very ceremonies.

Robert Gardner's Films

Robert Gardner's *Dances of the Kwakiutl* (1951) is yet another film that stresses the importance of dance as the essential expression of Kwakwa̲ka'wakw ceremony. The twelve-minute film is colour footage that Gardner shot in Blunden Harbour in 1950 while making a twenty-minute black-and-white film called *Blunden Harbour*. Both films are somewhat enigmatic. While Curtis's film was clearly made for commercial audiences and Boas's film was made as visual record to accompany his field notes, Gardner's objectives are not so obvious. The films were produced by Orbit Films for release through Dimensions, Inc., but no record of their commercial release seems to exist, and aside from the writings of Morris and Jacknis, they seem to have escaped the academic scrutiny that Gardner's other films have attracted. Even in Gardner's own writings, the films are ignored.[39] He mentions his time in Seattle but alludes only to the fact that he had "made a number of efforts and experiments in cinematography" before making *Dead Birds*, a film about two warring groups of Dani in what is now Irian Jaya.[40] Ira

Jacknis notes that when Gardner and Sidney Peterson founded Orbit Films, one of their goals was to "make an art of the anthropological film."[41] Gardner did speak about his Kwakwa̲ka'wakw films in an unpublished interview with James Blue and describes the project as "a poetic lyric documentary of the Kwakiutl nation."[42] In his own writings, Gardner mentions the anthropological theories to which he was attracted. Interestingly, he notes that the only current concept that appealed to him at that time was called "culture and personality," focusing on the interaction and tension between "individual will and cultural constraint."[43] The "culture and personality" approach was used by Ruth Benedict, a student of Boas, in *Patterns of Culture*,[44] which examined several Native groups, including the Kwakiutl. However, Gardner does not seem to use this approach in *Blunden Harbour* as he does in *Dead Birds*. There are no individual characters and no explanation of community ceremonials, as in his later works. It is difficult to know how much of *Blunden Harbour* was Gardner's conception and how much belonged to his cinematographer, William Heick; both Gardner and Heick claim to have been the editors, but it seems clear that Heick was responsible for the filming.[45]

In contrast to later films, Gardner's voice-over in *Blunden Harbour* provides no omniscient narrative. It rarely comments on the visual image, and when it does, the connection is tentative rather than definitive. The film begins with a myth that explains the origin of the village: "I am Helestes and I go spouting around the world but I wish to become a real man in this place. So I built my house in Blunden Harbour." This origin story accompanies images of the village taken from a motorboat offshore. The camera then moves to shots of the boardwalk on which women are spreading seaweed to dry. Although we see the village and are told that this is Blunden Harbour, no names of the people, their tribal identity, or their geographic location are given. As the camera follows a group of people collecting clams and other seafood, the narrative continues:

> No struggle for survival.... No men against the sea. These ones have an ancient formula for success, ancient and simple. From the water, food. From the woods, a way of life. Each day a little different from the next, gathering, saving, cooking, eating, sleeping. There is time and place for everyone, the old, the young, the dead,

FIGURE 4: Willie Seaweed fishing for crabs from Robert Gardner's *Blunden Harbour*. As seen in *Potlatch: A Strict Law Bids Us Dance*, published courtesy of the U'mista Cultural Society, Alert Bay, British Columbia.

the quick. There is as much to look back upon as there is ahead. Old methods with new tools. Old tools with new methods. This sliver of humanity has done well by the judgment of a whale.

Morris notes that where the voiceover does not specify the image, it "opens up the film and generalizes it, taking it onto a plane of universality."[46] The film combines shots of everyday life with modern amenities (cups, saucers, canned food, motorized fishing boats) and ancient technologies (crab spearing, dried seaweed cakes, traditional carving knives, log drums, and masks) (fig. 4). All of the imagery is accompanied by the sound of songs sung in Kwakwala. Shots of mortuary boxes in trees and the close-up of a carved eye on a mask are accompanied by "A way of life and death." The final scene in the film begins with Willie Seaweed speaking at a ceremony. The voiceover tells us, "A way of life, a way of death, and a way to remember." The scene continues with half a dozen different dancers all accompanied by a single song (fig. 5).

Morris's observations on the universality of the film are reinforced by the overall mood of serenity and stability. There is no conflict, no drama. "The film renders the life of Blunden Harbour utterly familiar,

FIGURE 5: Owl dancer, Joe Seaweed from Robert Gardner's *Blunden Harbour*. As seen in *Potlatch: A Strict Law Bids Us Dance*, published courtesy of the U'mista Cultural Society, Alert Bay, British Columbia.

there is nothing chaotic about it, nothing unpredictable."[47] Even the dance scene, whose masks and costumes should seem exotic and alien, relinquishes its dramatic power to the tranquility and composure of the film as a whole. *Blunden Harbour* is purposefully ahistorical. It presents images from 'Nak'waxdáx̱w life as iconic moments of the essential Kwakwak̲a'wakw character. An eternal ethnographic present whose essence despite material changes is, at its core, immune to change.

For its part, *Dances of the Kwakiutl* consists of colour footage that was shot concurrently with the filming of *Blunden Harbour*. The same dancers, singers, and witnesses appear in each film. The film has only one short bit of narration, which is even more enigmatic than that presented in the longer film. After the appearance of the title, the film begins with close-up shots of the singers' hands and faces. As the image moves to take in the dancer, the narration begins:

> Fifty years ago the Kwakiutl Indians of British Columbia held their Winter Ceremonial in order to bring back the youth who were staying with the supernatural protector of their society. The songs and dances which belong to this ritual were vital to the success of

the ceremony. Lately both the intention and performance of the Winter Ceremonial have been substantially altered. The dancers are no longer significant within the ceremonial complex and their performance depends now an individual and spontaneous will to recreate a very old syncopated dance form.

Here perhaps is a hint of the tension between individual personality and cultural constraint; however, there is no further explanation, no identification of the dancers or the ceremonial complex. Again, as in *Blunden Harbour*, despite the varied appearance of the dancers and their distinctive movements, the songs do not change with each new participant. These films do, in fact, seem to be experiments in visual poetics—an attempt, as Gardner wrote, to do "something that might lift up humanity and also belong to Art ... a longing to capture human reality in ways that might reveal its essence of significance."[48]

Films by the U'mista Cultural Society

The jump from Robert Gardner's 1951 productions to the films of the U'mista Cultural Society two and three decades later is a large one. The intervening years changed anthropology, ethnographic filmmaking, and Native rights. The 1960s and 1970s led the way for a re-evaluation of Native rights in both the United States and Canada. Interest in the art of British Columbia's Native people resulted in two shows by the Vancouver Art Gallery in the late 1950s, and in 1967 Doris Shadbolt organized the gallery's acclaimed *Arts of the Raven* exhibit. These shows marked the beginning of a trend. Between 1967 and 1983, the British Columbia Provincial Museum, the Vancouver Art Gallery, the Vancouver Centennial Museum, and the University of British Columbia, put on over thirty temporary exhibitions.[49] The catalogue for *Arts of the Raven* reflects the role that Native art played in defining a new Canadian regional identity as well. The art was to be seen as an aesthetically valuable tradition, one that was alive and well and being practised by British Columbia's first residents. The images were becoming part of regional history: "But now these are arts in a different sense. Though truly enough of Indian descent, they are now Canadian art, modern art, fine art."[50]

This attitude led to government subsidies for Native projects, including a grant from the British Columbia provincial government to the U'mista Cultural Society to produce their own ethnographic film in 1975, entitled *Potlatch...A Strict Law Bids Us Dance*. The film was originally conceived as a National Film Board production, budgeted at $90,000 for a half-hour documentary. When the Kwagiulth District Council learned that the film was not intended to make a profit that they could use to establish a cultural centre, they fired the NFB. The project was then taken over by the District Council. The U'mista Cultural Society was the executive producer of the film, Tom Shandell produced it, and Dennis Wheeler directed it. With a $45,000 budget, they produced a fifty-three-minute film.[51]

Focusing on the importance of the potlatch and the loss of ceremonial regalia, the film juxtaposes Kwakwaka'wakw elders remembering Dan Cranmer's 1921 Village Island potlatch, with shots of Doug Cranmer's 1974 memorial potlatch for his brother Danny, and recreations of the 1922 prosecution of forty-five people for dancing and giving or receiving gifts at the 1921 potlatch. Despite the theme of loss and unjust punishment, the film is not a memorial for the past, but a celebration of endurance *despite* loss. This is demonstrated by recollections of the infamous Village Island potlatch that are intercut with images of the contemporary potlatch.

Unlike the reconstructions used by Curtis, Boas, and Gardner, the dancing here is not staged solely for the camera, and modern-day adaptations are not banished from the view of the camera. Contemporary concerns and the history of the film's subjects are highlighted: Alfred Scow describes seeing his possessions illustrated in museum catalogues; Lucy Brown discusses her role in the Village Island potlatch; the recollections of Dan Cranmer about the ramifications of his potlatch are read by his daughter Gloria Cranmer Webster. Webster also explains the importance of wealth and power, and the role of coppers in Kwakwaka'wakw society. Although the film is obviously made with the non-Native viewer in mind—there is a lot of explanatory narration—the speeches given at the potlatch on the transfer of a copper, though translated into English from Kwakwala, are not totally understandable by the non-Native viewer because formal Kwakwala rhetoric is used (fig. 6).

FIGURE 6: Presentation of a copper. Billie Sandy Willie of Kingcome Inlet (holding the copper) with James Sewid. As seen in *Potlatch: A Strict Law Bids Us Dance*, published courtesy of the U'mista Cultural Society, Alert Bay, British Columbia.

The writing of the film was a collaboration by Gloria Cranmer Webster—the film's narrator (along with Robert Joseph)—Dennis Wheeler, Brian Shein, and Tom Shandell. According to Webster, the fact that the filmmakers were not Native was not a problem because they supplied the technical knowledge while the band controlled content.[52] Dennis Wheeler wrote,

> We knew that we were making a film with the Kwakiutl, not about them. That was an important distinction from the beginning. It was very concrete inasmuch they were the owners of the film. But the film had to do several things at once. It had to give an intense feeling of the potlatch without mystifying it or romanticizing it, as well as a sense of what the history of it was in political and mythological terms.[53]

The importance of the potlatch as an ongoing institution is emphasized through the use of texts and images created by people outside of the culture. Boas's record of a speech made to him in 1896 is read to accompany footage from Associated Screen News films.[54] The speech challenges Boas's right to witness the ceremony and insists on his respect for Kwakwaka'wakw laws governing land ownership and dancing.

> Is this the white man's land? We are told that it is the Queen's land; but no! It is mine!… Where was the Queen when our God gave the land to my grandfather and told him, 'This will be thine'?… Do we ask the white man, 'Do as the Indian does'? No, we do not. Why then do you ask us, 'Do as the white man does'? It is a strict law that bids us dance. It is a strict law that bids us distribute our property among our friends and neighbours. It is a good law. Let the white man observe his law, we shall observe ours. And now, if you are come to forbid us to dance, be gone; if not, you will be welcome to us.

The footage of the contemporary potlatch is directly followed by a series of images from the Curtis and Gardner films.[55] A still photograph of the Thunderbird dancing in the prow of the canoe, from the Curtis film, affirms the long tradition of dancing that *Potlatch* emphasizes (fig. 3). The ownership that the Kwakwaka'wakw people feel for these traditions—and for their participation in the Curtis film—is exemplified in an anecdote from the making of *Potlatch*. Dennis Wheeler originally wanted to include footage from *In the Land of the Head-Hunters* rather than stills taken during the filming. Apparently, the royalties requested for use of film footage made it too expensive for the project. Webster simply said, "Dennis, let's just use it, we don't have to pay for it, it's ours."[56]

There was no such problem with the footage from *Blunden Harbour* or *Dances of the Kwakiutl*; Gardner provided the film footage at no charge.[57] The images taken from his films are especially telling. Of all the dance footage in those films, the chosen moments include only those points in the film where the dancers look directly into the camera (fig. 5). These scenes engender confrontation that pulls the viewer into the action, effectively questioning the role of the film's observers and bringing them into the potlatch setting where they are made witnesses to the events. This was by all appearances a purposeful choice on the part of the filmmakers. Just as the speech to Boas challenged his respect for traditions over one hundred years ago, the U'mista film challenges our role as observers.

The film concludes with an explanation of the concept of U'mista, the return to the family of someone who had been taken by another group, or the return of an item of importance. Webster explains that they are fighting for the return of the confiscated potlatch goods that have languished like prisoners in the storerooms of Canadian museums.

Box of Treasures (1983) is the sequel to *Potlatch*. The U'mista Cultural Society succeeded in its struggle for the repatriation of the masks and regalia confiscated from the 1921 Cranmer potlatch. The film documents the celebration of their return, with the opening of the cultural centre, and a concurrent potlatch given by the Cranmer family on November 1, 1980.

Prior to these celebrations, Gloria Cranmer Webster was approached by Chuck Olin, who was making a film for a Maritime Peoples exhibit at Chicago's Field Museum of Natural History, and wanted to film in Alert Bay. When this was proposed to the band council, they agreed that Olin could work in Alert Bay if he would film the opening of the Cultural Centre for them. Not knowing what to film and what to omit at the opening, Olin filmed it all. He later asked Webster to come to Chicago to see the footage and suggested that U'mista make a film with it, feeling that there was a message there for other Native groups.[58] The film took three years to produce and included six trips by Olin to Alert Bay. Olin was inspired by the people he met—their successes in cultural survival, and their struggles with the larger political, social, and economic issues of the day. He felt that it was "a jewel of a culture with everything conspiring against it." He understood that there was a continuity of tradition within the culture but that it had been stretched thin.[59] It is interesting that Olin's original draft of the film was unsatisfactory to the band because it had a happily-ever-after ending suggesting that the return of the masks addressed many of the band's concerns. They wanted a stronger message about both the repatriation of property and the strengthening of cultural traditions. According to Webster, they wanted the filmmakers to go back to the interviews because "the real stuff is already in there, in the interviews that we did with various people that this is a battle we'd won, but the war is still

FIGURE 7: *Nimpkish Producer* coming into the harbour with dancers on top of the wheelhouse during the opening ceremonies of the U'mista Cultural Centre, November 1980. Tony Westman, the cameraman for *Box of Treasures*, can be seen in the foreground filming the dancers on the beach in front of the Cultural Centre. [Photo by Robin Wright.]

going on and this is just part of the story. So that change happened and we were happy with that."[60]

One of the most powerful shots in *Box of Treasures* is not reappropriated old footage, as was used in *Potlatch*, but new footage that quotes the most famous moment of the Curtis film, in which the Bear and Thunderbird each dance in the prow of a war canoe. During the opening ceremonies for the new cultural centre, a fishing boat arrives with similarly costumed dancers performing on top of the wheelhouse (fig. 7). The event was certainly not planned for its cinematic impact, but the sequence of shots as the boat enters the harbour deliberately plays on familiarity with the Curtis scene.[61] Had *Box of Treasures* been shot fifteen years later in the late 1990s, these dancers once again would have arrived by canoe.

Morris quotes John Berger's inquiry into the role of film and photography: "All photographs are of the past, yet in them an instant of the past is arrested so that, unlike a lived past, it can never lead to the present. Every photograph presents us with two messages: a message concerning the event photographed and another concerning the shock of discontinuity."[62] Films like *Potlatch* and *Box of Treasures* that quote old images, either by using them directly, or by framing new images in the likeness of the old, can confront this "shock of discontinuity." Although she is not speaking specifically about these instances of visual quotation, Morris asks pertinent questions about Native use of information—visual or textual—compiled by non-Native anthropologists and filmmakers:

> We can and must ask of recent films whether and to what extent they make use of old concepts and symbols to tell different stories, and to what extent such filmic intertextuality supports or undermines an attempt to undo the narrative of an earlier era. These are urgent questions, for those earlier narratives were both determined by and complicit with the institutional policies aimed at the elimination of aboriginal cultures.[63]

Morris argues that the use of old concepts and symbols risks re-inscribing the ideologies of salvage ethnography and assimilationist policy. While she doesn't insist that these old ideologies are reproduced in the U'mista films, neither does she recognize the important, perhaps essential, function of incorporating the Curtis, Boas, and Gardner images. I believe that the use of earlier devices does not necessarily subject the filmmaker to the policies or politics of their non-Native predecessors. Denying Native people the ability to adopt and adapt non-traditional technologies or information confines them within the very limits they are working to destroy. It may be that using the same tropes is the best way to undermine or invert earlier narratives—converting and subverting them. Any other approach might simply create a whole new path that would not intercept and confront old paradigms of paternalism and assimilation.

This concept is exemplified in the U'mista Cultural Centre itself. Within the museum, objects are arranged in a manner reflecting the temporal sequence of the rituals for which they were made. As a viewer travels through the galleries, he or she re-enacts the process of witnessing each object and validating its presence in the sequence. This is a new hybrid concept of "museum," one that has been adapted and "transculturated" to become "a cultural center and a site of storytelling, of indigenous history and of ongoing tribal politics."[64] The

FIGURE 8: Dan Cranmer dances as Hamatsa with Gloria Cranmer Webster at the opening ceremonies for the U'mista Cultural Centre, November 1980. [Photo by Robin Wright.]

museum and the films are simply tools by which the Kwakwaka'wakw may now exercise their inherent rights to reclaim and recontextualize these objects, texts, and images.[65] The strength of these claims is emphasized in the closing scene of *Box of Treasures*, which, like all of the films discussed here, features ceremonial dancing: Dan Cranmer and Gloria Cranmer Webster participating in the Hamatsa dance. This image is accompanied by Gloria Webster's moving text: "But most of all we celebrate the fact that we're still alive, we're still here. We've survived and we'll continue to survive and we're always going to be here" (fig. 8).

All six of these films focus on ceremonial dancing as the essential institution of the Kwakwaka'wakw people. Certainly, this was not a coincidence. The Native subjects of the films were high-ranking families whose role within the potlatch complex was key to their experience within their culture.[66] The Curtis and Boas films, despite the participation of Native actors, insist on a historical reconstruction that denied contemporary realities of Kwa-gulth life. Gardner acknowledges the intrusion of modern-day commodities and subsumes them into a poetic snapshot of Kwakwaka'wakw life. Only the U'mista films insist on a combination of cultural history—emphasizing continuity of tradition—with the specificity of individual experience and contemporary realities. In their productions, images created by earlier non-Natives filmmakers are reappropriated to serve their own narrative. Images of family members wearing long-lost regalia—taken by others and used for outside purposes—have been returned to the culture. Thus, like the physical objects in the cultural centre, they too are U'mista.

Notes

1 In the 1983 film *Box of Treasures*, Gloria Cranmer Webster states that the Kwakwaka'wakw are "probably the most highly anthropologized group of Native people in the world." See *Box of Treasures*, directed by Chuck Olin (U'mista Cultural Society, 1983). Film.

2 For an extensive history of the making of the film and the relationship of Curtis and Hunt, see Bill Holm and George Irving Quimby, *Edward S. Curtis in the Land of the War Canoes: A Pioneer Cinematographer in the Pacific Northwest* (Seattle: University of Washington Press, 1980).

3 Bill Holm spoke with over fifty people who had been involved with the film or present at the filming (Ibid., 16–17).

4 Brian Winston, "Before Grierson, Before Flaherty... Was Edward S. Curtis," *Sight and Sound* 57, 4 (1988): 278.

5 Holm and Quimby, *Edward S. Curtis*, 113–14. It is interesting to note that Curtis is using the word *documentary* to validate his pursuits more than a decade before Grierson defines the documentary as a category of anthropological filmmaking in his 1926 review of Flaherty's *Moana*. See Eliot Wienberger, "The Camera People," in *Beyond Document: Essays on Nonfiction Film*, ed. Charles Warren (Hanover: Wesleyan University Press, 1996), 139.

6 A film made by Pliny Goddard in 1922 no longer survives. *Totemland* was produced by the Associated Screen News of Montreal in 1930. Also in 1930, Franz Boas filmed the research footage considered here. See Ira Jacknis, "George Hunt, Collector of Indian Specimens," in *Chiefly Feasts: The Enduring Kwakiutl Potlatch*, ed. Aldona Jonaitis (New York: American Museum of Natural History, 1991), 205n12.

7 Jacknis, "George Hunt," 206.

8 A number of artifacts and props from the film are now in the collection of the Burke Museum. These include the Duntsik boards (seen growing and receding during the dance scene), more than a dozen cedar bark head and neck rings, two basketry hats, three whalebone clubs, and Naida's headdress.

9 Holm and Quimby, *Edward S. Curtis*, 55.

10 Ibid., 57.

11   Bill Holm, personal communication, October 10, 2000; Lois Speck, "Interview with Gloria Cranmer Webster," *U'mista Cultural Society Newsletter* (Summer 2000): 18.

12   Holm and Quimby, *Edward S. Curtis*, 57.

13   Ibid., 58, 60.

14   Ibid., 121–25.

15   Although George Hunt was half-white, half-Tlingit by birth, he was raised within the Fort Rupert community and his native tongue was Kwakwala. Hunt's mother, a foreigner to the community, established her position through traditional methods; thus from an early age Hunt was aware of the Kwa-gulth system of social validation. At the age of nine, Hunt was initiated in a Kwa-gulth ritual, and throughout his life he participated fully in the ceremonial and social life of the Fort Rupert Kwa-gulth. See Jeanne Cannizzo, "George Hunt and the Invention of Kwakiutl Culture," *Canadian Review of Sociology and Anthropology* 20, 1 (1983): 44–58.

16   Quoted in Holm and Quimby, *Edward S. Curtis*, 13.

17   Ibid., 14.

18   Rosalind C. Morris, *New Worlds from Fragments: Film, Ethnography, and the Representation of Northwest Coast Cultures* (Boulder: Westview, 1994), 40.

19   Holm and Quimby, *Edward S. Curtis*, 96, 102.

20   These included the Sea Monster House at the Pacific Science Center, the Burke Museum, the Portland Art Museum, the Royal Columbia Provincial Museum, the American Museum of Natural History's *Chiefly Feasts* exhibit, and most surprisingly, in the Vancouver Art Gallery's *Down from the Shimmering Sky*—an exhibition that prided itself on showing art in a *gallery* setting without the usual anthropological context.

21   Jacknis, "George Hunt," 181.

22   Holm, personal communication, October 10, 2000.

23   The film, as edited by Holm, is available at the University of Washington. A copy of some 1930 Boas footage is still available unedited by Holm at the National Anthropological Archives in Washington, DC. This copy has fifteen minutes of the dance scenes (but not the Games and Technologies reel) in an order different from the one in which they appear in the Holm version. One short reel shows Boas himself dancing as well as some non-Native children playing. This copy was given to the archives by Columbia University and may have been in the possession of Boas's student, Dr. David Effron. Thanks to Aaron Glass for bringing this copy to my attention.

24   Holm, personal communication, October 10, 2000. In Helen Codere's edited volume of Boas's *Kwakiutl Ethnography*, she reported that the film was lost. See Franz Boas, *Kwakiutl Ethnography*, ed. Helen Codere (Chicago: University of Chicago Press, 1966), 171. Morris repeats this information and adds that Boas thought the footage had been stolen. See Morris, *New*

Worlds from Fragments, 56. In 1953, Gunther recorded songs, sung by Mungo Martin, to go with the film, but that project was never completed (Holm, personal communication, November 11, 2000).

25 Holm, personal communication, October 10, 2000. Holm's explanations of the activities were informed by his interviews with the surviving actors in the film who were asked to explain the scenes. Holm spoke with Mungo Martin, Mary Johnson, Mr. and Mrs. James Knox, and Bob Wilson, who all participated in the film. Other actors included Mr. and Mrs. George Hunt, Sam Hunt, Frank Walker, Sarah Hunt Ohmid, and Charles Wilson, many of whom had been key informants for Boas. See Bill Holm, *Notes on "The Kwakiutl of British Columbia": A Documentary Film by Franz Boas*, prod. Franz Boas, ed. Bill Holm (Seattle: University of Washington Press, 1973), 1.

26 Ira Jacknis agrees that the film was never intended to be presented to a general audience. See Ira Kacknis, "Visualizing Kwakwaka'wakw Tradition: The Films of William Heick, 1951-63," *BC Studies* 125 and 126 (2000): 103.

27 Holm, *Notes on the Kwakiutl*, 1; Holm, personal communication, October 10, 2000.

28 The dances had to be staged outside to provide enough light for the cameras. Because the windup camera held a limited amount of film, the dance sequences were by necessity abbreviated (Holm, *Notes on "The Kwakiutl,"* 2).

29 Morris, *New Worlds from Fragments*, 56.

30 Ibid., 61.

31 Ibid., 56-62.

32 Ibid., 62.

33 Ibid., 63.

34 Morris asserts that "not even Holm could interpret the image-track that Boas left behind." However, this is exactly what he did in compiling the text (ibid., *New Worlds from Fragments*, 59).

35 Ibid.

36 It seems clear that Morris did not read Holm's text, because there are discrepancies between her descriptions and the information provided in Holm's notes. She does cite Colin Browne's annotation of the film, which states that the film is "available with copious excellent notes by Bill Holm." See Colin Browne, *Motion Picture Production in British Columbia 1848-1940: A Brief Historical Background and Catalogue* (Victoria: British Columbia Provincial Museum, 1979), 190. Morris seems to feel strongly that the film should be analyzed on its own merits without considering any texts (Morris, *New Worlds from Fragments*, 59).

37 Morris, *New Worlds from Fragments*, 63. The film, similar to Boas's field notes, records information from his informants about activities that Boas considered to be "traditional." However, the milled-lumber houses of Fort

Rupert appear in the background and the actors are wearing early-twentieth-century Western clothing—characteristics that certainly would not have appeared in a Curtis production. The undisguised trappings of twentieth-century life support the notion that the film sequences were intended as field notes rather than as part of a film production.

38 Morris, *New Worlds from Fragments*, 64.

39 Gardner made an additional film in Fort Rupert, located directly across Queen Charlotte Straights from Blunden Harbour, in June 1950. Gardner, in response to an inquiry from Bill Holm, denied having made the film (Bill Holm, personal interview, November 11, 1999). However, Ira Jacknis discusses the circumstances of the filming in Fort Rupert. The footage was apparently made into a finished film, although the present whereabouts of the film is unknown (Jacknis, "Visualizing Kwakwaka'wakw Tradition," 108–109).

40 Robert Gardner, "The Impulse to Preserve," in *Beyond Document: Essays on Nonfiction Film*, ed. Charles Warren (Hanover: Wesleyan University Press, 1996), 174.

41 Jacknis quotes avant-garde filmmaker Stan Brakhage (Jacknis, "Visualizing Kwakwaka'wakw Tradition," 107).

42 Ibid., 108.

43 Gardner, "The Impulse to Preserve," 173.

44 Ruth Benedict, *Patterns of Culture* (Boston: Houghton Mifflin, 1934).

45 Jacknis, "Visualizing Kwakwaka'wakw Tradition," 110n31.

46 Morris, *New Worlds from Fragments*, 104.

47 Ibid., 105.

48 Gardner, "The Impulse to Preserve," 172.

49 Karen Duffek, *The Contemporary Northwest Coast Indian Art Market* (MA thesis, University of British Columbia, 1983), 33.

50 Wilson Duff, Bill Reid, and Bill Holm, *Arts of the Raven: Masterworks by the Northwest Coast Indian* (Vancouver: Vancouver Art Gallery, 1967), 8.

51 Speck, "Interview with Gloria Cranmer Webster," 18.

52 Ibid.

53 Dennis Wheeler, "Director's Statement," *Potlatch... A Strict Law Bids Us Dance.* (U'mista Cultural Society, 1975).

54 These scenes are from *Fish and Medicine Men*, 1928, and *Totemland*, 1930. Thanks to Dan Savard for identifying these clips.

55 One provocative angle for viewing these films may be to consider the ramifications of performances enacted specifically for the camera and those filmed while in progress for a traditional audience. For an informative discussion of dances performed for non-Natives and what aspects must be included, regardless of audience, see Judith Ostrowitz, *Privileging the Past: Reconstructing History in Northwest Coast Art* (Seattle: University of Washington Press, 1999), 84–104.

56 Speck, "Interview with Gloria Cranmer Webster," 18.

57 Ibid.

58 Ibid.

59 Ibid.

60 One benefit of this collaborative project was the "Salmonista Video Project," which grew out of Olin's time at Alert Bay. One of his crew, Judy Hoffman, came and taught a video workshop, instructing students in handling of video equipment, lighting, sound dubbing, history of video, maintenance of equipment, and interviewing techniques. See Speck, "Interview with Gloria Cranmer Webster," 18. One of the students in this workshop was Barbara Cranmer, who went on to direct *Mungo Martin: A Slender Thread*, I'Tusto: *To Rise Again*, and Tlina: *The Rendering of Wealth*.

61 The arrival of a big canoe for a potlatch was one of the scenes recorded in the now-lost footage that Gardner shot at Fort Rupert in 1950 (Jacknis, *Visualizing Kwakwaka'wakw Tradition*, 109n28).

62 Morris, *New Worlds from Fragments*, 39.

63 Ibid., 116-17.

64 James Clifford, "Four Northwest Coast Museums: Travel Reflections," in *Routes: Travel and Translation in the Late Twentieth Century* (Cambridge: Harvard University Press, 1997), 212.

65 For a discussion of the reclamation and reorganization of objects and texts in the U'mista Cultural Center see Clifford, "Four Northwest Coast Museums, 107-45. A number of his observations can be applied to the recontextualized images that appear in the U'mista films.

66 See Barbara Saunders, "Contested *Ethnie* in Two Kwakwaka'wakw Museums," in *Contesting Art: Art, Politics and Identity in the Modern World*, ed. Jeremy MacClancy, 85-130 (New York: Oxford, 1997), for a discussion of the self-conscious construction of a Kwakwaka'wakw *ethnie* by the U'mista Centre and the Hunt-Cranmer family, based on the Boas texts and the repatriated Potlatch collection.

Bibliography

Benedict, Ruth. *Patterns of Culture*. Boston: Houghton Mifflin, 1934.

Blunden Harbour. Directed by Robert Gardner. Orbit Films, 1951. Film.

Boas, Franz. *Kwakiutl Ethnography*. Ed. Helen Codere. Chicago: University of Chicago Press, 1966.

Box of Treasures. Directed by Chuck Olin. U'mista Cultural Society, 1983. Film.

Browne, Colin. *Motion Picture Production in British Columbia 1848-1940: A Brief Historical Background and Catalogue*. Victoria: British Columbia Provincial Museum, 1979.

Cannizzo, Jeanne. "George Hunt and the Invention of Kwakiutl Culture." *Canadian Review of Sociology and Anthropology* 20, 1 (1983): 44–58.

Clifford, James. "Four Northwest Coast Museums: Travel Reflections." In *Routes: Travel and Translation in the Late Twentieth Century.* Ed. James Clifford. Cambridge: Harvard University Press, 1997.

———. "Museums as Contact Zones." In *Routes: Travel and Translation in the Late Twentieth Century.* Cambridge: Harvard University Press, 1997.

Dances of the Kwakiutl. Directed by Robert Gardner. Orbit Films, 1951. Film.

Duff, Wilson, Bill Reid, and Bill Holm. *Arts of the Raven: Masterworks by the Northwest Coast Indian.* Vancouver: Vancouver Art Gallery, 1967.

Duffek, Karen. *The Contemporary Northwest Coast Indian Art Market.* MA thesis, University of British Columbia, 1983.

Gardner, Robert. "The Impulse to Preserve." In *Beyond Document: Essays on Nonfiction Film.* Ed. Charles Warren. Hanover: Wesleyan University Press, 1996.

Holm, Bill. *Notes on "The Kwakiutl of British Columbia": A Documentary Film by Franz Boas.* Produced by Franz Boas. Ed. Bill Holm. Seattle: University of Washington Press, 1973.

Holm, Bill, and George Irving Quimby. *Edward S. Curtis in the Land of the War Canoes: A Pioneer Cinematographer in the Pacific Northwest.* Seattle: University of Washington Press, 1980.

In the Land of the Head-Hunters. Directed by Edward Curtis. Continental Film Company, 1914. Film.

Jacknis, Ira. "George Hunt, Collector of Indian Specimens." In *Chiefly Feasts: The Enduring Kwakiutl Potlatch.* Ed. Aldona Jonaitis. New York: American Museum of Natural History, 1991.

———. "Visualizing Kwakwaka'wakw Tradition: The Films of William Heick, 1951–63." *BC Studies* 125 and 126 (2000): 99–146.

Jonaitis, Aldona, *From the Land of the Totem Poles.* New York: American Museum of Natural History, 1988.

———, ed. *A Wealth of Thought: Franz Boas on Native American Art.* Seattle: University of Washington Press, 1995.

The Kwakiutl of British Columbia: A Documentary Film by Franz Boas. Directed by Franz Boas, 1930. Ed. Bill Holm. University of Washington Press, 1973. Film.

Loizos, Peter. *Innovation in Ethnographic Film: From Innocence to Self-consciousness, 1955-1985*. Manchester: Manchester University Press, 1993.

Morris, Rosalind C. *New Worlds from Fragments: Film, Ethnography, and the Representation of Northwest Coast Cultures*. Boulder: Westview, 1994.

Ostrowitz, Judith. *Privileging the Past: Reconstructing History in Northwest Coast Art*. Seattle: University of Washington Press, 1999.

Potlatch...A Strict Law Bids Us Dance. Directed by Dennis Wheeler, executive producer. U'mista Cultural Society, 1975. Film.

Saunders, Barbara. "Contested *Ethnie* in Two Kwakwaka'wakw Museums." In *Contesting Art: Art, Politics and Identity in the Modern World*. Ed. Jeremy MacClancy, 85-130. New York: Oxford, 1997.

Speck, Lois. "Interview with Gloria Cranmer Webster." *U'mista Cultural Society Newsletter* (Summer 2000): 10-14.

———. "U'mista Cultural Center 1980-2000." *U'mista Cultural Society Newsletter* (Summer 2000): 17-25.

Webster, Gloria Cranmer. "The Contemporary Potlatch." In *Chiefly Feasts: The Enduring Kwakiutl Potlatch*. Ed. Aldona Jonaitis. Seattle: University of Washington Press, 1991.

Wheeler, Dennis. "Director's Statement" *Potlatch...A Strict Law Bids Us Dance*. U'mista Cultural Society, 1975.

Wienberger, Eliot. "The Camera People." In *Beyond Document: Essays on Nonfiction Film*. Ed. Charles Warren. Hanover: Wesleyan University Press, 1996.

Winston, Brian. "Before Grierson, Before Flaherty...Was Edward S. Curtis." *Sight and Sound* 57, 4 (1988): 277-79.

13

A Way of Seeing the World: Connecting Text, Context, and People

Bernie Harder

TEACHING THE LITERATURE WRITTEN by contemporary First Nations authors in North America can provide one way of beginning to acknowledge Aboriginal peoples. As a non-Native professor, I have found the opportunity to develop and teach undergraduate and graduate courses in the fiction, poetry, and drama of Native authors to be an exciting challenge but also a serious responsibility that depends on much help from Native individuals and communities. I began developing the courses because of my interest in knowing Native people better and understanding the related justice issues; however, their willingness to help me inside and outside the classroom is essential because the approach to knowledge embodied in the literature differs significantly from dominant Euro-American concepts. An elder told me about an experience he had in his youth that somehow stayed in his mind. Twenty years later he needed a certain plant and remembered exactly where he could find it and understood what had happened. He was telling me to be patient about understanding things that might seem puzzling. This is an approach very different from what has to happen in a classroom where students are trained to understand a subject quickly and to have the answers ready for the exams. Knowledge is often sought through guidance where the classroom might be the bush, a fast, or a sweat lodge, and the teachers include the medicines, the animals, and the rocks that are respected as people. The literature by Aboriginal authors often draws from this different world and exposes the tension with the dominant ideologies of institutionalized education. It can create doorways for a better understanding. But freeing our minds and relationships from stereotypical concepts requires respecting indigenous peoples and experiencing life with them just as they are. This approach might make it possible to challenge the colonization that affects all of us, whether we are aware of it or not.

The students find that the painful stories of oppression in indigenous literatures are balanced by a way of life that can contribute to personal growth and provide a direction for social change. The focus is not just on knowledge and intellectual growth, because the mind, the spirit, the body, and the emotions are all equally important and connected to each other, to the community, and to the universe. While the literature cannot avoid the destructive results of European colonization, it also celebrates the original way of life and the survival and affirmation of the original peoples of North America. Reading the literature in the context of the history and contemporary life of the original peoples in conjunction with a greater awareness of continuing colonization helps to expose the tension of the tightrope but also suggests solutions that might transform the conflicts to allow hope for harmony. The need for a safe ground for discussion that is identifiable like an island but has no boundaries is obvious, because colonization attempts to engulf everyone, even though its effects and our understanding of its forms can differ.

Interpreting Native Literatures

Native authors have discussed the importance of evaluating the possible theoretical approaches to the literature in order to avoid subjecting the interpretation to the assumptions of the dominant society, another form of colonization. In an article identifying some of the distinctive themes in Native literature, Armand Garnet Ruffo, Anishinabe (Ojibway) author and literature professor at Carleton University, explains the importance of developing an appropriate theoretical approach. In an essay entitled "Why Native literature?" that discusses some of the theoretical problems related to characterizing Native literature, Ruffo warns against imposing external theories: "The literature itself tells us what it is; theories of criticism, ways of approaching the literature, will necessarily come from the literature and not be foisted upon it."[1]

The writings may help explain existing theories in academically interesting ways, but the theories developed in the dominant society are not sufficient for interpreting the literature.

Furthermore, the interpretation depends on a sense of Native communities since they are essential to shaping the meaning of the literary expression. As Ruffo explains in the same essay, "Native writers, while writing from individual perspectives, are in a sense adjuncts of the collective experience, of what we may call 'community.' This is no doubt a very different frame of reference from that of non-Native writers, who traditionally place great emphasis on individuality and hence personal isolation."[2] In other words, a beginning point for interpreting Native literature requires a continual attempt to become familiar with Native individuals and communities. The most challenging advice a Native author gave me was that if you want to understand the literature, you have to spend time in Native communities. There I learned that two basic requirements are respect and a willingness to listen with the heart, not just the head. Listening in this way includes getting involved through action.

When we experience the importance of land in its natural state during a traditional activity, then it becomes easier to understand how destructive agriculture and development can be to a traditional way of life. A Lakota teacher once tried to explain to me that our mind is not in our body, but out there with the land. We can try to understand what it says to us. Trying to grasp that is a continuous process, not just a concept.

Ruffo's *Grey Owl: The Mystery of Archie Belaney*

The importance of community is subtly embodied in Ruffo's book of poetry, *Grey Owl: The Mystery of Archie Belaney*. The Ojibway of Northern Ontario seem to be the context of the story about Grey Owl, but as context they are central to the story—both within the book and outside it. Without them, Grey Owl could not have promoted his constructed identity. Ruffo's reconstruction of Grey Owl's character in the book is a result of the mixture of historical facts, oral stories, and Ruffo's own imagination that raises interesting intellectual and moral questions. These questions are not resolved but lead to the realization that Archie Belaney's inner life is a mystery that has its roots in the Native people and community. Belaney's identity, including his imagined relationship to the public, is embedded in the Ojibway community and the Native people of Northern Ontario and beyond, revealing who they are and the problems they have with the settlers. Ruffo, coming from the same families and community that welcomed Archie, represents the Ojibway people both in the manner and in the content of the story. The Tema-Augama Anishinabai, in the poem "Gitchi-Saganash,"[3] welcome Archie and support his interest, even though they know he is not an Indian. As in other responses to Archie, the respect and gentleness of their response is based in the values of their way of life. Although Native people have reasons for being cautious about people who come into their communities, there is still an enormous willingness to share and welcome visitors who come with respect and a willingness to listen and learn and be with them.

Much of the representation is implied or left in the silence of thoughts. In the poem, "Jane Espanial, 1923,"[4] Jane dyes Archie's hair, aware that "between my fingers it feels fine, not like Indian hair." She tries to joke about his nervousness about hiding his appearance, but he suddenly "becomes pensive, as if from the shadows / of the surrounding bush we call our backyard." The problem of changing his identity is not just physical but deeply rooted in the relationship to the land. What he calls "Wilderness" and "an untouched virgin territory"[5] in his autobiography is their home and all that is implied in it being their "backyard." Similarly, in "To Become,"[6] Archie thinks of the new lodge he is building in terms of more money, more tourists and jobs, but for Angele, his first wife, and all the Indians, jobs means being "servants in their own land." The poetry identifies the importance of the connection of land to people but does not attempt to explain it. These differences in attitudes briefly indicate how much is involved in who the Ojibway people are, pointing to a world of meaning that exists beyond words.

Archie changes from trapper to conservationist to spokesperson and entertainer. He even addresses questions of justice and oppression. In spite of his success and usefulness, he is unable to represent the Ojibway, since they are always different from his portrayal. They furnish him with the icons of his construction of himself and Indians, even when they know that the icons are not representing them. There is always a huge gap between Archie's representation and the voices of the individual Ojibway. The poem "Annie Espaniel, 1923,"[7] demonstrates this problem. When he says he wants to organize an Indian War Dance, Annie asks what it is, but when he argues that "you can't have an Indian War Dance without a costume," she says "I agree" and helps him. Archie's use of the word *costume* implies a lot about his willingness to appropriate and adapt traditional regalia for dramatic purposes, and Annie Espaniel's response indicates the gentleness and tolerance she shows for his attitudes, because she knows the difference.

The Ojibway people speak through the individual voices in the poems, suggesting but not explaining their way of life. Grey Owl's representation is his own creation, even though it is his life with the Anishinabe people that gives him credibility. Ruffo's focus is not Grey Owl's representation of the Anishinabe people but rather, as Rolland Nadjiwon, Potawatami author and educator, commented, "It is the Anishinabe in juxtaposition to Archie Belaney's representations. Grey Owl always gets the spotlight even though it is the foundation of the Anishinabe that he is built on."[8]

The poem "You Ask"[9] identifies the distance between the voices in Archie and Anahareo's relationship. The poem begins with the question of what it is like for Archie to still use the films of his former relationship with Anahareo, who was essential in shaping his carrier as his wife but hasn't lived with him for years. He responds to these questions and affirms the distance between the fiction and the identity he projects in his lectures: "Surely I've lost myself, to this man I've become, / this man I am, to this work I've taken on, to the public." Nevertheless, the distance between the voices does not annihilate the mystery of Archie's character or the validity of his achievement. John Tootoosis, who helped Archie recognize the importance of the justice issues facing Indian people expressed in the poem "Grey Owl, 1936,"[10] affirms Grey Owl's message and achievement in a council with the Cree: "We know Wa-She-Quon-Asin is not born of us, and we say nothing." They know but remain silent about his self-representation and encourage him "to dance with us, as you can." They know he does not dance like an Indian but save their words instead of wasting them because "in this struggle of generations / they are our strongest medicine." Their opportunity to be heard, to use their medicine, may come later, but for now, they "are thankful he has chosen our side."

Ruffo's sensitive examination of the complexity of representation emphasizes the importance of listening to Native people without our own agenda in order to understand the significance and validity of representations. The process often begins when Native speakers come to the classroom; students learn the value of getting to know Native people and finding the connections between the literature and the human realities. Their education can move beyond the walls of the educational institution as well as their personal walls to include what they can learn and experience directly from their involvement with Aboriginal people. This process is a way of understanding the significance of what the authors are writing about that is difficult to grasp from the books alone. It contributes perhaps in a small way to the decolonizing of both our minds and the dominant society that generally excludes Aboriginal peoples and marginalizes their history, knowledge, and way of life.

Aboriginal Knowledge

Native literature is based on an understanding of knowledge and meaning that is rooted in the community. These concepts are significantly different from the dominant assumptions embedded in the educational system and the dominant society. This difference is difficult to articulate but is an integral part of understanding Native literature and the approach to meaning in the communities. In the novel *Keeper'n Me* by Richard Wagamese, Ojibway author and journalist living in Ottawa, the main character Garnet explains some of the teachings he is learning from Keeper who is trying to pass on the original teachings. He explains,

> Land is the most sacred thing in the Indian way of seeing. It's where life comes from and all the teachings and philosophy that kept Indians alive through everything that happened to them all over all these years comes from the land. Lose that connection you lose yourself, according to people around here. Lose that connection you lose that feeling of being part of something bigger than everything. Kinda tapping into the great mystery. Feeling the

spirit of the land that's the spirit of the people and the spirit of your-self.[11]

The central teaching is based on the philosophy that everything is connected: the individual is connected to the land, to the people, and to the great mystery. Knowledge depends on experiencing that connection and cannot be isolated in autonomous texts without great loss.

A little later, Garnet explains that knowledge can come directly from the silence of the land: "A beautiful roaring silence. A silence that is full of everything. When your ears get used to it you start to hear things you never heard in all your life."[12] The land is not just the context, but also the direct source of knowledge, and functions as the teacher. The value that the dominant system usually assigns to printed texts is attributed to the connection to the land in Wagamese's novel. This teaching may sound mystical and could be interpreted as merely part of the fiction but is in fact an important aspect of the Native way of life. Meaning depends on the way everything is connected. In an article entitled "We Belong to This Land: A View of 'Cultural Difference,'" Kateri Akiwenzie-Damm, a member of the Chippewas of Nawash, Cape Croker Band on Georgian Bay in Ontario, explains that the connection to this land is a fundamental difference between Native peoples and the dominant culture:

> It is our connection to the land that makes us who we are, that shapes our thinking, our cultural practices, our spiritual, emotional, physical, and social lives.... Land, community, culture, and spirituality are intricately woven together. This interconnectedness is expressed and reinforced through our arts, language, ceremonies, songs, prayers, dances, customs, values, and daily practices, all of which have been developed over generations over thousands and thousands of years of living on the land.[13]

She explains how this interconnectedness is essential to Native literatures because writing is "a way to share, to reaffirm kinship, to connect with the sacredness of creation."[14] In her poem "what the earth might say," in her collection called *my heart is a stray bullet*, she also, like Wagamese, expresses the idea that meaning can come directly from the land:

> there is no true silence
> everything every bird and blade of grass
> calls out its story as it must
> and though you may see nothing
> even the empty places are filled with meaning.[15]

As she explains in her article in a quotation from Paula Gunn Allen's "Iyani," "the Earth is the mind of the people as we are the mind of the earth."[16] Experiencing this difference to even a small degree can open the mind to at least realizing that there is a totally different way of understanding the world, human beings, and the nature of knowledge. If we do not understand the difference, we can at least acknowledge and respect it instead of imposing our concepts on Native peoples in the education system. One might even begin to suspect that it is Euro-American epistemology that is unnatural, since peoples throughout the earth who are still connected to the land seem to share similar views.

The significance of the land can be seen in the way values and language function in the literature as well as everyday life. The relationships are an intrinsic part of the way the values are associated with experiences and with the meaning that English expresses, including how language itself is viewed and used. The meaning of values and language is based on the assumption that everything is related, in contrast to the Western ideas about individuality and exclusive categories. Relationships are fundamental, although the content and teachings may vary endlessly among the First Nations. The literature makes us aware of the significance of relationships as it applies to values and language, even if we understand it only in a limited way. It's very simple in some ways, but also part of the great mystery of Creation that cannot and does not need to be explained, even though it can be experienced and understood to the extent that the community and the individual are capable. Kateri Akiwenzie-Damm describes this apparent paradox in a beautiful way in her essay:

> When Indigenous people study and come to understand our own literatures, languages, cultures, and aesthetics, there comes the realization that everything is connected. There comes the realization that there are few simple answers except when there is no understanding, or when understanding is so profound that connections can be understood at a glance, with language and mean-

ing carved into a simple design that reflects the larger pattern. There comes the realization that words are sacred.[17]

The language already seems too limited for what she is saying, but it opens a world of meanings that has no limits. The spiritual and sacred in words cannot be adequately represented with words,[18] but words can be connected to experiences that give them meaning. "Words are sacred" is infinite in meaning and possibilities; we may not realize that they can connect us with healing, with love, the land, the community, and the great mystery.

Values as Relationships

The value of experiences is inseparable from these relationships. In Lee Maracle's novel *Ravensong*, the heroine Stacey is trying to understand the difference between what death means in her Salish community and what it means to the people in the white town across the river. She is trying to understand her thought that "death does not count in the white town the same as it does in the village."[19] She considers the possibility that the death of an individual does not relate to the community in the same way:

> She could see the meaning of death to the village. She watched the numbers terrify everyone. The loss was total.... Every single person served the community, each one becoming a wedge of the family circle around which good health and well-being revolved. A missing person became a missing piece of the circle which could not be replaced.
>
> White people didn't seem to live this way. No one individual was indispensable. Their parts didn't seem to be bonded to the whole. It wasn't that they didn't feel their losses, it was that their losses didn't seem to have much value.[20]

The meaning of an individual's death is inseparable from relationship to the community. Life and the relationship does not end in death. Similarly, the stories about love, sex, abuse, the search for identity, healing, and so on, all assume the importance of the relationship of the individual to community, the land, and the spiritual reality. For example, in her book about American Indian literature, Paula Gunn Allen, Laguna Pueblo/Sioux author and literary critic, explains how the main character in Leslie Marmon Silko's novel, *Ceremony*, demonstrates the healing movement from isolation to a sense of relationship:

> So Tayo's initiation into motherhood is complete, and the witchery is countered for a time, at least for one human being and his land. Tayo has bridged the distance between his isolated consciousness and the universe of being, because he has loved the spirit woman who brings all things into being and because he is at last conscious that she has always loved them, his people and himself.[21]

The "spirit woman" in Silko's novel is also physically real so that Tayo's sexual and emotional experiences with her also connect him to her spiritually; there is no boundary between them.

Specific values are also understood in relationship to land, people, and the spiritual. Part of this is possible because there are no definite boundaries and no hierarchies in creation. Animals, rocks, and things are also people; rocks can be grandfathers, for example, that deserve the same respect and have functions similar to those of teachers, providing guidance and wisdom. In Wagamese's novel, Keeper explains that when they want the young people to learn humility and respect, they send them out onto the land: "Us, we needed that humble feelin' workin' in us all the time and out there's where you find it. So we send people out there to find the humility an' respect they're gonna need to appreciate ceremony. Get that an' ceremony's always gonna mean more. Teach you more."[22] In Keeper's story about respect, the animal that has the most respect and is the greatest warrior is the mole, because "he lives in constant touch with Mother Earth. All his life always stays in touch with her. That way he gets wise."[23] He is always aware of all the animals around him, and the other reason is that the "mole always takes time to investigate what he feels. That's why. And you gotta have that same medicine power to be a great warrior."[24] Values are understood as relationships; humility is important because even a mole can teach us a lot about respect and power.

The total respect for the natural world is ironically the opposite of the value system imposed on indigenous peoples through colonization. In their book on multiculturalism and the media, *Unthinking Eurocentrism*, Shohat and Stam explain that, in the dominant colonial value system, "animalization forms part of the larger, more diffuse mechanism of naturalization: the reduction of the cultural to the biological, the tendency to associate the colonized with the vegetative and the instinctual rather than the learned and the cultural."[25] Similarly, Ruffo explains how Northrop Frye also identified a similar difference between the Native and non-Native perspective in his discussion of Canadian poetry: "Thus Frye moves us along a trajectory in which nature becomes the embodiment of the unanswerable denial of human and moral values, equated with all that is uncivilized."[26] The two perspectives seem to create two completely different worlds and value systems. Animals and plants are equal to humans, not placed on a hierarchy.

The Language Is the People

The First Nations theories about language and the everyday, as well as literary Native use of English, vividly demonstrate how knowledge is the result of relationships. The meaning of words like *moon, earth, bear, eagle,* and *tobacco* seem straightforward and simple enough, but when Native people use these words they can include culturally complex meanings that might be virtually impossible to define even though they are understood. When a Native person says that he saw a bear, it might have been a bear in the standard Canadian sense of the word, but a bear is also spiritual power and sacred, and connected to the medicine wheel in specific ways that vary according to specific cultures and teachings. The bear is also the protector of the land and the animals and one of the clans. The particular person may also have a specific emotional, spiritual, physical, or intellectual relationship to bear, and in the specific instance the bear may have even conveyed a message to him about something that was happening at the time. The social, spiritual, and physical contexts are all important to the meaning. These ideas become a human reality—a young girl telling us about seeing a bear and exactly what the bear said to her. We have to learn not to doubt or question another person's experience. I learned that even our language naturalizes this doubt. I came to my friend with my grandson after driving along a bush road and reported that he said he saw an eagle. My friend stopped me abruptly and explained why, and ended up telling me that if my grandson said he saw an eagle, then he saw an eagle. Even "he said" casts doubt. It is so easy to expose children to doubt, and important to protect them from it.

One easy mistake is to think of words as symbols in order to explain the complex meanings, but this approach sets up a boundary between the word and its meanings that distorts the connections, as they are experienced within the culture. A corn stalk is not like a woman; it is a woman. Or maybe it is both. Our universe is made of stories.

A particular experience can enrich the meaning of words beyond definitions or concepts. I was exploring a mountain for the first time and was exhausted and not sure which way to go. It was getting late in the afternoon, and there was some thunder echoing through the hills. I sat down on a log to rest and was surprised by a hummingbird right in front of me. I didn't even know they were in the mountains. It stayed there for a while and then flew to my right, facing me. I remembered hearing that hummingbirds are messengers and decided to go in the direction it would take. Then it went to my left for a moment and then in front of me again. By this time I was fascinated by its flight, because those seemed to be the best choices, but I wasn't sure which to take. It came right up to me and touched the feather in my hand and then shot off in a straight line towards my right. I followed and immediately saw an eagle gliding in the same direction. I knew there could be difficult marshes and steep bluffs but felt safe and found myself heading down a gentle slope towards a lake where I was able to drink water and go for a swim and lie on a smooth rock in the warm sun. After that, there was an old logging trail that took me to the road just in time for some loggers to come by and give me a ride to my camp. We had a good chat, but their main comment was about whether I had asked for protection before going into the bush. Hummingbirds. And a river or a fire can tell stories that clarify what is going on inside us. It's a natural way of connecting for many people, but that does not mean that generalizations of this sort can be used as prescriptions for determining identity.

English has become "a powerful tool of oppression" in Canada,[27] but Native authors are consciously resisting the process. They are appropriating the English language to express the meaning and knowledge of their culture. The opening lines of the poem "Autumn Morning," by

Peter Blue Cloud, of the Mohawk Nation at Kahnawake, for example, could be read as a romantic description of the scenery:

> Full moon and the whispering leaves
> of dry corn stalks touched by wind
> a low mist swirls the river's surface
> in gentle dance.[28]

In this poem, the moon, the corn, and the small whirlwind of mist introduce a lot of cultural meanings that create and express a profound experience of the morning in simple language, leading to a seemingly simple but again profound conclusion because of the cultural meaning of language: "And dawn is a praise of silence / to be respected."

In the poem, the land is making the statement of praise to which the poem points. As in Akiwenzie-Damm's poem, it is the silence that speaks; the poet becomes part of the creation because he notices and respects it. The cultural meanings are not being imported into the language; instead, the language is appropriated into the cultural meanings that existed long before the English language even came into being. In her essay "Land Speaking," Jeanette Armstrong, Okanagan and director of En'owkin Native Education Centre in Penticton, British Columbia, explains some of the distinct ideas about language. She says that according to her Okanagan ancestors, it was the land that gave the people the language, and, "my own father told me that it was the land that changed the language because there is special knowledge in each different place. All my elders say it is the land that holds all knowledge of life and death and is a constant teacher. It is said in Okanagan that the land constantly speaks. It is constantly communicating."[29] Speaking is sacred because words contain power and spirit and are able "to realize the potential for transformation of the world."[30] Even the "perception of the way reality occurs is very different from that solicited by the English language. Reality is very much like a story: it is easily changeable and transformative with each speaker."[31] Human beings, in this view, are part of the land and participate in the expression of knowledge that originates from the land; they are not the source of language or knowledge. Armstrong, like other Native authors, struggles to incorporate the differences into her use of English so that "it will also display, through its altered syntax, semantic differences reflecting the view of reality embodied in the culture."[32] Writing for her, as for other Native authors, becomes a way of resisting the "invasive imperialism upon my tongue."[33] The use of English is a way of re-establishing the connections to land, community, history, and culture that the colonial process attempts to sever.

Creating Connections

Native people, individuals, communities, and nations have countless ways of creating and maintaining the connections. The relationships exist in the nature of the world, but they must also be continuously formed through actions; there are always processes within and outside the community, the family, and the individual's life that threaten the connections. Native literature, like the ceremonies, indigenous education, the oral tradition, and all the other activities, contributes towards establishing, celebrating, and acknowledging those connections and also towards identifying the disruptions that threaten and destroy them. As Ruffo shows in his essay, the four main themes in Native literature are the connections to the land, to the community and family, to history, and to the mythological or the sacred elements. "Native literature," as he explains, "in its oral form was spiritually centered in that it was, and is, informed by an Indigenous worldview that sees humans not at the top of an evolutionary pyramid but rather as a link in a circle of creation in which every entity is endowed with spirit."[34] Contemporary Native writers continue to explore and affirm the experience of this link. They write, Ruffo states, because they are determined "to liberate themselves and to choose life over death" and because they want to "address Native people themselves so they can empower and heal themselves through their own cultural affirmation, as well as to address those in power and give them the real story."[35]

Acknowledgements

I would like to thank the people who have helped me with this paper. The list is long but includes grandfathers and grandmothers, the fire, water, animals, birds, plants, and all my relations. Many thanks!

Notes

1 Armand Garnet Ruffo, *Native North America: Critical and Cultural Perspectives*, ed. Renée Hulan (Toronto: ECW Press, 1999), 114.

2 Ibid.

3 Armand Garnet Ruffo, *Grey Owl: The Mystery of Archie Belaney* (Regina: Coteau Books, 1996), 18.

4 Ibid., 34.

5 Ibid., 12–13.

6 Ibid., 19.

7 Ibid., 37.

8 Rolland Nadjiwon, e-mail to author, 9 August 2000.

9 Ibid.

10 Ibid.

11 Richard Wagamese, *Keeper 'n Me* (Toronto: Doubleday Canada, 1994), 156.

12 Ibid.

13 Kateri Akiwenzie-Damm, "We Belong to This Land: A View of 'Cultural Difference,'" in *Literary Pluralities*, ed. Christl Verduyn (Peterborough: Broadview Press/Journal of Canadian Studies, 1998), 84.

14 Ibid., 89.

15 Ibid., 29.

16 Ibid., 84.

17 Ibid., 89–90.

18 Bernie Harder, "Limitations of the Media in Representing Aboriginal Cultures in Canada," *Media Development* 42 (1995): 21–23.

19 Lee Maracle, *Ravensong: A Novel* (Vancouver: Press Gang), 25–26.

20 Ibid., 26.

21 Paula Gunn Allen, "The Feminine Landscape of Leslie Marmon Silko's *Ceremony*," in *Studies in American Literature*, ed. Paula Gunn Allen (New York: The Modern Language Association of North America, 1983), 133.

22 Wagamese, *Keeper 'n Me*, 180.

23 Ibid., 152.

24 Ibid.

25 Ella Stohat and Robert Stam, *Unthinking Eurocentrism: Multiculturalism and the Media* (London and New York: Routledge, 1994), 138.

26 Ruffo, *Native North America*, 111.

27 Bernie Harder, "The English Language against the Anishinabeg in Canada," *Australian-Canadian Studies* 14 (1996).

28 Blue Cloud, "Autumn Meeting," *Gatherings: The En'owkin Journal of First American Peoples* 5 (1994): 56.

29 Jeannette Armstrong, "Land Speaking," in *Speaking for the Generations: Native Writers on Writing*, ed. Simon J. Ortiz (Tuscon: University of Arizona Press, 1998), 176.

30 Ibid., 183.

31 Ibid., 191.
32 Ibid., 193.
33 Ibid., 194.
34 Ruffo, *Native North America*, 118.
35 Ibid., 120.

Bibliography

Akiwenzie-Damm, Kateri. "We Belong to This Land: A View of 'Cultural Difference.'" In *Literary Pluralities*. Ed. Christl Verduyn, 84-91. Peterborough: Broadview Press/Journal of Canadian Studies, 1998.

Allen, Paula Gunn. "The Feminine Landscape of Leslie Marmon Silko's *Ceremony*." In *Studies in American Literature*. Ed. Paula Gunn Allen, 127-33. New York: The Modern Language Association of America, 1983.

Armstrong, Jeanette. "Land Speaking." In *Speaking for the Generations: Native Writers on Writing*. Ed. Simon J. Ortiz, 174-94. Tucson: University of Arizona Press, 1998.

Blue Cloud, Peter/Aroniawenrate. "Autumn Meeting." *Gatherings: The En'owkin Journal of First American Peoples* 5 (1994): 56.

damm, kateri. *my heart is a stray bullet*. Cape Croker: Kegedonce Press, 1993.

Grey Owl. *Pilgrims of the Wild*. Toronto: Macmillan, 1990.

Harder, Bernie. "The English Language against the Anishinabeg in Canada." *Australian-Canadian Studies* 14 (1996): 207-21.

———. "Limitations of the Media in Representing Aboriginal Cultures in Canada." *Media Development* 42 (1995): 21-23.

Maracle, Lee. *Ravensong: A Novel*. Vancouver: Press Gang, 1993.

Ruffo, Armand Garnet. *Grey Owl: The Mystery of Archie Belaney*. Regina: Coteau, 1996.

———. "Why Native Literature?" In *Native North America: Critical and Cultural Perspectives*. Ed. Renée Hulan, 109-21. Toronto: ECW Press, 1999.

Shohat, Ella, and Robert Stam. *Unthinking Eurocentrism: Multiculturalism and the Media*. London and New York: Routledge, 1994.

Wagamese, Richard. *Keeper 'n Me*. Toronto: Doubleday, 1994.

14

Representation of Aboriginal Peoples in Rudy Wiebe's Fiction: *The Temptations of Big Bear* and *A Discovery of Strangers*

Janne Korkka

Introduction

PERHAPS THE BEST-KNOWN WRITER in Western Canada, Rudy Wiebe is most often noted for his interest in the Aboriginal peoples of Canada and his fictional re-creations of their past, although his desire to abolish definitive and biased narratives or histories becomes evident throughout his works. What is characteristic of Wiebe's works is that he often takes up a historic chain of events that is considered familiar, and shows that aspects of these stories have been seriously neglected. This is how the problem of representation of the Aboriginal peoples becomes such a prominent feature in his works: until recent decades, their experiences have usually been marginal or ignored in traditional history writing—the main type of discourse that has mediated between the past and the present in Western societies.

Today, there are a number of prominent First Nations writers working in Canada. Hence the question of whether non-Native writers should continue to tell Native stories has become much more widely debated than in 1973, when Wiebe's first major work drawing on the past of the First Nations of Canada, *The Temptations of Big Bear*, was published. This is not to suggest that Native peoples would not have felt the need to openly discuss questions of cultural appropriation at that time and before. Rather, wider recognition for the sensitivity of the subject and the creation of forums for Native peoples to speak about their concerns to larger audiences are developments of recent decades. Like its predecessor, Wiebe's second work under examination here, the novel *A Discovery of Strangers* (1994), stems from similar concern for incomplete histories. Both works are prime examples of Wiebe's desire to prioritize understanding of Aboriginal people's experience, but this latter novel faces a different, more complex world as it is read, interpreted, and measured against more numerous and more widely available stories involving Native Canadian voices—as writers, characters, or both.

Wiebe's active writing career now spans over forty years. His works include nine novels, three books of non-fiction, numerous short stories, and various shorter non-fictional pieces. Only a few of these works do not involve the First Nations or Métis at all. For example, his first novel, *Peace Shall Destroy Many* (1961), concentrates on a Mennonite community in the Prairies, but Aboriginal communities are living nearby. First Nations are therefore present at the margins, much like in the Canadian society of the time: the thought that Aboriginal peoples were going to disappear and its unfortunate repercussions—for example, the residential school system—were perhaps about to collapse, but had not yet been fully abandoned. In Wiebe's novel, the Mennonite community seeks no real contact with the First Nations, but the young protagonist finds that as he seeks to understand more about his surroundings, the margin is actually where he needs to look. The land carries little evidence of a century of Anglo-Canadian or Mennonite presence, but the millennia of Aboriginal presence, if not always visible in the land, is preserved in its stories. Wiebe's next novel, *First and Vital Candle* (1966), involves both Native and white characters, but its most successful passage concentrates on an Inuit community destroyed by famine. The disaster is not brought about by Inuit inability to adopt a more Anglo-Canadian way of life; instead, new contacts erase old taboos about over-exploitation of resources in the fragile Arctic, and disappearing traditions lead to the disappearance of the community.

From *The Temptations of Big Bear* onwards, the First Nations emerge as the main focus of the majority of Wiebe's works. This change parallels the increasing attention to First Nations issues in Canada in recent decades. First Nations voices in fiction as written by First Nations authors from the 1970s onwards are numerous: the list of influential authors who have drawn attention from outside their own communities could start with Maria Campbell, Beatrice Culleton, Tomson Highway, and Thomas King. Granted, Rudy Wiebe is not a Native Canadian, but he is arguably one of the first Canadian authors to interpret the range of First Nations experience in fiction and to challenge uninformed, stereotypical views. His works have invited further exploration of such themes from different sides of ethnic boundaries, as well as caused controversy among readers. In my interview with Wiebe,[1] he recognized that writing about the First Nations is a delicate issue; for example, he felt ambivalent about writing *Stolen Life* with Yvonne Johnson in the 1990s. However, he also recalled being encouraged by many Native people, because Johnson, who was imprisoned, was in no position to tell her story alone.[2] Wiebe's fiction is therefore in a crossroads between pressures unrestricted to the study of Canadian literature: exploring Native experience is a necessity for non-Natives as well for upholding interaction between different cultures. At the same time, differences in value systems that concern retelling stories and creating fictional voices should not be ignored, either.

As Wiebe's major works are fictional texts uniting references from varied written sources and at least implying reference to oral ones, their analysis calls for consideration of polyphony as discussed by Mikhail Bakhtin,[3] and Linda Hutcheon's ideas on historiographic metafiction.[4] Wiebe's texts clearly fit Hutcheon's definition of the genre, because they are strongly rooted in the history and the socio-political structures of the surrounding society and are consistently concerned with the processes of its own formation. What makes this process even more complex is that Wiebe's main characters in both novels live in oral cultures: their way of passing on knowledge to each other and younger generations is radically different from the writer's medium and the text-oriented colonizing culture—not to mention contemporary Canada or Western societies in general. Wiebe's novels are therefore textual hybrids: using textual form and drawing mainly from the remaining written sources, they reconstruct the conflict between an oral and a text-oriented culture. At the same time, they have to acknowledge the different rhythms of an oral society and transform them into a literary form, an undertaking not without its problems. Offering a general discussion of this complex process and its possible problems is beyond the scope of this article; however, its repercussions can be seen in the formation of Wiebe's literary work, and its relevance to it will be discussed.

The interaction of written and spoken genres and discourses is made more complex when Bakhtin's approach to polyphonic acquisition of meaning is considered. As Holquist—Bakhtin's biographer and his leading interpreter—summarizes one of the most pervasive ideas in Bakhtin's major texts, "There is no word directed to no one."[5] In Wiebe, meaning arises from interaction, not seclusion, and that calls for application of a Bakhtinian approach. For Bakhtin, the essence of polyphony in a novel is the free interaction of independent voices.[6] In other words, independent voices engage each other in a dialogue, and are not controlled by either the other voices in the narrative or the author. However, their discourses are not meaningful on their own, either; only in relation to other discourses as "one language can, after all, see itself only in the light of another language."[7] Hence the interpretation of voices depends on their interaction, and also on their cultural background, because no voice can speak independently of it. As it comes to Native voice, Native peoples today are successfully using written text to make their own voices heard in a predominantly literary society. And that literary society is becoming more and more aware of the importance of oral history as one possible way of preserving a culture. However, a clash between an oral and a literary culture at the time of first contact, as discussed in Wiebe's texts, seems unavoidable. Neither can immediately absorb the other's patterns in creating and preserving cultural knowledge; it cannot even be taken for granted that one will recognize the validity of the other, as in the colonizers' treatment of Native peoples in North America.

The Temptations of Big Bear: Fiction Reopens the Past

The Temptations of Big Bear reimagines the story of the Plains Cree chief Big Bear, beginning with his refusal to select a reserve as required by treaty and by Canadian expansion in 1876. The story reaches its climax with the defeat of the subsequent Native uprising and Big Bear's imprisonment in 1885, despite his refusal to take part in the hostilities. The novel concludes with his death in 1888. Big Bear lived on his own land but in his lifetime he was forced to witness a change. Even if the changes that drove the Cree to reservations and completely disrupted their buffalo-dependent economy were forced on them, Big Bear most definitely became a part of Canadian history, though it must also be remembered that Cree history extends millennia beyond that of Canada. This period is not made insignificant by the last 200 years that have created the parallels between Plains Cree and Canadian histories. Strangely, though Big Bear's effect on the latter, too, is undeniable, he remained for almost a century a little-known and badly neglected part of them.

In the field of literary research, *The Temptations of Big Bear* has most often been discussed in connection with Wiebe's fifth novel, *The Scorched-Wood People* (1977), which recounts the Métis self-government movement centred upon Louis Riel in Manitoba between 1869 and 1885. Thus these two novels share historical background in their description of the Native and Métis sides of the Northwest rebellion, to the extent that central characters in one novel are referred to in the other. However, less often explored, and possibly more interesting parallels can also be found between Big Bear's story and Wiebe's later novel *A Discovery of Strangers* (1994). The novel starts from a similar frame of reference—the incompatibility of European and Native American cultural traditions. One might even be tempted to say that the latter novel reworks the themes of *The Temptations of Big Bear*, transposed a thousand miles north; this would, however, take too much attention from its undeniable merits as an independent work of fiction.

In *The Temptations of Big Bear*, the traditional Cree way of life is becoming irrevocably altered on the prairies, and the narrative in *A Discovery of Strangers* presents a people on the first steps of a parallel change in the subarctic North. Despite the disruptions, the Cree still survive, and their traditions are constantly being revitalized. By contrast, the Tetsot'ine (or Yellowknife), the Native people seen in the latter novel, have been absorbed into neighbouring peoples and no longer exist as a distinct nation. The experiences of cultural change vary greatly in the two novels and are not always parallel. Parallels between the two narratives can, however, be seen in the way these experiences are described. Both make use of several different, often conflicting voices and discourses, which emphasizes the importance of analyzing their polyphonic and dialogic elements, which are of fundamental importance in both works.

Adopting a polyphonic approach to *The Temptations of Big Bear* is quite logical, as the events that it describes did not involve any single group of people totally isolated from others. Understanding Big Bear's life requires equal consideration for his and his people's experiences and the experiences of those involved in Canadian expansion. In the novel, individual voices (Native and white) form a choir of voices that speak not so much about themselves but in relation to Big Bear and his unsuccessful struggle to preserve his way of life, which is threatened by Canadian expansion and the near-extinction of the buffalo. Consider the conflicts between different voices: Kitty McLean is a sketch-like character presented only through her admiration of Big Bear: "I want to be more like you. A Person."[8] Though naive and romanticized, the characterization is still not beyond plausibility as it describes a fairly inexperienced young person. By contrast, Big Bear is presented as a complex amalgamation of personal vision and reflections of the experience of an entire people when their cultural traditions are disrupted. This is illustrated, for example, by his final words in his trial after the uprising is suppressed:

> Before many of you were born I ran buffalo over this place where you have put this building, and white men ate the meat I gave them. I gave them my hand as a brother; I was free, and the smallest person in my band was as free as I because the Master of Life had given us our place on the earth and that was enough for us. But you have taken our inheritance, and our strength. The land is torn up, black with fires, and empty. *You have done this.* And there is nothing left now but that you must help us.[9]

A representative for the colonizer, the judge responds in official rhetoric, which disregards the Native peoples' distress:

> I have no objection to hear what you have to say, but on one point you must be corrected. *This land never belonged to you.* The land was and is the Queen's. She has allowed you to use it. When she wanted to make other use of it, she called you together through her officers and let you decide which of the choicest parts of the country you wanted, to reserve them for yourself. Your people can live there because the Queen has graciously given it to them. The land belongs to the Queen.[10]

Among these discourses are also the linguistically complex, highly formal written charges made against Big Bear. When brought together with conflicting discourses, they appear as constructs, deliberately made in order to incriminate a man who had become inconvenient for the colonizing power and to legitimize a questionable judicial process:

> That Mis-ta-hah-mus-qua, otherwise called Big Bear, not regarding the duty of his allegiance, but wholly withdrawing the love, obedience, fidelity and allegiance which every true and faithful subject to our Lady the Queen does, and of right ought to bear towards our said Lady the Queen,... did, within the Dominion of Canada, compass, imagine, invent, devise and intend to levy war against our said Lady the Queen, within Canada.[11]

Though reflecting very different attitudes, all discourses thus turn towards Big Bear's character, often both as an individual and as a reflection of the Plains Cree community. In Bakhtinian terms, the narrative thus does not represent a closed character, or show who the protagonist is according to the author; instead, it shows "*how* he is conscious of himself."[12] Even further, it expands this view and shows also how others are conscious of the protagonist and how this inevitably shapes their world views.

Even if the voices heard in the novel are all directed towards one character, he is in no way in control of their views of him. In an interview with Wiebe, Juneja et al. raise the question of Big Bear's being idealized in the narrative.[13] Granted, Big Bear is presented as an admirably wise man, but as Wiebe points out in his response in the interview, he is still completely unable to convince his people not to start a hopeless conflict against the whites.[14] His strength lies in his ability to see that violent resistance will not help the Cree regain their traditional way of life. While Big Bear was a figure of considerable influence among his people, the society had no role for a dictator of any kind. He does not try to tell his people what should be done and he has no tools to impose his views on others.

Perhaps this is one reflection of the conflict between oral and written: in the prairies, the colonizer receives his orders and authority from Ontario and, at least symbolically, from the Queen in London. The oral community of the Cree functions differently: Big Bear must live among the people over whom he wishes to have direct influence, and any authority he may have stems from this everyday contact. His influence is immediate; it stems from the social situation and is not absolute. There is little chance for orders given from a distance. But the colonizer does not have the same problem: there is a long, impersonal chain of command in which the final authority remains a distant abstraction, a name written on a piece of paper—yet there are intermediaries seeing that this authority is unquestioned. Big Bear's declining influence in his own community is illustrated by his words about the killings of white men at the Frog Lake settlement:

> My friend, I am very sorry for what has been done.... There was a time when young men sat around me to listen; I was the greatest chief of the First People. But now they laugh at me. For some time they have been trying to take away the good name I have lived so long, and now they have done that very well. It will do them no good, but they have thrown away my name. It is gone, and I am old. That is the way things are.[15]

The careful consideration of different aspects of the protagonist's characterization and his influence on others is the most satisfying aspect of the narrative: while Wiebe's sympathy for the Cree in their struggle is evident, he does not erase voices that are unfavourable to them or make the Cree flawless as characters. The danger of idealizing a single voice and thus working against the principles of dialogism that strongly influence the narrative is clear. However, as the protagonist is not only an individual but a reflection of a community as well, the successes or failures of either one are incorporated into the other.

Including historical documentation and fictional text in the same work creates a certain tension between these two elements: neither component can be interpreted as it would if separated from the other. Because Cree culture was (and still is) transmitted orally, the historical documentation in *The Temptations of Big Bear* reveals little beyond the white regime's approach to Big Bear. Also, the texts that claim to present Big Bear's original voice come to us only through mediating voices, not Big Bear's. Thus there are considerable gaps between what has actually happened and what written history has recorded. In recent decades, as has for instance been argued by Hayden White,[16] there has emerged a much wider recognition that the story plays a considerable role in history, and this boundary has become widely questioned both in fiction and in theoretical debates. In effect, *The Temptations of Big Bear* stems solely from known history, but it systematically problematizes and even denies the interpretations that history offers. The novel is, therefore, not only a story of one man, but also a story of how our expectations of the history we think we know are abandoned as its inadequacy becomes evident.

Wiebe's reimagination of the story thus evokes Big Bear on three levels:

1. *As a real-life character*, for which there is little direct evidence; available documents and photographs mostly represent Anglo-Canadian views. Though by no means eradicated, oral traditions preserving knowledge have suffered from the disruptive effects of Canadian expansion and the imposition of cultural strategies not of Cree origin.

2. *As historically documented*, which deals with Big Bear and those affected by his actions.

3. *As a fictional re-creation*, which can incorporate historical documentation and redefine the reader's understanding of it.

As Hutcheon has shown, level 1 is separated from the other two by a fixed boundary, across which the other two can absorb material only through textual mediators—though one should not exclude strictly oral sources, where they can be found. By contrast, any boundary between levels 2 and 3 is unsteady and dependent on subjective interpretation.[17] Hutcheon's ideas on the relationship between history, fiction, and the past prove to be directly applicable to the interaction of these three levels in *The Temptations of Big Bear*:

1. *The past*, which can be accessed only through *textual* evidence.

2. *History*, which depends upon how the remaining evidence has been interpreted.

3. *Fiction*, which can reconsider any evidence, and even venture beyond direct evidence.[18]

History and fiction are each trying to gain access to a closed body of events. The majority of historical and fictional texts follow certain principles characteristic of each genre, but it is impossible to set or locate a boundary across which fiction could not absorb interpretations from more historically motivated discourses and incorporate them into itself. Most important, what may have been a closed body at the beginning of fictional interpretation becomes open-ended again, as the meanings that possibly arise from the interpretation of past events cannot be limited to well-defined sets of options.

Wiebe's Big Bear is therefore the result of a dialogue between three elements: historical documentation and fictional text, which are both a means to access the past through textual evidence. Documentation tends to represent the view of the dominant Canadian expansion. The fiction reinserts an understanding of the Native people's experience into a narrative from which it has been erased by the writing of history. The forms utilized in these Western historical narratives are overwhelmingly textual: they rely on other written sources that have already interpreted their reference materials, and themselves make further generalizations and erase the individuality of actors. Wiebe takes a different approach: he cannot dismiss the written sources, as they are valid interpretations of one point of view. However, he also needs to restore the individuality of Big Bear's experience in order to genuinely remake past events into a fiction that examines the meanings arising from the past. This fiction cannot be a mere collection of dates, names, and condensed reports of events—as an approach would be if it were based solely on and drew only from incomplete and biased written documents. It cannot be a direct reproduction of oral historical narratives, either: the novel as form does not function on the same terms. The possibilities for reproducing the patterns of an oral society are therefore limited.

Wiebe's fiction thus often shows how lacking the historical perspective is by itself, if one hopes to consider the effects of events in the novel on people and institutions that were involved in them. The absolute facts of past events have already been blurred by time; there have never been absolute interpretations of their meanings. Wiebe's primary interest therefore lies in exploring the possible interpretations and meanings of those events, and they can be constantly re-evaluated through dialogue between the elements involved. His primary concern is not recreating the smallest detail of what actually happened, but in recreating circumstances in order to explore the possibilities of interpreting lives led in a lost world.

Northern Worlds: A Discovery of Strangers

Twenty years after *The Temptations of Big Bear*, Wiebe returned to the themes of incompatible histories, dialogue between cultures, and forms of knowledge in *A Discovery of Strangers*. The novel is situated in the years of the first Franklin overland expedition to the arctic coast of Canada, 1819–1822. The narrative concentrates on the incompatibility of European and Native Tetsot'ine (or Yellowknife) cultures. The Tetsot'ine were a northern Dene people who was gradually absorbed into neighbouring peoples in the late 1800s and early 1900s.[19]

As in *The Temptations of Big Bear*, Wiebe does not rely on the plot in his attempt to arouse the reader's interest, because the disastrous end of the expedition is already known. Instead, he explores the unknown elements of the story: how did the Natives relate to the Europeans? How did they receive knowledge about the future in a dream? Why—as was the case in the 1973 novel—did knowing the future change nothing? The answers to some of these questions are elusive, but the last one is answered when the dialogic relationships in *The Temptations of Big Bear* and *A Discovery of Strangers* are considered: in each case, a voice warns about the disastrous effects of a certain action. This voice is ignored, and the disaster it has foretold becomes reality. Thus, refusing to enter into dialogue with divergent discourses deprives the chain of events of its open-endedness, an element inherent in the novel, as Bakhtin argues that it is the only literary genre still developing.[20]

Declaring the two novels reflections of each other would, however, be a mistake. *The Temptations of Big Bear* represents a complex reimagination of a critical period in the history of a major Native Canadian people. It is achieved by intertwining the experiences and voices of the Plains Cree through one of their most influential leaders, other Plains nations, the military colonizing force, the settlers following in its wake, and, at least indirectly, the political authorities in control of the expansion and the judicial processes after the Native uprising is suppressed. *A Discovery of Strangers* is structurally more straightforward, as it revolves around the re-creations of a limited number of voices— those of a small nation living in the Arctic and a small company of explorers. Like its surroundings, the arctic landscape, the narrative is more restricted; the voices it employs are in direct contact throughout the course of the novel. However, landscape dictates the interaction in both novels: though immense, its resources are limited, and it provides everything the Cree and the Tetsot'ine need, requiring them to refrain from over-exploitation. The newcomers, both in the Plains and in the Arctic, seek more to overcome the natural limitations of the land and to mould it to their needs. Though different in absolute scale, the extinction of the immense buffalo herds in the Canadian plains and the failure of the Franklin expedition hunting methods that were proven elsewhere show that the newcomers' approach disrupts the natural rhythms of the landscape.

Plurality of Experience or Appropriation?

In *A Discovery of Strangers*, the Native people represent wisdom gained from centuries of experience. This shows them to be, in some respects, wiser than the whites, none of whom survive the harsh conditions of the subarctic, but the novel also shows this that wisdom is not idealized: it is a consequence of life in a region for which voyagers from more temperate climates could not be prepared. Nevertheless, the officers of Franklin's expedition are convinced that their methods of exploration will get them to the Polar Sea (which the Tetsot'ine refer to as the Everlasting Ice). The Tetsot'ine, for their part, know from the very moment they meet the Europeans that the explorers will perish during their journey. Again, like the defeat of the Native uprising in *The Temptations of Big Bear*, the disastrous final stages of the expedition's journey and deaths of several members of the expedition crew are a historical fact. So they do not provide the possibility for extensive reinterpretation of historical material—the central element in many of Wiebe's works. Instead, he concentrates on the lack of dialogue between the whites and the Native people, which, in the end, proves disastrous for many of Franklin's men. This is amply illustrated by Franklin's reaction to the warning of Keskarrah (the tribe seer) against continuing the journey to the Everlasting Ice:

> "Now tell them: if they travel to the Everlasting Ice when the long light comes, we will not see them again."
>
> Lieutenant Franklin nods thoughtfully to St. Germain's translation. "What does he mean?" he asks in his ponderous way. "If we go to the Polar Sea, who will die, they or we?"...

"The land teaches us how to live, not how to kill ourselves. We know the names of every place you will meet. And we have seen this: your journey will end at the double rapids on the river of the Copperwoman."[21]

As in *The Temptations of Big Bear*, the warning of a future disaster is not taken seriously. Consequently, future events already familiar to central characters in each narrative become set to unfold:

And Lieutenant Franklin's excellent English manners cannot prevent him from smiling slightly. Which smile Keskarrah sees, and understands its arrogance perfectly....

"Tell him, in the name of my Expedition, I thank him for telling me this. Tell him also that I am sure, their land being so very large as we already know, that with this warning we will thankfully be able to avoid, wherever they may be, those fatal double rapids."[22]

The refusal to enter into dialogue proves fateful: after reaching the Obstruction Rapids in the Copperwoman River when returning from the Polar Sea, Franklin's men go hungry, resort to cannibalism, and many of them die, because Franklin is unwilling to consider the possibility that the Native people know how to survive in this wilderness and he does not. In other words, he severs dialogue by refusing to listen to a voice that provides vital information, but whose knowledge is incompatible with his own views and is acquired by methods unknown to him. As a result, his men perish. In the case of his expedition, there literally is no life without dialogue.

In the novel, the excerpts from the Franklin expedition's diaries invoke the juxtaposition and questionability of *the familiar* and *the real*. The diary excerpts tell a story that is familiar, but, as the overtly fictional parts show, is unavoidably one-sided. They are based on real experiences, but they omit others' equally real experiences, and only incidentally refer to elements that are essential in any attempt to properly understand the story:

Thursday August 3rd 1820   Great Slave Lake

At 4 a.m. we proceeded to the head of the lake channel, where we found Bigfoot and his party waiting to guide us. We were soon surrounded by a little fleet of canoes, containing the Yellowknives,

their wives and children, and in company with them we entered
a river 150 yards wide, with banks well covered by pines and
poplars, but the naked hills behind them betrayed the barrenness
of the country. We named it the Yellowknife River.[23]

As the quote shows, the people they meet have been renamed. Upon
their entry to the river that the Dene call Dehcho, the expedition
rename the river as well. Thus they appropriate the land, without consideration for its past. The element lacking from the story told in the
diary excerpts is consideration of the Aboriginal experience, unfamiliar and containing elements beyond mainstream Western experience,
yet entirely real to a people whose world is organized differently. Wiebe
reinserts this experience into a narrative from which it has been erased,
an act of censorship that has compromised the entire narrative. Wiebe
cannot, of course, access the original events: his endeavour is to reconsider remaining evidence and incorporate it into a fictional world. Thus
the narrative explores the possibilities of interpretation and meanings
that arise from the combination of direct historical documentation
and fictional material as seen from the point of view of the other, whose
centrality to any discourse Bakhtinian theory emphasizes.

The presence of otherness is, of course, inevitable in a narrative
incorporating characters from completely different cultural backgrounds
and even further, a writer from a different time and cultural reality.
Bakhtin argues that consciousness is always multiple,[24] and therefore
understanding or describing any event includes more than a single individual's point of view. Although the issue of non-Natives writing about
First Nations has become a major concern in the study of Canadian literature, the primary question still cannot be "What right does Wiebe
have to write about another people?" While the matter is sensitive and
must not be overlooked, reducing a critical approach to a work of fiction to this single question is unsatisfactory, as any fictional text always
goes beyond the mind of the writer and touches another's consciousness. Thus the question can be only about the effects or degrees of otherness: how does the fact that one writes about the other effect the
narrative? Even more important, how does this affect the possibilities
of interpreting a narrative that incorporates multiple consciousnesses?
What are the characteristics of a certain people that a writer needs to
take into account—such as the Native people's fundamentally different

approach to stories—although writers should not automatically feel intimidated if they choose to discuss them? Further, does awareness of the writer's own experiences reflect some aspect of the text in a way that adds to the possibilities of interpretation? In connection to these questions, historiography and the polyphonic qualities of the novel that Bakhtin emphasizes become acutely important: the word is always socially bound, reflecting the experiences of others.[25] As a text, it is the only mediator of historical constructs[26] as well as rooted in those same constructs. On its own, without being placed in an intricate network of references, the word would be left outside any frame of reference and could hardly be understood. Wiebe's understanding of the First Nations he writes about is therefore deeply rooted in the historical references of the text (the experiences they include and exclude), the very same material whose authority he finds suspect and ventures beyond in *The Temptations of Big Bear* and *A Discovery of Strangers*. Similar concern for the process of interpretation, especially of material with strong historical references, is consistently shown in Wiebe's other works as well.

If one voice, then, always *reflects* another, trying to *assume* another is problematic. The title of First Nations author Lenore Keeshig-Tobias's oft-quoted essay "Stop Stealing Native Stories" (1997) reveals the core of the problem: Native North American traditions in the use and importance of stories, or the medium used to convey them (oral vs. written), are not, as such, compatible with their Western counterparts. The essay title might suggest that the issue is simple, but Keeshig-Tobias's comments in an interview with Lutz[27] reveal that it is not: Wiebe is one of the writers she gives credit for "promot[ing] a greater understanding of Native culture," although she emphasizes that non-Native writers are not capable of assuming a Native voice. As far as Wiebe is concerned, this seems quite accurate: there may well be something "Mennonite" in Big Bear's quest for peace, reflecting the author's own background. However, there is also a genuine attempt to understand a person living in an alien cultural tradition, not a mere reproduction of stereotypical images, which would be the downfall of any serious work of fiction. The problem appears to be less that non-Native writers who show sensitivity to Native peoples claim to assume a genuine Native voice. It is more that readers and critics often treat these works as if they did.

Thus they instigate a negative response from Native readers, not only to previous readings of a work but the original text as well.

Thus the continuing debate on appropriation seems to arise partly from the break from tradition that occurs with the change of medium: when Native traditions were passed on in their oral form only, stories could be told in cycles. For example, as Dyck[28] points out, trickster stories were told only at a certain time of year and under specific conditions. In such a cyclical rhythm of life, it is possible to abstain from even referring to certain types of stories at other times. But when the stories are written down, this cyclical pattern of an oral culture is broken: the story is there to be read at all times. The writer can, of course, show that the story is tied to certain rhythms and patterns, from which it derives a part of its meanings—but the actual process of telling the story cannot remain identical to the original, oral one. As Keeshig-Tobias continues, writing reaches more people, but storytelling loses its intimacy in the shift to written form.[29] Native writers themselves are making more and more use of the written text, so they, too, are adopting new patterns that are at least partly incompatible with the traditional rhythms of an oral society. The issue becomes highly problematic if seen in terms of either development or deterioration. If instead it is seen as change, and the value judgements laid onto it as constructs of their own, does the problem appear the same? Change in cultural patterns and their linguistic expression seems inevitable; whether they are treated as development or deterioration is a question of interpretation.

Looking at *A Discovery of Strangers* and its interpretation of the Arctic, Hulan raises the question of the changing images of the North as a part of a Canadian identity and its reflections in literature about the North. In her extensive study on northern experience, she discusses a wide range of topics from traditional ethnographic views to different perceptions of national identity. Her study touches on a number of important authors for whom North has been a point of special interest, but among these accounts, the most extensive one is on Rudy Wiebe. Hulan criticizes both Wiebe's desire for an authentic Northern experience and recognition of it as central to Canadian national identity: she finds that growing interest in the north has meant that "speakers in [critical discourse] gain epistemic privilege through experience *in* the north rather than experience as a northern inhabitant."[30] As a result, the intrinsic difference between the two is being eradicated, and the view that northern experience would be best understood through national identity is gaining ground. Hulan regards the latter concept as a myth, as Canadians do not come from a uniform ethnic or cultural stock. Also, the great majority of Canadians live south of regions that they would regard as north.

However, Hulan welcomes Wiebe's fictional representation of the North. She commends especially *A Discovery of Strangers* as it does not employ common, clichéd views on the Canadian north, but instead engages with the problems of representing cultural contact in the region.[31] Further, in her view, the novel's dialogic form "highlights the cultural difference that make cultural encounter perilous."[32] As I have argued above, one of Wiebe's main goals is to reintroduce voices all but erased from the narrative. As for the questions of cultural appropriation often raised in such a process, Hulan accepts Wiebe's method of accessing experience inherent to the other: what makes his understanding of the other highly meaningful is meticulous research into existing documentation representing both the colonizer's and the Native's point of view, the willingness to cite those sources and the attempt to give all of them serious consideration—including those that have marginalized others.[33] Although I am arguing that one key feature in Wiebe's fiction is a desire to abolish definitive narratives, his preference for multi-voiced narratives shows, of course, that this cannot be achieved through eradication. Instead, for Wiebe, the inclusion of what has been a dominant voice opens the possibility to subverting its position and, for example, reopening closed or strongly biased discourses on the past. One such discourse is the story of the first encounter between cultures in *A Discovery of Strangers*.

An understanding of the arctic land that the Aboriginal people show in *A Discovery of Strangers* is, naturally, necessary for survival there and logically a result of a way of life completely dependent on the land. The ease of fictional re-creation, however, stops there: there are, of course, Native peoples who continue to live in the region, historical sources on their past such as the Franklin expedition's diaries and other travel narratives, but the Tetsot'ine themselves were almost destroyed and the survivors absorbed into other peoples almost a century ago. How does an author develop an understanding of such a people and convey it to his readers? An answer lies in polyphony and the plurality of experience Wiebe seeks in his work: detached descriptions of a community are likely to be much less helpful to understanding a community that no longer exists than detailed accounts of different individuals, their understanding of life within the community, and their interaction with others. A further challenge to a white reader is that knowledge based on premonition is usually considered a delusion in Western cultures. As this is the way the Tetsot'ine receive part of their knowledge in *A Discovery of Strangers*, this element of their life is beyond mainstream Western culture.

Wiebe does not, however, contend with oversimplified juxtapositions such as Native wisdom and white ignorance: the Tetsot'ine are convinced that the whites will perish, but some do manage to trace a route to their destination, the Arctic Sea, and some do survive the harsh conditions. The whites, for their part, are clearly ill-prepared for arctic exploration as they are, for example, completely dependent on Native hunters and still fail to adopt their methods of survival. However, they also quite calmly and rationally try to protect indispensable supplies that the Tetsot'ine are destroying when they mourn the deaths of some of their hunters. In accordance with Bakhtinian theory, this implies that it is impossible to dismiss or take for granted any view only because it seems self-evident or trivial from the point of view of a single consciousness. The Native people's strategies are, of course, the norm for survival in their homeland, but the expedition's different approach had been successfully applied in different circumstances. Franklin's mistake is not only in imposing his methods, but more important, his failure to realize that from the very beginning, new surroundings require a new approach that cannot necessarily be derived from methods proven elsewhere.

The necessity to consider other possible approaches is also why I cannot discuss the Tetsot'ine only, even though I find their side of the story the more intriguing one, as it is less familiar. After all, their side of this story—first contact between two cultures—is incomplete without the other side and could not be understood alone. It is possible to concentrate on their experience, and it is quite appropriate to do so because it was once neglected. However, it is impossible to restore balance by erasing the white influence, which is a historical fact, no matter what the present opinion of its impact is.

At irregular intervals, the narrative in *A Discovery of Strangers* advances through Keskarrah's wife, Birdseye, and her dreams, which become visions of the expedition's unavoidable failure. In these passages the juxtaposition of Franklin's rigid belief in his own capabilities and the Native people's view that the land alone dictates how to survive in the arctic sometimes seems too straightforward; it is as if one could see into the thoughts of the author. In a narrative that otherwise utilizes polyphonic structures and concentrates on the plurality of possible experience, one would not expect such an experience. If it occurs, the text seems to say too much too directly. That limits the reader's possible response and understanding of the unfamiliar, which is often what the author concentrates on, too.[34] Wiebe's novel as a whole is, however, too complex to be approached from this perspective. In *A Discovery of Strangers*, each voice presents its own understanding of the events, and while the juxtapositions sometimes surface very clearly, they are left unsolved. Granted, Franklin's expedition might have been clearly successful if he had listened to the Tetsot'ine; however, had his crew not reacted at all when the Natives were destroying shared resources in their grief, future survival of both parties would have been compromised even more dangerously.

The narrative thus explores plurality of experience through different interpretations of shared knowledge, and the difficulty of understanding another's point of view. The plurality of any experience is most clearly shown when the Native peoples and their understanding of the land or the animals become the focus. There are numerous instances throughout the narrative. The one reproduced here is an example that brings together aspects of the other or the less familiar: the Native people, their mythical understanding of the world that the animals share, and the difference between those views and what for most readers represents the familiar, Western cultural traditions:

> The caribou cow with three tines on each of her antlers lay curled, bedded and at momentary rest with her calf in the lee of her body. She had once been a woman; in fact, she has already been born a woman twice. But she has never liked that very much, and each time she is born that way she lives human only until her dreams are strong enough to call her innumerable caribou family, and they come for her. One morning people will awaken, and finally notice

the two pointed tracks that come to their lodge in the hard travelling snow, and the three tracks that leave. Then the Tetsot'ine—
Those Who Know Something a Little—understand what has
happened.

"We have lost another good child to the caribou," they begin
to wail. "She will never play or make fire with us, or dance, or sew
clothes, or bear strong children, or comfort us when we are hungry and sick. No-o-o-o, oh no, no. We will never see that good
child again."[35]

Thus the novel offers instances of discourse that is shaped or chosen by the author, but conveyed through other voices. In these cases,
it accomplishes the difficult task of exploring the plurality of possible
experiences. First, the representation of otherness encompasses a northern land of extreme conditions that have not changed in 200 years.
Despite technological advances, the land still remains alien to most.
Second, this narrative also represents the animals of the Arctic as beings
on a level of consciousness similar to that of its human inhabitants.
Finally, in the key roles, the narrative presents a Native people who no
longer exist, and Franklin's party, an expedition that never attempts to
properly interpret the nature of any of the above. Most important, the
narrative tries to represent a multitude of points of view and experiences
and show that none of them can be understood separately from all of
the others.

Stolen Life

Wiebe's latest work of non-fiction, *Stolen Life: The Journey of a Cree
Woman* (1998), brings him back to the themes raised already in *The
Temptations of Big Bear*. The book is a collaboration with Yvonne
Johnson, a Native Canadian sentenced to life in prison for murder. Of
the four people involved in and accused of the crime, Johnson received
by far the most severe punishment, while *Stolen Life* shows that evidence for the case could be seen to incriminate other suspects equally.

If we consider Wiebe's interest in the problematic history of Natives
forced to enter a white-dominated society, taking up a contemporary
incident that raises similar questions may not appear surprising. It is,
however, worth noting that Yvonne Johnson is related to Big Bear, and
the basic problem in both her and her ancestor's situation seems iden-

tical: both are taken into a predominantly white society that wants to control its Native members, but is uninterested in providing them with means to survive in it. In the book, Johnson describes similar experiences of displacement in both the United States and Canada. Thus what Wiebe in his previous works has been struggling to unearth from an unbalanced history emerges in the present as well: retelling the past leads to the equal necessity of retelling the present before either can be understood.

For Wiebe, Big Bear symbolizes the past of Native Canadians, and Yvonne Johnson the present, where sometimes alarmingly little seems to have changed since the late 1800s. Wiebe's endeavour has previously been to re-create images from the past, to show how strongly it is a part of the present. His connection with Johnson most forcefully corroborates this view. It also makes Wiebe's obsession with history tangible for the reader: a part of telling the story of Yvonne Johnson is becoming a part of it oneself, even more deeply than as a person who is looking back on a distant past and engaging in a dialogue with its texts. The line between narrator, protagonist, and any element of the story becomes as close to erasure as possible. *Stolen Life* shows that Wiebe indeed is no spectator; as he anticipated in his short story "Where is the voice coming from?" (1982), he has "become *element* in what is happening at this very moment."[36] The storyteller is no longer distinguishable from the telling of the story.

However, in light of the question of appropriating Native voice, Wiebe's position may seem awkward. As mentioned in the introduction, he recognized these pressures during the writing. He is yet another white person who enters Yvonne Johnson's life, and the telling of her story will definitely be shaped by Wiebe's involvement. Is Johnson giving up her individual voice, or is it taken from her? Should Wiebe be telling her story at all? In this case, however, these questions are trivial at best: Johnson herself has sought Wiebe's contribution to the work, and her right to make a personal choice in telling her own story cannot be questioned. Instead of asking whether Wiebe should tell Johnson's story, one must ask whether her story would have become available at all without Wiebe, or someone like Wiebe. Would anything even resembling her voice have reached a larger audience without Wiebe? The answer is most likely no.

Does this, then, suggest that Native peoples may still find themselves pushed into a marginal position, in danger of being deprived of their own voice? Yes, it does. What it does *not* mean is that no white person should ever be involved in telling Native stories. An injustice will not be remedied if all dialogue is severed. Though clashes of views will emerge as long as the dialogue continues, they do reflect the ongoing interaction between Native peoples and the mainstream Anglo-Canadian society. At least for the latter, erasure of this dialogue could mean erasure of stories coming from the other. If there is no one willing to work as a mediator, or no one who is allowed to do so, there is no chance at all of changing an unbalanced relationship between different peoples.

Towards Further Possibilities

All three works discussed demonstrate the difficulty of constructing and utilizing clear categories and juxtapositions in the interpretation of such a variety of experiences as seen in the texts. The insightful complexity of the narratives cannot be denied. Though in a more condensed form than *The Temptations of Big Bear*, the narrative in *A Discovery of Strangers* presents a comparable multiplicity of experience established from the outset. It varies from the Natives to the whites and the voyageurs working for them, as well as the Natives' understanding of the animals, which everyone in the barren north is dependent on. Wiebe's greatest accomplishment in these two novels is not in solving the problems he sets out to discuss or presenting a definitive view of the past of two Native peoples, but precisely the opposite: he presents a new interpretation that can instigate further responses. As a work of non-fiction, *Stolen Life* utilizes different strategies in telling a story, but does not divert from the path defined by Wiebe's other works: the plurality of experiences incorporated into the narratives shows that any established interpretations of past or present human experience can always be supplemented with new ones.

A final quote from Wiebe reflects both his position on accusations of appropriation of voice and the nature of retelling the past of another people: "But these stories are there. Dig them up, if you want to, if you're crazy enough and obsessive enough to do it. I don't own them.

I own the way I tell it, but you can tell it in a different way."[37] The comment reflects the traditional First Nations approach to stories, which Keeshig-Tobias sums up in her essay: "So potent are stories that, in native culture, one storyteller cannot tell another's story without permission."[38] Ownership of a story is established as a delicate question by both writers, but the nature of a story may be elusive: is the owner a person who has lived through it, a descendant, or the first person who told that story? What if, as may be the case with both Big Bear and the Tetsot'ine, these patterns have been so badly disturbed by colonial influence that no such people exist any more, or the story has become unknown to them as well? Further, although Yvonne Johnson's voice is reshaped through her collaboration with Wiebe, her experiences of life-long abuse and marginalization—also in a very concrete, physical sense during her imprisonment—would otherwise seem to lead to complete erasure of voice.

Therefore, Wiebe opens a path to interpreting both First Nations and mainstream Canadian experience against each other with his reintroduction of an understanding of the Aboriginal experience to Western, textually oriented understanding of the past. This necessarily reopens both elements for further examination. Although the matter is sensitive, exclusion of voice is precisely what has created problems in the relations between mainstream Canada and First Nations. The situation cannot be remedied simply by reversing the roles; varied responses are essential for the survival and reshaping of any tradition. It would be presumptuous to state that Wiebe's example as an interpreter of First Nations experience in the past forty years has prompted Native people themselves to transform their traditional stories into forms available to others. However, denying this possibility altogether would also be hasty because his work has drawn strong responses from them. Certainly, the best response or challenge to his way of telling a story would be to tell another story, sharing something of great value. Most important, Wiebe's novels do not invite readers to view remnants of a story. Instead, readers are invited to engage in an ongoing remaking of neglected or suppressed stories and seek to understand the elements they may not have stopped to consider before.

Notes

1 Janne Korkka. "Where Is the Text Coming From? An Interview with Rudy Wiebe." *World Literature Written in English* 38, 1 (1999): 69–85.
2 Janne Korkka, "Making a Story That Could Not Be Found: Rudy Wiebe's Multiple Canadas," in *Tales of Two Cities: Essays on New Anglophone Literatures*, ed. John Skinner (Turku: University of Turku, 2000), 70.
3 Mikhail Bakhtin, *The Dialogic Imagination* (Austin: University of Texas Press, 1981), and *Problems of Dostoevsky's Poetics* (Minneapolis: University of Minnesota Press, 1984).
4 Linda Hutcheon, *The Canadian Postmodern* (Toronto: Oxford University Press, 1988), and *A Poetics of Postmodernism* (New York and London: Routledge, 1988).
5 Michael Holquist, *Dialogism: Bakhtin and His World* (London and New York: Routledge, 1990), 27.
6 Bakhtin, *Dialogic Imagination* and *Dostoevsky's Poetics*.
7 Ibid., 12.
8 Rudy Wiebe, *The Temptations of Big Bear* (Toronto: McClelland and Stewart, 1973), 313.
9 Ibid., 398 (italics in original).
10 Ibid., 399 (italics mine).
11 Ibid., 352–53.
12 Bakhtin, *Dostoevsky's Poetics*, 48–49.
13 Om P. Juneja and Chandra Mohan, eds., *Ambivalence: Studies in Canadian Literature*. New Delhi: Allied Publishers, 1990.
14 Ibid.
15 Wiebe, *The Temptations of Big Bear*, 267.
16 Hayden White, *Metahistory* (Baltimore: Johns Hopkins University Press, 1973).
17 Hutcheon, *Poetics of Postmodernism*, 92–93.
18 Ibid.
19 For details, see Beryl C. Gillespie, "Yellowknife," in *Handbook of North American Indians*, vol. 6, *Subarctic*, ed. June Helm, (Washington: Smithsonian Institution, 1981), 285–90.
20 Bakhtin, *Dialogic Imagination*, 7.
21 Rudy Wiebe, *A Discovery of Strangers* (New York: Quality Paperback Book Club, 1994), 206.
22 Ibid., 206–207.
23 Wiebe, *A Discovery of Strangers*, 40 (italics in original).
24 Bakhtin, *Dostoevsky's Poetics*, 288.
25 Bakhtin, *Dialogic Imagination*, 292.
26 Hutcheon, *The Canadian Postmodern*, 14.
27 Hartmut Lutz, *Contemporary Challenges: Conversations with Canadian Native Authors* (Saskatoon: Fifth House, 1991), 80.

28 Ted Dyck, "The Places of Aboriginal Writing 2000 in Canada: The Novel," <http://www.wtc.ab.ca/tedyck/abor.00.htm>.
29 Lutz, *Contemporary Challenges*, 81.
30 Renée Hulan, *Northern Experience and the Myths of Canadian Culture* (Montreal: McGill–Queen's University Press, 2002), 15.
31 Ibid., 171.
32 Ibid, 174.
33 Ibid, 172–73.
34 Maria Frühwald, "A Discovery of Strange Things in Rudy Wiebe's *A Discovery of Strangers*," in *New Worlds: Discovering and Constructing the Unknown in Anglophone Literature*, ed. Martin Kuester, Gabriele Christ, and Rudolf Beck (Munich: Ernst Vögel, 2000), 144.
35 Wiebe, *A Discovery of Strangers*, 3–4.
36 Rudy Wiebe, "Where Is the Voice Coming From?" in *The Angel of the Tar Sands and Other Stories* (Toronto: McClelland and Stewart, 1982), 85.
37 Korkka, "Where Is the Text Coming From?" 76.
38 Lenore Keeshig-Tobias, "Stop stealing Native stories," in *Borrowed Power: Essays on Cultural Appropriation*, ed. Bruce Ziff and Pratima V. Rao (New Brunswick, NJ: Rutgers University Press), 73.

Bibliography

Bakhtin, Mikhail. *The Dialogic Imagination*. Austin: University of Texas Press, 1981.
———. *Problems of Dostoevsky's Poetics*. Minneapolis: University of Minnesota Press, 1984.
Dyck, Ted. "The Places of Aboriginal Writing 2000 in Canada: The Novel." <http://www.wtc.ab.ca/tedyck/abor.00.htm>.
Frühwald, Maria. "A Discovery of Strange Things in Rudy Wiebe's *A Discovery of Strangers*." In *New Worlds: Discovering and Constructing the Unknown in Anglophone Literature*. Ed. Martin Kuester, Gabriele Christ, and Rudolf Beck, 133–47. Munich: Ernst Vögel, 2000.
Gillespie, Beryl C. "Yellowknife." In *Handbook of North American Indians*. Vol. 6, *Subarctic*. Ed. June Helm, 285–90. Washington: Smithsonian Institution, 1981.
Holquist, Michael. *Dialogism: Bakhtin and His World*. London and New York: Routledge, 1990.
Hulan, Renée. *Northern Experience and the Myths of Canadian Culture*. Montréal and Kingston: McGill-Queen's University Press. 2002.
Hutcheon, Linda. *The Canadian Postmodern*. Toronto: Oxford University Press, 1988.

——— . *A Poetics of Postmodernism*. New York and London: Routledge, 1988.

Juneja, Om P. and Chandra Mohan. *Ambivalence: Studies in Canadian Literature*. New Delhi: Allied Publishers, 1990.

Keeshig-Tobias, Lenore. "Stop Stealing Native Stories." In *Borrowed Power: Essays on Cultural Appropriation*. Ed. Bruce Ziff and Pratima V. Rao, 71–73. New Brunswick, NJ: Rutgers University Press, 1977.

Korkka, Janne. "Making a Story That Could Not Be Found: Rudy Wiebe's Multiple Canadas." In *Tales of Two Cities: Essays on New Anglophone Literatures*. Ed. John Skinner, 21–35. Turku: University of Turku, 2000.

——— . "Where Is the Text Coming From? An Interview with Rudy Wiebe." *World Literature Written in English* 38, 1 (1999): 69–85.

Lutz, Hartmut. *Contemporary Challenges: Conversations with Canadian Native Authors*. Saskatoon: Fifth House, 1991.

White, Hayden. *Metahistory*. Baltimore: Johns Hopkins University Press, 1973.

Wiebe, Rudy. *A Discovery of Strangers*. New York: Quality Paperback Book Club, 1994.

——— . *First and Vital Candle*. Toronto: McClelland and Stewart, 1966.

——— . *Peace Shall Destroy Many*. Toronto: McClelland and Stewart, 1961.

——— . *The Scorched Wood People*. Toronto: McClelland and Stewart, 1977.

——— . *The Temptations of Big Bear*. Toronto: McClelland and Stewart, 1973.

——— . "Where Is the Voice Coming From?" In *The Angel of the Tar Sands and Other Stories*, 78–87. Toronto: McClelland and Stewart, 1982.

Wiebe, Rudy, and Yvonne Johnson. *Stolen Life: The Journey of a Cree Woman*. Toronto: Alfred A. Knopf, 1998.

Contributors

Lenore Keeshig-Tobias, Cape Croker First Nation

Ute Lischke, associate professor of German cultural and film studies, Department of Languages and Literatures, Wilfrid Laurier University

David T. McNab, assistant professor of Native studies, School of Arts and Letters, Atkinson Faculty of Liberal and Professional Studies, York University

Drew Hayden Taylor, Curve Lake First Nation

Philip Bellfy, associate professor, writing, rhetoric, and American cultures, Michigan State University

David Newhouse, principal, Gzowski College, and associate professor, Department of Native Studies, Trent University

Dawn T. Maracle, doctoral candidate in education, OISE, University of Toronto

Mark Dockstator, chair and associate professor of Indian studies, Department of Native Studies, Trent University

Olive Patricia Dickason, adjunct professor of history, University of Ottawa and Professor Emerita of History, University of Alberta

Karl Hele, assistant professor, First Nations Studies Program, University of Western Ontario

Winona Wheeler, dean and associate professor of Indian studies, Saskatoon campus, First Nations University of Canada

Stephen Bocking, associate professor, Environmental and Resource Studies Program, Trent University

Dennis A. Bartels, professor of anthropology and sociology, Sir Wilfrid Grenfell College, Memorial University of Newfoundland, and Alice Bartels, writer, Toronto

Kathryn Bunn-Marcuse, doctoral candidate in art history, University of Washington

Bernie Harder, associate professor, Department of English Language, Literature, and Creative Writing, University of Windsor

Janne Korkka, doctoral candidate in English, University of Turku, Finland